Gender, Violence and the State in Asia

While gender-based violence occurs in all societies irrespective of the level of development or cultural setting, whether in conflict or peacetime, the challenges for legal responses to gender-based violence are particularly acute in Asia. This book addresses the lack of academic discourse on gender-based violence in Asia beyond domestic violence, by demonstrating that gendered violence exists within many different contexts and is perpetuated by multiple actors.

Bringing together scholars, legal practitioners and human rights advocates, the book examines the intersections between gender, violence and the state in Asian contexts. It considers the role of state institutions in perpetuating and preventing violence based on gender and identity, and thus contributes to growing scholarship around due diligence standards under international law. Analysing both physical and structural gender-based violence, it scrutinises how such violence exists within a landscape shaped by distinct cultural norms, laws and policies, and grapples with how to practically translate international human rights standards about state responsibility into these complex domestic environments. Contributors from diverse backgrounds draw on case studies and empirical research to ground this academic scholarship in lived experiences of individuals and their communities in Asia.

By bridging the divide between policy, laws and practice to offer a unique insight into both theoretical and practical responses to how gender-based violence is understood within communities and state institutions in Asian countries, this book will appeal to students and scholars of Asian Studies, Gender Studies and Law.

Amy Barrow is Assistant Professor in the Faculty of Law at The Chinese University of Hong Kong, where she is a founding member of the Centre for Rights and Justice.

Joy L. Chia is a program officer with the East Asia Program at the Open Society Foundations.

Routledge Research on Gender in Asia Series

For a full list of titles visit www.routledge.com/Routledge-Research-on-Gender-in-Asia-Series/book-series/RRGAS

Recently published titles:

Unmarried Women in Japan
The Drift into Singlehood
Akiko Yoshida

Postcolonial Lesbian Identities in Singapore
Re-thinking Global Sexualities
Shawna Tang

Intimacy and Reproduction in Contemporary Japan
Genaro Castro-Vázquez

Gender, Violence and the State in Asia
Edited by Amy Barrow and Joy L. Chia

Motherhood and Work in Contemporary Japan
Junko Nishimura

Social Transformation in Post-conflict Nepal
A Gender Perspective
Punam Yadav

Gender, Governance and Empowerment in India
Sreevidya Kalaramadam

Women and Conflict in India
Sanghamitra Choudhury

Gender, Violence and the State in Asia

Edited by Amy Barrow and Joy L. Chia

Routledge
Taylor & Francis Group
LONDON AND NEW YORK

First published 2016
by Routledge
2 Park Square, Milton Park, Abingdon, Oxon OX14 4RN

and by Routledge
711 Third Avenue, New York, NY 10017

Routledge is an imprint of the Taylor & Francis Group, an informa business

British Library Cataloguing in Publication Data
A catalogue record for this book is available from the British Library

Library of Congress Cataloging in Publication Data
Names: Barrow, Amy (Law teacher), editor. |
Chia, Joy L. (Joy Li Fen) editor.
Title: Gender, violence and the state in Asia/Edited by Amy Barrow and Joy L. Chia.
Description: New York, NY: Routledge, 2016. | Series: Routledge research on gender in Asia; 13 | Includes bibliographical references and index.
Identifiers: LCCN 2015049071| ISBN 9781138101722 (hardback) |
ISBN 9781315656731 (ebook)
Subjects: LCSH: Sex discrimination against women–Law and legislation–Asia.
| Sex discrimination–Law and legislation–Asia. | Women–Violence against–Asia. | Women–Crimes against–Asia. | Violence–Government policy–Asia.
Classification: LCC KM145.W64 G46 2016 | DDC 342.508/78–dc23
LC record available at http://lccn.loc.gov/2015049071

ISBN: 978-1-138-10172-2 (hbk)
ISBN: 978-1-315-65673-1 (ebk)

Typeset in Times New Roman
by Sunrise Setting Ltd, Brixham, UK

Contents

Tables

Notes on contributors

Amy Barrow is Assistant Professor in the Faculty of Law at the Chinese University of Hong Kong, where she is a founding member of the Centre for Rights and Justice and a member of the Gender Research Centre. Amy's research expertise includes UN Security Council Resolution 1325 and the development of norms on women, peace and security; gender and the law; human rights; institutional mechanisms for the advancement of women; and socio-legal research methods. Amy has a keen interest in how international law filters down to the grass-roots level and is used by multiple actors in society. Within her work Amy adopts an interdisciplinary approach and draws upon empirical research methods. She is a member of the WILPF Academic Network, a think tank that focuses on issues of gender, peace and security, and a founding coalition member of Everywoman Everywhere, a project of the International Commission on Violence against Women and Girls, which grew out of research conducted by the Initiative on Violence against Women at the Harvard Kennedy School's Carr Center for Human Rights.

Joy L. Chia is a program officer with the East Asia Program at the Open Society Foundations. She was a visiting scholar (honorary) at the Centre for Rights and Justice at the Faculty of Law, Chinese University of Hong Kong from 2012 to 2015. Joy was previously the Asia Law and Justice Fellow at the Leitner Center for International Law and Justice at Fordham Law School, and has worked on myriad human-rights issues, including gender and sexuality, the rights of refugees and immigrants, public health, and the protection of Chinese human-rights defenders and lawyers. She has also been an Adjunct Professor at the Chinese University of Hong Kong and at Fordham Law School. Prior to her fellowship with the Leitner Center, she was a complex commercial litigation associate at two large New York law firms, with a strong commitment to pro bono work in asylum and family law. Joy is a graduate of Yale University and Columbia University School of Law, where she was a Harlan Fiske Stone Scholar.

Christine Chinkin, FBA, is currently Director of the Centre for Women, Peace and Security, a former Professor of International Law at the London School of Economics, a William C. Cook Global Law Professor at the University of Michigan Law School and an academic member of Matrix Chambers. She has degrees in law from the Universities of London, Yale and Sydney. She is the author of many articles on issues of international law, of *Halsbury's Laws of Australia, Title on Foreign Relations* (2nd edition 2001) and *Third Parties in International Law*

(1993); and co-author of *Dispute Resolution in Australia* (2nd edition 2002), *The Boundaries of International Law: A Feminist Analysis* (2000) and *The Making of International Law* (2007). In April 2001 she was awarded the American Society of International Law's Certificate of Merit for 'outstanding contribution to scholarship' and in 2006 the Society's Goler T. Butcher Medal 'for outstanding contributions to the development or effective realization of international human rights law' (with H. Charlesworth). Professor Chinkin has been a consultant on trafficking in women to the UN Office of the High Commissioner on Human Rights; and on Peace Agreements and Gender to the UN Division for the Advancement of Women and UNIFEM. She was a scientific expert to an Ad Hoc Committee of the Council of Europe on the drafting of the Istanbul Convention on Preventing and Combating Violence against Women and Domestic Violence, 2011. She is currently a member of the Kosovo Human Rights Advisory Panel.

Susanne Yuk-ping Choi is Professor at the Department of Sociology, the Chinese University of Hong Kong. Her current research interests include gender, family, health and migration. She has written extensively on issues related to violence against female sex workers in Chinese societies. Her co-authored work *Masculine Compromise: Migration, Family and Gender in China* is to be published by University of California Press. She has also been published by journals such as *American Journal of Sociology*, *Journal of Marriage and Family*, *International Migration Review*, *The China Quarterly*, *Social Science and Medicine*, *Violence against Women*, *Culture, Health and Sexuality*, *Journal of Interpersonal Violence*, *Aids Care*, *Sexually Transmitted Diseases*, *Sociology of Health and Illness* and *British Journal of Sociology*.

Surabhi Chopra is an Assistant Professor at the Faculty of Law, Chinese University of Hong Kong. She researches national security laws, mass violence and the rights of the poor in South Asia. She co-edited "On Their Watch: Mass Violence and State Apathy in India" (New Delhi: Three Essays Collective 2014). Professor Chopra has worked as a barrister and human rights consultant. Her experience includes work with, *inter alia*, the International Development Research Centre, Tooks Chambers, Human Rights Watch, ActionAid, UNICEF and India's National Commission for the Protection of Child Rights. She studied law, human rights and anthropology, and was educated at Cambridge and Harvard Universities and the London School of Economics.

Lynette J. Chua is a law and society scholar with research interests in law and social change, and law and social movements. She is conducting fieldwork and writing on the emergence of sexual minority rights mobilisation in Myanmar at a time of political transition. She has also conducted an ethnographic study of Singapore's gay and lesbian movement to analyse the emergence, development, and strategies and tactics of the movement, and explore the complex role of law and meanings of rights. Her book, *Mobilizing Gay Singapore: Rights and Resistance in an Authoritarian State*, received the 2015 Distinguished Book Award from the Sociology of Law Section of the American Sociological Association. Her work is also published in *Law and Society Review*, *Human Rights Quarterly* and the *Asian Journal of Law and Society*.

David Gilbert is a PhD candidate in the College of Asia and the Pacific, Australian National University. His research examines transgender everyday life and belonging in urban Myanmar. David's research and writing on Myanmar has also been published in *Human Rights Quarterly*, *Sojourn*, *Arena* and the *Vagabond Press Asia Pacific Writing Series*.

Shyamala Gomez is the Country Director of FOKUS WOMEN, the Sri Lanka country office of FOKUS, a women's organisation based in Oslo. She has held different posts, including that of Gender Advisor to the UN Office of the Resident Coordinator in Sri Lanka and Senior Programme Manager of the Women's Housing Rights Programme at the Centre on Housing Rights and Evictions (COHRE). Shyamala also taught law for many years at the Faculty of Law, University of Colombo. She has written and published widely on issues of violence against women, women and their land rights, migrant workers, reproductive rights, masculinities and, more recently, on women, peace and security. She has also engaged and consulted with the corporate sector on tackling sexual harassment in the workplace. She undertook a baseline study on the status of UNSCR 1325 in Sri Lanka for FOKUS in 2011 and also wrote the country paper for a five-country study that assessed the implementation of UNSCR 1325 in Sri Lanka for the 10th anniversary celebration of UNSCR 1325. She is a lawyer and Fulbright Scholar, and holds an LLB from the University of Colombo and an LLM from Georgetown University.

Amrita Gurung is a recipient of the Matthias Moyersoen Research Apprenticeship Fellowship and has earned a Post-Graduate Diploma in Social Sciences from Nepa School of Social Sciences and Humanities. She previously served: as a coordinator for the Certificate Course in Voluntarism and Social Work as part of advocacy for the promotion of a volunteerism-based society in Nepal; as a journalist with *The Kathmandu Post*; and as a documentation associate for the Food-first Information and Action Network, Nepal. At the same time, she volunteered and advocated for the promotion of volunteerism in the national development framework under the National Development Volunteer Service. As part of the US Embassy International Visitors Leadership Program, Amrita is running a project to form a club with girls from squatter communities in Kathmandu by building their capacities to take action. She is currently working as a research assistant at the Social Science Baha's Centre for the Study of Labour and Mobility in Kathmandu.

Sara Hossain is a barrister practising in the Supreme Court of Bangladesh, mainly in the areas of constitutional, public interest and family law. She is a partner at the law firm of Dr. Kamal Hossain and Associates (www.khossain.com), and currently serves pro bono as the Honorary Executive Director of the Bangladesh Legal Aid and Services Trust (www.blast.org.bd). Sara ran the South Asia Programme at INTERIGHTS and was a founding board member of the South Asia Women's Fund. Sara's casework on women's rights has included challenging 'fatwa' violence, 'forced veiling' and the use of the 'two finger test', before the Supreme Court of Bangladesh, and amicus/third party briefs on marital rape before the Supreme Court of Nepal, challenging the requirement of proof of force to establish rape (*MC v Bulgaria* before the European Court of Human Rights).

Sara writes and speaks on public interest law, human rights and women's rights and access to justice. Her publications include 'Confronting Constitutional Curtailments: Attempts to Rebuild Independence of the Judiciary in Bangladesh', in Paul Brass (ed) *Handbook of Politics in South Asia* (Routledge, 2010), 'Wayward Girls and Well-Wisher Parents: Habeas Corpus, Women's Rights to Consent and the Bangladesh Courts' in Aisha Gill (ed) *Forced Marriage* (Zed, London 2010); (with Bina de Costa) 'Redress for Sexual Violence Before the International Crimes Tribunal in Bangladesh: Lessons from History, and Hopes for the Future' in *Criminal Law Forum*, Volume 21, Number 2, 331–359; (co-edited with Lynn Welchman) *'Honour': Crimes, Paradigms and Violence against Women* (Zed Books, London, 2005) and (co-edited with Dina M. Siddiqi) *Human Rights in Bangladesh 2007* (ASK, Dhaka, 2008). Sara was educated at Wadham College, Oxford (MA (Hons) 1988), called to the Bar from Middle Temple (1989), enrolled in the High Court Division of the Supreme Court of Bangladesh (1992) and then in the Appellate Division in 2008. She has received various awards for her work, including from the Lawyers Committee for Human Rights (now Human Rights First), and been selected as a World Economic Forum Fellow and an Asia 21 Fellow.

Puja Kapai is an Associate Professor of Law, Director of the Centre for Comparative and Public Law, and the Director of the Social Justice Summer Internship at the Faculty of the Law at the University of Hong Kong. Her research expertise lies in international human rights law and political theory. Her writing spans a broad range of subjects including equality and non-discrimination, minority rights (including ethnic, religious and sexual minorities, children, women and the elderly), identity politics, theories of justice, deliberative democracy and civic participation, citizenship studies, domestic violence, and comparative law and legal transplants. Puja has been a consultant to various non-governmental organisations and is currently on the Board of Directors for Unison Hong Kong, the Asian Migrants Centre and the Association for Concern for Legal Rights of Victims of Domestic Violence. She was awarded the US Secretary of State's Hong Kong Woman of Courage Award in 2015.

Kay McArdle joined PathFinders as its first CEO in October 2013. She is responsible for PathFinders' overall strategic development with special focus on government, consular, academic and agency relations, access to justice and communications. Kay is a lawyer and CEDR-accredited mediator. She was first admitted to practice law in England and Wales and in 1997 in Hong Kong. Her main practice areas are employment, litigation and discrimination. Before PathFinders, Kay worked at Mayer Brown JSM. Prior to that she held regional management positions at Goldman Sachs in Hong Kong for 11 years. Kay is Vice-Chair of the Executive Committee of the Child Development Centre NGO (board in 2007) and Board Chair Emeritus of The Women's Foundation NGO (board in 2007–14; chair 2011–14). She has guest lectured at the Faculty of Law at the Chinese University of Hong Kong. Kay is a passionate advocate for the rights of minorities and historically under-served and under-represented populations including women, special needs children and ethnic minorities. Kay is married and has three sons.

Rita Shackel is Associate Professor at Sydney Law School. Her research interests focus on sexual abuse and violence against women and children. Currently Rita is lead investigator on an Australian Government funded project – *Transitional Justice for Women in Uganda, Kenya and DRC* – which is examining the efficacy of transitional justice for women and women's justice needs and priorities. Rita is also currently engaged in research for the *Royal Commission into Institutional Responses to Child Sexual Abuse* being conducted in Australia. Rita is particularly interested in the psycho-social needs of victims of crime and survivors of sexual abuse and sexual violence. Rita's research is strongly interdisciplinary in nature and draws on empirical methodologies.

Lily Thapa is the founder of Women for Human Rights, which brings together Nepalese widows, many of whom were the young wives of men killed in Nepal's eleven-year insurgency, out of isolation and dependency in their husbands' homes and connects them with each other in groups that help build their economic and political strength. Lily was herself widowed at 29 when her husband, an army medical doctor, died while serving in the UN Peace Mission in the Gulf War of 1991. Lily is a lecturer at the University of Nepal, Vice President of the Network of Women for Peace and Democracy and General Secretary of the South Asian Network for Widow's Empowerment in Development. Lily has worked in the social development sector for more than 20 years. Currently she is a research scholar (PHD) in Sociology at Tribhuwan University, Kathmandu, Nepal, focusing on the sociological aspects of the impact of conflict in Nepal. She also completed the Post-Graduation in Women in Management course at Lulea University of Technology, Sweden.

Gao Wei is a research fellow with the Wuhan University Public Interest and Development Law Institute (PIDLI) and a principal researcher of Wuhan East-Lake Institute for Social Advancement. She earned her Bachelor's in Law from Wuhan University in 2008 and her Master's in Human Rights Law from the Central European University in 2010. She has worked with PIDLI since 2010 and is now directing the Human Rights Research program at PIDLI, which involves a wide range of activities, including training and undertaking research targeting various disadvantaged groups in China. She has worked closely on rural justice over the years and particularly with rural women leaders in Hubei Province in China during the past two years.

Huang Zhong is a research fellow of Wuhan University Public Interest and Development Law Institute (PIDLI) and a principal researcher of Wuhan East-Lake Institute for Social Advancement. She earned her LLB from Wuhan University in 2007 and a Master's in Applied Human Rights from the University of York (UK) in 2009. She started working with PIDLI in 2010 and the main projects she has been involved in include Legal Empowerment in China and Occupational Safety and Health Protection, and Empowerment of Rural Migrant Women Workers in Hubei. She has a keen interest in rural justice issues, especially the status of women, and has been working in community legal education for vulnerable groups in rural areas for many years.

Acknowledgements

This book was conceived in the summer of 2013 during discussions and planning towards the Faculty of Law's Centre for Rights and Justice's international conference on *Gender, Violence and the State in Asia* which was held on 8–10 May 2014 at The Chinese University of Hong Kong (CUHK). We thank Dr. Eva Pils, former Director of the Centre for Rights and Justice (CRJ), for her scholarly insight, encouragement and support throughout this process but especially for recognising our overlapping interests and for providing the spark for this fruitful collaboration.

The Centre for Rights and Justice's conference provided an ideal springboard to bring together scholars, practitioners and human rights advocates from across Asia and internationally to discuss the multiple forms in which gender-based violence manifests itself and to consider the role of the state and its actors in responding to and, in some cases, perpetuating gender-based violence. We would not have been able to organise the conference without the generous support of the CRJ in the Faculty of Law at the CUHK as well as the Taiwan Foundation for Democracy. We would especially like to thank our colleagues in the Faculty of Law and at the CRJ: then Director of the CRJ, Prof. Nina Jorgensen; Dr. Flora Sapio; Prof. Luke Marsh; Alainna Wrigley for her technical expertise and wizardry; Prof. Mike McConville, Emeritus Professor and Founding Dean of the Faculty of Law, who all gave very helpful advice and suggestions during the planning process; and Karrie Li and her team for their administrative support.

We would like to extend our thanks to all the contributors to the conference on *Gender, Violence and the State in Asia* and particularly the authors of this book for their generosity of time to reflect on their work and practice and who have been steadfastly patient and committed throughout the writing and editorial process. We are delighted to bring together both accomplished and rising scholars, practitioners and human rights advocates in Asia and internationally, each of whom has significant insight into gender-based violence and questions of gender, equality and the law. Individual authors extend special thanks at the start of their respective chapters.

We are indebted to Stephanie Rogers and Rebecca Lawrence at Routledge for their enthusiastic support in getting the book to print and to the anonymous reviewer whose comments helped us immensely during the editorial process.

Our respective families and friends from both near and far have supported us along the way with patience and good humour, particularly our partners, Rebecca and Roger. The process of working collaboratively has been richly rewarding and we hope to continue to collaborate on scholarly endeavours in the future. Finally, and by no means least, this book is dedicated to our daughters, Evelyn, who arrived shortly before the book went to print, and Sophia, in the hope that one day they can live in a world free from gender-based violence.

Table of international legal instruments

1930 International Labour Organisation, C029 Forced Labour Convention, 1930 (No. 29) Convention concerning Forced or Compulsory Labour (entry into force: 5 September 2013).

1948 UN General Assembly, Universal Declaration of Human Rights, 10 December 1948, GA Res. 217 A (III).

1957 International Labour Organisation, C107 Indigenous and Tribal Populations Convention, 1957 (No. 107) Convention concerning the Protection and Integration of Indigenous and Other Tribunal and Semi-Tribal Populations in Independent Countries (entry into force: 2 June 1959).

1965 UN General Assembly, International Convention on the Elimination of All Forms of Racial Discrimination, 21 December 1965, 660 UNTS 195.

1966 UN General Assembly, International Covenant on Economic, Social and Cultural Rights, 16 December 1966, 993 UNTS 3.

UN General Assembly, International Covenant on Civil and Political Rights, 16 December 1966, 999 UNTS 171.

1979 UN General Assembly, Convention on the Elimination of All Forms of Discrimination against Women, 18 December 1979, 1249 UNTS 13.

1984 UN General Assembly, Convention against Torture and other Cruel, Inhuman or Degrading Treatment or Punishment, 10 December 1984, 1645 UNTS 85.

1989 International Labour Organisation, C169 Indigenous and Tribal People's Convention, 1989 (No. 169) Convention concerning Indigenous and Tribal Peoples in Independent Counties (entry into force: 5 September 1991).

UN General Assembly, Convention on the Rights of the Child, 20 November 1989, 1577 UNTS 3.

1990 UN General Assembly, International Convention on the Protection of the Rights of All Migrant Workers and Members of Their Families, 18 December 1990, A/RES/45/158.

1994 Organization of American States (OAS), Inter-American Convention on the Prevention, Punishment and Eradication of Violence against Women ("Convention of Belem do Para"), 9 June 1994 (entry into force: 5 March 1995).

1995 United Nations, Fourth World Conference on Women, Beijing Declaration and Platform for Action A/CONF.177/20, 15 September 1995 (endorsed by GA Res. 50/203, 22 December 1995).

2003 African Union, Protocol to the African Charter on Human and People's Rights on the Rights of Women in Africa, 11 July 2003.

2010 UN General Assembly, Convention on the Rights of Persons with Disabilities, 13 December 2006, A/RES/61/106, Annex I.

2011 Council of Europe, Council of Europe Convention on preventing and combating violence against women and domestic violence, 11 May 2011 CETS No.210 (entry into force: 1 August 2014).

International Labour Organisation, C189 Domestic Workers Convention, 2011 (No. 189) Convention concerning decent work for domestic workers (entry into force: 5 September 2013).

Introduction

Framing gender, violence and the state in Asia

Amy Barrow and Joy L. Chia

This book explores the intersections between gender, violence and the role of the state in Asia. Drawing on a range of examples from jurisdictions across Asia, legal academics, practitioners and human-rights advocates examine how gender and violence are articulated and understood through international and national legal regimes in Asia. Their chapters challenge perceptions that often limit legal discourse about gender and violence to domestic violence within the family and spousal violence. These perceptions are pervasive within governments and communities in Asia, and often frame anti-violence efforts in ways that lead to the marginalisation of other equally entrenched forms of gender-based violence. In challenging these perceptions, this book aims to expand how gender and violence is theorised to consider structural violence and the ways in which laws and policies can actively undermine gender equality. Specifically, the book explores how the perpetuation of gender-based violence is often shaped by distinct cultural norms, laws and policies. While gender-based violence occurs in all societies irrespective of the level of development or cultural setting, whether in conflict or peacetime, the challenges for legal responses to gender-based violence are particularly acute in Asia.

Asia is a richly diverse region in terms of culture, economic development, legal systems and political regimes. Many Asian states, including the People's Republic of China (the PRC), are experiencing massive social and economic transformations, while other countries, such as Myanmar, are on the cusp of political transition. A number of states in the region, including Nepal, Sri Lanka and East Timor, have emerged from periods of protracted conflict, many of which have been marred by gender-based violence during conflict and its aftermath. Further, the legacy of colonial rule weighs heavily on the region, and archaic penal and other laws remain on many statute books. The sheer geographic heft of the Asian continent and the wide variance across Asian societies are two important factors that render efforts to generalise or simplify their historical experiences to a single narrative extremely difficult; they have also stymied attempts to develop region-wide governance structures, or Asia-specific human-rights treaties.

Historically, resistance by Asian states, including the PRC and Singapore, to the imposition of what is often perceived as a Euro-centric human-rights regime has invariably shaped national responses to international human-rights norms.

Across Asia, United Nations member states' engagements with international human-rights treaties remain weak even as states within Asia are increasingly gaining prominence in international affairs. Although all countries in Asia have ratified or acceded to the Convention of the Elimination of All Forms of Discrimination against Women (CEDAW), many of these countries have also entered reservations to core treaty obligations such as Article 2 (policy measures to eliminate discrimination against women) and Article 16 (equality in marriage and family life) thus significantly undermining the scope of the Convention's application. Given the limited scrutiny of gender-based violence within Asian contexts, regionally and internationally, this book offers a unique space to consider country-specific comparisons, including those in Bangladesh, China, East Timor, Hong Kong, India, Nepal, Myanmar and Sri Lanka.

A key aim of the book is to bridge policy and practice by drawing together both theoretical analyses of gender-based violence and practical experiences in Asian contexts. The chapters in this book are informed and influenced by the contributors' significant insights into gender, its intersections with other aspects of identity, violence and the state at academic, practical and often personal levels. The book brings together a collection of papers delivered at an international conference, *Gender, Violence and the State in Asia*, in May 2014. The conference was held at the Centre for Rights and Justice (CRJ) in the Faculty of Law at The Chinese University of Hong Kong with the generous support of the Taiwan Foundation for Democracy (TFD). We are indebted to Professor Christine Chinkin, a highly esteemed scholar on gender, human rights and international law, for situating gender-based violence in Asian contexts within the broader international human-rights framework. Drawing on a feminist analysis of international law, Professor Chinkin's seminal work broached previously unasked questions of women's status and identity within international law.

Chinkin, together with Hilary Charlesworth, exposed the 'silences and fundamentally skewed nature of international law' (Charlesworth *et al.* 1991), which have proven to be detrimental to the recognition of women as legal subjects in international law. Applying a feminist analysis, Charlesworth and Chinkin explored the way in which the structure and institutions of international law privileged male experiences, ignoring issues of sex and gender, which effectively sustained the unequal status of women globally (Charlesworth and Chinkin 2000). Chinkin drew attention to the narrow scope and remit of international law and jurisprudence, including its public-sphere bias, and advocated a redrawing of its boundaries to include the experiences of women, the majority of whose lives continue to be located in the private sphere (Chinkin 1999). While the UN Decade for Women (1976–85) was instrumental in raising the profile of women's rights, specifically the adoption of CEDAW in 1979, weak accountability mechanisms have undermined the Convention. As Charlesworth and Chinkin explain:

> *Many of the issues that concern women thus suffer a double marginalisation in the terms of traditional international law making: they are seen as the*

> *'soft' issues of human rights and are developed through modalities of law making that allow states to accept such principles while minimising their commitments.*
>
> (Charlesworth and Chinkin 2000, p. 66)

The Beijing Declaration and Platform for Action 1995 and subsequent legal instruments, including UN Security Council Resolution 1325 on Women, Peace and Security (2000),[1] which considers women's experiences during armed conflict and its aftermath, have sought to mainstream gender in international law and policy-making. It is hard to envisage that these developments would have occurred without the sustained activism of the transnational women's movement (and its respective caucuses) throughout the UN Decade for Women and at the Commission on the Status of Women, as well as the feminist analysis and scholarship of prominent academics including Chinkin, Charlesworth and Radhika Coomaraswamy, the former UN Special Rapporteur on Violence against Women (1994–2003).

While CEDAW sought to recognise women's rights and strengthen gender equality, Coomaraswamy suggested that a discrete focus on non-discrimination had effectively allowed the international legal system to take the 'easy way out' by avoiding engagement with all of equality's intricacies (Coomaraswamy 1994, p. 47). Further, within its structure, CEDAW itself lacks a clear focus on violence against women and its circumspect provisions do not adequately capture gender-based violence as a breach of a fundamental human right, which makes it difficult to hold states accountable. This significant gap in the framework of CEDAW has also allowed states to perpetuate inadequate understandings of, and responses to, all forms of gender-based violence by both states and non-state actors.

Given the absence of explicit provisions on violence against women within CEDAW, it is perhaps not surprising that state reporting often conflates gender-based violence with domestic violence, nor is it surprising that such reporting is often inadequate. State reports to CEDAW fail to consider other forms of violence against women including physical violence that falls outside the realm of spousal violence as well as structural violence that perpetuates gender inequality such as discriminatory laws or policies.

It was only in 1992, within General Recommendation No. 19, that the CEDAW Committee clarified that violence against women is to be recognised as a form of discrimination against women (Chinkin 2012, pp. 444–5). General Recommendation No. 19 specifically states that '[gender-based violence] includes acts that inflict physical, mental or sexual harm or suffering, threats of such acts, coercion and other deprivations of liberty' (General Recommendation No. 19, para. 6). However, this definition in itself does not adequately capture the multiple ways in which violence against women is manifested.

The Council of Europe Convention on Preventing and Combating Violence against Women and Domestic Violence (*Istanbul Convention 2014*), which entered into force on 1 August 2014, focuses specifically on multiple forms of violence against women, including domestic violence and '[recognises] . . . that violence against women is a manifestation of historically unequal power relations between women and men, which have led to domination over, and discrimination against, women by men and to the prevention of the full advancement of women' (Preamble). Further, the *Istanbul Convention 2014* clearly defines multiple forms of violence against women including sexual harassment (Article 40), stalking (Article 34), sexual violence and rape (Article 36), as well as psychological violence (Article 33), forced abortion and forced sterilisation (Article 39). While this is an important development internationally, the Convention's application is limited to member states of the Council of Europe.

Unlike Europe (*Istanbul Convention 2014*) and Latin America (Convention of Belém do Pará 1994) which have specific, continent-wide treaties targeting violence against women, and Africa, where the Protocol to the African Charter on Human and Peoples' Rights on the Rights of Women 2003 mainstreams provisions on violence, there is no Asia-specific treaty concerning women's rights or addressing violence against women directly. CEDAW, therefore, remains an important framework through which we can analyse women's rights and gender equality in Asia since the majority of states in Asia have ratified or acceded to it. At the sub-regional level all member states within the Association of South East Asian Nations (ASEAN) region[2] have ratified CEDAW, which has been influential in regional policy-making (Tan 2011, p. 153). In 2004, ASEAN adopted the Declaration against Trafficking in Persons Particularly Women and Children 2004 and the Declaration on the Elimination of Violence against Women in the ASEAN Region 2004. The adoption of these Declarations led to the formation of the ASEAN Commission for the Promotion and Protection of the Rights of Women and Children (ACWC) in 2009 (Tan 2011, p. 154). Thus there has been a gradual institutionalisation of human rights within the ASEAN region, particularly in relation to recognition of legal protections for women and children.

In 2013, the Declaration on the Elimination of Violence against Women and Elimination of Violence against Children in ASEAN was adopted. Significantly, this Declaration specifically acknowledged that women's and children's rights should be promoted, and that they should be protected from all forms of violence, abuse and exploitation. Further, the Declaration identifies domestic violence, sexual exploitation, cyber pornography and cyber prostitution, trafficking, women in armed conflict, ethnic and indigenous groups as well as stateless women and children as examples of women and children's vulnerability to violence, abuse and exploitation. On paper, the scope of this definition is broad, but the Declaration's implementation and enforcement in practice may be undermined by the nature of ASEAN as an organisation. In contrast with the European Union, which is a supranational organisation, ASEAN membership is strongly underpinned by the principles of consensus, sovereignty and non-interference in the affairs of its member states (Tan, 2011, p. 141).

Across the Asia-Pacific region, as of November 2015, thirty-one states have adopted some form of legislation to address violence against women, yet significantly only thirteen states criminalise marital rape.[3] While ASEAN recently adopted a Regional Plan of Action on Ending Violence against Women on 25 November 2015, it remains to be seen if the political will to end gender-based violence really exists within ASEAN or subsists only on paper.

One of the primary goals of this book is to highlight and discuss the inadequacies in state responses to gender-based violence. The 1993 Declaration on the Elimination of Violence against Women clearly stated that states have a duty to 'exercise due diligence to prevent, investigate and, in accordance with national legislation, punish acts of violence against women, whether those acts are perpetuated by the State or by private actors' (Article 4(c)). Due diligence goes beyond pro forma enactment of formal legal provisions and requires that states also assess the systems that they have put in place to combat violence against women for the intended result and effectiveness (UN Human Rights Council 2006, p. 10). In her 2013 report to the Human Rights Council, Rashida Manjoo, the former Special Rapporteur on Violence against Women (2009–15), proposed that due-diligence standards used in the context of evaluating the human-rights responsibilities of transnational corporations could in turn serve as useful assessment tools in the violence against women context (UN Human Rights Council 2013, pp. 7–8). These four elements are: (a) the identification and assessment of actual or potential adverse human rights impacts; (b) whether appropriate actions have been taken based on information from such assessments; (c) tracking the effectiveness of the response; and (d) effective communication with relevant stakeholders concerning the response (ibid.). In examining how state institutions interact with gender-based violence in Asia, this book attempts to expose state failings under the due-diligence rubric as well as flesh out how these elements may be effectively applied in the Asian context.

While much of the discourse on violence against women in Asia has revolved around violence perpetuated by non-state actors and state responsibility to address such violence, this book also turns the same critical eye to state action and inaction that has not been examined through a gender lens. In highlighting the often overlooked gender differences within the state's application and development of its laws and policies (such as in the administration of national security laws, transitional justice mechanisms and rural justice reforms), this book demonstrates the urgent need to mainstream a gender perspective in evaluating and implementing justice mechanisms throughout state systems.

A final issue that must be addressed is whether gender-based violence and violence against women are interchangeable concepts. While gender-based violence disproportionality impacts women, both men and women often face violence and discrimination because of perceptions that they have deviated from binary gender norms and stereotypical expectations. This book grapples with the theoretical and practical difficulties imposed by existing frameworks that reflect these gender binaries and stereotypes tied to gender roles. These underlying theoretical tensions were also drawn out in dynamic discussions at the May 2014 conference on which this book is based. These discussions also highlighted the need for more in-depth research on gender-based and gendered violence in the context of sexual minorities and gender non-conforming communities.

The authors of this book offer complex and nuanced analyses of gender-based violence and the intricacies of securing gender equality in Asia, paying particular attention to how gender and violence interact with state institutions and legal frameworks. The contributors to this book bring a wealth of formidable experience and insight, many have bridged scholarship and human-rights practice in their professional lives. The book benefits from the frontline work of legal practitioners and human-rights activists whose advocacy and service provision have focused on the rights of marginalised populations (including women from ethnic or religious minorities, rural women, single women/widows, migrant domestic workers and LGBT individuals). The book also draws upon the cutting-edge scholarship of our academic colleagues, many of whom have adopted empirical methods in their work and work directly with civil-society organisations and other stakeholders. By drawing together scholarly and practitioner perspectives, the book provides a rich insight into the conceptual and practical challenges of addressing gender-based violence in Asian contexts, while underscoring the importance of marrying theoretical scholarship with practical insight from on-the-ground human-rights advocacy and activism.

The book is structured around three core themes: 'Gender, violence and states in transition' (Part I), 'Gender, violence and access to justice' (Part II) and 'Transcending borders and boundaries: negotiating gender, identity and violence' (Part III). As an overarching framework to the book, Chinkin's chapter situates each of these themes within the broader international human-rights framework, including CEDAW and the ensuing obligations of Asian states under international law to examine *Gender, violence and access to justice in international law*.

By focusing on gender, violence and states in transition, the chapters within Part I explore the fragility of transition and its impact on state responses to gender-based violence. Drawing on experiences of instability and transition in East Timor and Sri Lanka, Rita Shackel's chapter explores the continuum of violence that occurs during times of transition, which suggests that violence against women is not extraordinary or episodic, but often forms the backdrop to the everyday lives of women and girls, whether during conflict or in its aftermath. While periods of transition may entrench patterns of gender-based violence, such periods potentially allow for positive social changes as a result of shifts in social hierarchies.

Shyamala Gomez's case study of Sri Lanka critically examines the state's response to gender-based violence in the aftermath of the civil war. While national policy frameworks exist, including the Lessons Learnt and Reconciliation Commission (LLRC) and the National Action Plan for the Promotion and Protection of Human Rights (NHRAP), Gomez suggests that the reality of women's lives on the ground needs to be more effectively bridged by such policy frameworks. Within her analysis of how the conflict has impacted women's lives, Gomez exposes the complexity of documenting and responding to sexual violence.

Similarly, Amrita Gurung and Lily Thapa's case study and analysis of *Violence, women and conflict in Nepal* reinforces the continuum of violence that women experience during times of transition. Exploring the structural inequality and physical violence experienced by women, Gurung and Thapa highlight the importance of moving beyond the homogenisation of women's experiences in post-conflict settings, drawing on the example of single women (widows) in Nepal as a distinct identity group to challenge mainstream narratives of conflict-affected victims, which fail to consider the intersection of gender with other identity characteristics, including caste and ethnicity.

Amy Barrow's chapter considers how international legal responses to gender-based violence in armed conflict filter down to national level, examining the implementation of Security Council Resolution 1325 (SRC 1325) at state level through a content analysis of National Action Plans (NAPs) on women, peace and security. Analysing the NAPs of the Philippines, Nepal and the Republic of Korea, Barrow seeks to draw out the practical challenges of implementing SCR 1325 including ensuring accountability for NAPs monitoring and evaluation. Within her analysis, Barrow seeks to evaluate whether there are any particular structural or other obstacles within the Asian context, which have implications for the effective implementation of SCR 1325.

In exploring the intersections between gender, violence and access to justice, Part II of the book investigates how women engage with formal justice systems to seek redress for gender-based violence. The consequences of engagement can sometimes prove detrimental and serve to further exacerbate violence experienced by women and minority groups.

Surabhi Chopra explores the way in which the state engages and interacts with female suspects, detainees and defendants under national security laws in India. A proliferation of security laws which give the Executive broad-reaching powers has weakened the individual rights of suspects and detainees, though to date how women suspected of security offences are disproportionately vulnerable to sexualised forms of extra-legal violence by state actors has been afforded little scrutiny. In examining two cases, Chopra exposes the state's passive response toward victims of sexual assault by state personnel.

In her chapter on *Public interest litigation on violence against women in Bangladesh: possibilities and limits*, Sara Hossain explores the experiences of legal aid lawyers working for the Bangladesh Legal Aid Services Trust (BLAST) in undertaking public interest litigation to challenge and seek remedies for violence against women. She focuses on two cases, one relating to the investigation and prosecution of *fatwa* violence, and another concerning the collection of medical evidence in rape cases, to draw out the possibilities and limitations of public interest litigation as a strategy to secure redress.

Huang Zhong's chapter examines the rural justice system in China, with a particular focus on the role of basic level judicial offices. Drawing upon case studies from Huang's research in a remote ethnic minority area in Hubei Province, the chapter considers several case studies involving the resolution of matrimonial disputes by judicial offices. The chapter demonstrates that a lack of gender awareness in laws and judicial practices may result in the marginalisation of rural women during the process of access to justice, and eventually prejudice the fulfilment of their rights.

Drawing on research conducted with ethnic minority (EMI) women in Hong Kong, Puja Kapai argues that the effectiveness of protective measures to combat violence against women is highly dependent on the state's understanding of the internal (cultural) and external (situational) context and how these factors combine to influence EMI women's help-seeking behaviour and their access to justice. Kapai argues that the adoption of an intersectional analysis is imperative for framing responses to gender-based violence in order to deliver contextualised justice in cases concerning violence against EMI women.

The chapters in Part III, *Transcending borders and boundaries: negotiating gender, identity and violence*, explore the intersection of gender with other identity characteristics, such as sexuality and immigrant status, and the distinct challenges experienced by minority and other vulnerable groups in responding to gender-based violence. The theme covers violence that occurs as a result of the movement across physical and imagined boundaries, including geographic and jurisdictional borders, as well as the boundaries of permissible gender expression, sexuality and identity. A principle focus of this section is to consider how laws and policies may actively perpetuate structural violence. A range of case studies explore the myriad ways in which structurally violent laws and policies fundamentally impact upon the lives of minority and other vulnerable identity groups within society.

Lynette Chua and David Gilbert draw on ethnographic empirical research undertaken with sexual minorities in Myanmar, specifically *apwint*. Biologically male, *apwint* act and appear as feminine. In exploring the social oppression, police abuse and state-sanctioned violence toward *apwint*, Chua and Gilbert expose the endemic corruption at all levels of governance in Myanmar and the arbitrary application of the rule of law, while considering how human-rights violations against *apwint* may be effectively addressed.

Joy Chia explores the intersectionality of gender, sexuality and violence in the Chinese legal system and argues that structural inequalities embedded within Chinese laws and policy-making structures have privileged the male experience of violence by (1) framing 'real' violence as violent acts perpetuated by strangers, rather than those familiar to the victim; and (2) prioritising physical violence over other forms of violence. Chinese laws perpetuate gender stereotypes while rendering the violence experienced by many minority populations invisible. Chia then argues that current legal reform in the Chinese context in the area of family violence is undermined by state tolerance of (even perpetuation of) gender-based violence in the public sphere.

Kay McArdle draws upon her work with PathFinders, a non-governmental organisation that works on the frontline with pregnant, migrant domestic workers, to consider how the legal and policy landscape in Hong Kong falls short of providing adequate protection. The outsourcing of care services for the young and elderly by the Hong Kong Government effectively perpetuates a cycle of migration from South East Asia to Hong Kong. Immigration policies – including the 'two week' rule, whereby migrant domestic workers must return to their home country if their contract is terminated – disempower migrant domestic workers, placing them in a vulnerable position. Exploring the economic and social context in which migrant domestic worker's lives are situated, McArdle highlights how migrant women are particularly vulnerable to abuse given their lower socio-economic status, ethnicity and gender, which is compounded during and after pregnancy.

Gao Wei's chapter examines the challenges that rural women leaders in China face in negotiating their different identities, and how conflicts brought up by the different roles they are expected to play can impact rural women's rights. Rural women leaders are usually the first institutional point of contact when women in rural communities encounter gender-related disputes, however, as representatives of the state they are also obligated to implement the government's law and policies in regard to family planning, which are both physically and structurally violent against women. The chapter examines how rural women leaders engage with these dual professional identities, while also remaining embedded in their communities. Drawing on a case study of rural women leaders in Hubei, China, the chapter suggests that the empowerment of rural women leaders through proper training may lead to better protection for rural women's rights and to attitudinal changes in other male rural leaders.

In her examination of client-perpetrated violence toward sex workers in Hong Kong, Susanne Choi explores how the varying conditions of sex workers across different settings and venues influence and shape legal responses to sex work, resulting in diverse vulnerabilities. In aiming to move beyond previous research which focuses on the distinction between indoor and outdoor sex work, Choi argues that greater understanding is needed of the hierarchy of the sex industry and how this leads to inequality between different groups of sex workers and to a distinct risk of violence.

While there is no single argument stemming from the book, the diverse chapters provide an insight into how women and minority gender groups experience gender-based violence across jurisdictions in Asia. Although each jurisdiction is unique in its social, legal and political landscape, there are clear parallels that can be drawn in terms of the acute challenges experienced by women, whether during periods of transition from conflict to peace, in women's access to justice or in how women and minority gender groups negotiate gender and other aspects of identity in addressing violence. While discourses often construct gender-based violence within the private domain focusing almost exclusively on intimate partner violence, the diverse and multiple forms of violence presented here, challenge the assumption that gender and violence are hidden from the public domain. Conversely, gender and violence are clearly visible within the public domain and such violence takes multiple forms, both physical and structural. Paradoxically this 'visibility' often translates into 'blindness' or impunity in practice. Thus, the challenges for responding to gender-based violence in both public and private domains are critical in Asia, particularly given the complex and diverse cultural, religious and social dynamics upon which women's lives are often hinged.

Notes

1 UN Security Council (2000) Resolution 1325, 31 October 2000, UN Doc. S/RES/1325.
2 ASEAN is comprised of ten member states: Brunei, Cambodia, Laos, Indonesia, Malaysia, Myanmar, the Philippines, Singapore, Thailand and Vietnam.
3 United Nations ESCAP 'On the International Day for the Elimination of Violence against Women – UN underlines need to transform commitments into action in Asia-Pacific' (25 November 2015) G/54/2015 [online] http://www.unescap.org/news/international-day-elimination-violence-against-women-%E2%80%93-un-underlines-need-transform-commitments

Bibliography

Charlesworth, H. and Chinkin, C. (2000) *The Boundaries of International Law: A Feminist Analysis* Manchester University Press, Manchester, UK.

Charlesworth, H. Chinkin, C. and Wright, S. (1991) 'Feminist Approaches to International Law' *The American Journal of International Law* vol. 85, no. 4, pp. 613–45.

Chinkin, C. (1999) 'A Critique of the Public/Private Dimension' *European Journal of International Law* vol. 10, no. 2, pp. 387–95.

Chinkin, C. (2012). 'Violence against Women' in Freeman, M. Chinkin, C. and Rudolf, B. (eds.), *The UN Convention on the Elimination of All Forms of Discrimination against Women: A Commentary*, Oxford University Press, Oxford, U.K.

Coomaraswamy, R. (1994). 'To Bellow like a Cow: Women, Ethnicity, and the Discourse of Rights' in Cook, R.J. (eds.), *Human Rights of Women: Natioanl and International Perspectives* University of Pennsylvania Press, Philadelphia, Pennsylvania, U.S.A., pp. 39–57.

Tan, H.L. (2011). *The ASEAN Intergovernmental Commission on Human Rights: Institutionalising Human Rights in Southeast Asia*, Cambridge University Press, Cambridge, UK.

UN Human Rights Council (2006), Special Rapporteur on Violence against Women, *The Due Diligence Standard as a Tool for the Elimination of Violence Against Women*, E/CN.4/2006/61.

UN Human Rights Council (2013), *Report of the Special Rapporteur on Violence against Women, Its Causes and Consequences, Rashida Manjoo*, A/HRC/23/49.

1 Gender, violence and access to justice in international law

Christine Chinkin

Introduction

The authors in this book have a very evident wealth of expertise about gender and violence across Asia, the different social contexts, the manifestations of violence and the legal frameworks for addressing it. Since I cannot contribute to this detailed local knowledge and since gender-based violence is a global phenomenon, this chapter addresses the topic from the perspective of state obligations under international human-rights law,[1] in particular with respect to access to justice for victims of gender-based violence.

In 1992 the Committee on Elimination of all Forms of Discrimination against Women (CEDAW Committee) explained that '[g]ender-based violence is a form of discrimination that seriously inhibits women's ability to enjoy rights and freedoms on a basis of equality with men' (CEDAW Committee 1992 General Comment No. 19, para. 1[2]), thereby conflating women and gender. This understanding encompasses gender-based violence neither against men nor against persons because of their sexual orientation or gender identity. This was unsurprising for at least two reasons. First the Committee is the monitoring body for the Convention on the Elimination of all Forms of Discrimination (CEDAW), which is the only gender-specific UN human-rights treaty. Unlike, for instance, the Universal Declaration of Human Rights (UDHR), the International Covenant on Civil and Political Rights (ICCPR) and the International Covenant on Economic Social and Cultural Rights (ICESCR), which require guarantees of rights without discrimination *inter alia* as to sex (UDHR, Art. 2; ICCPR, Art. 2(1); ICESCR, Art. 2(2)), CEDAW condemns discrimination only against women. Second, the concept of violence targeted against women, because they are women, was entering the international agenda in the early 1990s (Chinkin 2012), while the broader (and controversial) concepts of sexuality, gender and gender identities had not yet done so. Indeed, in 1998, the inclusion of persecution on the basis of gender as a crime against humanity was hotly contested at Rome during the negotiations for the International Criminal Court[3] and it was not until the twenty-first century that the Office of the High Commissioner of Human Rights examined discrimination and violent acts committed against individuals on the grounds of their sexual orientation or gender identity (UNHCHR 2011). In 2011 the Council of Europe

Convention on Violence against Women (*Istanbul Convention*) was the first human-rights treaty explicitly to include (in Article 2(3)) non-discrimination on the grounds of sex, gender, sexual orientation or gender identity. Nevertheless, while recognising the importance of further examination of such forms of violence and the responses to them, this chapter focuses on gender-based violence against women.

The legal framework

There is no international treaty on the prevention and prosecution of violence against women, although there have been calls for such a treaty to be negotiated. Nor is there an Asia-specific treaty, such as those in Latin America, Africa and now Europe.[4] Asian states' obligations in this regard are therefore somewhat diffuse, deriving from a range of international human-rights treaties which are supplemented by multiple 'soft law' instruments and the jurisprudence of international institutions such as the UN human-rights treaty bodies, especially the CEDAW Committee. Accordingly, states' legal obligations must be discerned from these sources, in particular from the statements and jurisprudence of the CEDAW Committee. All states parties to CEDAW (which includes the majority of Asian/Pacific states) must submit their periodic reports to the Committee (Article 18) and the concluding observations provide guidance as to how the Committee – the authoritative interpretative body established under the Convention[5] – understands states' obligations, tailored to the state in question. Accordingly this chapter will take particular account of the issues the Committee has raised with Asian states through the reporting process. The state-specific concluding observations are supplemented by the Committee's General Recommendations, of which there are currently thirty-two. However, there does appear to be a reluctance among Asian states to engage with CEDAW; only a handful have accepted the 1999 Optional Protocol to CEDAW[6] and many regional states are behind with their reporting obligations, or combine a number of reports together. But it is not only through CEDAW that states' obligations under international law can be discerned as other treaty bodies, such as the UN Human Rights Committee (UNHRC) and Committee on Economic, Social and Cultural Rights (CESCR), have integrated violence against women into the terms of their gender-neutral treaties, thereby bestowing gender specificity into these core human-rights instruments (see UNHRC General Comment No. 28[7]; CESCR General Comment No. 16[8]; UN Human Rights Council 2008). There is also an observable synergy between institutions; for instance the Inter-American and European human-rights courts draw upon the work of the CEDAW Committee,[9] and vice versa, thereby building up a coherent set of understandings around which there is growing consensus at the institutional level. These are in addition to and alongside those developed through the Security Council's continuing commitment to women, peace and security.[10]

CEDAW does not explicitly address violence against women. It condemns discrimination against women and requires parties to pursue without delay a policy of eliminating discrimination against women. Importantly, the CEDAW Committee has confirmed that the Convention also applies to girls since they 'are part of the larger community of women' (General Recommendation No. 28, para. 21[11]). In a groundbreaking step in its 1992 General Recommendation No. 19 on violence against women the Committee interpreted the definition of discrimination in CEDAW to include gender-based violence 'that seriously inhibits women's ability to enjoy rights and freedoms on a basis of equality with men' and set out states' obligations in this regard (para. 1). It also intimated that it would expect states to report on the steps they were taking with respect to addressing violence against women, and subject those steps to scrutiny. Although a General Recommendation is not of itself legally binding, the fact that states have indeed reported on violence against women and have responded – at least to some extent – to the Committee's recommendations to them has given General Recommendation No. 19 greater authority (Chinkin 2013, p. 80). The Committee's concluding observations have also added content and specificity to both the Convention and General Recommendation No. 19.

The process of bringing violence against women into international human-rights law did not stop with the adoption of General Recommendation No 19; also supplementing CEDAW are a number of 'soft law' instruments, including the Beijing Declaration and Platform for Action 1995 and the subsequent five-, ten- and fifteen-year follow-up processes, resolutions of the United Nations General Assembly (UNGA), the Human Rights Council and the Commission on the Status of Women (CSW).[12] The reiteration of the basic principles in these international instruments, typically adopted by consensus or by overwhelming majorities, affirms that they create expectations of compliance. These are the 'top-down' instruments; they have provided civil society, including most importantly local women's groups, with the legal framework around which they have organised, lobbied and campaigned. It remains evident that the vision of a world free from gender-based violence has not been achieved, but without the work, commitment and innovations of such groups that have sought to turn legal form into reality the story might well have gone no further.

Defining 'violence against women'

It is perhaps useful to consider first what is meant by violence against women. In General Recommendation No. 19 the CEDAW Committee defined gender-based violence as 'violence that is directed against a woman because she is a woman or that affects women disproportionately. It includes acts that inflict physical, mental or sexual harm or suffering, threats of such acts, coercion and other deprivations of liberty' (General Recommendation No. 19, para.6). The General Assembly importantly added structural violence which is 'a manifestation of historically unequal power relations between men and women'. The violence does not just happen to occur to women, but is motivated by sex and gender,[13] such as the assertion of male power and control in both the public and private spheres, enforcement of assigned social gender roles, and the punishment of perceived deviant behaviour. It is thus deeply rooted in cultural, religious and social norms and is often perpetuated by a culture of denial and silence.

Violence against women has multiple forms. It occurs in the family (domestic, intimate partner and interfamilial violence, incest and, so-called, honour killings), the community (for instance in work, educational and religious establishments, or in outbursts of communal violence such as in Gujarat[14] or sexual harassment of women in Tahir Square[15]) and the state (in military institutions, welfare institutions, police stations[16] and prisons,[17] social agencies). Some forms of violence against women are rooted in custom and cultural traditions, or are maintained through enduring stereotypes defining women's roles and responsibilities, but which are discriminatory and perpetuate their subordination within the family and society.[18] Human-rights bodies have identified and expressed their concern to some Asian states about particular forms of violence that occur within their countries that constitute violations of women's human rights, for example: to Pakistan about child and forced marriages, *karo-kari*, stove burning and acid throwing, marriage to the Koran, polygamy and honour killing (CEDAW Committee 2013a); to India about dowry, *sati*, the *devadasi* system, and witch-hunting (CEDAW Committee 2007a, para. 26); to Timor-Leste about polygamy, bride price and dowry (CEDAW Committee 2009b, para. 27); to Laos about the practices of some ethnic groups within the country with respect to the rape of young girls before puberty (CEDAW Committee 2009c, para. 22); to Papua New Guinea about 'brutal torture' and killings of women accused of witchcraft (CEDAW Committee 2010a, para. 27);[19] to Indonesia about a law permitting medical practitioners to perform female genital mutilation (CEDAW Committee 2012b, para. 21; UNHRC 2013, para. 12); to Nepal about child marriage, the dowry system, son preference, witchcraft accusations and *chaupadi*, *jhuma*, *deuki* and *dhan-khaane* (CEDAW Committee 2011a, para. 17). Some types of widespread and targeted killings of women, committed essentially with impunity, have been labelled femicide, for instance in South Asia killings associated with 'cultural practices in the region such as female infanticide, preadolescent mortality of girls and dowry-related deaths' (Special Rapporteur on Violence Against Women 2012, paras. 22, 56–60, 77–81). Ill-treatment, sometimes amounting to the extreme levels associated with torture, of domestic workers invariably women and often foreign women,[20] is another concern relevant to a number of Asian states that are both recipients and suppliers of domestic servants.

Gender-based violence is not the same as sexual violence, but there is no generally accepted definition of the latter in international law. One suggested definition is 'any violence, physical or psychological, carried out through sexual means or by targeting sexuality' which includes 'both physical and psychological attacks directed at a person's sexual characteristics, such as forcing a person to strip naked in public, mutilating a person's genitals, or slicing off a woman's breasts' (UN Sub-Commission on the Promotion and Protection of Human Rights 1998, paras. 21–2). Although harms caused through sexual violence often incur particular social stigma, ostracism and isolation, a focus on sex crimes or sexual violence incurs the risk of perceiving women solely through the lens of sexual activity, thereby failing to recognise them as holistic beings and denying their agency. A particular aspect of the sexualisation of women has been raised in the context of Singapore. The CEDAW Committee has expressed its concern at the pervasiveness of advertising for products and services that urge women to improve their body image and conform to societal expectations; 'such cultural overemphasis on women's beauty . . . reinforce[s] the image of women as sex objects and constitute serious obstacles to [all] women's enjoyment of their human rights' (CEDAW Committee 2012a, paras. 21–2). In the words of the Committee 'the over-sexualized depiction of women strengthens the existing stereotypes of women as sex objects and continues to generate girls' low self-esteem' (CEDAW Committee 2009a, para. 29).[21]

Violence against women is not solely physical and a holistic understanding includes non-physical violence – economic, psychological and verbal violence. Sexist and discriminatory remarks from public officials, which are repeated in the media, become accepted as normal expressions and reinforce social stereotypes of women; this in turn underlines the status of women as second-class citizens. The Committee has accordingly urged Japan 'to take measures, including the criminalization of verbal violence, to ensure that Government officials do not make disparaging remarks that demean women and contribute to the patriarchal system which discriminates against women' (CEDAW Committee 2009a, para. 30).

The concept of economic violence has been much contested; in negotiating the *Istanbul Convention*, some delegates refused to countenance any such notion and expressed scepticism as to how it could be understood or articulated.[22] A case before the CEDAW Committee, *V.K. v. Bulgaria* (Communication No. 20/2008), illustrates what is meant. The complainant had alleged that her husband

> decided on the spending of the family's income and provided the author with money only for the basic needs of the family. She had no additional money for herself and was not allowed to spend money given to her for other purposes than those strictly specified; nor was she informed about how the rest of her husband's income was spent. As a result, she was economically entirely dependent on her husband.

The Committee criticised 'an overly restrictive definition of domestic violence' that neglected her emotional and psychological suffering. But this is economic violence at the individual level. What is more challenging is how accepted economic policies – austerity, privatisation and structural adjustment programmes coupled with the concentration of women in export centres and minimal regulation of trade and working conditions – all contribute to women's unequal access to economic and social rights, to the feminisation of poverty[23] and vulnerability to violence. The former Special Rapporteur on Violence against Women, Yakin Ertürk, has explained how power operates through coercion and through the structural relations of production and reproduction, controlling the allocation and use of resources, benefits, privileges and authority in the state, in society and in the home – the sites of violence against women. She identifies three 'key structural elements highlighted by the political economy approach' that contribute to the unequal delivery of economic and social rights, and hence to violence against women: the sexual division of labour; the 'global, macroeconomic environment'; and the gender dimensions of armed conflict (UNHRC Special Rapporteur on Violence Against Women 2009a, paras. 28–34).

Access to justice

This chapter now turns from an understanding of what constitutes violence against women to its central theme: states' obligations with respect to victims' and potential victims' access to justice – their engagement with law enforcement and judicial bodies from their first encounter through to any trial and subsequent appeal process. It thus encompasses seeking protection, filing complaints, dealings with those collecting forensic and medical evidence, proceedings in civil and criminal courts, and enforcement processes. At the core of obligations with respect to access to justice are the rights to a fair trial and to equality before the law, 'key element[s] of human rights protection' which serve as the 'procedural means to safeguard the rule of law'.[24] The Human Rights Committee has recommended that states provide information with respect to whether women enjoy access to justice on equal terms with men[25] but in its General Comment 32 on Article 14 of the ICCPR, it failed to develop its earlier reasoning on this topic or to add any gender analysis. Failure to ensure victims of such violence *de jure* and *de facto* access to justice is both a consequence of sex and gender-based discrimination and constitutes further discrimination. States' obligations with respect to access to justice cannot be isolated from all other state obligations, for an adequate response to gender-based violence that is compliant with international standards must be state-wide, comprehensive, integrated and joined up across all relevant departments, agencies and stakeholders, including importantly men and boys. In July 2015 the CEDAW Committee filled an important gap by its adoption of a comprehensive General Recommendation on women's access to justice (General Recommendation No. 33), recognising its importance in optimising the 'emancipatory and transformative potential of law'. It accordingly considers the obstacles that restrict women's access to justice, reinforces earlier work of the Committee and identifies six interrelated and essential components to the concept across all areas of law: 'justiciability, availability, accessibility, good quality, accountability of justice systems and the provision of remedies for victims' (para. 14). These themes resonate throughout the following account, which focuses on access to justice in the particular context of violence against women.

In order to clarify states' obligations with respect to gender-based violence, the CEDAW Committee has adopted and developed the typology of layered obligations: that states must 'respect, protect, and fulfil women's right to non-discrimination and to the enjoyment of equality' (General Recommendation No. 28, para. 28; *A.T. v. Hungary*). It is within this framework that access to justice can be analysed. The first level obligation to respect requires the state to ensure that public officials, whose acts and omissions are attributable to the state, do not commit such violence (International Law Commission 2001). Violence against women must be justiciable for victims to be able to claim their rights and legal entitlements, including with respect to acts that occurred in the past (General Recommendation No. 33, para. 14(a)). For instance, the CEDAW Committee reminds states of their continuing obligations with respect to the violent acts of a previous regime which have not been adequately addressed and where the pain and social injustice are ongoing. For instance, it has regretted Japan's failure 'to find a lasting solution for the situation of "comfort women" victimized by the Japanese military during the Second World War and expresses concern at the deletion of references to this issue in school textbooks' (CEDAW Committee 2009a, para. 30). In 2013 it urged Cambodia 'to provide effective redress' including with respect to the 'sexual violence, against women committed during the Khmer Rouge regime and consider to develop effective non-judicial transitional justice programmes, including the provision of adequate reparation and psychological and other appropriate support' (CEDAW Committee 2013b, para.15).[26]

Furthermore, since violence against women is rooted in women's social and economic inequality and itself constitutes a form of discrimination, the obligation to respect women's right to be free from violence includes the duty to ensure that all laws – criminal, civil, administrative and labour – are not discriminatory.[27] This requires gender analysis to identify which laws are directly or indirectly discriminatory, to repeal those that are, and to 'refrain from making laws, policies, regulations, programmes, administrative procedures and institutional structures that directly or indirectly result in the denial of the equal enjoyment by women of their civil, political, economic, social and cultural rights' (General Recommendation No. 28, para. 9).

The second level obligation to protect requires the state to take positive measures to protect women from gender-based violence not only when committed by public officials but also by non-state actors. The third level obligation – the duty to fulfil – requires the state to take positive, forward-looking and long-term policies and programmes for the actual enjoyment of human rights (ibid.); for instance, ongoing equality awareness training of all relevant officials in *inter alia* law enforcement (including those working in informal justice processes such as village mediation units [CEDAW Committee 2009c, para. 24]), health and social services, and the education of women and men about equality. This requires research into the root causes of violence against women (Marks 2011) to gain a fuller picture of its incidence and context through the collection and collation of adequate and reliable statistical data on domestic and sexual violence disaggregated by sex, age, nationality and relationship between victim and perpetrator (CEDAW Committee 2012a, para. 23(e); CEDAW Committee 2007b, para. 17). The CEDAW Committee consistently reminds Asian states of the need to do this. Other forward-looking steps include combating pornography and banning the sale of video games and cartoons involving rape and sexual violence against women, steps which require media regulation and which pit women's right to be free from violence against commercial interests and market principles (e.g. CEDAW Committee 2009a, paras. 30 and 36). Ultimately, the obligation to fulfil looks to addressing gender ideology that sustains the structural and systemic inequality of women, thereby transforming gender relations (Holtmaat 2012, p.144).

The obligation to protect women from violence committed by non-state actors and thus to ensure women's right to be free from violence has been conceptualised and made more concrete through the duty and standard of due diligence (UNHRC 2006; UNHRC 2013). Thus 'States may also be responsible for private acts if they fail to act with due diligence to prevent violations of rights or to investigate and punish acts of violence, and for providing compensation' (General Recommendation No. 19, para. 9);[28] this obligation arises 'under general international law and specific human rights covenants' (*Fatma Yildirim (deceased) v. Austria,* para. 12.1.1). The due diligence requirements to prevent, protect against, prosecute and punish gender-based violence are all linked and, taken together, constitute the obligation to ensure access to justice to all victims and to transform the societal values and institutions that sustain gender inequality.

The standard of due diligence is not one of strict liability but requires the state to act with the means at its disposal; nevertheless the standard is high and increasing. Law enforcement officials must respond to gender-based violence with the same level of commitment to prevent, prosecute and punish it as they would to all other crimes, whoever the perpetrator. It must not be trivialised as 'solely domestic', 'private', or a waste of police time. Victims must be recognised as victims of serious crimes in accordance with the Declaration of Basic Principles of Justice for Victims of Crime and Abuse of Power (UNGA 1985). The CEDAW Committee (in line with the European and Inter-American Human Rights Courts) has applied the duty of due diligence in the contexts of domestic violence (*A.T. v. Hungary*; *Fatma Yildirim (deceased) v. Austria*; *Şahide Goecke v. Austria*), sexual violence against a child with disabilities (*VPP v. Bulgaria*), the commission of rape (*Vertido v. The Philippines*; *RPB v. The Philippines*) and failure to protect the daughter of a victim of domestic violence from the continuing effects of that violence (*Angela González Carreño v. Spain*).

Determining the measures that should be taken by states to meet the standard of due diligence is context specific and any attempted list will not be exhaustive. The obligation to prevent acts of gender-based violence may be explained in the general terms of state responsibility for the commission of an internationally wrongful act as 'best effort obligations requiring States to take all reasonable or necessary measures to prevent a given event from occurring, but without warranting that the event will not occur' (Crawford 2002, p. 140). A primary level prevention strategy requires an informed assessment of risk of death or serious injury,[29] both in general and specific, to particular incidents or individuals of which the authorities are aware, or should be aware.[30] The former requires an evaluation by relevant authorities across agencies of the overall situation and the system-wide factors that incur the risk of violence against women,[31] for example structural discrimination and stereotyping of women, as well as the increased risk incurred by women made especially vulnerable by their circumstances, such as those from rural communities who migrate to seek employment in towns (General Recommendation No. 19, para. 21), living in conditions of poverty or extreme poverty, prevailing community violence, disadvantaged by caste (CEDAW Committee 2007a, para. 21), ethnicity (CEDAW Committee 2009c, para. 22), foreign wives (CEDAW Committee 2011b, para. 20), immigrant (CEDAW Committee 2009a, para. 30), or rural women (CEDAW Committee 2009b, para. 30). In individual instances this requires attention to the specific situation of the woman who has been brought to the attention of the authorities. Determining whether the authorities 'knew or should have known' of the danger of violence is context specific, as illustrated by the facts in *Fatma Yildirim v. Austria*. Fatma Yildirim – an Austrian national of Turkish origin – suffered violence at the hands of her husband, including threats to kill her and her children if she were to divorce him. Although she obtained an injunction prohibiting him from returning to the couple's apartment, the immediate surroundings and her workplace, he continued to contact her in person and by phone and to threaten her. There were regular police interventions but a request to the public prosecutor to detain her husband was refused. Another factor that increased the danger was that the husband (a non-Austrian national) stood to lose his residence permit in Austria if the marriage was terminated. Her husband stabbed her to death near her apartment. The CEDAW Committee determined that the failure of the authorities to detain her husband breached the due diligence obligation to protect Fatma Yildirim from him; they did not take the decisive steps when the facts showed that they knew, or should have known, of the extreme danger she was in.

The State's duty to protect women from violence includes the provision of adequate, available and affordable legal remedies and effective ways of accessing these remedies,[32] even for the poorest and most marginalised women. National legislation should provide for adequate civil orders, such as emergency barring, restraining or protection orders. Protective orders must be known to law enforcement officials so they can advise on their issuance, be speedily obtainable, and effective (e.g. CESCR 2010, para. 24). Bureaucratic restrictions should not be allowed to constrain their accessibility, for instance through hearings scheduled some weeks ahead, restrictive time limits imposed for reporting violence, or protective measures only being made available if a certain level of injury has been incurred (*V.K. v. Bulgaria*). The CEDAW Committee has repeatedly approved states' adoption of appropriate legislation and programmes and the establishment of national machinery responsible for oversight of women's rights, but has expressed regret where such reforms have not been introduced, or where introduced have not been made effective in achieving substantive equality.[33] As it observed in *Fatma Yildirim*, although Austria had put in place a comprehensive framework to address domestic violence, including

> legislation, criminal and civil-law remedies, awareness raising, education and training, shelters, counselling for victims of violence and work with perpetrators . . . in order for the individual woman victim of domestic violence to enjoy the practical realization of the principle of equality of men and women . . . the political will that is expressed in the aforementioned

> comprehensive system of Austria must be supported by State actors, who adhere to the State party's due diligence obligations.
>
> (*Fatma Yildirim v. Austria*, para. 12.1.2)

The processes and institutions for accessing justice have been described as a 'justice chain'[34] that women must be able to navigate; accordingly, obstacles to that navigation must be identified and addressed. Obstacles may be practical, for instance: unavailability of services within remote areas; lack of transport; linguistic barriers and lack of interpreters (*RPB v. The Philippines*); high rates of illiteracy (CEDAW Committee 2012c, paras. 21–2); lack of knowledge or the means of acquiring reliable and timely information about whom to contact or how to do so; the costs of proceedings and lack of financial and other resources. Other obstacles are institutional, for instance: corruption; absence of an independent judiciary; a plurality of mechanisms making navigation uncertain or impossible; too great a reliance on traditional justice systems (ibid., para. 21); or diverting cases to mediation where power imbalances are not moderated by law.[35] Still others are cultural: conflicting social policies, for example a social emphasis on family unity and reconciliation rather than on women's safety; a tolerance of violence against women; an attitude that 'she brought it on herself', provoked or deserved it. Some barriers can be addressed by a commitment to women's rights and gender sensitivity, but others are deep-rooted and require an overall institutional and structural reform that brings together rule of law initiatives, capacity building and ensuring access to justice for women. Conflicting rights may also be argued as a reason for denying women protective orders. For instance, Austria maintained that an arrest warrant against Fatma Yildirim's husband would be disproportionately invasive. The CEDAW Committee rejected this position emphasising that a 'perpetrator's rights cannot supersede women's human rights to life and to physical and mental integrity' (*Fatma Yildirim v. Austria*, para. 12.1.5).[36]

In civil or criminal proceedings women victims of violence need adequate representation by legal professionals who are trained and have expertise in such cases.[37] Available and affordable legal assistance may be achieved through a legal aid scheme (CEDAW Committee 2012c, para. 30; General Recommendation No. 33, paras. 17(a), 36 and 37), or through court-appointed attorneys or public defenders.[38] Whatever the means through which legal assistance is secured, quality control of lawyers' work is important. Information in the form of guides and manuals to improve access to justice should be prepared, made available in multiple venues frequented by women such as shopping centres, markets, housing authorities, clinics, and in local languages. Women cannot always access remedies for themselves and step by step guidance should be available through the entire civil or criminal law process. Authorities also need to be alert to take special measures themselves commensurate with the gravity of the situation.

A holistic approach to the state's duty to protect combines civil law protection measures, the use of the criminal law, and practical measures for the immediate physical care of victims of violence, involving co-ordination and co-operation between services for physical and psychological health, social welfare services and the law enforcement services (e.g. CEDAW Committee 2009a, para. 32; General Recommendation No. 33, para. 16(b)). Ideally all such services – or at least details about where to find them – should be available in a single 'one-stop' location (General Recommendation No. 33, para. 17(f)). Access to state agencies should be facilitated, for example through a properly resourced 24-hour free hotline through which contact in emergency situations can be made and to which there is an immediate response (CEDAW Committee 2009a; CEDAW Committee 2011b). The state's duty to ensure physical care includes access to an adequate number of secure refuges or shelters, available throughout the country on a temporary basis, so that women do not have to remain in violent and abusive relationships.

The duty to prosecute challenges impunity and demands accountability. It requires an adequate and effective investigation of the violence, legislation that criminalises the diverse forms of violence against women and defines them appropriately to ensure justiciability, a readiness to prosecute alleged perpetrators under national laws, not allowing defences under customary or religious laws, and effective trial proceedings. Each of these has been addressed by the Committee in its concluding observations to Asian states.

First, there must be criminalisation of gender-based violence and appropriate definitions of the relevant crimes. Choices have to be made about what crimes should be criminalised and how they should be defined.[39] Thus the Committee has expressed concern about laws that inadequately criminalise domestic violence or incest (CEDAW Committee 2009a, para. 33), or that distinguish between 'seriously harmful and less harmful acts of violence, the latter of which are exempted from penal liabilities' (CEDAW Committee 2009c, para. 23) and are thereby socially legitimised and accompanied by a culture of silence. Other expressed concerns are defining sexual assault as a crime against morality rather than as against physical security and integrity (CEDAW Committee 2009a, para. 33), failing to include marital rape in the legal definition of rape,[40] or restricting it only to cases where the spouses no longer live together (CEDAW Committee 2012a, para. 23(a)). Non-criminalisation of rape in marriage perpetuates the conception of wives as the sexual property of their husbands, justifying rough or violent treatment to ensure submission to intercourse (Cook and Cusak 2010, pp. 27–8). Along with criminalisation is the ascribing of penalties that must be commensurate with the seriousness of the crime.[41] Where violence against women is not criminalised, is made subject to lower penalties than other forms of violence, lesser penalties are imposed even where the law allows for more severe penalties, or the accused is allowed to apologise,[42] that violence is popularly understood as not serious and women's right to equality is denied.

The CEDAW Committee has clarified that rape is to be understood as violating a woman's right to 'personal security and bodily integrity' (*Vertido v. The Philippines*, para. 8.7) and has urged legislation that defines rape by placing 'lack of consent at its centre' and which removes any requirement that sexual assault be committed by force or violence and that penetration be proved. The Committee has encouraged states to minimise the secondary victimisation of rape survivors that occurs when they are subjected to an aggressive or insensitive institutional response, for instance through court room questioning that focuses on their behaviour rather than that of the accused. To minimise this the Committee has controversially recommended that the definition of sexual assault should require either,

> the existence of unequivocal and voluntary agreement and requiring proof by the accused of steps taken to ascertain whether the complainant was consenting; or . . . that the act take place in "coercive circumstances" and includes a broad range of coercive circumstances.
>
> (ibid., para. 8.8 (b)(i)–(ii))[43]

The concept of 'coercive circumstances' resonates with international criminal law. The appellate chamber for the *ad hoc* international criminal tribunals for former Yugoslavia and Rwanda has determined that 'consent [for the purpose of defining rape] must be consent given voluntarily, as a result of the victim's free will, assessed in the context of the surrounding circumstances'.[44] Similarly the elements of the crime of rape within the jurisdiction of the International Criminal Court include 'taking advantage of a coercive environment'.[45] While this shifts attention from the state of the victim's mind (was she consenting?) to the objective realities of the situation, it nevertheless retains the relevance of consent.[46] Although it has made its own recommendations as to the definition of rape, the Committee has also recommended that states consult widely with women's groups when reforming laws and procedures relating to rape and sexual abuse.

Prompt, thorough, impartial and serious investigation of all allegations of violence against women is an essential prerequisite to the right of access to criminal, civil or administrative courts and to providing an effective remedy (*González et al.*, para. 287). Obstacles to a serious, impartial and effective investigation of violence against women abound,[47] contributing to and resulting in a low rate of reporting of such cases.[48] Putting the burden on the woman so that a crime of sexual violence is prosecuted only upon complaint by the victim is one such obstacle; so too are limitation periods for reporting rape,[49] or financial disincentives to reporting, for instance charges for forensic examination after rape or for the acquisition of a medical certificate, but prosecution without such evidence may be impracticable. Still another is requiring that reporting an assault to the authorities takes priority over seeking medical attention, with the result that victims may not seek the health, psychological or legal support they require (CEDAW Committee 2008). The reception a survivor expects from the police and prosecutors and the priority (or otherwise) given to cases of violence against women when reported both impact on whether a crime is reported. One suggested reform is to require that such cases are dealt with by women law enforcement officers (and to increase their number)[50] or to have special police stations. Victims of violence must be treated with sensitivity during medical and forensic examination by staff trained in the trauma caused by the commission of these offences.

Access to justice may be delayed or impeded due to gender stereotyping such as 'the persistence of patriarchal attitudes and deep-rooted stereotypes regarding the roles and responsibilities of women and men within the family and society at large' that maintain the concept of 'head of the household' (CEDAW Committee 2012a, para. 21). The CEDAW Committee CEDAW Committee considered that allowing a man with a history of domestic violence against the mother of his daughter unsupervised visitation rights with respect to his daughter and which led to her murder:

> reflect a pattern of action which responds to a stereotyped conception of visiting rights based on formal equality . . . the authorities of the State party, in deciding on the establishment of an unsupervised scheme of visits, applied stereotyped and therefore discriminatory notions in a context of domestic violence and failed to provide due supervision.
>
> (*Angela González Carreño v. Spain,* paras 9.4 and 9.7)

Stereotyping is maintained by the media, in educational textbooks[51] and curricular materials, which impact upon girls' educational choices, their future careers and thus to the unequal sharing of family and domestic responsibilities, resulting in their disadvantaged situation in the labour market and their under-representation in political and public life and decision-making positions (CEDAW Committee 2009a, para. 29). CEDAW Article 5 requires states to

> modify the social and cultural patterns of conduct of men and women, with a view to achieving the elimination of prejudices and customary and all other practices which are based on the idea of the inferiority or the superiority of either of the sexes or on stereotyped roles for men and women.

Core to this obligation, the Committee has emphasised the importance of integrating educational programmes on women's rights and gender equality into curricula and the role of the media in challenging gender stereotypes (General Recommendation No. 33, paras. 32–4). Law enforcement agencies and the judiciary should be at the forefront in fulfilling this obligation (Cook and Cusak 2010), but instead gendered myths and stereotypes distract from adequate protection, prompt and expeditious investigations, prevent charges being brought and pervade the trials of those accused of committing violent crimes against women, undermining women's ability to navigate the various stages of the criminal process.[52]

Some gender-based myths and stereotypes are specific to the particular locale but others are repeated across societies, including Asian societies. One is a culture of disbelief whereby women reporting violence are assumed to be lying with respect to its incidence and seriousness, or that 'an accusation for rape can be made with facility' (*Vertido v. The Philippines*, para. 8.5). This engenders contempt towards women complainants of violence and sympathy for the accused, and disregard of women's evidence, imposing a burden upon women within the justice system that is not shared by men and is thus discriminatory. In *Vertido v. The Philippines*, the complainant listed multiple such myths and misconceptions that founded her claim that she had been revictimised by the state in the criminal proceedings, where her alleged rapist was acquitted. The CEDAW Committee explained the general principle that

> stereotyping affects women's right to a fair and just trial and that the judiciary must take caution not to create inflexible standards of what women or girls should be or what they should have done when confronted with a situation of rape based merely on preconceived notions of what defines a rape victim or a victim of gender-based violence.
>
> (*Vertido v. The Philippines*, para. 8.4)

The Committee also explained that an expectation that the complainant should have resisted her attacker reinforces 'the myth that women must physically resist the sexual assault' (ibid., para 8.5) and thus that there 'should be no assumption in law or in practice that a woman gives her consent because she has not physically resisted the unwanted sexual conduct, regardless of whether the perpetrator threatened to use or used physical violence' (ibid.). In a subsequent rape case the local court had considered that the complainant's

> demeanour was inconsistent with that of an ordinary Filipina whose instinct dictates that she summons every ounce of her strength and courage to thwart any attempt to besmirch her honour and blemish her purity. . . . It is unnatural for an intended rape victim . . . not to make even a feeble attempt to free herself despite a myriad of opportunities to do so.
>
> (*RPB v. The Philippines*, para. 8.9)

Coming to the trial, proceedings must be expeditious, impartial and fair. Concerns include laws that undermine the value of women's testimony, require corroboration, or assess it in a gender-biased manner (as was the case in *Vertido*). Where prosecution of violence against women is not perceived as a high priority, delay in commencing proceedings and excessively long proceedings deny justice to the victim, maintain her anxiety and may weaken her evidence if, for example, she has forgotten details, which in turn add to the secondary victimisation and violate the right to prompt and effective remedies.

As well as punishment of perpetrators, there has been an increasing focus on states' obligations to ensure that victims of gender-based violence receive remedies that are affordable, accessible, appropriate and timely (General Recommendation No. 28, para. 34).[53] Reparations awarded in response to violence against women should reflect the realities of that violence and its gendered impact.[54] The former Special Rapporteur on Violence against Women, Rashida Manjoo, has highlighted the 'neglect of women in the reparations domain' (UNHRC 2010, para. 25). She also explains the difference between reparations which are directed at the individual victim whose rights have been violated and rehabilitation measures which are a matter of social assistance and wider social policy. The latter are

> addressed at the entire population to ensure that each and every person can meaningfully enjoy all rights recognized by the State. They are inspired by notions of redistributive justice and should primarily target those sectors of the population which have traditionally been discriminated against and structurally disadvantaged, including women.
>
> (UN Human Rights Council 2010, paras. 19–20)

In a later report Rashida Manjoo has explained how the state's due diligence obligations extend to reparations and the transformative potential of reparations:

> Systemic due diligence refers to the obligations States must take to ensure a holistic and sustained model of prevention, protection, punishment and reparations for acts of violence against women. At a systemic level, States can meet their responsibility to protect, prevent and punish by, among other things, adopting or modifying legislation; developing strategies, action plans and awareness-raising campaigns and providing services; reinforcing the capacities and power of police, prosecutors and judges; adequately resourcing transformative change initiatives; and holding accountable those who fail to protect and prevent, as well as those who perpetrate violations of human rights of women. Also, states have to be involved more concretely in overall societal transformation to address structural and systemic gender inequality and discrimination.
>
> (UN Human Rights Council 2013, para. 71)

In response to individual communications, where it has found violations of the state's obligations with respect to violence against women, the CEDAW Committee has made recommendations both with respect to the situation of the individual complainant and more general recommendations to address the systemic issues of discrimination raised by the case.

Conclusion

'The right to access to justice for women is essential to the realisation of all the rights protected under the Convention on the Elimination of All Forms of Violence against Women' (General Recommendation No. 33, para. 1). Gender-based violence against women is both a denial of women's human rights themselves and inhibits women's enjoyment of other rights. Accordingly, when women are unable to access justice following crimes of violence committed against them, it constitutes a violation of the fundamental principle of equality before the law and exacerbates the direct consequences of that violence. Where continuing tolerance by state organs is not limited to individual cases it becomes a pattern. The culture of impunity – the culture of silence – is a factor in the normalisation of societal violence, which as it continues becomes ever harder to reduce. Denial of access to justice is only one aspect of this normalisation and must be seen alongside other ways in which women are marginalised and subordinated. For instance, unequal access to economic, social and cultural rights increases women's dependency and vulnerability to violence, while failure to secure women's protection from violence further limits their access to economic and social rights. This in turn reduces women's contributions to the achievement of social goals, to the overall detriment of the state.

But justice systems also provide women with a forum to confront those who have committed violations against them and where those wrongs are redressed. It is thus important that women are able to participate at all stages of the 'justice chain' and are equally represented in all roles, for instance in the judiciary, 'as magistrates, judges, prosecutors, public defenders, lawyers, administrators, mediators, law enforcement officials, judicial and penal officials and expert practitioners' (General Recommendation No. 33, para. 15(f)). The former Special Rapporteur on Violence against Women, Rashida Manjoo, has also stressed the importance of women's participation in discussion and processes for reparations, especially taking into account the concept of 'transformative' reparations.[55]

> Without the participation of women and girls from different contexts, initiatives are more likely to reflect men's experience of violence and their concerns, priorities and needs regarding redress. Additionally, without such participation, an opportunity is missed for victims to gain a sense of agency that may in itself be an important form of rehabilitation, especially when victims come to perceive themselves as actors of social change.
>
> (UN Human Rights Council 2010, para. 29)

Indeed, where formal justice systems have failed women, they have regained some sense of agency through informal peoples' tribunals where survivors have been heard and validated (Chinkin 2006, p. 201). A former Special Rapporteur on Violence against Women, Yakin Ertürk, has argued that interventions aimed at enhancing women's self-awareness, self-esteem, self-confidence and self-reliance enable women to understand that subordination and violence are not fate, to resist internalising oppression, to develop their capabilities as autonomous beings and constantly to renegotiate the terms of their existence in public and private spheres (UN Human Rights Council 2009b, para. 35). Women's tribunals have to some extent achieved this; the challenge for women is to make the formal justice system similarly empowering. Implementation of the slew of recommendations included in the CEDAW Committee's General Recommendation No. 33 on women's access to justice would go a very long way towards achieving this essential component of a transformative rule of law.

Notes

[Editors' Note: This chapter draws upon a paper written for the Commonwealth Ministers' Conference in May 2014 and published as Christine Chinkin (2014) 'Addressing violence against women in the Commonwealth within states' obligations under international law', Commonwealth Law Bulletin, 40:3, 471–501

1 There are further obligations with respect to gender-based violence under international humanitarian law and international criminal law, which the chapter does not address.

2 Committee on the Elimination of All Forms of Discrimination against Women (CEDAW Committee) General Recommendation No.19 (Violence against women), UN Doc. HRI\GEN\1\Rev.1, 29 January 1992.

3 Rome Statute of the International Criminal Court (ICC), 1998, Article 7 (1) (h).

4 The treaties are the *Inter-American Convention on the Prevention, Punishment and Eradication of Violence against Women* (Convention of *Belém do Pará*), adopted by the Organisation of American States on 6 September 1994; the *Protocol to the African Charter on Human and Peoples' Rights on the Rights of Women in Africa*, adopted by the African Union on 13 September 2000; and the *Istanbul Convention* which came into force on 1 August 2014. Unlike the *Istanbul Convention* and the *Convention of Belém do Pará* the *Protocol* is not directed solely at violence, which instead is mainstreamed throughout.

5 The International Court of Justice (ICJ) has recognised that the opinion of a UN human-rights treaty body – 'an independent body established specifically to supervise the application of that treaty' – should be given 'great weight'; *Ahmadou Sadio Diallo (Republic of Guinea v. Democratic Republic of the Congo)* para. 66. The ICJ was referring to the Human Rights Committee.

6 Excluding the Central Asian Republics and Pacific Islands only Cambodia, Mongolia, Nepal, the Philippines, the Republic of Korea, Sri Lanka, Thailand and Timor-Leste are parties to the Optional Protocol.

7 UN Human Rights Committee General Comment No. 28: Article 3 (The equality of rights between men and women), 29 March, CCPR/C/21/Rev.1/Add.10

8 Committee on Economic, Social and Cultural Rights (CESCR) General Comment No. 16, The equal right of men and women to the enjoyment of all economic, social and cultural rights, UN Doc. E/C.12/2005/4, 11 August 2005.

9 For instance, the Inter-American Commission has explained that 'while the organs of the Inter-American System are not bound to follow the judgments of international supervisory bodies, their jurisprudence can provide constructive insights into the interpretation and application of rights that are common to regional and international human rights systems'. *Jessica Lenahan (Gonzales) v. United States* (2011), para. 135.

10 UNSC Res. 1325 (31 October 2000) UN Doc. S/RES/1325; UNSC Res. 1820 (19 June 2008) UN Doc. S/RES/1820; SC Res. 1888 (30 September 2009) UN Doc. S/RES/1888; UNSC Res. 1889 (5 October 2009) UN Doc. S/RES/1889; UNSC Res. 1960 (16 December 2010) UN Doc. S/RES/1960; UNSC Res. 2106 (24 June 2013) UN Doc. S/RES/2106; UNSC Res. 2122 (18 October 2013) UN Doc. S/RES/2122; and UNSC Res. 2242 (13 October 2015) UN Doc. S/RES/2242.

11 CEDAW Committee, General Recommendation No. 28 on the core obligations of States parties under Article 2 of the Convention on the Elimination of All Forms of Discrimination against Women, CEDAW/C/GC28, 16 December 2010.

12 Especially important are the UNGA's *Declaration on the Elimination of Violence against Women 2003* (DEVAW) UNGA Resolution 48/104, and, *The elimination and prevention of all forms of violence against women and girls 2013*, U.N. Doc. E/CN.6/2013/L.5, passed by the Commission on the Status of Women.

13 Gender, as distinct from sex, is defined by the CEDAW Committee as the 'socially constructed identities, attributes and roles for women and men and society's social and cultural meaning for these biological differences resulting in hierarchical relationships between women and men and in the distribution of power and rights favouring men and disadvantaging women' (CEDAW General Recommendation No. 28, para. 5).

14 The CEDAW Committee sought an exceptional report from India on the impact of the Gujarat massacre on women (CEDAW Committee 2010b).

15 The African Commission on Human Rights found that Egypt failed to protect four women journalists from violence during protests in Tahir Square (*Egyptian Initiative for Personal Rights and Interights v. Egypt*).

16 CEDAW Committee 2010a, para. 29 ('deep concern about reports of sexual abuse of women upon arrest and in police custody, perpetrated by both police officers and male detainees').

17 For example, *Inga Abramova v. Belarus* (state found to be in violation of CEDAW and General Recommendation No. 19 through humiliating and degrading treatment and sexual harassment in prison).

18 For example, CEDAW Committee 2007b, para. 12 ('The Committee reiterates its concern about the persistence of patriarchal attitudes and deep-rooted stereotypes, including the preference for male offspring, regarding the roles and responsibilities of women and men within the family and society at large'); see also CEDAW Committee 2012b, para. 23.

19 See also UNHRC Special Rapporteur on Violence against Women 2012, para. 40 (suspected witches – mainly widows or other vulnerable elderly women – thrown from cliffs, tortured, dragged behind cars, burned or buried alive).

20 For example, CEDAW Committee 2012a, para. 31 ('the Committee remains concerned at the situation of foreign domestic workers, in particular with regard to the mandatory regular testing for pregnancy and sexually transmitted diseases, the prohibition against marrying Singaporeans and the lack of a mandatory day off'); see generally CEDAW General Recommendation No. 26 on women migrant workers, CEDAW/C/2009/WP.1/R, 5 December 2008.

21 The Special Rapporteur on violence against women has also expressed concern about the sexualisation of women, for instance by the media in the U.K. and the over-sexualisation especially of young girls (OHCHR 2014).

22 However, the *Istanbul Convention* Article 3(a) includes economic harm and 3(b) includes economic violence in the definitions of violence against women and domestic violence, respectively.

23 Fourth World Conference on Women, Declaration, UN Doc. A/CONF/177/20, Beijing, 15 September 1995, 'Women and Poverty'.

24 UN Human Rights Committee (2007) General Comment No. 32: Article 14 (Right to equality before courts and tribunals and to a fair trial), 23 August, CCPR/C/GC/32.

25 The Committee highlighted as issues it especially wished states to address in their reports legal provisions that prevent women from enjoying autonomous access to the courts, provisions relating to women as witnesses, equal access to legal aid and whether certain women are denied the presumption of innocence (UN Human Rights Committee General Comment 28, para. 18).

26 The Human Rights Committee has similarly expressed concern about the 'prevailing culture of impunity' following the conflict in Nepal, including for crimes of sexual violence (UN Human Rights Committee 2014, para. 5).

27 Direct and indirect discrimination creates many difficulties for women who are seeking access to justice; CEDAW General Recommendation No. 33, para. 22.

28 CEDAW General Recommendation No. 33 on Women's Access to Justice, para. 51(a) recommends that States parties, 'Exercise due diligence to prevent, investigate, punish and provide reparation for all crimes committed against women'.

29 Article 51 of the *Istanbul Convention* on risk assessment and risk management requires parties to 'take the necessary legislative or other measures to ensure that an assessment of the lethality risk, the seriousness of the situation and the risk of repeated violence is carried out by all relevant authorities in order to manage the risk and if necessary to provide co-ordinated safety and support'.

30 The state must assess the threat posed to an individual: *Opuz v. Turkey* (2009) para. 147; Jessica *Lenahan (Gonzales) v. United States* (2011) at para. 132.

31 On generalised risk of violence to women, see *González et al. ('Cotton Field') v. Mexico* (2009) para. 283: once the state 'was aware that there was a real and imminent risk that the victims would be sexually abused, subjected to ill-treatment and killed, . . . an obligation of strict due diligence arises'; in her concurring opinion Judge Cecilia Medina noted that as soon as the state became officially aware of the pattern of violence against women in Ciudad Juárez 'there was an absence of policies designed to try and revert the situation' (ibid. para. 18).

32 The CEDAW Committee has recommended that remedies be 'adequate, effective, promptly attributed, holistic and proportional to the gravity of the harm suffered' CEDAW General Recommendation No. 33, para. 19 (b).

33 Substantive equality requires not only redressing the disadvantageous practical impact of apparently neutral laws and practices but also focusing on the 'asymmetrical structures of power, dominance and disadvantage at work in society' (Byrnes 2012, pp. 54–5).

34 The Committee recommends that cases of violence against women are 'under no circumstances referred to any alternative dispute resolution processes', CEDAW General Recommendation No. 33 on women's access to justice, CEDAW/C/GC/33, 23 July 2015, para. 58 (c).

35 Including mediation by police in cases of alleged rape (CEDAW Committee 2012b, para. 25(b)).

36 *See* also *A.T. v. Hungary*, para. 9.3: 'Women's human rights to life and to physical and mental integrity cannot be superseded by other rights, including the right to property and the right to privacy'; *Şahide Goecke v. Austria*, para. 12.1.5.

37 For example, the CEDAW Committee urged India to provide 'free legal services to poor and marginalized women in rural and tribal areas in addition to urban areas and to monitor the quality and impact of such services in regard to ensuring women's access to justice' (CEDAW Committee 2007b, para. 19).

38 The CEDAW Committee expressed its concern to Cambodia that such legal aid as was available was funded primarily through non-governmental organisations. It was also concerned that corrupt practices increased court expenses (CEDAW (2013b) Concluding Observations, Cambodia, para. 12).

39 The *Istanbul Convention* requires states parties to criminalise stalking, psychological, physical and sexual violence, sexual harassment, forced marriage, female genital mutilation, forced abortion and sterilisation, and domestic violence.

40 For example, Lao, CEDAW/C/LAO/CO 16-18, 13 April 2012; CEDAW Committee 2012b, para. 25(d); UNHRC, Concluding Observations, Mongolia, CCPR/C/MNG/CO/5, 2 May 2011, para. 18; CESCR, Concluding Comments, Sri Lanka (2010), para. 25 (concern expressed that 'cultural sensitivities are used as a justification by the State party not to criminalize marital rape in all circumstances').

41 CEDAW Committee 2012b, para. 25(d) (payment of a fine as settlement of the case); UNHRC Concluding Observations, Nepal (2014), para. 13.

42 CEDAW Committee 2010a, para. 29 (traditional apologies as a form of resolution for offences committed against the victims, including in the context of the village courts).

43 This recommendation has not led to any review of the legislation with respect to rape in the Philippines; *RPB v. The Philippines*, para. 8.10.

44 *Gacumbitsi v. Prosecutor*, ICTR-01-64–A, 7 July 2006, paras. 147–57. This formulation is also to be found in the *Istanbul Convention*, Article 36 (2).

45 International Criminal Court, Elements of Crimes (2011), Article 7 (1) (g)-1 Crime against humanity of rape.

46 For a critique, see Mackinnon 2006, p. 237.

47 'Inadequate case management and evidence collection' can result in 'systematic failures in investigation' in cases brought by women (General Recommendation No. 33, para. 25(a) (vi)).

48 For example, CEDAW Committee 2011b, para. 20 ('low rate of reported cases does not correspond with the actual number of cases of domestic violence occurring in the State party'); CESCR 2009, para. 24 ('rate of mandatory reporting of domestic violence is very low, that legal action against perpetrators is seldom taken and that a number of settled cases have resulted in non-prosecution'); CEDAW Committee 2009c, para. 23.

49 UN Human Rights Committee (2014), para. 13 (35 day limitation on reporting rape).

50 The Committee has also expressed concern about the limited number of women police officers available to deal with cases of sexual and domestic violence; e.g. CEDAW Committee 2011b, para. 20.

51 Cook and Cusak give the example of the Thai government recognising that school text books over-represented men as leaders and administrators in the community (Cook and Cusak 2010, pp. 132–3).

52 General Recommendation No. 33, para. 26 states that 'Stereotyping and gender bias . . . impede women's access to justice in all areas of law, and may particularly impact upon women victims and survivors of violence'.

53 *Vertido v. The Philippines* is a landmark ruling in that the Committee determined CEDAW, Article 2 (c) provides a right to a remedy.

54 *Basic Principles and Guidelines on the Right to a Remedy and Reparation for Victims of Gross Violations of International Human Rights Law and Serious Violations of International Humanitarian Law*, GA Res. 60/147, 2005. For a gendered analysis of principles relating to reparations, see *Nairobi Declaration on Women's and Girls' Right to a Remedy and Reparation*, http://www.womensrightscoalition.org/site/reparation/signature_en.php.

55 The concept of transformative reparations that seek to repair the social situation of the victim is widely associated with the reparative orders made by the Inter-American Court of Human Rights in the case of *González et al.* (2009).

Bibliography

Byrnes, A. (2012) 'Article 1' in Freeman, M., Chinkin, C. and Rudolf, B. (eds.) *The UN Convention on the Elimination of All Forms of Discrimination Against Women: A Commentary*, Oxford University Press, Oxford, U.K. pp. 54–5.

Chinkin, C. (2006) 'Peoples' Tribunals: Legitimate or Rough Justice? *Windsor Yearbook of Access to Justice*, vol. 24, pp. 201–20.

Chinkin, C. (2012) 'Violence against Women' in Freeman, M., Chinkin, C. and Rudolf, B. (eds.) *The UN Convention on the Elimination of All Forms of Discrimination Against Women: A Commentary*, Oxford University Press, Oxford, U.K., pp. 444–7.

Chinkin, C. (2013) 'Sources' in Moeckli, D., Shah, S. and Sivakumaran, S. (eds.) *International Human Rights Law*, 2nd edition, Oxford University Press, Oxford, U.K.

Cook, R. and Cusak S. (2010) *Gender Stereotyping Transnational Legal Perspectives*, University of Pennsylvania Press, Philadelphia, U.S.A.

Crawford, J. (2002) *The International Law Commission's Articles on State Responsibility. Introduction, Text and Commentaries*, Cambridge University Press, Cambridge, U.K.

Holtmaat, R. (2012) 'Article 5', in Chinkin, C. and Rudolf, B. (eds.) *The UN Convention on the Elimination of All Forms of Discrimination Against Women: A Commentary*, Oxford University Press, Oxford, U.K., p. 144.

MacKinnon, C. (2006) 'Defining Rape Internationally. A Comment on *Akayesu*', in MacKinnon, C., *Are Women Human? And Other International Dialogues*, Harvard University Press, Cambridge, Massachusetts, U.S.A., pp. 237–46.

Marks, S. (2011) 'Human Rights and Root Causes', *The Modern Law Review*, vol. 74, pp. 57–78.

Cases

A.T. v. Hungary, Communication No. 2/2003, 26 January 2005.

Ahmadou Sadio Diallo (Republic of Guinea v. Democratic Republic of the Congo) (2010) Merits, Judgment, ICJ. Reports.

Angela González Carreño v. Spain, Communication No. 47/2012, 15 August 2014, CEDAW/C/58/D/47/2012.

Egyptian Initiative for Personal Rights and Interights v. Egypt, ACHPR Communication 323/06, 12 October 2013.

Fatma Yildirim (deceased) v. Austria, Communication No. 6/2005, 6 August, 2007, CEDAW/C/39/D/6/2005.

Inga Abramova v. Belarus, Communication No. 23/2009, CEDAW/C/49/D/23/2009, 27 September 2011.

Jessica Lenahan (Gonzales) v. United States, Report No. 80/11, Case 2.626, 21 July 2011.

Gacumbitsi v Prosecutor, ICTR-01-64 –A, 7 July 2006.

González et al. ('Cotton Field') v. Mexico, 16 November 2009, (Preliminary Objection, Merits, Reparations, and Costs) Series C No. 205.

Opuz v. Turkey, (ECtHR) (Application no. 33401/02), 9 June 2009.

RPB v. The Philippines, Communication No. 34/2011, 12 March 2014, CEDAW/C/57/D/34/2011.

Şahide Goecke v. Austria, Communication No. 5/2005, 6 August, 2007, CEDAW/C/39/D/5/2005.

V.K. v. Bulgaria, Communication No. 20/2008, 17 August 2011, CEDAW /C/49/D/20/2008.

VPP v. Bulgaria, Communication 31/2011, 27 November 2011, CEDAW/C/53/D/31/2011.

Vertido v. The Philippines, Communication No 18/2008, 1 September 2010, CEDAW/C/46/18/2008.

United Nations Documents

CEDAW Committee (2007a) Concluding Observations, India, CEDAW/C/IND/CO/3, 2 February 2007.

CEDAW Committee (2007b) Concluding Observations, Vietnam, CEDAW/C/VNM/CO/6, 2 February 2007.

CEDAW Committee (2008) Concluding Observations, Myanmar, CEDAW/C/MMR/CO 3, 7 November 2008.

CEDAW Committee (2009a) Concluding Observations, Japan, CEDAW/C/JPN/CO/6, 7 August 2009.

CEDAW Committee (2009b) Concluding Observations, Timor Leste, CEDAW/C/TLS/CO/1, 7 August 2009.

CEDAW Committee (2009c) Concluding Observations, Lao People's Democratic Republic, CEDAW/C/LAO/CO/7, 14 August 2009.

CEDAW Committee (2010a) Concluding Observations, Papua New Guinea, CEDAW/C/PNG/CO 3, 30 July 2010.

CEDAW Committee (2010b) Concluding Observations, India, CEDAW/C/IND/CO/SP.1, 3 November 2010.

CEDAW Committee (2011a) Concluding Observations, Nepal, CEDAW/C/NPL/CO 4-5, 11 August 2011.

CEDAW Committee (2011b) Concluding Observations, South Korea, CEDAW/C/KOR/CO 7, 10 August 2011.

CEDAW Committee (2012a) Concluding Observations, Singapore, CEDAW/C/SGP/CO/4/Rev.1, 16 January 2012.

CEDAW Committee (2012b), Concluding Observations, Indonesia, CEDAW/C/IDN/CO/6-7, 7 August 2012.

CEDAW Committee (2012c) Concluding Observations, Timor Leste, CEDAW/C/TLS/CO 1, 18 October 2012.

CEDAW Committee (2013a) Concluding Observations, Pakistan, CEDAW/C/PAK/CO/4, 27 March 2013.

CEDAW Committee (2013b) Concluding Observations, Cambodia, CEDAW/C/KHM/CO/4-5, 28 October 2013.

CESCR (2009) Concluding Observations, South Korea, E/C.12/KOR/CO/3, 17 December 2009.

Committee on Economic, Social and Cultural Rights (CESCR) (2010) Concluding Comments, Sri Lanka, E/C.12/LKA/CO/2-4, 9 December 2010

International Law Commission (2001) *Articles on Responsibility of States for Internationally Wrongful Acts*, UNGA Res. 56/83.

OHCHR (2014) 'Special Rapporteur on violence against women finalizes country mission to the United Kingdom and Northern Ireland and calls for urgent action to address the accountability deficit and also the adverse impacts of changes in funding and services', 15 April [online] http://www.ohchr.org/EN/NewsEvents/Pages/DisplayNews.aspx?NewsID=14514&LangID=E

UN High Commissioner for Human Rights (2011) *Discriminatory Laws and Practices and Acts of Violence against Individuals based on their Sexual Orientation and Gender Identity*, UN Doc. A/HRC/19/41, 17 November 2011.

UN General Assembly (1985) *Declaration of Basic Principles of Justice for Victims of Crime and Abuse of Power*, UNGA Resolution 40/34.

UN Human Rights Committee (2014), Concluding Observations, Nepal, CCPR/C/NPL/CO/2, 15 April 2014.

UN Commission on Human Rights (2006) *Report of the Special Rapporteur on Violence against Women, Its Causes and Consequences on the Due Diligence Standard as a Tool for the Elimination of Violence against Women*, E/CN.4/2006/61, 20 January 2006.

UN Human Rights Council (2008) *Report of the Special Rapporteur on torture and other cruel, inhuman or degrading treatment or punishment, Manfred Nowak, on strengthening the protection of women against torture*, A/HRC/7/3, 15 January 2008.

UN Human Rights Council (2009a) *Report of the special rapporteur on violence against women, its causes and consequences: Political economy of women's human rights*, UN Doc. A/HRC/11/6.

UN Human Rights Council (2009b) *Report of the Special Rapporteur on Violence against Women, Yakin Ertürk (Addendum): 15 Years of the United Nations Special Rapporteur on Violence against Women (1994–2009) – A Critical Review*, UN Doc. A/HRC/11/6/Add.5.

UN Human Rights Council (2010) Special Rapporteur on Violence against Women, Reparations for Women Subjected to Violence, UN Doc. A/HRC/14/22.

UN Human Rights Council (2012) *Report of the Special rapporteur on Violence against Women, Rashida Manjoo, Gender Related Killings*, UN Doc. A/HRC/20/16.

UN Human Rights Council (2013) *Special Rapporteur on Violence against Women, Rashida Manjoo, State responsibility for eliminating violence against women*, UN Doc. A/HRC/23/49.

UN Sub-Commission on the Promotion and Protection of Human Rights (1998) *Final report submitted by Ms Gay J McDougall, Special Rapporteur, Contemporary forms of slavery: systematic rape, sexual slavery and slavery-like practices during armed conflict*, E/CN.4/Sub.2/1998/13.

Part I

Gender, violence and states in transition

2 From transition to transformation in gender equality

Lessons from Asia

Rita Shackel

Introduction

Currently there are over forty active armed conflicts of various kinds around the globe (International Institute for Strategic Studies n.d.). Additionally, many countries worldwide face internal conflicts or are struggling for independence, a stable state or peace. In Asia specifically there are far-ranging pockets of conflict and instability across the region and in neighbouring areas: political violence in Bangladesh (Society for the Study of Peace and Conflict 2014, p. 6); the ongoing Maoist conflict in India (ibid., p. 8); attacks by militant outfits in Pakistan (ibid., p. 12); and struggles between the Sri Lankan government and the Liberation Tigers of Tamil Eelam (LTTE) and other Tamil Diaspora groups (ibid., p. 13). In South and East Asia several states continue to face challenges in their democratic transitions and integration of minorities, including in Nepal, Bangladesh, Burma (Myanmar) and Sri Lanka (Goswami 2014). Indeed, no continent in the world is spared conflict or political unrest. While local contexts vary and the genesis of instability is impelled by diverse political, economic and social forces, some commonalities are nevertheless discernible, particularly when it comes to the plight of women and children, and their experiences of violence, discrimination and oppression. Women and children are unquestionably the most vulnerable during periods of conflict and instability (Beerli 2013) and are disproportionately the victims of sexual and gender-based violence during conflict and post-conflict (ibid.).

This chapter argues that women face a continuum of violence during and outside times of conflict. Recognising this continuum and displacing the fallacious view that depicts violence – particularly sexual violence – against women during conflict as 'extraordinary', is key to addressing sexual and gender-based violence and its root causes, and to formulating effective strategies that respond to the lived experiences and needs of women affected by such violence in ways that are empowering for women and with a long-term effect. The next section provides the contextual background for this discussion by examining the general nature of violence experienced by women, particularly in conflict and post-conflict settings. The section on transition for opportunity examines how periods of conflict and instability within states may act as an agent for social change, thereby creating opportunities for the repositioning of women in society and for a greater recognition of the rights of women, particularly the right to live free from actual or threatened violence and discrimination. Two examples from Asia – Timor-Leste and Sri Lanka – explore how post-conflict rebuilding may present such opportunities, as well as the intractable challenges, that often arise at such times and which risk stifling efforts towards greater gender equality and ending the culture of impunity for sexual violence against women. The penultimate section examines some specific domains and priorities in the rebuilding of states that are key to strengthening women's position in society, restoring their health and well-being, and building a platform for future action in recognition and vindication of women's rights. The final section concludes.

The continuum of violence experienced by women

Women and girls around the globe continue to experience violence on a massive scale with profound and devastating impacts (World Health Organisation [WHO] 2013, p. 2). Today's picture of violence against women reflects a sustained history and age-old practices of violence and discrimination perpetrated against women that have been documented in every corner of the world (Nobel Women's Initiative 2011, p. 4; Hynes *et al.* 2004, p. 294). Violence against women takes a myriad of forms and occurs in every sphere of women's lives (WHO 2013). The Declaration on the Elimination of Violence against Women defines 'violence against women' as 'any act of gender-based violence that results in, or is likely to result in, physical, sexual or psychological harm or suffering to women, including threats of such acts, coercion or arbitrary deprivation of liberty, whether occurring in public or in private life' (United Nations General Assembly [UNGA] 1993, Article 1).

Gender-based violence includes but is not limited to domestic violence, incest, rape, trafficking and forced prostitution, arranged marriages and child marriages, dowry-related violence, female genital mutilation, female infanticide, forced pregnancy and enforced sterilisation. Violence against women may be perpetrated within the family, the broader community or sanctioned by the state. The United Nations has recognised that violence against women is a 'manifestation of historically unequal power relations between men and women', which has engendered discrimination against, and the subordination of women (UNGA 1993). A key objective then for achieving greater gender equality must be the disruption and recalibration of traditional gender hierarchies and structures of power between men and women in society.

In 2013 the WHO reported that thirty-five per cent of women worldwide had experienced either physical and/or sexual intimate partner violence or non-partner sexual violence. This statistic, although grave in itself, only reveals a snapshot of the reality and magnitude of the violence experienced by women. In some countries, as many as seventy per cent of women have experienced physical and/or sexual violence by an intimate partner (WHO 2013). In Asia, the prevalence of sexual violence among women aged fifteen years and older has been estimated at over forty per cent (WHO 2013). In conflict settings, violence against women is a rampant tactic to overpower, destabilise and shame communities into submission (United Nations Security Council 2008). In particular, women are disproportionately the targets of sexual and gender-based violence – '[e]stablished gender norms endow sexual violence with destructive power' (Crawford 2013, p. 510).

Women are also more often the casualties of economic and political violence (UNIFEM, n.d.). In the face of intractable conflict, insecurity, unrelenting violence and the threat of mortal danger, women and girls – targeted on the basis of their gender – are more often forced to flee and bear the brunt of their displacement and that of their children (United Nations High Commissioner for Refugees [UNHCR] 1993, p. 87; UNHCR 2013; International Committee of the Red Cross [ICRC] 2001, p. 30; ICRC 2013a; Refugee Studies Centre, University of Oxford 2011). It is estimated that women and children comprise seventy to eighty per cent of internally displaced persons globally (Internal Displacement Monitoring Centre 2007, p. 6). It has been noted that '[i]t is more dangerous to be a woman than to be a soldier in modern conflict' (Former Deputy Force Commander of the United Nations Mission to the Democratic Republic of Congo 2008, as cited in Nobel Women's Initiative 2011, p. 2).

Moreover, periods of conflict and instability within a state often bring with them heightened violence against women within their own homes and families, and the social and cultural subordination of women (Abeysekera 2003, p. 530; Rehn and Sirleaf 2002; Wirtz *et al.* 2014, p. 10). Such periods are often accompanied by an increased militarisation of the entire society with which comes the widespread sanctioning of violence, both politically and socially, as a legitimate means for conflict resolution (Abeysekera 2003, p. 524). Violence thus is normalised in both public and private spheres of life. Altered masculinities and femininities during conflict may also fuel violent masculinities and thereby contribute to increased domestic violence (Myrttinen 2005, pp. 233–44).

In Asia, sexual violence has been documented across the region in conflicts in Afghanistan, Burma, Cambodia, India, Nepal, the Philippines, Sri Lanka, Tajikistan, East Timor, Indonesia, Papua New Guinea and the Solomon Islands (Nobel Women's Initiative 2011, p. 8). Women have been subjected to sexual harassment, rape, sexual torture, sex slavery and forced prostitution on a mass scale (ibid., p. 8). In Asia the trafficking of women and girls for sexual exploitation is a serious problem and armed conflicts tend only to aggravate this situation (Nobel Women's Initiative 2011, p. 9; Rehn and Sirleaf 2002, pp. 12–14).

The impacts of violence against women are far reaching and extend beyond the individual woman to their children and the broader community. Women are often under extreme levels of stress to manage and cope with the violence, or threat of violence, within and outside the family home (Swaine 2003). Evidence suggests that violence is associated with high levels of psychological distress and impaired social functioning (ibid.). Sexual violence may also have a number of short- and long-term economic, health, social and cultural consequences. First, sexual violence may result in the loss of life: a woman may be killed by the perpetrators or even by husbands and others within her own community who may be unaccepting of women's extramarital sexual contact, even when it is forced upon them through violence, brutality and terror (UNHCR 2008, p. 17); children born of rape may be killed; women may suffer serious and debilitating injuries due to rape that ultimately result in death (UNHCR 2008, p. 75); and women may seek to, or do, take their own lives after rape, due to psychological trauma, social rejection and profound feelings of despair in the face of rape and its various sequelae (ICRC 2013b; Van Vliet 2010, pp. 258–60).

After rape, women may become isolated, may live in fear of revictimisation and may experience strong feelings of unworthiness and shame (Van Vliet 2010, p. 258). Medical trauma following sexual violence may include gynaecological fistula, sexually transmitted infections and HIV/AIDS (Nobel Women's Initiative 2011, p. 14). Rape may also have dire economic consequences for women, further entrenching them in a life of poverty and excluding them from their communities and from social support systems:

> Sexual violence limits women's freedom of movement in relation to subsistence activities . . . Also, the lack of economic opportunities for displaced populations often results in commercial and exploitative sex as one of the few options for income generation to meet basic needs.
>
> Women who have been attacked, as well as children born out of rape, are stigmatized and ostracized as a consequence of these crimes. In certain areas, husbands disown their wives and the high levels of discrimination cause the destruction of family and social relationships that make up the fabric of society.
>
> (Nobel Women's Initiative 2011, p. 14)

Importantly, although every woman's experience of violence is unique and personal a tendency towards homogenising them serves to render the individual voice opaque and risks 'oversimplification and generalization' of those experiences (Corrin 2008, p. 171). Nevertheless, some commonalities in women's experiences of violence are discernible, particularly in regard to women's needs in post-conflict settings. As we survey the globe, we see varied contexts and cultural settings that frame women's lives and their experiences of violence. The degree to which women in different regions and parts of the world have recounted similar experiences of violence is shocking, as is the pervasive lack of access to justice, both through formal and informal mechanisms, and in a state's (un)responsiveness to women's 'real' needs in the face of such violence, particularly in post-conflict and transitional states.

Transition as opportunity for positive change

Periods of conflict, instability and transition in the life of a state offer enormous challenges to governments, which may extend from having to rebuild an array of physical infrastructures, social networks and legal systems and stabilising the economy, to responding to a wide range of social issues, including the reintegration of displaced people and former combatants. One of the greatest, yet often unaddressed, challenges confronting post-conflict states and communities is responding to change in the social configuration and structure of a society which has been precipitated by the conflict and unrest.

Conflict is undoubtedly an agent for social change. Changes in women's traditional roles and responsibilities during conflict are well documented (Hall 2009), in particular women's increased participation in politics and the paid labour force (Rehn and Sirleaf 2002). Other prominent changes to women's roles, positions and identity during conflict include displacement, widowhood, assuming the headship of the household, imposed independence and changing from being a mother and wife to becoming an armed militant (Oosterveld 2012, pp. 15–17; Refugee Studies Centre, University of Oxford 2011). Thus conflict can push women into unfamiliar spaces and roles.

On the one hand, women may struggle and experience newfound hardships through such changes but, on the other hand, women may gain more autonomy and confidence and become more visible in society:

> In such circumstances, women cross public barriers, assert their right to be present in the marketplace or in government offices, in police stations and army camps, staking a claim to be treated as decision-makers and as citizens on an equal footing with men . . . The social structures and formal institutions in which these women interact accept their presence in roles and locations in which they had previously been virtually invisible.
>
> (Abeysekera 2003, p. 534)

With transition, therefore, opportunities also emerge to effect positive changes for women and society more generally (Björkdahl and Selimovic, 2015). In the immediate aftermath of conflict – during periods of peace-building and in post-conflict communities – societies have an opportunity to consolidate and build upon some of the more positive social changes triggered by the conflict (Abeysekera 2003, p. 525): '[t]ransitions are rare periods of rupture that offer opportunities to reconceive the social meaning of past conflicts in an attempt to reconstruct their present and future effects' (Aguirre and Pietropaoli 2008, p. 357). Unfortunately, such opportunities are all too often missed as a gateway for achieving transformative and sustainable changes to hegemonic gender norms with improved status for women.

Why? One primary reason is a lack of political will and/or state inaction (Wiseman 2008; Refugee Studies Centre, University of Oxford 2011). States have a fundamental role to play in, and indeed hold primary responsibility for, recognising the changes that have occurred within a society and to respond in ways that will facilitate the rebuilding of communities in a productive manner moving forward. This means that states must recognise the changes in women's roles and act to strengthen these new pillars for societal growth and gender equality. To ignore these changes is dangerous – this is clearly demonstrated by the often seen fragmentation of family in many post-conflict settings (Oosterveld 2012). As men and women experience shifts in femininities and masculinities and in their gender identities, gender roles may become morphed – women often strive for greater autonomy and independence; while men, in contrast, may struggle with a loss of power and become socially disengaged (Walker 2009, p. 32; Refugee Studies Centre, University of Oxford 2011). The result is tension and antagonism within families, which all too often is vented through violence (Walker 2009, p. 32; Duggan and Abusharaf 2006).

Increased levels of domestic and social violence against women in post-conflict communities are well-documented (Duggan and Abusharaf 2006). This is counter-productive to rebuilding communities both in the short- and long-terms – it risks setting up a dynamic in society that perpetuates a cycle of violence and disadvantage. Thus, in post-conflict settings, women often may be confronted with intense pressures to return to pre-conflict gender roles 'associated with discrimination and inequality' (Aguirre and Pietropaoli 2008, p. 357) and accept a life of dependence and subordination relative to men even if, ultimately, the result is dysfunctional and counterproductive for society as a whole (Hall 2009, p. 310).

I now use two examples from Asia, first Timor-Leste and then Sri Lanka, to explore briefly the different opportunities that post-conflict settings and unstable social spaces may offer to study how states in transition can leverage the changes invoked by societal instability, and the accompanying fracture in normative structures and traditional gender roles, to achieve sustained and productive social changes for the greater empowerment of women.

Timor-Leste

The conflict in East Timor was borne of over twenty-four years of occupation by the Indonesian military. During this period of occupation several thousand people were forcibly displaced and 'made to live in extreme conditions without adequate food, shelter and health facilities' (Justino *et al.* 2011, p. 8). By the end of the Indonesian occupation, at least 200,000 lives had been lost (United Nations Development Programme [UNDP] 2002, p. 71). In 1999, the people of East Timor overwhelmingly voted for independence from Indonesia (Allden 2007), which triggered a backlash from pro-integration militia groups and Indonesian armed forces and culminated in a wave of violence marked by extraordinary brutality (UNDP 2002, p. 72).

Between one and two thousand people were killed during this period of violence and one-third of the population was forced into refugee camps in West Timor and neighbouring islands. Another third took refuge in the mountains of East Timor (ibid.). By the end of this conflict, seventy-five per cent of the population had been displaced and seventy per cent of the country's infrastructure destroyed (The World Bank 2014). In response to international pressure, the UN Security Council authorised a multinational force to restore peace and security in the region and soon after established the United Nations Transitional Administration in East Timor (UNTAET) to oversee East Timor's transition to Independence (ibid.). The Independent Republic of Timor-Leste was born in 2002. However, since independence, Timor-Leste has continued to experience periodic waves of violence (Dolven *et al.* 2012, pp. 1–2).

It is well documented that women in East Timor experienced extreme poverty and pervasive rates of violence during the period of conflict and post-conflict (The World Bank 2014). A study conducted by the Reproductive Health Response in Conflict Consortium showed that one in four women reported violence perpetrated by someone outside their family during the crisis in East Timor (Hynes *et al.* 2004). Of these, a striking 68.8 per cent of incidents involved the perpetrator threatening to kill the woman and ninety-two per cent of women reported being threatened with a weapon (ibid.). This study also found that forty-seven per cent of women in relationships reported some form of violence perpetrated by their partner in the year preceding the crisis and forty-three per cent in the preceding year post-conflict. Evidence suggests that, in the majority of cases, no action was taken against the perpetrator (Swaine 2003). These statistics highlight the continuum of violence experienced by Timorese women in public and private spheres of life, in periods of conflict and post-conflict, and during periods of no conflict.

Violence against women on this scale is engendered by traditional patriarchal values and attitudes that position women as inferior to men in a society. In traditional Timorese society, women are seen as responsible for care-giving, they are sold and bought into marriage, and are unable to own property (Swaine 2003). Women lack power and authority; a reality exacerbated by the wide-scale poverty that exists in East Timor (UNDP 2013).

Following Indonesia's withdrawal from East Timor, the country was left with no constitution, no functioning justice system and a United Nations administration. This created a unique space for the rebuilding of East Timor; a space shaped by changed social and political configurations borne of the conflict, the presence of the United Nations with a mandate to promote universal human rights, and a *tabula rasa* in terms of constitutional, judicial and legislative structures. Importantly, this space created an opportunity for women's rights to be recognised, and principles of gender equality and non-discrimination to become entrenched in legal, political and economic developments. It also created a unique political space for development of a strong and unified offensive against violence towards women, particularly domestic violence (Hall 2009).

Such opportunity, however, is not without its challenges. As Allden (2007) has argued, one key challenge of such opportunity rests in reconciling the promotion of international human-rights standards with local traditional values and customs. For this to be achieved, '[t]he process of promoting women's rights needs to be internally validated and framed in a familiar language in order to become accepted' and '[i]t cannot be a process that is externally promoted without any internal support' (ibid., p. 9).

In the case of East Timor, the post-conflict period enabled the Timorese people to develop a new legal order and framework for justice, which articulated the rights of men and women on equal terms for the first time. Central to this new order was the Timorese Constitution 2002, which explicitly recognised the equal status of men and women. Article 17 of the Constitution provides that '[w]omen and men shall have the same rights and duties in all areas of family, political, economic, social and cultural life'. This status of equality between men and women is further fortified in Article 39 of the Constitution, which provides that marriage shall be based on 'terms of full equality of rights between spouses', and Article 63, which recognises the need for '[d]irect and active participation by [both] men and women' in a democratic political system and protects 'equality in the exercise of civil and political rights and non-discrimination on the basis of gender for access to political positions'. These new and expressly articulated foundations for equality between men and women have arguably translated into some tangible positive results for women in Timor-Leste (Porter 2011). Women are, for example, well represented in parliament, even against the high watermark of international standards, as a consequence of the *Electoral Law 2006*, which established a twenty-five per cent quota for women's participation. Since 2011, the rate of female participation in the Timor-Leste Parliament has been twenty-nine per cent (Krook 2013, p. 10).

Other legislative developments have also improved the position of women. Most notable are provisions contained in the *Penal Code 2009* (Decree Law 19/2009) and the *Law Against Domestic Violence 2010* (*LADV*) (Law no. 7/2010). The *Penal Code 2009* established the offence of 'Mistreatment of a spouse'. Article 154 renders '[a]ny person who inflicts physical or mental mistreatment or cruel treatment upon a spouse or person cohabiting with the perpetrator in a situation analogous to that of spouse' liable to be found guilty of a crime punishable with between two to six years' imprisonment. The *LADV 2010* goes further in expanding the definition of domestic violence in Article 2(1) to

> [a]ny act or sequence of acts committed within a family context, with or without cohabitation, by a family member against any other member of that family . . . which resulted, or may result, in physical, sexual or psychological injuries or suffering, economic abuse, including threats such as intimidating acts, bodily harm, aggression, coercion, harassment, or deprivation of freedom.

Further, Article 35 of the *LADV 2010* lists a series of crimes in the *Penal Code 2009* which, if committed specifically within the family context, amount to crimes of domestic violence.

These constitutional and legislative milestones are, without question, important and represent an achievement towards empowering women and improving their lives, but, of themselves, such reforms are insufficient. Not only is there a need to constantly interpret international human-rights standards into the local context, but what is fundamentally needed is cultural change that neither condones human-rights violations generally nor gender-based violence specifically.

The successes achieved in Timor-Leste also reveal another important dimension of rebuilding with power to influence, the capacity to drive political agendas through partnerships between government, civil society and the international community. In Timor-Leste, considerable traction around gender equality and domestic violence was obtained from the presence of the United Nations and the influx of international donors and NGOs seeking to partner with local NGOS. This

> introduced new norms and gave East Timorese women discursive power to work on gender-based violence [while] the arrival of the international

> community paved the way for gender-based violence to be dealt with on a larger scale and for norms of women's rights and gender equality to reach a much larger proportion of the East Timorese population.
>
> (Hall 2009, p. 315)

These factors had a potentially transformative influence on traditional norms and attitudes that perpetuate violence against women, particularly domestic violence. However, despite such a dynamic partnership in activism, challenges nevertheless arose in Timor-Leste, which resonated with Allden's caution that norm diffusion across a society requires the language and ideas that underpin gender equality to be translated into local cultural contexts – '[f]or this to happen, the process needs to be internally vindicated in order to challenge popular beliefs and attitudes, and to change common practice' (Allden 2007, pp. 8–9). Importantly, internal validation must also extend beyond the middle class to rural populations where strong patriarchal attitudes and practices are commonly the most deeply entrenched (Roynestad 2003).

If transition is to translate into transformative impact on the status of women and on women's lives more generally, a further element is also necessary; the capacity for strategies and solutions to bridge traditional and formal structures within society and to respond in multiple and diverse ways in different fora to the legal, social and cultural pluralities which exist within a society, and thereby harness women's advantage and benefit.

Sri Lanka

The case of Sri Lanka demonstrates a different set of opportunities and challenges in the wake of conflict, which may enable women's enhanced participation and agency in peace processes and post-conflict rebuilding.

The conflict in Sri Lanka was borne of almost two decades (1983–2001) of armed struggle between the LTTE, for an independent Tamil homeland, and the Sri Lankan government. This conflict witnessed millions of people being displaced throughout the country (Rajasingham-Senanayake 2004, p. 155). Women were subjected to rape, sexual torture, sexual abuse, kidnapping and various other brutalities (Abeysekera 2003, p. 535). For women the conflict caused a widespread loss of male kinship and changes in cultural practices and structures that impacted variously on women's roles during the conflict (ibid., pp. 533–4). Importantly, the conflict in Sri Lanka, which was grounded in strong ethnic divisions, served to highlight that 'changes do not manifest themselves in the same degree or even in the same way among all women' (Rajasingham-Senanayake 2004, p. 157) during conflicts and periods of instability. While the conflict in Sri Lanka, on the one hand, permitted Tamil women to play various new public roles, on the other hand, it restricted the mobility of Muslim women (ibid.). This example demonstrates, as raised above, the need for caution in not homogenising women's experiences of conflict, violence and rebuilding.

Many of the opportunities for women's empowerment that presented in Sri Lanka during the conflict and post-conflict phase were borne of changes in traditional roles for many Tamil women who found themselves widowed and with no male kinship. These women were forced to take on leadership roles within the family and contend with altered familial structures. Many of these women also faced a displacement which, despite arguably creating an ambivalent space for women marked by both the distress of dislocation as well as the hope for future freedom, created unique windows of opportunity for 'greater personal and group autonomy as well as experiments with identity and leadership' (ibid., p. 159). One example of an opportunity for empowerment and gender reconfiguration is seen in young Tamil widows' rejection and redefinition of the traditional role of the unmarried woman and the Hindu widow:

> Consciously and unconsciously, they appear[ed] to be redefining conceptions of the 'good woman' as one who lives within the traditional confines of caste, kin group and village. As they struggle[ed] with new gender roles and identities, many of these young widows also struggle[d] to find a language and cultural idiom to speak of their changed roles. They refuse[d] to wear the prescribed garb of widowhood and appear[ed] to break with the ideology of Kanaki (Paththini), the exemplary faithful wife and widow of Tamil mythology and ideology. Rather, they seem[ed] to evoke the sign of the *devadasi* – Kanaki's alter ego – who transcended conventional gender roles; the professional woman married to immortality for her talent and skill, most familiar to South Asian audiences in the name of the famed dancer and courtesan, Madhavi of the Tamil Hindu–Buddhist epic, *Silla-paddikaram*. [footnotes omitted]
>
> (ibid., p. 160)

This type of reconstruction of womanhood has profound implications for post-conflict humanitarian interventions and government relief. It suggests that development thinking must move beyond conventional 'victim ideology [and seek] to work out *culturally* appropriate and effective strategies for women's empowerment in the context of the social transformations that have occurred over years of armed conflict and displacement' (ibid.). As discussed further below, post-conflict humanitarian and government responses can fortify positive social changes borne of the conflict. However, poorly conceived and gender-biased, or even gender-neutral, responses risk unravelling such positive developments and returning women to the pre-conflict status quo in gender relations.

Thus, not only must changes in social structures and gender hierarchies be acknowledged and integrated in post-conflict rebuilding as a pathway for consolidating positive social changes towards women's empowerment, but women's changed position and roles in society must also translate into activity and influence in shaping rebuilding processes. Women in Sri Lanka were successful in achieving this to some extent; they gained increased visibility post-conflict, taking on a range of unorthodox roles from policing to diplomacy (Harris 2004). However, questions still arose about whether women's participation was representative of the different voices of 'woman' and whether women's marginalisation excluded women from certain peace-building processes, and accordingly stifled the capacity of actual decision-makers to develop and implement holistic, multi-layered and integrated gender-inclusive policies (Abeysekera 2003). A particular challenge in the Sri Lankan context was overcoming deep divisions between women themselves:

> Women who belong to communities where group identity is the defining factor in self-identification find themselves torn between different loyalties – to their community and to that of women. They are inhibited from raising issues that are significant for women or that advance equality within the community, since this is often perceived as being contrary to the interests of the community. Also, they cannot easily maintain contact with women outside of the community, because outsiders often belong to other social groups and, consequently, are perceived as hostile.
>
> (ibid., p. 532)

The case of Sri Lanka also serves to highlight that, despite opportunities to reconceptualise womanhood and reconfigure gender hierarchies, difficulties in achieving sustained transformative change for women may persist because 'many of the changes in women's positions that are due to conflict, even years after the fighting has ended, are quite tenuous and fragile' (ibid., p. 537).

Areas of priority and whose responsibility?

This chapter has argued that periods of conflict and instability in a state or region tend to impel social changes within communities, including in traditional gender roles; and that the post-conflict and rebuilding phases in affected societies represent a unique, if not crucial, point of inflection at which positive social changes can be harnessed for transformative impact, particularly for improving the position and lives of women. There are multiple potential pathways, as discussed above, for driving such changes including: using the increased presence of international NGOs (although this may also pose risks: Efuk 2007) and other agencies in post-conflict communities to lobby and campaign around specific gender issues; capitalising on newly created opportunities for participation of women in political and peace-building processes; and developing gender-sensitive legislation and processes in the regeneration of decimated legal and judicial systems. Irrespective of the vehicle used, several prerequisites are arguably necessary to transform the reality of women's lives with greater empowerment, access to justice, equality and deconstructing the powerful scaffolding that has universally supported and entrenched age-old patriarchal attitudes, values and practices.

First, there must be an understanding of what women need and want to achieve for themselves in this transformation. This understanding must inform and drive the agenda for reform so as to ensure that outcomes are responsive to women's priorities, actual needs, and their lived experiences, particularly changes in women's roles and identity which arise out of the conflict. Moreover, this understanding must be sufficiently broad to encompass the needs of the individual woman and must not simply cater to, nor become a tool for reinforcing, hegemonic gender and cultural norms; at the same time, the reality of local and cultural contexts must be recognised (Gready and Robins 2014). Second, there is a need to implement unified and sustainable strategies of action that provide complex multi-layered responses and solutions within the different spheres of women's lives. Third, there is the need to pursue actions and implement reforms that challenge and influence patriarchal and gender-based discriminatory societal attitudes and practices.

Increasingly, research is recognising the need to draw on the voices of women and is recognising the power of women as agents of change (Rehn and Sirleaf 2002; Srinivasan 1990). Where should attention and resources be directed to leverage most effectively the position of women during periods of transition and in the rebuilding of states and communities? It is becoming clear in listening to women's voices and learning from past experiences of conflict across the globe that formal legal justice, of itself, is neither always necessary nor sufficient to meet women's justice needs in post-conflict and transitioning states. Women often prioritise other needs over and above formal justice and, in particular, over the prosecution and punishment of perpetrators (Ajetunmobi 2012). Women's needs are shaped by their long-standing position of disadvantage and subordination relative to men and their greater vulnerability to the impacts of poverty. Thus the justice priorities of women extend to greater economic, social, health and political justice. One principal need that women have is access to psychosocial support (Harris and Freccero 2011, pp. 7–12). Coupled with this is the need for women to have spaces in which they can share their experiences of violence with other women (Leslie and Boso 2003). These spaces must be safe and secure and must provide women with adequate support to share their experiences, particularly of sexual violence, free of fear of judgement or stigmatisation. These spaces can serve a multiplicity of functions. First, they create opportunities for women to come together, to network, to build a collective identity and shared agency. The experiences of the individual woman and collective group can be shared and validated; this can be an important step towards truth telling and reconciliation. Second, such spaces may help women find 'a culturally appropriate idiom to articulate, legitimate and support' their changed roles and identity for long-term impact (Rajasingham-Senanayake 2004, p. 162). Third, such spaces can form an important component of the psychosocial support provided to women. Evidence suggests that access to appropriate psychosocial support for women affected by violence is often lacking in post-conflict settings and yet this represents one of the main justice needs that women identify and is key to their recovery and to rebuilding families and communities (Usta *et al.* 2008, p. 797).

Importantly, attention in rebuilding post-conflict must also recognise the inextricable link between women's needs and the needs of their children. For example, women's psychosocial needs go hand in hand with addressing the psychosocial needs and well-being of children. Women often find it difficult to move on and start healing themselves, if their children are still suffering. Recognising this mutually interactive connection between maternal and child well-being is not to seek to essentialise the role of women as mothers, but rather serves to highlight the fact that the needs of women must be situated and holistic, and must recognise the varied roles and responsibilities that women face as part of their lived experience, particularly as impacted by conflict and instability. Moreover, women's economic needs are also linked to their children's well-being and future development, especially access to education. Economic independence represents another primary need for women in rebuilding. Economic justice for women must not only recognise the historical disadvantage that women face but also the new responsibilities that have been thrust on them by the conflict and instability within the state. Economic justice for women demands reforms that delivers their economic independence in a sustainable and productive way for long-term impact. In this respect, one of the most urgent reforms for women post-conflict, as indicated in many states across the globe, is access to and ownership of property, particularly land rights (Manjoo and McRaith 2011; Adelman and Peterman 2014, p. 591). Property rights often represent an urgent post-conflict justice issue for women as they attempt resettlement, frequently with the newly acquired status of widow. In many countries women in such situations are deprived of the use of their land, stripped of any right of ownership, and land is stolen and redistributed amongst the former husband's family with the total exclusion of her and her children (Lastarria-Cornheil 2005, pp. 3, 8).

Additionally, the continuum of violence faced by women must be recognised. Ongoing violence against women serves to subordinate and oppress them when they are entitled to live a life free of actual and threatened violence (UNGA 1993, Articles 1–3). As noted above, research suggests that, in particular, violence within the home and intimate partner violence increase post-conflict and during periods of transition. This has been linked to a number of factors, including: men's disenfranchisement during conflict and post-conflict; the changed role of women and men in society during periods of instability; the availability of weapons; and the use of, and reliance on alcohol in fragmented communities (UNDP 2013; Rehn and Sirleaf 2002, p. 14).

Having identified significant areas of priority for women's needs, a final question for consideration is that of responsibility in responding to these needs and for creating pathways during periods of transition towards greater gender equality. A survey of post-conflict and transitioning states suggests that often NGOs and the international community take responsibility for such areas and in addressing the needs of women generally (Leslie and Boso 2003, p. 30). The provision of psychosocial support and financial assistance to women are two examples where this commonly occurs. However, the services and economic assistance provided to women by NGOs and international agencies is often short-term, fragmented and not sustained. If women's lives are to be transformed, psychosocial support and economic programmes need to be integrated, holistic and sustainable; otherwise their traditional position of disadvantage and subordination will continue (Gready and Robins 2014). This means that states themselves must be charged with taking action, delivering programmes and services to women, and driving reform in areas that ensure that women's changed position in society is recognised and maintained. States themselves need to take greater responsibility for the psychosocial well-being and economic empowerment of women. This call accords with the right to development (UNGA 1986), which recognises: the individual citizen as rights bearer; the primary role of the state as domestic duty bearer (Articles 2(3); 3(1); 8); and economic empowerment and reforms as central to fulfilling this duty and eradicating social injustices (Article 8(2)).

Conclusion

This chapter has argued that conflict, insecurity and periods of transition in the life of a state may represent important and unique opportunities for positive social changes borne of such societal disruption, to be consolidated and amplified for a transformative effect on women's lives. Many situations of conflict around the globe have been marked by women's widowhood, changed roles within the family and new economic and leadership responsibilities. The responses of NGOs and governments in post-conflict settings may harness these changes for long-term impact or alternatively dilute these developments with a retrograde effect on women's status in society. As Rimmer notes: '[t]he formal ending of violence does not necessarily mean the achievement of peace, rather it provides a new set of opportunities that can be grasped or thrown away' (Rimmer 2010, p. 145). This requires that all actors, and especially state actors, 'in political negotiations and civil rights groups involved in peace-building should be sensitive to the roles and opportunities afforded to them by the process' (Abeysekera 2003, p. 525). Thus the unique opportunity that instability, transition and rebuilding represents must be seized with creativity and recognised as a transformative moment by the state itself, which must be accompanied by rethinking existing paradigms of development, relief and rehabilitation, and even fundamental notions of peace and war. As Rajasingham-Senayake has eloquently argued:

> Th[e] lacuna in the understanding of conflict and its effects has much to do with how we conceptualize peace – as a return to the (gender) status quo. Peace we still think constitutes a return to things the way they used to be: the certainties of familiar, older, ways of being and doing. But, to conceptualize peace thus is another kind of (epistemic) violence . . . In this context, peace is necessarily a third place divorced from the past, utopia perhaps, somewhere arguably between the old and the existing, the past and the present.
>
> (Rajasingham-Senanayake 2004, pp. 164–5)

For transitions to translate into transformative impacts for women and their status in society, the gender politics of conflict must be leveraged in the rebuilding of communities for a redistributive impact and utilitarian end for all women, men, children, families and the entire community.

Bibliography

Abeysekera, S. (2003) 'Maximizing the Achievement of Women's Human Rights in Conflict-Transformation: The Case of Sri Lanka', *Columbia Journal of Transnational Law*, vol. 41, pp. 523–40.

Adelman, S. and Peterman, A. (2014) 'Resettlement and Gender Dimensions of Land Rights in Post-Conflict Northern Uganda', *World Development*, vol. 64, pp. 583–96.

Aguirre, D. and Pietropaoli, I. (2008) 'Gender Equality, Development and Transitional Justice: The Case of Nepal', *The International Journal of Transitional Justice*, vol. 2, pp. 356–77.

Ajetunmobi, A. (2012) 'Victims' responses after mass atrocities: a note on empirical findings', *Contemporary Justice Review: Issues in Criminal, Social, and Restorative Justice*, vol. 15, no. 1, pp. 39–56.

Allden, S. (2007) 'Internalising the Culture of Human Rights: Securing Women's Rights in Post-Conflict East Timor', *Asia-Pacific Journal on Human Rights and the Law*, vol. 1, pp. 1–23.

Beerli, C. (2013) *Vulnerabilities in Armed Conflicts*, Speech presented at the International Red Cross 14th Bruges Colloquium, 17 October, accessed 28 September 2014 [online] http://www.icrc.org/eng/resources/documents/statement/2013/10-18-protected-person-bruges.htm.

Björkdahl, A. and Selimovic, J. (2015) 'Gendering Agency in Transitional Justice', *Security Dialogue*, vol. 46, no. 3, pp. 165–82.

Corrin, J. (2008) '*Ples Bilong Mere*: Law, Gender and Peace-Building in Solomon Islands', *Feminist Legal Studies*, vol. 16, pp. 169–94.

Crawford, K. (2013) 'From Spoils to Weapons: Framing Wartime Sexual Violence', *Gender & Development*, vol. 21, pp. 505–17.

Dolven, B., Margesson, R. and Vaughn, B. (2012) *Timor-Leste: Political Dynamics, Development and International Involvement*, Congressional Research Service, Report No. R42585 [online] http://fas.org/sgp/crs/row/R42585.pdf

Duggan, C. and Abusharaf, A. (2006) 'Reparation of Sexual Violence and Democratic Transition: In Search of Gender Justice', in De Greiff, P. (ed.), *The Handbook of Reparations*, Oxford University Press, New York, pp. 623–49.

Efuk, S. (2007) 'Humanitarianism that Harms: A Critique of NGO Charity in Southern Sudan', *Civil Wars*, vol. 3, no. 3, pp. 45–73.

Goswami, N. (2014) 'Asian conflict "ayes" have it wrong', *Asia Times Online*, 10 January, [online] http://www.atimes.com/atimes/World/WOR-01-100114.html.

Gready, P. and Robins, S. (2014) 'From Traditional to Transformative Justice: A New Agenda for Practice', *The International Journal of Transitional Justice*, vol. 8, pp. 339–61.

Hall, N. (2009) 'East Timorese Women Challenge Domestic Violence', *Australian Journal of Political Science*, vol. 44, pp. 309–25.

Harris, S. (2004) 'Gender, participation, and post-conflict planning in northern Sri Lanka', *Gender & Development*, vol. 12, pp. 60–9.

Harris, L. and Freccero, J. (2011) *Sexual Violence: Medical and Psychosocial Support*, Working Paper, Sexual Violence and Accountability Project, Human Rights Centre, University of California, Berkley [online] https://www.law.berkeley.edu/wp-content/uploads/2015/04/Sexual-Violence_-Medical-and-Psychsocial-Support-SV-Working-Paper.pdf

Hynes, M., Ward, J., Robertson, K. and Crouse, C. (2004) 'A Determination of the Prevalence of Gender-based Violence among Conflict-affected Populations in East Timor', *Disasters*, vol. 28, no. 3, pp. 294–332.

Internal Displacement Monitoring Centre (2007) *Internal Displacement: Global Overview of Trends and Developments in 2006*, Geneva, Switzerland.

International Committee of the Red Cross (2001) *Women and War*, Geneva, Switzerland [online] https://www.icrc.org/eng/assets/files/other/icrc_002_0798_women_facing_war.pdf

International Committee of the Red Cross (2013a) *Protection of Women in Situations of Armed Conflict*, 5 June 2013 [online] https://www.icrc.org/eng/resources/documents/field-newsletter/2013/india-e-newsletter/legal-opinion-05-2013.htm.

International Committee of the Red Cross (2013b) *Sexual Violence in Armed Conflict: Questions and Answers*, 10 November 2013 [online] https://www.icrc.org/eng/resources/documents/faq/sexual-violence-questions-and-answers.htm#%20Who%20is%20affected%20and%20how?

International Institute for Strategic Studies n.d., *Armed Conflict Database*, IISS, London [online] https://acd.iiss.org/.

Justino, P., Leone, M. and Salardi, P. (2011) *Education and Conflict Recovery: The Case of Timor Leste*, MICROCON Research Working Paper 55, Brighton.

Krook, M. (2013) 'Electoral Gender Quotas: A Conceptual Analysis', *Comparative Political Studies*, 19 July 2013 [online] http://cps.sagepub.com/content/early/2013/07/14/0010414013495359.

Lastarria-Cornheil, S. (2005) *Gender and Property Rights within Post Conflict Situations*, USAID, Issue Paper No. 12, April.

Leslie, H and Boso, S. (2003) 'Gender-Related Violence in the Solomon Islands: The work of local women's organisations', *Asia Pacific Viewpoint*, vol. 44, no. 3. pp. 325–33.

Manjoo, R. and McRaith, C. (2011) 'Gender-Based Violence and Justice in Conflict and Post-Conflict Areas', *Cornell International Law Journal*, vol. 44, pp. 11–32.

Myrttinen, H. (2005) 'Masculinities, Violence and Power in Timor Leste', *Revue Lusotopie*, vol. 12, no. 1, pp. 233–44.

Nobel Women's Initiative (2011) *War on Women: Time for Action to End Sexual Violence in Conflict*, Canada [online] http://nobelwomensinitiative.org/2011/05/war-on-women-time-for-action-to-end-sexual-violence-in-conflict/

Oosterveld, V. (2012) *Report No. 29: Women and Girls Fleeing Conflict: Gender and the Interpretation and Application of the 1951 Refugee Convention*, prepared for United Nations High Commissioner for Refugees [online] http://www.unhcr.org/504dd7649.html.

Porter, E. (2011) 'Gender Inclusivity in Transitional Justice Strategies: Women in Timor Leste' in Stanley, R. and Buckley-Zistel S. (eds.) 2011, *Gender in Transitional Justice*, Palgrave Macmillan, UK, pp. 221–40.

Rajasingham-Senanayake, D. (2004) 'Between Reality and Representation: Women's Agency in War and Post-Conflict Sri Lanka', *Cultural Dynamics*, vol. 16, no. 2–3, pp. 141–68.

Refugee Studies Centre, University of Oxford (2011) *Conflict-induced displacement*, Forced Migration [online] http://www.forcedmigration.org/research-resources/expert-guides/gender-and-forced-migration/conflict-induced-displacement#section-6.

Rehn, E. and Sirleaf, E. (2002) *Women, War and Peace: The Independent Experts' Assessment on the Impact of Armed Conflict on Women and Women's Role in Peace-building*, UNIFEM, New York.

Rimmer, S. (2010) 'Sexing the Subject of Transitional Justice', *Australian Feminist Law Journal*, vol. 32, pp. 123–61.

Roynestad, E. (2003) 'Are women included or excluded in Post-Conflict Reconstruction? A case study from Timor Leste', United Nations Division for the Advancement of Women, EGM/PEACE/2003/EP.8. [online] http://www.un.org/womenwatch/daw/egm/peace2003/reports/EP8Roynestad.PDF.

Society for the Study of Peace and Conflict (2014) 'Armed Conflict and Crisis', *South Asia Conflict Monitor*, vol. 12, no. 1.

Srinivasan, A. (1990) 'The Survivor in the Study of Violence' in Veena Das, (ed.), *Mirrors of Violence: Communities, Riots and Survivors in South Asia*, Oxford University Press, Oxford, UK, pp. 305–20.

Swaine, A. (2003) *Traditional Justice and Gender-Based Violence*, International Rescue Committee Research Report.

UNIFEM n.d., *Facts and Figures on Peace and Security* [online] http://www.womenwarpeace.org/.

United Nations Development Programme (2002) *East Timor Human Development Report 2002: Ukun Rasik A'an – The Way Ahead*, UNDP, Dili.

United Nations Development Programme (2013) *Human Development Report 2013: The Rise of the South: Human Progress in a Diverse World*, UNDP, New York.

United Nations General Assembly (1986) *United Nations Declaration on the Right to Development*: resolution/adopted by the General Assembly, 4 December, A/RES/41/128.

United Nations General Assembly (1993) *United Nations Declaration on the Elimination of Violence against Women*: resolution/adopted by the General Assembly, 20 December, A/RES/48/104.

United Nations High Commissioner for Refugees (1993) *The State of the World's Refugees 1993: The Challenge of Protection.*

United Nations High Commissioner for Refugees (2008) *Evaluation of UNHCR's efforts to prevent and respond to sexual and gender-based violence in situations of forced displacement* [online] http://www.unhcr.org/48ea31062.pdf

United Nations High Commissioner for Refugees (2013) *UNHCR Statistical Yearbook 2013* [online] http://www.unhcr.org/54cf9bd69.html.

United Nations Security Council (2008) 1820 on women and peace and security, SC Res. 1820, 19 June 2008, UN Doc. S/RES/1820 (2008).

Usta, J., Farver, J. and Zein, L. (2008) 'Women, War, and Violence: Surviving the Experience', *Journal of Women's Health*, vol. 17 pp. 793–804.

Van Vliet, J. (2010) 'Shame and Avoidance in Trauma' in Martz, E. (ed.), *Trauma Rehabilitation After War and Conflict: Community and Individual Perspectives*, Springer-Verlag, New York, pp. 247–65.

Walker, M. (2009) 'Gender and Violence in Focus: A Background for Gender Justice in Reparations' in Rubio-Marin, R. (ed.), *The Gender of Reparations: Unsettling Sexual Hierarchies While Redressing Human Rights Violations*, Cambridge University Press, New York, pp. 18–63.

Wirtz, A.L., Pham, K., Glass, N., Loochkartt, S., Kidane, T., Cuspoca, D., Rubenstein, L., Singh, S. and Vu, A. (2014) 'Gender-Based Violence in Conflict and Displacement: Qualitative Findings from Displaced Women in Colombia', *Conflict and Health*, vol. 8, no. 10 [online] http://www.conflictandhealth.com/content/8/1/10.

Wiseman, E. (2008) 'From Rhetoric to Inaction: The Failure to Implement Gender Norms in the United Nations Organisation Mission in the Democratic Republic of the Congo', Masters thesis, The University of British Columbia, Vancouver.

The World Bank (2014) *Timor-Leste Overview*, The World Bank [online] http://www.worldbank.org/en/country/timor-leste/overview.

World Health Organisation (2013) *Global and Regional Estimates of Violence against Women* [online] http://apps.who.int/iris/bitstream/10665/85239/1/9789241564625_eng.pdf

3 Women in post-war Sri Lanka

Linking policy to reality

Shyamala Gomez

Introduction

This chapter reflects on how, five years after the military defeat of the Liberation Tigers of Tamil Eelam (LTTE) and the dawn of an uneasy peace in Sri Lanka, the state has responded to the concerns of women affected by war by examining the reality of women's lives in a post-war context in Sri Lanka. Post-conflict Sri Lanka has seen a rise in female-headed households, the number of widows, the incidence of sexual violence and obstacles to women accessing their rights to land; and some preliminary research indicates an increase in underage marriage. These issues have been experienced both in the areas affected by the conflict and by women living in the 'border' villages.

At the national level, the Recommendations of the Lessons Learnt and Reconciliation Commission (LLRC), the LLRC Action Plan (LLRCAP) and the National Action Plan for the Promotion and Protection of Human Rights (NHRAP) provide a framework for the state to address women's concerns in a holistic manner. The chapter first considers the international and national frameworks that can be drawn upon to address women's concerns. It examines gender-based violence and other post-war issues that have arisen through the lens of United Nations (UN) Security Council Resolution 1325[1] (hereafter SCR 1325) and subsequent Security Council resolutions dealing with sexual violence. Sri Lanka ratified the Convention on the Elimination of Discrimination against Women (CEDAW) in 1981. The CEDAW reporting process is another avenue through which national policy commitments and UN Security Council resolutions can be channelled. These resolutions on women, peace and security, together with CEDAW and the policy statements of the Sri Lankan government, will be used as a framework to examine the state's responsibility to ensure that women's security and other concerns are met.

Second, the chapter examines the situation of women affected by conflict, the relevant provisions of international instruments and the national policy documents that can be used by the state to address women's concerns. The chapter takes the position that when responding to the concerns of women affected by war, especially when addressing women's security and other interrelated rights, the state must take into consideration national policy documents, such as the LLRCAP and the NHRAP, and take steps to implement them using the UN Security Council resolutions on women, peace and security and CEDAW as a framework. Specifically, the chapter argues that the link between international legal instruments and national policies must be strengthened by the Sri Lankan state if it is to meaningfully respond to how women have been affected by the war.

International and national frameworks: UNSCR 1325 and CEDAW

SCR 1325 recognised the disproportionate impact of armed conflict on women and the role women play in international peace and security. Internationally, the biggest hurdle has been the lack of political will and the lack of an accountability mechanism to implement SCR 1325 meaningfully in specific country contexts. The Resolution has conceptual gaps and lacks proper guidelines so many countries fail to implement it in practice (Porter 2007, p. 3).

In Sri Lanka, the state generally distances itself from international instruments and mechanisms established by the UN, preferring to rely on domestic mechanisms to address human-rights violations. Sri Lanka does not have a National Action Plan (NAP) on SCR 1325 and efforts to formulate a NAP are at a standstill. Although the Ministry of Child Development and Women's Affairs has discussed the adoption of a NAP or other alternatives, such as incorporating a section on women's post-conflict issues into a draft National Action Plan on Women (NAPW), one is yet to be finalised.

In the absence of a specific NAP, SCR 1325 itself provides a useful framework to address post-war realities faced by women in Sri Lanka. Conflict prevention, conflict resolution, peace-building and encouraging women to participate in decision-making in conflict prevention and resolution are comparatively non-contentious. Similarly, restructuring efforts can be carried out within the framework of SCR 1325 without much resistance by the state. However, when sexual violence in post-war is discussed the Sri Lankan State is non-cooperative.

SCR 1325 lacks an implementing body and the resolution does not provide for time frames, nor does it name and shame countries or maintain lists of such countries (Steinberg 2011, p. 118). States must be creative and find means of operationalising the Resolution, which may be used in tandem with CEDAW. If the links between CEDAW and SCR 1325 are drawn explicitly, the CEDAW Convention can potentially provide a mechanism to operationalise the Resolution. This is especially true for Sri Lanka where the state is slow to take on board the content of the international instruments it ratifies and the obligations that arise from being a UN Member State. The state has been engaged with the CEDAW process for many years and it could be used to address concerns of women's peace and security.

Other Security Council resolutions on women, peace and security

The Resolutions that were adopted by the Security Council subsequent to SCR 1325 elaborate on the issue of violence against women. The value of Security

Council Resolution 1820[2] (hereafter SCR 1820) lies in the recognition that sexual violence can be a threat to international peace and security. SCR 1820 recognises sexual violence as a tactic of war. Similarly, Security Council Resolution 1888[3] (SCR 1888) adopted in 2009 under the women, peace and security agenda emphasises the role of the state in halting sexual violence as a tactic of war and addresses the modalities of implementing SCR 1820 and this further reinforces the stand of the Security Council that sexual violence in war should be taken seriously.

In 2010, the Security Council adopted Security Council Resolution 1960[4] (SCR 1960), which addresses impunity and provides guidance on the prevention and protection from sexual violence in conflict. SCR 1960 also emphasises that sexual violence is a serious violation of international human-rights standards. Measuring progress on the implementation of SCR 1325 is not an easy task. Security Council Resolution 1889[5] (SCR 1889) called on the UN Secretary-General to compile a set of indicators that would ensure more effective and co-ordinated implementation.

These Security Council Resolutions provide an extensive framework for states to respond to the situation of women and girls in armed conflict and the aftermath. While some of these provisions apply specifically to armed conflict, they remain relevant in post-conflict contexts. Sexual violence in conflict and its consequences have a bearing on international peace and security and this factor should compel states to tackle sexual and gender-based violence at every level. However, many states deny that sexual violence takes place in conflict settings or report very low numbers of victims. The LLRC report provides a useful framework to address the incidence of sexual violence and concerns of war-affected women. However, the LLRC does not directly address sexual violence.

Lessons Learnt and Reconciliation Commission (LLRC)

In May 2010, the President appointed a Lessons Learnt and Reconciliation Commission (LLRC), consisting of eight members, to inquire into and report on violations that took place in the period between 21 February 2002, when the ceasefire agreement came into operation, and 19 May 2009, which marked the end of the war. The Commission was tasked with examining the circumstances that led to the failure of the ceasefire agreement and the lessons that can be learnt to ensure that there will be no recurrence. It also mandates the Commission to look into methods of restitution to any persons affected by these events. However, there is no mention of women's concerns in the mandate. This is another instance where the opportunity to integrate women's concerns into future action plans of the state appears to have been lost. A NAP to operationalise the recommendations of the Commission was subsequently formulated. The NAP mandates that the state shall:

> *Establish an Inter-Agency Task Force mandated to address in a comprehensive manner the needs of women, children, elderly and other vulnerable groups such as disabled affected by conflict, and provide necessary relief.*[6]

Further, this section also states that, in order to achieve this objective, the activities laid down in the National Action Plan for the Protection and Promotion of Human Rights have to be implemented.

National Action Plan for the Protection and Promotion of Human Rights (2011–16) (NHRAP)

The NHRAP was a response to calls from the Sri Lankan citizenry to examine the human-rights situation as a result of the armed conflict.[7] The government also pledged to develop a plan during the Universal Periodic Review (UPR) process at the Human Rights Council in May 2008 (NHRAP, 2011–16, p. 5). The NHRAP, which has eight thematic areas, was developed with input from civil society. The section on women affected by conflict only has a minor reference to war widows and female ex-combatants. The section on violence against women makes no reference to gender-based violence during or after the conflict. Non-discrimination in women's access to land has been addressed within the report's section on the rights of internally displaced persons. Although the NHRAP is comprehensive, its implementation remains weak. The LLRCAP refers to the NHRAP and asks that certain activities be carried out with reference to both documents. However, the LLRCAP and the NHRAP are not legally enforceable documents. They lack legal 'teeth' and this factor accounts for the lack of importance they are accorded in society. They remain government policy documents to be referred to only when needed. Similarly, the resolutions on women, peace and security do not have an implementing body. Unless governments are committed to operationalising these policy documents, the provisions will remain merely on paper.

Gender-based violence in the post-war context

The war has significantly impacted on women, though incidences of sexual violence against women are rarely subject to discussion. This section analyses gender-based violence alongside relevant provisions in the LLRCAP and the NHRAP to consider how the state can utilise these policies to address the security concerns of women affected by the conflict, particularly sexual violence.

Reports of sexual violence by the armed forces in the former war-affected areas have been documented (European Center for Constitutional and Human Rights 2010; International Crisis Group 2011; Minority Rights Group International, 2013; Herath *et al.* 2012). A recent report highlighted the torture of men and women by the Sri Lankan armed forces during the war and cited victims of sexual and physical torture at the hands of the armed forces (Sooka 2014). An Oxfam report found that Batticaloa, a district affected by the war in the East, had the highest prevalence of abuse by the army, LTTE and other armed groups (Herath *et al.* 2012, p. 45).

Violence against women in other forms has also surfaced (Women's Action Network 2014). Women and children have been arbitrarily detained under the *Prevention of Terrorism Act 1979* for illegal acts allegedly carried out by their male relatives. Procedures under the Presidential Directives on Arrest and Detention were not followed during the arrests, which violates Article 13 of the Constitution. This Article affords protection against arbitrary arrest and detention and the state is obligated to release these detainees if there are no charges against them.

Domestic violence

The incidence of domestic violence has also increased in the Eastern Provinces of Sri Lanka. A study conducted by the Muslim Women's Research and Action Forum (MWRAF) found that a high number of Muslim women are victims of domestic violence (Women & Media Collective 2014a, p. 50) Early marriage, permitted under Muslim law, is common in these areas. These young women find it more difficult to discuss domestic violence openly due to socio-cultural constraints. Fifty-six case studies were collected by MWRAF from the Batticaloa and Ampara districts, areas affected by the war. The women had experienced violence at the hands of persons closely related to them. The Oxfam study, which interviewed 1,442 women, also found a high incidence (sixty-seven per cent) of spousal violence (Herath *et al.* 2012).

Female ex-combatants and sexual violence

The security of female ex-combatants has been further compromised due to the militarisation of the former war-affected areas. Women report that their movements are subject to continuous monitoring by military personnel (Herath *et al.* 2012). Some women allege that they have been asked for sexual favours when they report monthly to military establishments in their villages (Women & Media Collective 2014b). These incidents of sexual and psychological violence, although anecdotal, provide an insight into the lives of female ex-combatants and the difficulties they face in reintegrating into society. The reintegration of ex-combatants and the lack of security afforded to them by the state were referred to by the Rapporteur for Follow-up on Concluding Observations of the Committee on the Elimination of Discrimination against Women (CEDAW) on Sri Lanka's response to the situation of women in post-conflict (UN Office of the High Commissioner for Human Rights 2014). The Rapporteur specifically requested the Sri Lankan government to provide details on the rehabilitation of female ex-combatants.

The NHRAP and the LLRC recognise the need to reintegrate female ex-combatants into society. While the LLRCAP states that 2,274 ex-combatants have been rehabilitated, the NHRAP merely states that the government must ensure implementation of these plans to reintegrate these women. Although programmes to rehabilitate female former ex-combatants are carried out by the state, these programmes fall short in many aspects (Women & Media Collective 2014c, p. 31).

In its Concluding Observations, the CEDAW Committee has specifically emphasised reports of sexual violence allegedly perpetrated by the armed forces, the police and armed groups and urged the state to investigate, prosecute and punish acts of violence (CEDAW 2011). The CEDAW Committee requested that the state give a follow-up report on issues relating to the protection of Tamil women and female ex-combatants from human-rights violations, including their freedom of movement, and to provide for the socio-economic rights of internally displaced women. In response to Sri Lanka's follow up report, the CEDAW Committee stated that:

> sexual violence against Tamil women by State actors was perpetrated on a much larger scale, in particular at the end of the war. The Committee considers that the action taken by the State party has been so minimal given the scope of the problem that the Committee cannot consider that the recommendation has been implemented.
>
> (UN Office of the High Commissioner for Human Rights 2014)

This is a strong observation by the Committee that the state is not fulfilling its obligations under the CEDAW Convention.

Sri Lanka's follow-up report refers to the 'repeated attempts to draw a non-existent correlation between the presence of the military in the North and insecurity of women and girls in that region', (CEDAW 2013, p. 6) indicating the state's reluctance to formally acknowledge the connection between militarised settings and levels of gender-based violence. Specifically, the state report refers to the numbers of cases of sexual violence by the security forces both during and after the war. According to the report, from January 2007 to May 2009 seven security force personnel were involved in twelve incidents of sexual violence in the North and East during the conflict and during the post-conflict period from May 2009 to May 2012 ten personnel were involved in six incidents of sexual violence in the North, out of a total of 307 persons accused in 256 incidents in the Northern Province (ibid.).

The report states that the percentage of security force personnel 'accused' of being involved in sexual violence has decreased from 5.6 per cent during the conflict to 3.3 per cent in the post-conflict period, which the government uses as evidence that it is a myth to suggest that the presence of security forces in the North contributes to the insecurity of women and girls (ibid.). The report also states that legal action has been taken against these security forces personnel and, in two cases, three personnel were sentenced for between twelve to fourteen years (ibid.).

Despite the state's assertion, a military presence increases the risk of violence for women and this fact cannot be disputed in most conflict affected societies (see Shackel's analysis in Chapter 2). It is the obligation of the state to ensure that the security forces are held accountable for their acts. However, the Sri Lankan State perpetuates the myth that sexual violence is not common. This may be due to several factors, such as denial that such incidents take place, the general environment of impunity and a lack of accountability for such violations at the hands of the armed forces. Demilitarisation of the North and East will, to a certain extent, diffuse tension for the people living in these areas (European Center for Constitutional and Human Rights 2011).

Collection of data on sexual violence

A lack of data on sexual violence in Sri Lanka makes it harder to convince the government that action is needed to address the problem. The collection of 'hard numbers' on sexual violence will help to 'create sufficient political will' (Steinberg 2011, p. 127). Steinberg identifies three critical elements: first, 'credible data that the problem is real and pressing'; second, a link must be made between addressing the problem and achieving broader policy objectives; and third, a need to realise that the application of resources can help to solve the problem or even make a substantial improvement (ibid., pp. 127–8).

The task of collecting data has been recognised as a difficult one at the international level. SCR 1889 requested the UN Secretary-General to formulate indicators that could be applied globally to measure the implementation of SCR 1325. The inclusion of an indicator on the prevalence of sexual violence, type of perpetrator, type of violation, and groups affected may help to address this problem, though data is not easily accessible. In situations of conflict and post-conflict settings, reporting is often low due to security fears and there are no accessible databases that can be relied upon for advocacy purposes. Often, advocates have to rely on anecdotal evidence and secondary data to estimate the incidents of sexual violence that have taken place. Indicator 19 in the global indicators specifically refers to the 'percentage of referred cases of sexual and gender-based violence against women and girls that are reported, investigated and sentenced' (UN Women 2014, Annex 1). This indicator, in addition to the percentage of victims that report cases, also provides a measure of access to justice for victims of sexual violence. Again, due to fear of reprisal and threats to personal security and safety, very few victims access any form of justice. Similarly, the numbers of cases investigated and prosecuted remain low in most conflict-affected contexts.[8]

The CEDAW Committee, in its response to the state, commented on the fact that 'single women, war widows and former female combatants continue to suffer sexual violence, harassment and abuse at the hands of the military and from within their own community and that women who have come forward to challenge gender-based violence face many obstacles' (UN Office of the High Commissioner for Human Rights 2014). These obstacles deter women from reporting violations and silence them into inaction.

LLRC and violence

The only reference to women's security in the LLRCAP is to 'create a conducive environment in all areas of the country, especially the conflict affected areas, for women to feel that they live in a secure environment and their basic human dignity is safeguarded and protected'.[9] This passing reference to women's security concerns in the former war affected areas does not use the terminology of 'violence against women' or 'gender-based violence' and merely refers to the protection of women's dignity and to a safe environment for women.

NHRAP and violence

The NHRAP addresses violence against women in relation to access to services, sexual harassment in the public and private sectors, including the collection of gender-disaggregated data and co-ordination among the different service providers. There is no reference to violence against women during or after conflict. The section on 'women affected by conflict' only focuses on the reintegration of female ex-combatants and the development of policies for war widows. The NHRAP, like the LLRCAP, does not acknowledge the possibility of violence against women in a post-conflict context.

Addressing the issue of violence against women in the aftermath of conflict is all the more challenging when the issue is only referred to in passing in national policy documents. Limited engagement illustrates the state's lack of commitment and its denial that violence against women occurs during war and in post-war contexts. While both the LLRCAP and the NHRAP do not specifically address sexual violence in armed conflict or post-conflict settings, it is still possible to use these policy documents in tandem with the Security Council resolutions on women, peace and security and CEDAW. Civil society potentially plays an instrumental role by proactively promoting the application of CEDAW to urge the state to respond to women's concerns after the war. The state is then pressured to report every four years on the progress it has achieved towards CEDAW's objectives. States are effectively compelled to put in place institutional and other mechanisms to address the needs of women affected by the war.

Female-headed households and war widows

The thirty-year conflict brought about many changes to the core family unit, especially in areas affected by the war. Internal and, at times, multiple displacements meant that families were separated and resettled in different locations. The numbers of female-headed households rose in the North and East, areas affected by the war. Significantly, there are 54,532 female-headed households, among them 47,044 widows in the North (Sivachandran 2013a, 3). A 2012 study in the East estimated that more than fifteen per cent of the males in the households have lost their lives to war-related incidents (Herath *et al.* 2012, p. 39). Women have had to take on the burden of being the sole breadwinners within the family. Missing and 'disappeared' or abducted spouses, death of the spouse, spouses disabled as a consequence of the war, separation or divorce, spouses who had to migrate to other parts of the country to secure avenues of employment are some of the causes for the rise in female-headed households. Some men were also detained under emergency regulations (Sivachandran 2013a, p. 5). According to a study conducted by Sivachandran, the majority of women who head households are over fifty-five years old (ibid., p. 13). Further, 70 per cent of women-headed households consist of widows in the Jaffna district (ibid.).

However, there is no clear definition of a female-headed household, which means that some of these women are left out of development initiatives and beneficiary lists for different forms of assistance (Women & Media Collective 2014d, p. 23). Further, there is currently no national database of female-headed households, which is a major gap when civil society and state sponsored programmes targeting female-headed households are being designed. The lack of national data on female-headed households hampers development and other efforts, both by the state and by civil society. Widows and their families are more susceptible to violence due to the lack of a male in the household (Herath *et al.* 2012, p. 85). Many widows undergo sexual harassment at their workplace and on public transport (Sivachandran 2013a, p. 42). Female-headed households have also suffered abuse by the armed forces (ibid., p. 63). In 2013, the CEDAW Committee reiterated that specific groups, including widows, are at risk of violence, especially sexual violence (CEDAW 2013, para. 36).

A Memorandum drafted by civil society focuses on the security and safety of widows and calls upon the government to demilitarise the North and East.[10] The presence of the military threatens widows' physical security and exposes them to possible sexual violence. The Ministry of Child Development and Women's Affairs (MCDWA) has formulated a Widows' Policy, however, this remains in draft form and civil society has not had access to this document. The Ministry should have broad-based consultations with widows from North, East and South to ensure that the policy takes into account the needs and primary concerns of widows from both war affected areas and the concerns of the military widows from the South. The Widows' Policy may potentially serve as a policy guide for state-led initiatives to alleviate the status of widows in Sri Lanka. In drafting the Widows' Policy, the state should consider the LLRC recommendations and the NHRAP, which also provide a framework to operationalise the policy. According to the LLRC Report, the state undertakes to address the immediate needs of women, especially widows who most often have become heads of their households, by provision of livelihood and other income generating means to reduce immense economic hardships (Lessons Learnt and Reconciliation Commission Report 2011, para. 9.87, p. 366). The Action Plan focuses on livelihood and income generation but it does not clearly articulate what the immediate needs of women are in relation to stigma, trauma, violence and access to other socio-economic rights that are the immediate concerns of women in any conflict-affected society. Thus, it would also be useful for the policy to be framed more broadly to include the concerns of female-headed households, including widows, to ensure that these groups of women are also included in development initiatives.

The NHRAP notes the lack of policy on war widows that specifically addresses their economic rights and land and housing rights, as well as their vulnerability to exploitation. The NHRAP states the need for the 'formulation of a policy on war widows in all parts the country' including a mapping and needs assessment (NHRAP 2011–16, p. 69). Despite this acknowledgment, the NHRAP does not recognise that widows from the North and East have specific needs that must be addressed. While a policy on widows is to be welcomed, the needs of those who have been affected by the conflict must be addressed separately. The LLRCAP emphasises that female-headed households need to be assisted with services to deal with the trauma of missing family members, the provision of legal aid and, where possible, the provision of financial assistance where they have assumed the role of breadwinners. Read together, both plans will provide a framework to address the socio-economic needs of female-headed households and their vulnerability to exploitation and violence. While efforts are underway by the government, more needs to be done to address the situation of female-headed households and widows in a nuanced manner. SCR 1889 emphasises that strategies need to be adopted to increase women's role in conflict resolution decision-making and that states must promote women's participation in political and economic decision-making. Widows and female-headed households affected by the conflict must be given a voice in the peace-building process so that their concerns can be met.

Women's access to land

Land was a major factor in driving the thirty years of war in Sri Lanka. With multiple internal displacements due to the war and other factors, many women have been unable to access their rights to land. Documentation and deeds related to their lands have been misplaced or lost due to frequent movements. Acquiring new documentation is a difficult process and disputes related to land boundaries have also arisen (Sivachandran 2013b, p. 34). In the case of female-headed households, direct access to economic resources is needed for physical well-being (Agarwal 1994, p. 30). The ownership of land provides security for women as a source of income and livelihood.

The LLRC Recommendations on land do not specifically target women but generally identify the issues that need to be addressed, such as lost or destroyed land deeds, forged documents related to land and the transfer of land through fraudulent deeds. For example, state land allocated on permit has been transferred fraudulently as private land guaranteeing permanent ownership and land that has to undergo demining. The LLRC also highlights lands that have been taken over by the state to create High Security Zones (HSZ), some of which are ancestral lands. The LLRC also acknowledges that there is a need to grant legal ownership of land to internally displaced persons (IDPs) who have been resettled and that there is a notable absence of an official policy on return and resettlement of the internally displaced. Another serious consequence of the war has been illegal or secondary occupation as a result of landowners having to move away due to the war. Those IDPs who return to their own lands need to claim ownership where there could be secondary occupiers.

Women who have been displaced face severe hardships in getting back their lands. The armed forces have taken over arable land and engaged in cultivation (Sivachandran 2013b, p. 20). Some families were resettled in other areas and not allowed to go back to their own lands.[11] Land is also being acquired under the *Land Acquisition Act 1950*. Many families live on lands they do not possess legal documentation for. Approximately ninety per cent of the North is state land, the rest consists of private land. During the war, the LTTE mapped this land and allocated plots to individual families. However, these families do not have legal ownership and this has led to many land disputes.

The increase in land-related issues is further exacerbated by women's lack of awareness of the applicable land laws and circulars issued by the state.[12] Female-headed households also face difficulties when claiming their rights to land. For example, widows find it difficult to obtain death certificates for their deceased spouses as proof of death in order to apply for state allocation of land. In some cases, female-headed households are unable to claim lands because the permits and grants given by the state are in the names of their husbands.

Further, border villages remain forgotten in most development initiatives.[13] During the war, many cultivated lands were left unattended due to security concerns. Most villagers have cultivated unauthorised lands belonging to the government in the hope that land permits will be given to them in the future. A 2013 survey conducted by Rajarata Praja Kendraya, a community organisation, revealed that the land taken over by the state to erect police checkpoints and army camps during the war in these border villages has been given back to the original owners. However, some of these villagers have been given alternate lands with no legal ownership. Land used for cultivation has been taken over by security personnel and lands used for pasture has been taken over by the military for their cattle.

Women lack awareness on issues of legal land ownership and eighty-five per cent do not possess deeds of ownership as most of them occupy these state lands illegally (Rajarata Praja Kendraya 2013, p. 3). For them, occupying and cultivating the land gives them rights over the land, but this does not necessarily imply control over the land (Agarwal 1994, p. 20). The LLRC Action Plan states that the state shall, 'Grant the legal ownership of land to those [IDPs] who have been resettled'.[14] Women bear the responsibility to provide for the household and the state should take steps to regularise ownership of these lands. 'Titling women . . . and providing them infrastructural support could help increase output, by increasing their access to credit, and to technology and information on productivity increasing agricultural practices and inputs' (Agarwal 1994 p. 34). Given that these communities have been displaced from their own lands and have occupied and cultivated these state-owned lands as their own, the state should consider granting them the legal ownership.

Discriminatory land laws disentitle women from owning land. *The Land Development Ordinance (LDO)*, under which the state allocates land, stipulates a male preference whereby, in case of intestacy, the males of the family are given preference over females.[15] Under the *State Lands Ordinance 1949* land is allocated in single ownership as a practice, although the law does not preclude the giving of land in co-ownership. Most often it is the male that applies for land as he is considered the head of the household. Single ownership is given by the state to discourage fragmentation of land and for administrative convenience. These administrative practices preclude women from owning land and accessing other economic resources (COHRE 2011). The use of head of the household terminology also discriminates against women and disentitles them from owning land (COHRE 2008, p. 30).

Co-ownership of state-allocated land should be an option that is considered by the state for women displaced by the war. The NHRAP recognises that the head of the household concept discriminates against women and that, where possible, land should be given in co-ownership. The NHRAP also emphasises non-discriminatory land allocation in the return and resettlement of IDPs. The LLRCAP identifies the need for a systematic land programme that will take into account the different concerns of those affected by the conflict. It also acknowledges the lack of co-ordination among those involved in land administration and the shortage of land officials at all levels of government.

The CEDAW process provides an avenue through which the issues of women affected by conflict may be highlighted. CEDAW can be used as a framework to address issues such as sexual violence and other forms of violence against women, the discrimination faced by women when they attempt to access their rights to land and the discrimination faced by widows and female-headed households. Addressing the implementation of the LLRCAP and the NHRAP through the CEDAW process would ensure accountability on the part of the state.

Sri Lanka does not have a NAP on SCR 1325 and, to address this gap, it is important that the state implement existing national action plans and policies and consider international standards that will facilitate their implementation. In the absence of any accountability mechanism within Security Council resolutions on women, peace and security, it is vital that the state uses its domestic mechanisms to implement the resolutions from the ground upwards. National policies, SCR 1325 and other SCRs on sexual violence need to be read together by the state to better implement the resolutions and to meet minimum international standards. Similarly, the CEDAW process adds another dimension in that it has a regular reporting process that can be utilised by the state to hold itself accountable for the obligations that arise upon ratification of the Convention. The war also impacted on the socio-cultural customs and traditions of those living in the war affected areas.

Underage marriage

The issue of underage marriage is becoming more prevalent in Sri Lanka. According to the *Marriage Registration (Amendment) Act No.18, 1995*, if either party to a marriage is under the age of eighteen, it amounts to an illegal marriage. Traditionally, Sri Lanka does not have a high incidence of underage marriage (Centre for Reproductive Rights 2013). However, during the war and post-war periods the number of underage marriages has risen. During the war, underage girls were given away in marriage to avoid them being recruited by the LTTE, which did not recruit married women ('Rights of Women', Sri Lanka's National Action Plan for the Protection and Promotion of Human Rights 2011–2016, p. 69). Some even misrepresented their age in the marriage certificate in order to marry.

There are many causes for this phenomenon. Marriage by co-habitation is a common practice in the North and East of Sri Lanka. There is a lack of awareness within communities of the need to register the marriage and customary marriages are common where parties co-habit and are accepted by the community as husband and wife. Where there is no marriage certificate as proof of marriage, courts accept these forms of marriages after an inquiry and a certificate given by the *Grama Sevaka* (the local level government official) and the attestation of a religious leader.

Traditional family structures were destroyed due to the war and many communities experienced multiple displacement and school dropout rates were high. There is an increased incidence of early marriage among resettled communities in the North and East following the end of the war (Kumar 2013). Women who had to bear the burden of running their households as single parents gave their daughters away in marriage due to poverty and their inability to provide for them. This was seen as a way out for those women who suddenly had to be the sole providers for their households. A consequence of war is that early marriage appears to be followed as an acceptable custom, even in the aftermath of the war. After the war, an incentive for early marriage propagated inadvertently by the state is that priority is given to families over single women in the allocation of housing, state land and any other assistance. Tamil newspapers also report a high incidence of teenage pregnancies in the North. In 2013, out of a total of 10,435 pregnancies in the Northern Province, 318 were teenage mothers.[16]

During the war, the fear of sexual violence compelled parents of young daughters to permit marriage at an early age. A survey undertaken in the East found that 53.5 per cent of the women had married by the age of eighteen or had been co-habiting from a young age. Almost one in every ten of these young girls had begun to co-habit with their partners when they were below fifteen years of age. The post-war context is particularly disturbing. Almost one in five women who had married or co-habited before eighteen years of age, had done so following the end of the war in 2009. These figures indicate that underage marriages continue to take place even in a post-war context in the East (Women & Media Collective 2014b; Herath *et al.* 2012, p. 44).

An Oxfam survey found that forty per cent of all respondents had married before the age of eighteen. In Batticaloa, forty-four per cent of respondent women had married before the age of eighteen (Herath *et al.* 2012, p. 40). The link between early marriage and violence is also made in an Oxfam survey that stresses marriage at a young age may result in domestic violence (ibid., p. 85). Similar incidences of underage marriage have been reported from the North.[17] Reports from the border villages also indicate that rates of underage marriage are high and that there has been an increase in teenage mothers (Rajarata Praja Kendraya 2013). A reason for early marriage is the disruption of educational activities due to frequent displacement during the war (ibid.). This phenomenon indicates the structural and physical violence perpetuated against women in post-conflict settings.

Conclusion: linking resolutions and policies to reality

The outcome of having national policies and international standards in place that address the needs of women in the post-conflict period is to ensure that women's voices and their concerns are taken into consideration in post-war contexts. Lack of a political will to give adequate recognition to this issue means that the state fails in its duty to protect those women whose rights have been violated.

A society in transition creates a space for inequality and discrimination to be tackled. The post-conflict period also presents an opportune moment to introduce international norms and standards that can be creatively used to enhance the interpretation of national policies and standards already in place. Where states are reluctant to adhere to international standards and norms, there is nevertheless an obligation to adhere to the national policies and frameworks that have been put in place by the state. The LLRC recommendations and the NHRAP provide the state with the necessary framework to address the many issues that have surfaced as a result of the war. However, the Sri Lankan State must ensure that the reality is linked to these policies so that strategic and targeted interventions can be designed. At international level SCR 1325, and subsequent resolutions on women, peace and security, and CEDAW provide an overall framework to work within.

Drawing on the framework of international instruments and national policies will enable the state to examine the reality on the ground for women affected by the conflict and to take meaningful steps to address their concerns. It also affords a means of providing government support services and for designing interventions that will best address their problems. However, it is important that the state understands the reality for women, which is the first step in finding any meaningful solutions for the challenges that these women face.

Notes

1 United Nations Security Council (2000) Resolution 1325, 31 October 2000, UN Doc. S/RES/1325.
2 United Nations Security Council (2008) Resolution 1820, 19 June 2008, UN Doc. S/RES/1820.
3 United Nations Security Council (2009) Resolution 1888, 30 September 2009, UN Doc. S/RES/1888.
4 United Nations Security Council (2010) Resolution 1960, 16 December 2010, UN Doc. S/RES/1960.
5 United Nations Security Council (2009) Resolution 1889, 5 October 2009, UN Doc. S/RES/1889.
6 Section 9.92 of the Lessons Learnt Reconciliation Commission National Action Plan.
7 Introduction to National Action Plan for the Protection and Promotion of Human Rights (2011–16) (NHRAP), p. 5.
8 In response to the CEDAW Concluding Observations in 2013 the Sri Lankan government indicated that two cases had been successfully prosecuted (CEDAW 2013).
9 Lessons Learnt and Reconciliation Commission Action Plan Section 9.90.
10 *Memorandum: Concerns and Demands of Women Heads of Households,* on file with the author.
11 In Kepapulavu, 110 families were resettled on their own lands. A case has been filed in the courts in this regard and the decision is pending.
12 For example, women living in the North are ignorant about the Tesawalamai law that applies to Tamils living in the Northern Province.
13 Border villages are those bordering the North and East affected by the conflict and consist mainly of Sinhala communities.
14 Section 9.104 of the Lessons Learnt and Reconciliation Commission National Action Plan.
15 For a discussion on the LDO and the State Lands Ordinance, see the shadow report on land submitted to CEDAW by the Centre on Housing Rights and Evictions (COHRE 2011) to the CEDAW Committee 48th session, January 2011, http://www2.ohchr.org/english/bodies/cedaw/docs/ngos/COHRE_CEDAW_48th.pdf
16 *Tamil Thanthi*, 1st March, 2014. In Jaffna, a total of 46 teenage pregnancies have been recorded in 2013.

17 According to the Legal Aid Commission (LAC), Mannar, cases of customary unregistered marriages are brought to their notice after the birth of a child when the parents are unable to register the birth due to the lack of a marriage certificate.

Bibliography

Agarwal, B. (1994) *A Field of One's Own: Gender and Land Rights in South Asia*, Cambridge University Press, Cambridge, UK.

Centre on Housing Rights and Evictions (COHRE) (2008) *A Socio Legal Study on the Head of the Household in Sri Lanka, Women and Housing Rights Programme*, Colombo, Sri Lanka.

Centre on Housing Rights and Evictions (COHRE) (2011) Shadow Report to the CEDAW Committee 48th session, January, [online] http://www2.ohchr.org/english/bodies/cedaw/docs/ngos/COHRE_CEDAW_48th.pdf

Centre for Reproductive Rights (2013) *Child Marriage in South Asia: International and Constitutional Legal Standards and Jurisprudence for Promoting Accountability and Change*, Centre for Reproductive Rights, New York.

CEDAW (2011) Committee Concluding Observations, CEDAW/C/LKA/CO/7, 8 April 2011.

CEDAW (2013) Committee General Comment No. 30, 18 October 2013, CEDAW/C/GC/30.

CEDAW Committee (2013), Concluding observations on the combined fifth to seventh periodic reports of Sri Lanka, Addendum, Information provided by Sri Lanka in follow-up to the concluding observations, CEDAW/C/LKA/CO/7/Add.1, 24 September 2013.

European Center for Constitutional and Human Rights (2011) *Alternative Report on the Implementation of the UN CEDAW: Sri Lanka, 'Women and Armed Conflict'*, Berlin/Geneva [online] http://www2.ohchr.org/english/bodies/cedaw/docs/ECCHR_Sri_Lanka_for_the_session_CEDAW48.pdf

Herath, S., Sharma, K., Dissanayake, M., Senanayake, S., Nonis, R. (2012) *Survey Report on Gender Based Violence in the Oxfam Working Villages in the East of Sri Lanka*, study conducted by TNS Lanka (Pvt) Ltd, Oxfam GB, Sri Lanka.

International Crisis Group (2011) 'Sri Lanka: Women's insecurity in the North and East', 20 December 2011, http://www.crisisgroup.org/en/regions/asia/south-asia/sri-lanka/217-sri-lanka-womens-insecurity-in-the-north-and-east.aspx

Kumar, Prerna (2013) *Review of National Legislations and Policies on Child Marriage in South Asia*, Asian Forum of Parliamentarians on Population and Development and Australian Aid [online] http://www.afppddatabase.org/uploads/323-Review-of-National-Legislations-and-Policies-on-Child-Marriage-in-South-Asia.pdf

Lessons Learnt and Reconciliation Commission Report, November 2011, Sri Lanka [online] http://www.priu.gov.lk/news_update/Current_Affairs/ca201112/FINAL%20LLRC%20REPORT.pdf

Minority Rights Group International (2013) 'Living with insecurity: Marginalization and sexual violence against women in north and east Sri Lanka', 16 October 2013 [online] http://www.refworld.org/docid/528489bf4.html

National Action Plan for the Protection and Promotion of Human Rights (NHRAP) (2011–16), *Rights of Women*, Colombo, Sri Lanka.

Porter, E. (2007) *Peace building: Women in International Perspective*, Routledge, Abingdon, UK.

Rajarata Praja Kendraya (2013) *An Access to Way: An Ownership for the Unauthorized Land*, Sri Lanka.

Sivachandran, S. (2013a) *Women Headed Families in the Northern Province*, Centre for Women and Development, Sri Lanka.

Sivachandran, S. (2013b) *Land Rights and Women in the Northern Province of Sri Lanka: Post War Situation*, Centre for Women and Development, Sri Lanka.

Sooka, Y. (2014) *An Unfinished War: Torture and Sexual Violence in Sri Lanka 2009–2014* The Bar Human Rights Committee of England and Wales (BHRC) and the International Truth & Justice Project, Sri Lanka [online] https://barhumanrights.org.uk/sites/default/files/documents/news/an_unfinihsed_war._torture_and_sexual_violence_in_sri_lanka_2009-2014_0.pdf

Steinberg, D. (2011) 'An Agenda for Action', *Women and War, power and protection in the 21st Century*', Keuhnast, K., de Jonge Oudraat, C. and Hernes, H. (Eds.) US Institute for Peace, Washington DC, US.

United Nations Office of the High Commissioner for Human Rights (2014) Correspondence, AA/follow-up/SriLanka/57 [online] http://tbinternet.ohchr.org/Treaties/CEDAW/Shared%20Documents/LKA/INT_CEDAW_FUL_LKA_16994_E.pdf

UN Women, Peace and Security Section (2014) *Women, Peace and Security Statistics: Where We Stand and How to Move Forward*, Fifth Global Forum on Gender Statistics, November.

Women's Action Network (2014) 'Continuing Detention of Tamil Women and a Girl Child under the Prevention of Terrorism Act', 13 April 2014 [online] http://groundviews.org/2014/04/13/continuing-detention-of-tamil-women-and-a-girl-child-under-the-prevention-of-terrorism-act/http://womenclaimingrights.womenandmedia.org/?p=490

Women & Media Collective (2014a) 'Discrimination and Access to Justice: Muslim women seeking remedies for Domestic Violence in Selected Regions of the Amparai and Batticaloa Districts' in *Women Claiming Rights: Using Normative Frameworks of SCR 1325 & CEDAW, Study on Women Affected by Conflict in Post War Sri Lanka: Selected cases of Marginalization and Poverty, Female Headed Households, Female ex-combatants, Land Rights and Domestic Violence [online]* http://womenclaimingrights.womenandmedia.org/?p=490.

Women & Media Collective (2014b) *Responses to Concluding Observations of the CEDAW Committee dealing with Conflict, Shadow Report*, Sri Lanka.

Women & Media Collective (2014c) 'Female Ex-combatants in post war Sri Lanka: Experiences from selected regions in Jaffna, Kilinochchi, Mullaitivu, Mannar, Vavuniya, Batticaloa, Ampara and Trincomalee districts', *Women Claiming Rights: Using Normative Frameworks of SCR 1325 & CEDAW, Study on Women Affected by Conflict in Post War Sri Lanka: Selected cases of Marginalization and Poverty, Female Headed Households, Female ex-combatants, Land Rights and Domestic Violence*, Sri Lanka.

Women & Media Collective (2014d) 'Situation of Female Headed Households Post War in Selected Regions of Batticaloa, Jaffna and Vavunitya Districts', *Women Claiming Rights: Using Normative Frameworks of SCR 1325 & CEDAW, Study on Women Affected by conflict in Post War Sri Lanka, Selected Cases of Marginalization and Poverty; Female Headed Households; Female ex-combatants; Land rights and Domestic Violence*, Sri Lanka.

4 Violence, women and conflict in Nepal

Amrita Gurung and Lily Thapa

Introduction

After signing the Comprehensive Peace Accord in 2006, Nepal became a federal republic state, marking the end of a decade-long armed conflict. The institutional shift from a centuries-old monarchy to a federal republic signalled a new beginning for Nepal to make up losses on political, social and economic fronts by addressing the issues of a multi-cultural, multi-ethnic and multi-lingual state and its people. One notable change after the conflict was the growth in the representation of women. In 2006, Nepal's Parliament passed a special resolution to ensure thirty-three per cent of women's participation in all state structures and, as a result, close to that percentage of women from different castes and ethnic, geographic and religious groups are represented in the Constituent Assembly of Nepal. Further, the Nepalese government implemented some policies in the administrative and security sector which resulted in quotas of three per cent of women in the army and seven per cent of women in the police (Forum for Women Law and Development (FWLD), 2011, p. 3).

In the light of these developments, this chapter first considers the situation of women and girls in Nepal, including levels of gender-based violence and the impact of armed conflict and the transitional period on women. Second, the role of Nepal's National Action Plan (NAP) on Security Council Resolutions (SCRs) 1325[1] and 1820[2] is evaluated as to whether it allows for the meaningful reintegration and rehabilitation of conflict-affected victims in Nepal. However, while women's inclusion is important, the homogenisation of women undermines a more nuanced response to the situation of women and girls by the state. Thus this chapter argues that the 'Nepali women' narrative needs to be deconstructed to understand the specific needs of victims in Nepal. As part of this analysis, the chapter presents a case study of the widows' movement in Nepal, illustrating the importance of both international and national strategies in responding effectively to the situation of widows. Third, in exploring the difficulties faced by women victims in securing economic compensation, the chapter argues that economic compensation alone does not bring peace and justice and that the importance of women's inclusion in the peace-building process needs to be emphasised. Equally, the chapter stresses the need to promote the NAP on SCRs 1325 and 1820 to support its effective implementation.

Legal and social status of women in Nepal

Nepal has passed many laws to improve the status of women including the *Gender Equality Act 2006*, the *Human Trafficking and Transportation Control Act 2007* and the *Domestic Violence Control Act 2008. It has also* amended the *National Code* (*Muluki Ain*) and abolished the criminalisation of witchcraft. The recently adopted *Constitution of Nepal 2072* (20 September 2015) also recognises various rights of women, including the right to reproductive health and equal rights to property. However, despite the fact that close to thirty-three per cent of the Constituent Assembly are women, issues concerning gender discrimination have not been raised enough and women in Nepal continue to face physical violence and structural inequality on a daily basis. In addition, marginalised groups, including *Dalit*, *Madhesi* and indigenous women, continue to be excluded in decision-making processes. This exclusion is further aggravated by the political instability of the state and the culture of abuse of power by political leaders (Lawoti 2010, p. 1).

According to a study by the Women's Rehabilitation Centre (WOREC 2008), in general, women in Nepal mostly suffer from physical torture and domestic violence, and violence is inherently rooted in 'patriarchal norms, values and overwhelming discriminatory laws and policy of state' (ibid.). Data collected by the Informal Sector Service Center (INSEC) shows that there were 2,348 cases of violence against women across the country in 2013 that were related to 'domestic violence, violence faced in the name of witchcraft, polygamy, lack of pre and post-partum service, rape, rape attempt, sexual abuse, abortion and women trafficking' (INSEC 2013, p. 12). Between April and May 2014, WOREC Nepal documented a total of 411 cases of violence against women including 252 cases of domestic violence, fourteen murders of women, forty-nine cases of rape, twenty cases of attempted rape, twelve cases of sexual abuse and thirty-five cases of social violence (WOREC 2014). The report also highlights 'superstition, [a] culture of male dominance, women's sensitiveness and innocent behaviors', which often leads to the perpetration of domestic violence by husbands and family members. Given the fact that Nepal is a very conservative society, women tend to be silent victims of violence, which makes violence difficult to document and impacts upon women's access to justice. In addition to physical and sexual violence women are also the victims of structural violence in Nepal. A study conducted among Tharu and Brahmin ethnicities in rural Nepal reports 'lack of education', 'women's inability to negotiate with their husbands', 'traditional norms and cultural values' and 'lack of cash income' as the main causes of sexual violence (Lamichhane *et al.* 2011, p. 4).

The prevalence of domestic violence in Nepal is also linked to alcoholism, the dowry system, preference for sons and polygamous relationships (Voluntary Services Overseas (VSO Nepal) 2011, p. 24). While women and girls from all backgrounds are at risk of sexual violence and rape, *Saathi*, an organisation working on women's issues, highlights that 'women and girls from poor excluded marginalised groups are more at risk of rape, usually perpetrated by a distant relative or acquaintance whereas those from well-off Brahmin, Chhetri and Newari backgrounds are more vulnerable to incest' (Deuba and Rana 2001, p. 9). It can thus be said that violence against women is rooted in historical and structural inequality in power relations between women and men (ICFG 2013, pp. 6–7). Furthermore, it can be argued that in a Nepali context 'caste and gender discrimination, feudalistic suppression, lack of political representation/decision making, education system, economic inequality and exploitation' also lead to the perpetuation of gender-based violence (Shakya 2009, p. 3). Even though the then *Interim Constitution of Nepal* guaranteed that 'no physical, mental or other form of violence shall be inflicted on any women, and such an act shall be punishable by law', women in Nepal are victims of various cultural practices linked to their cultural backgrounds (ibid., p. 19). For example, cultural practices such as *badi*, *chaupadi*, and *jhuma* still exist in Nepal[3] and traditional practices, including the dowry system, are still very commonly practised in Nepal.

At present, Nepal is emerging from a period of transition, which has involved consideration of the problems faced by victims of the war. As part of the transitional period reconciliation between stakeholders in the peace-building process has been an important goal. Given that 'in traditional social structure as Nepal's, [where] women form the core to family as well as social networks' (ASPECT 2010, p. 6), the inclusion of women in the peace-building process has been advocated because women are perceived to be better at prioritising the issues of women and children; able to explain their own specific needs, experiences and suffering; and articulate these concerns to ensure that women's needs are being fulfilled as part of a meaningful reintegration and rehabilitation process. Accordingly, women should be provided with equal opportunities in decision-making at both polity and civil society levels. Further, a 2011 study conducted by VSO Nepal suggested that 'strategies for gender equity and improved gender relations need to incorporate the perspectives of both men and women' (VSO Nepal 2011, p. 5). Women and girl children were the most vulnerable population groups during the conflict as a result of actions by both the armed rebels (*Maoists*) and security forces. International legal instruments, including SCRs 1325 and 1820, may go some way to help address the status of women and girls in Nepal's transition from conflict to peace. SCRs 1325 and 1820 focus on the reintegration and rehabilitation of women and girls in society by including women at all levels of the peace-building process while, at the same time, addressing the sexual and physical abuse experienced by women in armed conflict to strengthen justice.

National Action Plan on Security Council Resolutions 1325 and 1820

Nepal launched its National Action Plan on 6 February 2011 to implement SCRs 1325 and 1820 and is the first state in South Asia to adopt a national level strategy to implement SCR 1325. The adoption of the NAP reflects the government's commitment to end gender-based violence perpetuated during and after the decade-long conflict in the country. SCR 1325 focuses on the importance of women's participation at all levels of the peace-building process and in conflict resolution, as well as addressing the protection of women from sexual violence. SCR 1820 focuses specifically on sexual violence in conflict and its aftermath. The five pillars of Nepal's NAP include: promotion; participation; prevention; relief and recovery; resource management, monitoring and evaluation. Each pillar of the NAP sets out activities to be carried out within five years of the NAP's adoption to ensure the full participation of women and girls at all levels of decision-making and in the peace-building process. Additionally, the NAP also focuses its attention on giving conflict victims skills-based training, psycho-social counselling, childcare facilities and economic compensation. However, translating these commitments into reality continues to be problematic.

Although, civil society has been active in promoting the five pillars of the NAP among conflict victims, their efforts are not enough. Apart from creating awareness about the NAP and SCRs 1325 and 1820, there has not been substantive progress in the NAP's implementation. The Ministry of Peace and Reconstruction, which has been assigned the main role of implementing the NAP, previously suggested that the delay in the release of the Nepal Peace Trust Fund had implications for the successful implementation of the NAP. The delay in the implementation of the NAP appears to sideline recognition of a number of issues relating to women and girls who suffered during the conflict.

According to the Ministry of Peace and Reconstruction, 17,886 persons were killed; 1,530 disappeared, with 79,571 internally displaced as a result of the conflict (Nepal Institute for Policy Studies 2013, p. 2). However, data on killings, abductions and other forms of violence varies between the government and civil society organisations (CSOs), with significant inconsistencies demonstrating the difficulties of collating data during periods of conflict and its aftermath. According to the *Nepal Human Development Report* among those who were killed, about 8 per cent were women and more than 3 per cent were children (UNDP 2009, p. 22). Gender-disaggregated data is yet to be identified; however, it is tentatively suggested that among all the conflict victims forty to sixty per cent of affected persons were women. Different CSOs, human-rights organisations, international non-governmental organisations (INGOs) and the media have revealed different data related to conflict-affected women and conflict-affected people. Due to the disparity in data, authentication of numbers of conflict-affected women for the purposes of justice is one of the major problems in the peace process.

Since women in rural areas are very much dependent on their husbands, having to live without male members in the house is usually very difficult for women. As a result they have an extra burden of work and have taken on agricultural and other tasks, including participation in the public sphere, which are ordinarily culturally forbidden (Upreti 2006, p. 14). With no support system and no source of income women suffer multiple forms of gender-based violence and psychological issues as a result of the war. They face difficulties in securing access to government compensation, their basic rights and resources such as land and public services. Additionally, women face stigma and social pressures, particularly as single women (widows) and as the sole breadwinner for their children and remaining household family members, leaving them vulnerable to physical, sexual and psychological violence.

Cases of rape, torture, violence and abuse during the conflict were exceptionally high (FWLD 2011, p. 16). The *National Code* (chapter 14, section 1, *Muluki Ain, 2020 [1963]*) fails to acknowledge and incorporate a broader definition of rape, which moves beyond traditional understandings of vaginal penetration, to include other forms of penetration. Rape crimes are time limited and incidents of rape must be reported within thirty-five days, which significantly hinders rape victims who are only able to report incidents of sexual violence after thirty-five days.

Girls who were used as rebels by the Maoists during the decade-long conflict also face challenges. Although these former child soldiers have been reintegrated back into society they are not fully accepted by their families and the communities they are living in and thus they continue to be stigmatised.

Some of the women victims who lost their husbands during the conflict or whose family members were subjected to enforced disappearances have received economic compensation. This compensation, as defined by the official directive, is up to one million rupees (ten *lakhs*) depending upon the degree of the loss. However, the 'compensation has not yet been received by all wounded or all the families of those killed' (UNDP 2009, p. 51), demonstrating the government's negligence towards the victims, both men and women. In considering how laws and policies have compounded women's experiences of gender-based violence in conflict and its aftermath, it is important to explore in detail how the homogenisation of Nepali women and their experiences in Nepal has led to a lack of engagement with the intersection between gender and other aspects of identity and the implications for women's legal and social status.

Homogenisation of Nepali women and implications for women's legal and social status

This section explores the process of homogenisation of women's identity in Nepal, including why women continue to face social stigma and discrimination, and in doing so it attempts to explain why both men and women continue to face challenges in asserting the multiplicity of individual identities during the transition from conflict to peace. Even though within the international community Nepal is a relatively small nation-state, significantly it has a highly diverse population marked by ethnic differences and cultural practices. According to the 2011 census, indigenous peoples, also known as *adivasi janjati* people, are estimated to comprise 36.31 per cent of the total population of Nepal. With indigenous peoples representing more than one third of the population, Nepal ratified the Convention of Indigenous and Tribal Peoples of the International Labour Organization (ILO), no. 169, to give a number of rights to indigenous people. However, the history of exclusion and marginalisation, and the socio-economic differences among various ethnic groups are palpably stark in Nepal (Center for Constitutional Dialogue 2009, p. 1).

Ethnic minority groups, including *Dalits* (sometimes referred to as untouchables), have traditionally faced serious challenges in their day-to-day life due to a multiplicity of identities and these are often the same groups or communities of people that are economically deprived of opportunities in modern Nepal. According to the *National Foundation for the Development of Indigenous Nationalities Act 2002* the definition of indigenous people is 'those ethnic groups or communities who have their own mother tongue and traditional customs, different cultural identity, different social structure and written or oral history'. However, Lawoti notes that 'underdevelopment, unemployment and marginalization, especially in the rural regions, [has] alienated a large number of people' (Lawoti 2007, p. 2). Ethnic minority and indigenous groups have been historically marginalised from the state infrastructure with little or no power thus excluding them ethnically, socially, politically and economically.

In the case of women, it is not just language that excludes ethnic minority and indigenous women from the mainstream but other factors also contribute to their exclusion, for example, levels of education, the kind of social background they come from and, more specifically, which place they come from and their ethnicity. While the same can be argued for men, given the high level of vulnerability to gender-based violence associated with women, it is crucial to examine how these groups of women continue to be marginalised from the state even after the participation of some as actors during the decade-long conflict. Ariño's analysis of the Maoist insurgency notes that 'Nepali women have been deeply affected by this armed conflict, and, as with many other conflicts, its origin and course had a notable gender dimension', which can be attributed to the large number of women combatants in the Maoist insurgency as well as high levels of gender-based violence (Ariño 2008, p. 5). However, women were largely excluded during the signing of the peace agreement in 2006.

It should be noted that apart from the shared experiences of suffering between women there are other issues that directly and indirectly affect women's status, including their different circumstances, such as whether they reside in rural or urban areas, whether they are rich or poor, educated or uneducated among other differences. Multicultural feminist theories address the important issue that 'all women are not created or constructed equal' (Tong 1989, p. 200). As the theory outlines it should not just be about 'sexism, but racism, ethnocentrism, classism, heterosexism, ableism, or ageism', which may also determine the living conditions of some women (ibid., p. 202). Further, post-colonial, post-structural and multi-cultural theories deconstruct power and hegemony, emphasising that needs are specific according to the individual's backgrounds.

In Nepal there is a consistent homogenisation of women, including of their specific needs, which may not be adequately addressed in terms of recognising their experiences and suffering during and after the war. Although there is a common demand on the part of women who claim that the government should provide them with adequate monetary compensation, this should not lead to the view that all women's suffering will come to an end with economic compensation. Many women are poor and lack a support system, which means they often do not have a strong backgrounds from which to bargain in the public domain. In efforts to implement SCRs 1325 and 1820, the subjugation of women and girl children has taken place and women have largely been designated as victims. Recognition of women as victims has overshadowed other aspects of women's identities, including where they come from, their upbringing and their educational and historical background. Generalising women as victims is problematic because the construction of 'Nepali women' is an essentialist portrayal as opposed to one which recognises the pluralist identities of women in Nepal, which all contributes to a process 'excluding and silencing radical diversity in the name of expediency and elite power brokering' (Tamang 2009, p. 61).

The general emphasis placed on women as conflict-victims, is one way of homogenising female identities that masks the multiple layers of women's identities. There is a high level of homogenisation, hegemony and essentialism expressed and exercised, especially at the policy level, which rules out the prospect of recognising these multiple identities and thus the multiple needs of the women who suffered during the war. This essentialised portrayal of women undermines the diversity of women in terms of ethnicities, experiences and their sufferings. For the proportionate representation of women at all levels of polity, society and economy, women's experiences should not be generalised, universalised and essentialised, as this potentially creates a power division between the victims, which risks the danger of imposing certain characteristics and features of some female victims on all women.

Instead, the Nepal Government, as well as human-rights organisations and CSOs working on the issues of women, should deconstruct and look into the power play and subjugation of women, and consider how society and the government construct the conflict and the victims in the way that they do, because 'objectivity is about limited location and situated knowledge' as opposed to 'partial, locatable and critical' understandings (Haraway 1988, pp. 583–4). Haraway further suggests that 'subjugated' standpoints are preferred because they seem to promise more adequate, sustained, objective, transforming accounts of the world' (ibid.). Therefore, in the government's legal and policy responses, it is important that Nepali women are not studied from subjugated standpoints because, in effect, this serves to homogenise Nepali women's experiences.

The Government's efforts to create awareness of the impact of the conflict on women and girls are not adequate. Specifically, there is a need for a clear mechanism to evaluate both how the NAP is being implemented and how the NAP is understood by both the victims and those stakeholders who implement it. There is a constant need to reflect upon the processes that take place between those who carry out programmes and those who are the beneficiaries in order to understand the power dimensions that underpin the subjugation of women. In the absence of clear mechanisms to establish accountability, 'how do the women elected know what the women who elected them want? By what right do they claim responsibility to represent women's concerns?' (Phillips 1998, p. 235). A lack of understanding about the NAP has created a gulf between victims and implementing actors in the same way that government programmes and facilities have failed to meet the specific needs of victims.

In addition to Nepal's diverse population, there are other categories of women, particularly widows, who face stigma and discrimination on the basis of their status, and these women have been systematically marginalised from decision-making processes and traditional power structures. Widows (or single women) have also been seriously affected by conflict, but have been rendered invisible within the essentialist construction of 'Nepali women'.

Case study: situational analysis of the status of widows in Nepal

The traditional word for widow, *vidhava,* is a symbolic identity for a woman whose husband is dead. The term is very old and can be traced beyond the Vedic language to Indo-European origin. There are many young widows in developing countries across South Asia, South East Asia, the Middle East and Africa due to war and conflict, HIV/AIDS, poverty and natural calamities. However, in conflict-affected countries many adult women are widows or wives of the disappeared, including young mothers of dependent children, who are forced to spend their lives in poverty and are thus vulnerable to abuse. In Nepal, the 2010 census states that six per cent of the female population is comprised of widows. Among them, seventy-eight per cent are entirely illiterate and, on average, these women have three to four children. The census also states that seventy-five per cent of widows were first married between the ages of ten to nineteen. According to a study by Women for Human Rights (WHR), sixty-seven per cent of Nepalese widows are under thirty-five years of age and the majority of them are working to survive in the informal sector, where they are subjected to physical, mental and sexual harassment (WHR 2010).

After their husband's death, widows are forced to follow inhumane cultural practices, such as discarding all their colourful red clothes, which are traditionally considered as auspicious. Further, widows are not allowed to be present during auspicious occasions because they are perceived as ill omens who will bring bad luck. Due to the loss of their husbands, widows are vulnerable to abuse and economic hardship, face social stigma in society and are susceptible to sexual exploitation. In addition to the loss of their husbands, many widows have lost their homes, their children, other family members, community members, social support mechanisms and financial and personal security. The husband's family usually has a claim over the property, which results in the eviction of widows from the family household. Even if a widow gains possession of the land, she may still be unable to access it due to land disputes brought on behalf of the husband's family. Widows often become the breadwinners for their families with children solely dependent on them for survival. Widows face an enormous financial burden upon entering widowhood. According to Nepal's 2011 Demographic Health Survey, early marriage is relatively common; 55 per cent of women aged 25–49 were married before the age of eighteen and 74 per cent were married by the age of twenty (MOHP 2012, p. 68). As a result, young widows face many obstacles since the cultural practice of early marriage still exists in Nepalese society.

Despite all these challenges, widow's groups are playing a key role in building peace in their communities. Through WHR, single women (widows) groups have been working exclusively with and for widows in Nepal since 1994.[4] WHR currently has 1,550 widows' groups in seventy-three districts with a membership base of more than 1 million single women who are trained and mobilised as change makers for the peace process, mediators and pressure groups and who advocate for widow's rights in their respective communities. In the districts, single women's groups are playing an active role in the peace movement and their work is supported at local and national levels. The unique feature of these groups is that they combine women from families of Maoists, the security forces and other political groups, decreasing the negative and vengeful attitudes within communities and thus also challenging the homogenisation of Nepali women. WHR is working with widows from all backgrounds and from many situations, including conflict-widows and victims of the insurgency, from both sides of the previously conflicting parties. WHR works to incorporate a gender perspective into the peace-building process, including reconciliation, reintegration and re-settlement through involving all conflict-affected widows. This initiative prioritises the involvement of single women as peacemakers by drawing upon the framework of SCR 1325, which emphasises the involvement of women at every step of the peace-building process.

WHR makes a unique contribution to reconciliation at the grassroots level by promoting the joint involvement of all categories of widows, no matter whether they are families of security personnel or Maoists, whatever their political background, caste, class or ethnicity, recognising only that they have related needs and interests in the same communities. Single women groups are trying to fully integrate their activities with the economic and social development of their respective communities by drawing on the CEDAW optional protocol, as well as SCRs 1325 and SCR 1820, to strengthen the rights of single women. To ensure the increased representation of women at all decision-making levels in national, regional and international institutions and mechanisms for the prevention, management and resolution of conflict, single women's groups have undertaken the task of building capacity for single women at the local level, with the mission of providing leadership training and educating single women about political participation. A network has been built up from agencies at local level (including ward and village development committee levels) to district development committee level. This network extends further to national and regional levels, where the South Asian Network for Widows Empowerment in Development (SANWED) has been instrumental in raising awareness about the legal and social status of widows in South Asia.[5] The various ministries and the National Women's Commission of Nepal have also incorporated single women's issues into their strategies and agendas for women's empowerment.

As a result of the strong advocacy and lobbying from the single women's groups at district level, there have been some changes made to the discriminatory laws, mostly through the 11th amendment to the *National Code of Nepal* (*Muluki Ain*) resulting in widow's rights to property and citizenship. The single women's groups have actively promoted single women as agents of change in the mainstream development process of Nepal, leading the government to adopt a National Plan of Action for Widows and to set up an emergency fund. The single women's groups, along with the central office, have lobbied national and regional stakeholders to endorse the principles of the *Widow's Charter*, which calls for the protection and fulfilment of the special needs of widows. Lobbying efforts were made by single women's groups at the grassroots level and by WHR at the national level, to incorporate elements of the *Widows' Charter* into the new constitution of Nepal, and the recently adopted Constitution does refer to the issue of widows, thus ensuring that the rights and needs of single women are addressed as fundamental rights.

Poverty, stigma and the marginalisation of widows and their children are widespread in society, resulting in gender-based violence, but the experiences of widows are often overlooked in mainstream discourses on women's gender equality, which tend to homogenise women's experiences. Therefore, it is important that the international community, the United Nations and respective governments give more attention to combating all forms of discrimination against widows, including harmful traditional practices, by providing widows with full rights to live with dignity. The number of widows remains high and requires the urgent attention of the Nepali government to consider the provision of basic services under the national programme on women's empowerment, particularly the adoption of a rights-based response to ensure that widows who are in their productive years continue to contribute effectively to national development, which will enhance their skills and capacities. The appointment of a special rapporteur on widowhood at the UN would support international recognition of the intersection of conflict, gender and widowhood. Besides, all the international instruments and declarations should identify clear indicators to measure the status of widows, including within NAPs on SCRs 1325 and 1820.

Further, the government of Nepal has the responsibility to address the complex and challenging issues of widowhood since armed conflicts, violence, revolutions, natural disasters, harmful traditional practices (such as child marriage) and HIV/AIDS have significantly increased the number of widows. Reparations are important for widows, as well as other women, in addition to skills-based training, psycho-social counselling, childcare facilities and economic compensation.

Compensation for victims

As discussed, the decade-long conflict has affected women and girls in various ways. Many women, of different ethnicities, were strategically used during the conflict, which is reflected in the high number of women participants in Maoist groups. Additionally, women suffered from domestic and sexual violence perpetuated by the war, including rape, beatings, torture and harassment due to being Maoists and belonging to rebel groups. As a result, many women lost their lives or husbands, and a significant number of children were orphaned. There is little or no support system for conflict-affected women from multiple backgrounds.

The NAP on SCRs 1325 and 1820 recognises multiple categories of women affected by the conflict and includes the provision of relief and recovery to these groups. However implementation of the NAP has been weak given the delay in the release of the budget by the Nepal Peace Trust Fund, which is the central mechanism for technical and financial support for the peace process and the state has obligations to fulfil 'women's specific security and peace building needs, including obligations to implement Security Council resolutions 1325, 1820, 1888, 1889 and 1960' (United Nations, 2011, p. 1). The United Nations points out that in programmes where the Nepal Peace Trust Fund has made provision for the inclusion of women's needs or gender considerations 'there has not been regular tracking of funds provided to meet these specific goals' (ibid.). The United Nations also highlights that since the establishment of Nepal Peace Trust Fund only a few projects have been implemented that have addressed or budgeted for women's needs.

Apart from this, most of the programmes and organisations that are working on the implementation of Nepal's NAP are Kathmandu-centric. This imposes a serious problem among local stakeholders (village development and local peace development committees, conflict-affected groups, local government, women development officers) as it excludes them from understanding the details of SCRs 1325 and 1820 and of the NAP itself, which is designed to respond to the needs of conflict victims, men and women alike.

The majority of men and women have been deeply affected by the decade-long conflict. Many people have experienced psycho-social problems as a result of losing loved ones; some individuals are disabled as a result of injuries, some victims have been mutilated; for others social roles have shifted significantly and they are now the main source of support for their family members. Women who are widows with no support system have become the object of abuse both at home and in their villages. The level of stigma attached to single women is echoed by their sense of low self-esteem and confidence. With children to look after and houses to run they face great despair. Former women combatants have settled down and started a new life but they are also not exempt from stigma and social pressures built around them by society. Economically burdened and with no bargaining power they look for new opportunities which will allow them to reintegrate into the army, thus giving them some economic leverage. Aside from these tensions, there is very little participation of women in government bodies and among local peace stakeholders. In particular, this prevents women from bargaining as victims for agents of change. Their sufferings and experiences are different and therefore a nuanced understanding of women's specific needs should be adopted and taken seriously by all levels of polity.

As discussed, to date those persons who lost their loved ones in the conflict or whose loved ones were subjected to enforced disappearances have received 300,000 rupees (three *lakhs*) of compensation and, according to the revised directive of the government, they are expected to receive 200,000 rupees (two *lakhs*) more. However, the victims are of the opinion that they should receive the full economic compensation of one million rupees (ten *lakhs*), which would at least give them economic leverage to run start-up businesses and support their family and children.

The suffering of male victims of the conflict is mostly visible as many were shot and wounded, beaten and harassed, accused and persecuted. In contrast, the suffering of many female victims is less visible because it is more subtle and carried out in the private sphere. For women whose husbands were killed or disappeared there is no sign of their return. In rural Nepal, where the majority of the population depends on subsistence farming as their only source of livelihood, it is difficult to come to terms with the aftermath of the war. The war took away human resources, especially men, and women have been left as the sole caretakers of children and older members of the community. Women who were hugely dependent on men economically are struggling to put themselves in the shoes of their male counterparts. Women's bargaining power is limited to the household and taking care of children, which is also often controlled by senior male members of the family. As a result, the experiences of women have largely gone unnoticed and have not been adequately addressed either by the state or government.

Even though the government has provided economic compensation to some women, this should not, in any case, be the only determining factor with regard to whether the government has fulfilled its responsibility in the peace and reconciliation process. What these women want is the truth about the whereabouts of their husbands who were beaten, put in detention and. in some cases, even killed. To include women as active participants in conflict resolution and the peace-building process, the government should provide the truth and facilitate legal procedures to seek justice for the persons who were disappeared or killed.

In July 2007 the government drafted the *Truth and Reconciliation Bill* under the Ministry of Peace and Reconstruction to constitute an independent and impartial commission to bring the actual facts to the public by investigating the truth regarding persons involved in gross violations of human rights and crimes against humanity, as committed by both the government and Maoists during the course of armed conflict between 13 February 1996 and 21 November 2007. After seven years the *Commission on Investigation of Disappeared Persons, Truth and Reconciliation Act 2014* was approved by Parliament on 25 April 2014 paving the way for the formation of two separate commissions, one on truth and reconciliation and one on disappeared persons. The Truth and Reconciliation Commission is focused on:

> finding out and documenting the violations of human rights and humanitarian laws and serious crimes, and making recommendation to competent agencies or government for criminal prosecution against the alleged perpetrators; reparation to the victims with the assurance of justice; and provide suggestions for institutional reform to stop repetition of such incidents in the future.
>
> (INSEC 2014, p. 5)

While the Commission for the Investigation of Disappeared Person's role is to search for disappeared persons and make their whereabouts public.

However, the process leading up to the enactment of the *Commission on Investigation of Disappeared Persons, Truth and Reconciliation Act in April 2014* proved to be seriously contentious. Activists and victims alike objected to provisions on mediation between victims and perpetrators, the granting of amnesty and the foreclosure of investigation and prosecution in cases where mediation is sought (Sharma 2014). During the drafting process a ruling by the Supreme Court in

January 2014 found the granting of amnesties to be unconstitutional and ordered the Maoist-led government not to grant amnesties to the perpetrators of serious crimes (ibid.). The Act has also been criticised for falling below international standards (Bisset 2014, p. 4).

More facilities and relief packages should be given to families, including those with women-headed households to lift them out of poverty and deprivation. Children should be given free education; and women from all backgrounds should be given opportunities and platforms where they can earn their livelihood without being vulnerable to any forms of domestic and physical violence. All women, irrespective of their background, should be encouraged and engaged to take part in social and governmental programmes, at both village development committee and district levels, thus uplifting their positions at local level. In other words, women should not only receive compensation but also be empowered politically, economically and socially.

Conclusion

The process of homogenisation, generalisation and essentialisation of women leads to a skewed view of Nepali women that is arbitrarily formed, undermining the individual characteristics of victims and their potential needs. Assumptions relating to women's status are not only based on their sex but may also extend towards their ethnicity, geographical location, profession, caste and religion. As a result, women's and girls' experiences of subjugation are more subtle and indirect than explicit and direct. The homogenisation of women and girls has continued even after the cessation of direct hostilities in Nepal, despite the existence of international legal instruments on women, peace and security, such as SCRs 1325 and 1820.

The implementation of the resolutions on women, peace and security is limited and universalises the experiences and sufferings of women and girls, thus restricting the opportunities to include and understand the multiple needs and demands of conflict-affected victims. Women and girls continue to bear the brunt of the conflict socially, economically and politically. Those women and girls who were previously Maoist combatants have been excluded from mainstream politics and the peace-building process. Women and girls were also subjected to various forms and degrees of domestic, sexual and physical violence both during and after the war. While gender-based violence occurs frequently during the conflict, it should not, nevertheless, be understood in reference to the conflict alone.

The tendency to essentialise conflict-affected victims will in turn exacerbate the exclusion of groups of women, especially those groups who have historically been marginalised and excluded from national and policy level debates and discourses. Furthermore, this will largely prohibit the excluded groups of women and girl children and marginalised communities like *Tharu* and *Dalits* from articulating their specific needs in national programmes and relief and recovery facilities. As these groups have been historically marginalised and socially excluded they are often perceived as backward, at all levels of the economy and polity. In addition, they are illiterate and deprived of health, nutritious food, housing, land rights and citizenship. In these circumstances these minority groups will only be pushed further towards the periphery if the programmes and policies are not in tune with their specific needs.

Therefore, it is important that the government adopts a nuanced approach, considering the specific needs of the 'victims', including developing reintegration and rehabilitation programmes which cater to specific minority groups according to their needs. Additionally, the truth should be brought out and justice given to the families of victims who were disappeared or killed, including the whereabouts of missing individuals. Apart from these programmes, training should be provided to women and girls to empower them and make them feel less vulnerable and susceptible to physical and sexual violence and abuse. The women who were former rebels should be given the opportunity to join the army, if they wish to do so.

It is of utmost importance that the government creates opportunities for the multiple groups of female conflict-affected victims to improve their living conditions and reduce economic hardship, including creating awareness programmes to prevent social stigma of single women and allow their meaningful reintegration and rehabilitation in society. It is therefore equally important that local peace and security stakeholders, district level government bodies such as the district administration office and local peace development committees, including other stakeholders, should be made aware of the NAP on SCRs 1325 and 1820 and be held accountable for implementing the NAP. The local officials and advocates, including civil society organisations, working for human rights have also agreed that a lack of awareness of the NAP among stakeholders is a serious limitation to its implementation. More importantly, transitional justice mechanisms, specifically the *Commission on Investigation of Disappeared Persons, Truth and Reconciliation Act 2014* needs to be amended in line with international law and should abide by the Supreme Court's ruling that amnesty should not be granted for gross human-rights violations.

Notes

1 United Nations Security Council (2000) Resolution 1325, 31 October 2000, UN Doc. S/RES/1325.

2 United Nations Security Council (2008) Resolution 1820, 19 June 2008, UN Doc. S/RES/1820.

3 *Badi* describes families who are professional sex workers. *Chaupadi* (similar to a cow shed, separate from the house) is a place where women have to be situated during menstruation. *Jhuma* is a woman who is devoted to God – in some particular ethnic castes, the middle daughter is offered to god.

4 Humiliation and agony are attached to the the word for a widow in Nepali. For this reason, WHR uses the term for single women in Nepali. WHR also works with divorcees, unmarried women over thirty-five years and with the wives of missing husbands. During the conflict, widows were often the first targets of rape and sexual slavery, being without male protection. They therefore suffer from multiple stigmas, as widows, as rape victims and because they are infected with the AIDS virus. In Nepal, poorest senior widows are demonised as witches and are targets for physical and psychological violence, even murder.

5 The South Asian Network for Widow's Empowerment in Development (SANWED) was instrumental in pushing for widow's issues to be incorporated into the Colombo

Declaration during the 15th SAARC Summit 2008, which supports regional cooperation for the elimination of all forms of discrimination and abuse against women in general and widows in particular, guaranteeing their rights to live freely in society in a dignified manner. Rights-based approaches to empower widows have only recently been adopted, as opposed to welfare approaches which had been adopted by NGOs and the government for a number of years. The integration of widows into the mainstream and the transformation of these excluded women into agents of change has been undertaken by SANWED, which comprises the National Forum for Single Women's Rights and the Guild of Services in India; Women for Human Rights in Nepal; the Small Fishers Federation in Sri Lanka; Aurat Foundation in Pakistan; National Forum for Women in Bangladesh; and HAWA in Afghanistan.

Bibliography

Ariño, M.V. (2008) *Nepal: a gender view of the armed conflict and the peace process*, Escola De Cultura De Pau, Spain.

ASPECT (Asian Study Center for Peace and Conflict Transformation) (2010) *Peace Process in the Context of Nepal*, Background Paper no. 1, 22 November, Kathmandu, Nepal.

Bisset, A. (2014) *Transitional Justice in Nepal, The Commission on Investigation of Disappeared Persons, Truth and Reconciliation Act 2014*, Bingham Centre Working Paper 2014/07 [online] http://binghamcentre.biicl.org/documents/334_nepal_update_-_bisset.pdf

Center for Constitutional Dialogue (2009) *Rights of Indigenous Peoples*, Nepal Participatory Constitution Building Booklet Series no. 6, Kathmandu, Nepal.

Deuba, A.R. and Rana, P.S. (2001) *A Study on the Psycho-Social Impacts of Violence Against Women and Girls with Special Focus on Rape, Incest and Polygamy*, Saathi and SNV, Nepal [online] http://www.childtrafficking.com/Docs/pshycho_social_impact_study_070402.pdf

Forum for Women, Law and Development (FWLD) (2011) *Shadow Report on the Fourth and Fifth Periodic Report by the Government of Nepal on CEDAW*, Kathmandu, Nepal.

Haraway, D. (1988) 'Situated Knowledge: The science in question and the privilege of partial perspectives', *Feminist Studies*, vol. 14, no. 3, pp. 575–99.

Informal Sector Service Center (INSEC) (2013) *Violence against Women/Girls: Assessing the situation of Nepal in 2013*, Kathmandu, Nepal.

Informal Sector Service Center (INSEC) (2014) *Transitional justice efforts in Nepal*, Kathmandu, Nepal.

Interdisciplinary Centre for Gender Studies (ICFG) (2013) *Factsheet violence against women – The missing MDG?* Federal Department of Foreign Affairs, Switzerland.

IRIN News (2006) 'NEPAL: Child marriage still common in rural southwest, Baskhora', 19 October [online] http://www.irinnews.org/printreport.aspx?reportid=61758

Lamichhane, P., Puri, M. Tamang, J. and Dulal, B. (2011) 'Women's Status and Violence against Young Married Women in Rural Nepal', *BMC Women's Health* 11:19.

Lawoti, M. (2007) *Looking back, looking forward: Centralization, multiple conflicts, and democratic state building in Nepal*, Policy Studies 43, East-West Center, Washington DC, USA [online] http://www.eastwestcenter.org/fileadmin/stored/pdfs/ps043.pdf

Lawoti, M. (2010) 'Inclusion and Accountability in a "New" Democratic Nepal' in Rita Manchanda, R. (Ed.) *States in Conflict with Their Minorities: Challenges to Minority Rights in South Asia*, Sage Publications India Pvt. Ltd.

Ministry of Health and Population (MOHP), New ERA, and ICF International Inc. (2012) *Nepal Demographic and Health Survey 2011*, Kathmandu, Nepal: Ministry of Health and Population, New ERA, and ICF International, Calverton, Maryland.

Nepal Institute for Policy Studies (2013) *Nepal's Peace Process: A Brief Overview* Policy Paper, July 2013, vol. 8, no. 1 [online] http://nipsnepal.org/uploads/files/Nepal's%20Peace%20Process_A%20Brief%20Overview_Eng%20(2).pdf

Phillips, A. (Ed.) (1998) *Democracy and Representation: Or, why should it matter who our representatives are*, Oxford University Press.

SANWED (2008) *Report of South Asian Network for Widows' Empowerment in Development*, SANWED.

Shakya, A. (2009) *Social Impact of Armed Conflict in Nepal: Cause and Impact* Social Inclusion Research Fund, Kathmandu, Nepal.

Sharma, M. (2014) TRC: Let's not make it Damocles' Sword' (22 April 2014) [online] http://setopati.net/opinion/1414/TRC:-Let%E2%80%99s-not-make-it-Damocles%E2%80%99-sword/.

Tamang, S. (2009) 'The politics of conflict and difference or the difference of conflict in politics: the women's movement in Nepal', *Feminist Review*, vol. 91, pp. 61–80.

Tong, R. (1989) 'Multicultural, Global and Postcolonial Feminism' *Feminist Thought: A Comprehensive Introduction*, Westview Press, Boulder and San Francisco, USA.

United Nations (2011) *Aid Effectiveness and the Implementation of SCR 1325 in Nepal* Kathmandu, Nepal.

United Nations Development Programme (UNDP) (2009), Nepal Human Development Report, Kathmandu, Nepal.

Upreti, B.R. (2006) *Nepal's Armed Conflict: Security Implications for Development and Resource Governance* Kathmandu, Nepal.

Voluntary Services Overseas (VSO Nepal) (2011) *Gender Backgrounder and Discussion Paper* Kathmandu, Nepal.

Women for Human Rights (WHR) (2010) *Report of International Conference on Widowhood*, Nepal.

Women's Rehabilitation Centre (WOREC) (2008) *Summary Report on Media Interaction on Violence Against Women* Kathmandu, Nepal, [on file with editor].

Women's Rehabilitation Centre (WOREC) (2014) *Monthly VAW Report (Mid-April–Mid-May 2014)* Kathmandu, Nepal.

5 Implementing Security Council Resolution 1325 in Asia

The role of national action plans on women, peace and security

Amy Barrow

Introduction

Unanimously adopted by the United Nations (UN) Security Council in October 2000, Security Council Resolution 1325[1] (hereafter SCR 1325) situates the experiences of women in armed conflict as a core security challenge, which potentially undermines the maintenance of international peace and security. SCR 1325 seeks to mainstream gender in a peace and security context, including the integration of a gender perspective in peacekeeping operations. Containing a preamble and eighteen operative paragraphs covering prevention, participation and protection, the resolution attempts to move beyond a victim-centred paradigm by recognising the agency of women and their multiple roles in armed conflict as actors and participants. Despite SCR 1325's transformative potential as a gender mainstreaming instrument, the framework of the resolution has been subjected to significant criticism.

SCR 1325 does not invoke Chapter VII of the UN Charter, which allows the Security Council to take action with respect to threats to peace, breaches of the peace and acts of aggression. Without legally binding UN Member States, international lawyers suggest that SCR 1325 lacks substantive 'teeth' (see, for example, Otto 2009). The resolution has also been widely lamented for failing to incorporate clear targets, benchmarks and indicators to measure progress in implementation (see Barrow 2009; Bell and O'Rourke 2010; Fujio 2008; Swaine 2009). Despite the lack of its enforcement women's organisations regularly refer to SCR 1325 as legally binding, which may be part of a wider advocacy strategy to transform what is effectively a soft-law instrument into a hard-law obligation (Fujio 2008, p. 227). Advocates point to Article 25 of the UN Charter, which stipulates that Member States should fulfil the decisions of the Security Council. Significantly, the Security Council's regular affirmation of the aims and objectives of SCR 1325, as well as continuous monitoring and evaluation of implementation efforts by civil society organisations (CSOs), have helped to maintain gender on the Security Council's agenda.

In 2002, a Security Council Presidential Statement directly called for Member States to develop National Action Plans (NAPs) on women, peace and security to strengthen SCR 1325's implementation in peace and security operations (UN Security

Council 2002). Further, the UN Secretary General's report of 13 October 2004 also encouraged Member States to develop NAPs (UN Security Council 2004). Initially driven by northern European states,[2] NAPs have been developed and adopted by a number of states emerging from protracted conflict.[3] Potentially, NAPs are a useful policy tool that allows for the formulation of domestic policies on, for example, protection from gender-based violence in conflict and the mainstreaming of gender in peacekeeping operations; but the question of whether NAPs support the broader objectives of women's empowerment and access to decision-making is subject to scrutiny. There has been limited, if any, evaluation of the development of NAPs in Asia.[4] The Philippines adopted a National Action Plan in 2010, followed by Nepal in 2011 and the Republic of Korea in 2014. Most recently, Afghanistan and Japan adopted NAPs in 2015 after lengthy development and drafting processes.

This chapter critically analyses the development of NAPs in Asia, focusing on experiences in the Philippines, Nepal and the Republic of Korea to evaluate NAPs' role in promoting the integration of a gender perspective in peace and security operations, including whether NAPs help to realise SCR 1325's broader objectives, including women's empowerment and access to decision-making. First, the aims and objectives of NAPs are considered. Second, a content analysis of the Philippine, Nepalese and Korean NAPs will be undertaken to consider how SCR 1325 is operationalised, if at all, at the national level. Drawing upon this analysis, the chapter aims to identify any particular economic, political, social or other challenges which hinder the adoption of national level initiatives on women, peace and security within Asia.

Aims and objectives of National Action Plans (NAP) on SCR 1325

UN Member States were first encouraged to develop national level initiatives to support the implementation of SCR 1325 in 2002. The President of the Security Council called upon Member States, as well as UN entities and civil society actors, to develop action plans which incorporate clear goals and a timetable for the implementation of SCR 1325. A failure to include benchmarks or indicators within the framework of SCR 1325 is indicative of a lack of institutional accountability for the resolution, though not wholly unsurprising given the nature of SCR 1325 as a soft-law instrument of the Security Council. Without any benchmarks or indicators it is difficult to assess, by either quantitative or qualitative means, whether SCR 1325 is being operationalised in practice. Conversely, NAPs potentially allow for the effective integration of benchmarks and indicators, particularly given that states usually attribute responsibility to government departments or entities to implement SCR 1325.

Benchmarks have a normative element; they focus on the minimum institutional standards that are required to achieve an institution's objectives (International Council on Human Rights Policy 2005, p. 10). For example, the character of an institution, including its independence and whether there are clear lines of accountability, would be considered as a benchmark. In contrast, quantitative, qualitative or participatory (developed with multiple stakeholders) indicators are used to measure progress towards institutional objectives such as gender equality. The United Nations Economic and Social Commission for Asia and the Pacific (2007) has noted the importance of developing targets and indicators as a way to measure the promotion of gender equality and women's empowerment, for example, legislation protecting women in the informal sector or on equal opportunities, which would give an indication of the integration of women's human rights in laws, the constitution and legal jurisprudence.

While the principal aim of NAPs is to help operationalise SCR 1325, action plans are not limited to the substantive aims of the resolution. Member States have been actively encouraged to focus more broadly on the constraints faced by women and girls in post-conflict situations, including issues such as: access to economic resources; land and property rights; and other factors not specifically identified within the framework of SCR 1325. Some NAPs also make reference to UN Security Council Resolution 1820[5] (hereafter SCR 1820), which, significantly was the first state-sponsored resolution on women, peace and security to be adopted following SCR 1325 and is perceived as a mechanism for addressing sexual violence in armed conflict. Potentially, however, SCR 1820 detracts from the transformative potential of SCR 1325 by returning to a victim-centred paradigm of women's experiences in armed conflict and its aftermath.

In the lead up to the tenth anniversary of SCR 1325, a flurry of resolutions on women, peace and security were adopted, including Security Council Resolutions 1888[6] and 1960[7]. While many of these resolutions centre on sexual violence, Security Council Resolution 1889[8] sought to revisit and reaffirm the core aims and objectives of SCR 1325 by adopting concrete strategies to strengthen implementation. Although the adoption of a series of resolutions helps to support the development of a normative framework on women, peace and security within the UN system, an awareness of the aims and objectives of SCRs 1325, 1820 and subsequent resolutions is lacking in government and policy circles, as well as in civil society including among women's organisations. The tenth anniversary of SCR 1325 saw a spike in the development of NAPs, though overall the rate of adoption of NAPs is relatively low, with fifty-two out of 193 Member States approving a NAP.[9]

The operationalisation of SCR 1325 is multi-layered. At a normative level operationalisation may be demonstrated through awareness of and receptiveness to SCR 1325 among elite security policy circles as a mechanism to address the situation of women in armed conflict and its aftermath. Normative operationalisation may be identified, for example, through national legal and policy responses to armed conflict, including whether SCR 1325 is effectively mainstreamed in peace agreements and other related programmes. Further, the integration of SCR 1325 into domestic law, including constitutional frameworks, would provide an indicator of normative receptiveness to SCR 1325 at the national level. Explicit references to the resolution or a clear articulation of what is meant by the inclusion of a gender perspective or gender equality may also indicate that SCR 1325 is being operationalised at the normative level (Bell and O'Rourke 2010).

While SCR 1325 may be operationalised at the normative level, it does not automatically follow that it will be operationalised in practice on the ground. Practically, its operationalisation may be measured quantitatively by, for example, how many women participate in formal peace negotiations or how many military personnel are prosecuted for sexually exploitative behaviour. Qualitative measures may include the way in which refugee camps are designed to take account of the differences between men and women, including basic security measures to prevent sexual violence, such as the location and design of toilets and adequate lighting.

First-generation NAPs[10] have largely been developed by donor states that play a significant role in peacekeeping operations and international development assistance. With the exception of conflict in Northern Ireland in the UK, the so-called Troubles,[11] these donor states have not emerged from protracted conflict. The framework of these NAPs as vehicles to drive the implementation of SCR1325 are not necessarily sophisticated enough to reflect the cultural, economic, political and social complexities of post-conflict settings, nor designed in a way to address the practical operationalisation of SCRs on women, peace and security. Thus the development of NAPs in countries emerging from protracted conflict potentially offers a clearer indication of how SCR 1325 may be effectively operationalised to respond to the situation of women and girls on the ground, in highly polarised settings where the problems are most acute.

Development of NAPs in Asia

To date there has been limited adoption of NAPs within Asia. The Philippines adopted a NAP in 2010, followed by Nepal in 2011, the Republic of Korea in 2014 and Afghanistan in 2015. Most recently, after a drawn out process of drafting, Japan adopted a NAP in September 2015. It is not immediately clear why the adoption of NAPs within Asia has lagged behind other regions. In part, this may be related to the, political landscape of Asia, which is incredibly diverse culturally, economically, legally and politically. A number of states within Asia have emerged from protracted armed conflict including Nepal, Sri Lanka and Timor-Leste. Further, without any regional Asia-wide human-rights mechanisms or bodies, there is perhaps a lack of institutional momentum to drive forward the development of NAPs. The ASEAN Intergovernmental Commission on Human Rights was founded in 2009, but the institution is relatively young and it is difficult to evaluate fully how the Commission will influence and shape the development of ASEAN-wide norms on gender equality and women's empowerment. Further, the Asian values debate in the early 1990s framed universal human-rights norms as a form of ideological imperialism and there was significant opposition from states, including China and Singapore, to the perceived hierarchy of rights, which elevated civil and political rights above economic, social and cultural rights. Scepticism towards the United Nations and the international human-rights regime remains.

In some Asian states there is continued resistance to the perceived imposition of eurocentric standards. For example, in Sri Lanka, the government has distanced itself from international legal instruments, preferring to rely on domestic mechanisms (see Gomez's analysis in Chapter 4). Other states have already adopted more general action plans focused on gender equality and do not see the value of creating an additional action plan focused on women, peace and security. Significantly, however, the aims and objectives of SCR 1325 and the linkage with women's experiences of armed conflict are often overlooked in broader gender equality concerns. The Convention on the Elimination of All Forms of Discrimination against Women (hereafter CEDAW), for example, does not explicitly address gender-based violence in armed conflict although it is one of the most widely ratified international treaties (though with the most reservations by states parties), and many states have drawn on CEDAW to adopt national level plans on gender equality.

A few Asian states have taken proactive steps to develop NAPs on SCR 1325 and other resolutions on women, peace and security. The framework of these NAPs may give an insight into the way in which SCR 1325 is currently operationalised at the national level in Asian settings including any particular constraints which hinder its effective implementation. Though the geopolitical landscape of each of these states is distinct, each country examined in detail within this chapter has experienced protracted armed conflict. The Philippines continues to be affected by multiple armed insurgency movements, particularly in the south. Nepal is currently in a fragile state of transition following a sustained armed Maoist insurgency movement. The Republic of Korea (ROK) occupies a unique geopolitical status as the only divided nation state under an armistice agreement following the Korean War of 1950–3. While the ROK is not actively engaged in armed conflict, sporadic border incidents have heightened ongoing tensions with the Democratic People's Republic of North Korea (DPRK).

Philippines National Action Plan

The Philippines has experienced protracted armed conflict since the 1960s, with multiple armed insurgent groups in operation. The New People's Army, a military wing of the Communist Party of the Philippines, has waged a nationwide armed communist insurgency against the government since the 1960s. Mindanao, the second largest island located in the south, has experienced periods of fighting and instability since the late 1960s as a consequence of the armed struggle for an independent state. Although the Philippines government and the Moro Islamic Liberation Front, a self-determination movement, signed the Comprehensive Agreement on the Bangsamoro on 17 March 2014, any peace is fragile in the region. Both movements have significantly impacted upon the security of citizens with extra-judicial killings and abductions. Violence against women has manifested itself in multiple forms, including sexual harassment, assault and sexual abuse, as well as in terms of economic dislocation, the displacement of women and the dispersal of women's organisations (Global Network of Women Peacebuilders 2011a, p. 250). Poverty, a lack of education and basic social services are also perceived to have exacerbated the armed conflict (Philippine NAP 2009, p. 3). The conflict has invariably impacted on women's roles with women taking on the role of providers or actively participating in the insurgency, though not necessarily carrying arms (Global Network of Women Peacebuilders 2011a, p. 250). Further, the prevalence of small arms, which are often used by armed insurgents but are also held by a wider cross section of society in the Philippines (Santos Jr. *et al.* 2010), has had serious consequences for incidences of gender-based violence and been linked to deaths, rape, intimidation and harassment (Philippine NAP 2009, p. 4).

All ASEAN States, including the Philippines, have signed or acceded to CEDAW and ASEAN adopted a Declaration on the Elimination of Violence against Women in the ASEAN region in 2004.[12] The Philippines' adoption of a series of laws addressing gender-based violence appears progressive when compared with other ASEAN states, such as Myanmar, which do not have specific laws on violence against women.[13] In addition to constitutional provisions on equality,[14] the Philippines has adopted a number of specific laws,[15] including the Magna Carta of Women[16] enacted in 2009, which is effectively a bill of women's human rights. Further, the Philippine Plan for Gender Responsive Development (1995–2025), lays the foundation for a long-term plan on gender equality. Although many ASEAN states also contribute troops to UN peacekeeping missions, there does not seem to be any collective momentum within ASEAN to drive forward the development of NAPs on women, peace and security, despite their potential role in pre-deployment training. This is why the Philippines' adoption of a National Action Plan on SCRs 1325 and 1820 seems particularly progressive.

The process leading up to the adoption of the NAP included multiple consultations with both CSOs and state agencies at the regional level and validation workshops at the national level, allowing for further revision of the NAP, which was finalised in March 2010. The framework of the NAP is designed around four purposes: (1) protection and prevention; (2) empowerment and participation; (3) promotion and mainstreaming; and (4) capacity development and monitoring and reporting. Under each purpose there are: an overarching outcome and indicators stipulated which are supplemented by specific action points; a result statement, which should be read as a projected outcome; indicators to measure implementation of the action point; a timeline; and the identification of key actors.

Purpose one of the NAP includes the protection of women's human rights and the prevention of violence against women from threats, injuries, rape, death and displacement, to ensure that women's rights are respected. Significantly, the NAP aspires to empower women and girls who have formally participated in armed conflict to ensure that they are socially and economically productive. Under purpose two, which focuses explicitly on empowerment and participation, the NAP recognises the importance of reaching out to marginalised groups of women within society, particularly indigenous and Moro women, through targeted training to enhance their leadership skills. While these intended outcomes suggest the transformative potential of NAPs as policy instruments, a reliance on quantitative indicators to measure progress towards such outcomes may not adequately evaluate whether NAPs help to operationalise SCR 1325 at either a normative or operational level.

A good illustration of how quantitative indicators may not accurately reflect whether women are supported adequately can be seen in provisions on rehabilitation and reintegration programmes. A key outcome of the NAP is to address the special needs of women and girls formerly involved in armed conflict, replicating the aims of operational paragraph 8(a) of SCR 1325. The principal indicator adopted to evaluate how women and their families are identified and addressed is a rapid needs assessment (RNA), which relies on a quantitative measurement of the number of women and girls assisted in psychology, health, alternative learning, law and livelihood. Although quantitative measures help to provide baseline statistics that allow for the mapping of levels of assistance over time, there is no qualitative evaluation or clear measurement of the way in which these assistance programmes benefit individual women and girls, or whether such assistance reaches all those persons in need of support.

There is also no indication within the NAP of how such RNAs will be funded, or the resources that will be allocated to support services. Although key state agencies are identified, principally the Department of Social Welfare and Development, local government units and CSOs, lines of accountability are by no means clear. There is little indication given of who is responsible for developing the RNA, what it entails or whether these assessment tools are designed to include both quantitative and/or qualitative measures. Additionally, it is not clear who will be responsible for providing assistance, or whether CSOs, which often have limited funding, will take primary responsibility for the provision of support services.

A major action point within the NAP is the enactment and enforcement of laws that regulate the possession of small arms. While often linked to armed conflict, the use of small arms and gun violence is highly prevalent in the Philippines. By including provisions on small arms and gun violence the Philippine NAP addresses the issue of disarmament simultaneously with broader concerns related to gender and gun violence within Filipino society. Indicators of progress towards this goal include the ratification of the International Arms Trade Treaty, which entered into force on 24 December 2014, and the adoption of appropriate legislation at local level. Further, the NAP focuses on arms control and the criminal prosecution of individuals possessing illegal arms.

The NAP aims to operationalise SCR 1325 at a normative level. Though not explicitly linked, the NAP appears to utilise evidence that gender issues are discussed in peace negotiations and agreements alongside the number of violations of human rights and international humanitarian law and gender-based violence as a measurable indicator of the outcome of gender responsive peace agreements. While the inclusion of a gender perspective within peace agreements is important to reflect the normative operationalision of provisions on women, peace and security, it is not clear how this impacts upon levels of gender-based violence on the ground. The inclusion of a gender perspective within legislation and peace agreements does not necessarily help to reduce levels of gender-based violence in the immediate aftermath of conflict and during peacetime. How these peace agreements filter down from national to local level, and the local means employed to respond to provisions such as education and prevention strategies, may have a greater impact on the practical operationalisation of international legal norms.

The NAP places a emphasis on the promotion of gender mainstreaming in conflict prevention, resolution and peacebuilding under purpose four. Significantly, the drafters of the NAP recognise the importance of further situating the provisions within local settings, evidenced by the move to mainstream the NAP in regional and local gender and development (GAD) planning processes and budgeting. Incorporating the NAP into GAD processes intrinsically links conflict prevention, resolution and peacebuilding with developmental goals, recognising the role of poverty and underdevelopment in exacerbating the armed conflict. Alongside these goals, the integration of peace, non-violence and gender education in formal and non-formal education curriculums, and the inclusion of gender- and culture-sensitive advocacy campaigns through the media, reflect the multi-layered promotional activities envisaged to support the mainstreaming of gender and awareness of women's multiple roles in peace and security processes.

The majority of action points are given a timeframe of 2010–16 to be completed – the lifetime of the NAP itself. As the first ASEAN state to adopt a NAP, the Philippines has demonstrated a clear commitment to addressing gender-based violence in conflict, though this does not appear to have influenced or compelled other ASEAN states to adopt NAPs.

Nepal National Action Plan

Nepal experienced a decade-long armed insurgency by Maoists from February 1996 to November 2006, when the Comprehensive Peace Accord was signed by both the Government of Nepal and the Maoists. While the insurgency has formally ended, the transition from conflict to peace in Nepal remains a fragile one. The Maoist insurgency movement was ideologically driven and sought to challenge the feudal governance system premised on complex structural hierarchies, including caste, class, gender and geographical factors[17] that have historically shaped Nepalese society and are perceived to have perpetuated inequality, exclusion and discrimination (Global Network of Women Peacebuilders 2011b). The armed insurgency and conflict between government security forces and Maoist rebels damaged infrastructure, killed thousands of men, women and children, and displaced more than 75,000 people, significantly impacting upon familial relationships (see Gurung and Thapa's analysis in Chapter 4).

The deeply gendered armed conflict impacted on women through multiple factors (Upreti 2006, p. 273), including whether they resided in conflict-affected areas, the political affiliation of their husbands and family members and, for some women, their direct role in the conflict as combatants (Global Network of Women Peacebuilders 2011b, p. 211). The conflict was marked on both sides by incidents of abduction, torture, rape and sexual violence. As a result of the conflict the number of female-headed households and widows (single women) has increased.

A raft of discriminatory legislation provisions in the *Muluki Ain* (Civil Code) have also exacerbated societal stigma towards single women, although, as a result of advocacy campaigns and pressure from CSOs, these provisions are gradually being repealed.[18]

At the normative level, the Nepalese government appears to be committed to the transformative potential of SCR 1325, with recognition of the state's responsibility for increasing women's participation in peacebuilding processes, within policy formation and at the implementation level. Further, the Nepalese government recognises the role of SCRs 1325 and 1820 as a framework for strengthening women's participation in the promotion of peace and security. The NAP succeeds in fleshing out SCRs 1325 and 1820 in a Nepalese context without focusing solely on sexual violence. The NAP is ambitious and far reaching, moving beyond the narrow remit of SCR 1325. In many respects it reflects the limitations of SCR 1325 by adequately capturing the complexity of multiple forms of violence that occur in conflict settings. Gender-based violence is framed quite narrowly in SCR 1325. This is not necessarily the result of SCR 1325's character as a universal, soft-law instrument, but is an indication of the role of the Security Council, which has traditionally focused on the cessation of direct hostilities and violence, cognisant of the negative peace paradigm.[19]

In many societies, as in Nepal, discrimination and gender-based violence are perpetuated not only through physical violence but also through structural cultural, legal, political and social strata that exacerbate inequalities. The negative peace paradigm does not adequately respond to structural gender-based violence. While the strengthening of the relationship between the Security Council, the Peacebuilding Commission and other entities within the UN is often articulated, the role and remit of the Security Council remains distinct and a shift to a broader interpretation of gender-based violence is yet to be identified. The Nepalese NAP (Government of Nepal 2011) provides a concrete example, at least on paper, of how SCR 1325 may be effectively translated and contextualised in highly polarised settings.

In addition to providing contextual background on the armed Maoist insurgency – including the specific impact on women and the constitutional, legal and policy provisions on women, peace and security – the NAP includes a detailed matrix framed around five pillars: participation; protection and prevention; promotion; relief and recovery; and resource management, monitoring and evaluation. Under each pillar strategic objectives, specific actions, expected results, indicators, implementing agencies and a timeframe are identified.

Significantly, the Nepalese NAP aims to move beyond the homogenisation of women (see Gurung and Thapa's analysis in Chapter 4), by recognising women's multiple roles, including how women's gender roles intersect with other aspects of identity. Fourteen sub-categories of women are identified as 'conflict affected-women and children' in section 7.1 of the Nepal NAP (Government of Nepal 2011), including former women combatants, single women (widows), disabled women and women in detention or imprisonment. Importantly, sexual violence includes sexually explicit behaviour or conduct, which may include words or activities against the sexuality of any person. This is a significant extension of the framework of SCR 1325, which, as with other Security Council resolutions, is heteronormative and does not include consideration of sexual orientation and gender identity.

Similar to the Philippine NAP, indicators of participation within the matrix are largely premised on quantitative measures, such as the numbers of women in peace negotiations or as candidates in elections. Other indicators are specifically targeted at improving the statutory legal framework, including the formulation of laws pertaining to confidentiality and other amendments to legal provisions to extend the statute of limitations for filing complaints in respect of allegations of rape. Again, similar to the Philippine NAP, the inclusion of women, peace and security issues within the school curriculum and other non-formal education programmes is advocated. Indicators are included to measure the effectiveness of programmes implemented at district level but there is no explanation of how 'effectiveness' should be measured. Both 'impact' and 'effectiveness' are notoriously hard to measure and often deeply subjective. The use of such indicators may prove to be problematic in practice, particularly if there are not the resources or capacity to monitor and evaluate the NAP over time.

In addition to specifying indicators, the NAP aims to improve transparency and accountability by identifying both responsible and supporting agencies in the implementation of strategic objectives. While it may be difficult to hold state agencies to account for a failure to fulfil duties under what are, in many respects, aspirational policy provisions, it nevertheless helps to foster a culture of accountability if state agencies have clear obligations that they must be answerable to.

Republic of Korea (ROK) NAP

In contrast to the armed insurgency movements which have marred economic, political and social development in the Philippines and Nepal, the Republic of Korea (ROK), although remaining under an armistice agreement, is perceived as a developed market (Woods 2013, p. 5), and actively contributes to international development assistance, which distinguishes it from the Philippines and Nepal.

The Republic of Korea (ROK) launched its National Action Plan (2014) to implement SCR 1325 in 2014, following a two-year drafting process which included discussions with CSOs in the 1325 Network. However, the finalised NAP does not include provision for continued engagement with civil society. The adoption of the NAP coincided with the ROK's role as non-permanent member of the UN Security Council during 2013–14. In contrast with other Asian NAPs the substantive content is somewhat limited in detail. While the NAP outlines international legal provisions on violence against women in armed conflict, very little context is provided in relation to the national framework of laws addressing gender equality. Though the ROK is not actively engaged in armed conflict tensions with the DPRK remain (heightened by sporadic border incidents), though the NAP's purpose and objectives do not discuss the implications of the armistice agreement for Korean women in any detail. Conversely, the drafters of the NAP are keen to point to the importance of women's protection during conflict, citing, in section B(1), the grave violations of Korean women's rights, principally the sexual slavery system of 'comfort women' at the hands of the Japanese Imperial Army during World War II (National Action Plan 2014). The issue has remained politically contentious, particularly given the lack of compensation and formal reparations by the Government of Japan to women survivors who were forced into sexual slavery. Such references to historical human-rights violations are a distinct feature of the ROK NAP.[20]

The ROK NAP is both inward- and outward-looking. Given the ROK's unique status under armistice and its role as a developed donor state, the NAP appears responsive to historical human-rights violations, with the inclusion of support service programmes to survivors of the comfort women system, while at the same time including multilateral and bilateral level action points which reflect the ROK's role as a developed donor state within the international community. The ROK NAP is framed around four areas: prevention; participation; protection; relief and recovery. Each area is further broken down into objectives, strategies, actions and the implementing agency identified. However, no indicators, either quantitative or qualitative, are included, neither is a timeframe specified.

At a normative level, the plan aims to sensitise multiple actors to the importance of conflict prevention. From pre-deployment training on the prevention of sexual violence and commercial sexual exploitation to the inclusion of human rights and humanitarian law topics (including sexual violence during armed conflict) in educational curriculums at elementary, middle and high school levels, the NAP's awareness-raising strategy is multifaceted. Given the historical significance of the comfort women system, a clear objective of the ROK's NAP is to educate individuals about how conflict impacts on women, including sexual violence, though curiously there is little engagement with the wider implications for women of the division between North and South Korea, including the dislocation of families. Framing the NAP's focus on women as victims of the comfort system, rather than as survivors, risks the perpetuation of stereotypical portrayals of women in conflict, which could be avoided by the inclusion of multiple representations of women in conflict within the design of curriculums.

Importantly, the NAP includes specific provisions on ratifying and implementing international legal instruments on human trafficking and on the revision of domestic legislation, demonstrating the ROK's commitment to the inclusion of human trafficking in broader protection policies, which go beyond the framework of SCR 1325. The NAP also includes affirmative action provisions, including the use of annual target quotas for female members in government and developing a database to identify national female experts in national defence, unification and foreign affairs. Further, under the protection pillar, the NAP aims to increase the number of female representatives in government delegations and peacekeeping talks, including the Inter-Korean dialogues and Six-Party Talks. Thus the ROK NAP includes both inward- and outward-looking strategies, which may reflect the ROK's position as a non-permanent member of the Security Council at the time that the NAP was formally developed.

Challenges for the adoption of NAPs in Asia

While the cultural, economic, political and social dynamics of the Philippines, Nepal and the Republic of Korea differ substantially, the design of each respective NAP, particularly those in the Philippines and Nepal, demonstrates the importance of demystifying SCR 1325 to move beyond what is often perceived as an aspirational, soft-law instrument that lacks enforceability, to conceptualise the spirit and intention of SCR 1325 in concrete and specific ways relevant to local settings.

In many respects SCR 1325 acts as a minimum framework that states should aspire to in their efforts to integrate a gender perspective into conflict prevention and resolution processes. As evidenced by the ambitious and broad reach of these NAPs, national level initiatives have the potential to bridge the gap between women's experiences in armed conflict with broader gender equality goals. However, the development of NAPs in Asia has been limited and a state's commitment to adoption may be influenced by a number of factors.

First, the slow adoption of NAPs in Asia may relate to the resistance of Asian states to universal human-rights norms, particularly given that northern European states have driven the development of NAPs. To date, the NAPs of many developed donor states focus on the operational aspects of SCRs 1325 and 1820, including peacekeeping operations and disarmament, demobilization and reintegration, which may not adequately engage with or capture the complex reality of the political, social and cultural situation on the ground, particularly in those states emerging from protracted conflict. Further, while NAPs address gender-based violence, they may nevertheless not be sophisticated enough to address intersectional violence based on gender in connection with other facets of identity, including race, ethnicity, caste, religion or other status that underpins the social fabric of Asian states. Thus it is important that European NAPs do not represent a blueprint for the development of NAPs in Asia. In this respect, the NAPs of the Philippines and Nepal in particular provide a good illustration of how states in Asia can adopt relevant national-level initiatives, including inward-looking strategies, which link broader gender equality and development priorities, while responding to international norms on women, peace and security.

Compared with other regions, Asia lacks an Asia-wide human-rights body or mechanism which could potentially provide the structural support necessary to foster the development of NAPs on SCR 1325. Within South East Asia, the Association for South East Asian Nations (ASEAN)[21] has taken steps to address gender-based violence in ASEAN policy-making. As discussed, all ASEAN Member States have signed or acceded to CEDAW. Further, the establishment of the ASEAN Intergovernmental Commission on Human Rights (AICHR) in 2009 formalised ASEAN states' commitment to the protection and promotion of human rights and fundamental freedoms. In contrast with other regional governance systems however, Tan suggests that the 'ASEAN Way', premised upon consultation, consensus[22] and a strong adherence to the principles of sovereignty and non-interference[23] distinguishes the body from other supranational organisations, such as the European Union (Tan 2011, p. 141).

Within Europe, for example, the adoption of a Common Security and Defence Policy (CSDP) provided for the framing of a common defence policy to develop the Union's civilian and military crisis management and conflict prevention, including gender mainstreaming in CSDP. Given that gender equality is a core value of the European Union, steps have been taken to support the implementation of SCR 1325. In 2008, the Council of the European Union adopted a policy document on a *Comprehensive approach to the EU Implementation of United Nations Security Council Resolutions 1325 and 1820 on women, peace and security* (European Union 2008). The adoption of any common defence and security policy of a similar nature does not seem conceivable in the ASEAN context, let alone more widely in Asia. While the AICHR is located under the auspices of the ASEAN Political-Security Community, there has been limited engagement[24] with SCR 1325, despite the fact that many ASEAN States contribute troops to UN peacekeeping operations.

As a region, Asia has witnessed significant periods of both international and intra-national armed conflict, which have been fuelled by ideological, territorial and other disputes. Conflict and underdevelopment have exacerbated women's inequality within society. Effectively, SCR 1325 may be perceived as a transitional justice mechanism to help support and transform women's status in conflict prevention and resolution. Given that states such as the Philippines and Nepal are significantly underdeveloped, and that this has compounded armed insurgency movements, the intrinsic linkage between development and conflict resolution requires consideration in the implementation of NAPs on SCR 1325. As D'Aguirre and Pietropaoli suggest (2008, p. 358), rights-based development programmes must be adopted in conjunction with transitional justice mechanisms. The linkage between peace, security and development, including the role of gender-based violence in undermining security, may need to be addressed more explicitly within the framework of some Asian NAPs, though this coupling of aims is not without its own problems.

To illustrate, Nepal's NAP appears progressive with broad-ranging, aspirational objectives, though the Nepalese state does not appear to have sufficient resources or the capacity to support the implementation of its NAP. The Nepal NAP explicitly states that additional resources need to be mobilised from donor partner organisations. States emerging from protracted conflict may be less well-positioned either to take ownership of the drafting process or to implement NAPs independently. Reliance on external support may risk the agenda of external organisations diluting the aims and objectives of NAPs, particularly given specific conditions attached to donor funding.

Without any external drivers pushing for the adoption of NAPs, including the role of donors or UN entities like UN Women and the Peace and Support Working Group, it is not clear that some states within Asia would be in a position to adopt NAPs independently. This situation is not unique to Asia, states in Africa and other regions have relied on assistance from UN entities and donor agencies to support the development of NAPs. Given the historical resistance towards the imposition of international human rights stemming from the Asian values debate, any perceived lack of ownership of NAPs may result in a backlash against the UN and other entities, undermining their legitimacy.

Conclusion

While SCRs 1325 and 1820 may resonate with states emerging from armed conflict, the adoption of NAPs by Asian states has lacked momentum. This may be due to a number of factors, not least a scepticism on the part of states and, in some instances, a clear resistance towards the United Nations and the international human-rights norms it promulgates. To illustrate, although many Asian states have signed or ratified CEDAW, significant delays in the human-rights reporting process undermine states parties' obligations and commitment to the treaty. Further, Asia as a region lacks collective human-rights mechanisms and, where these exist, a culture of non-interference, particularly in the realm of security, may detract from the development of a common strategy to foster the development of NAPs. Additionally, while the influence of external drivers such as international co-operation with the UN and donor states may help to support capacity building, it is important that such structural support should not unduly dictate the design of NAPs.

Both the Philippine and Nepalese NAPs demonstrate the importance of local ownership and framing national level initiatives on women, peace and security with wider gender equality and development goals. Though the geopolitical landscape of Asia is incredibly diverse, the adoption of NAPs by both developed and developing states explored within this chapter, illustrates the relevance of SCRs 1325 and 1820 to the region. The effective implementation of international norms and law, in general, is very much dependent on the political will of UN Member States. While NAPs potentially aid the implementation of international norms on women, peace and security, a lack of economic and social capacity may lead to superficial results. Given the lack of a structural framework to support international human-rights norms within the Asian context the challenges of implementation are even more acute.

Notes

1 United Nations Security Council (2000) Resolution 1325, 31 October 2000, UN Doc. S/RES/1325.
2 Denmark initially adopted a National Action Plan in 2005, followed by Sweden and the United Kingdom in 2006.
3 Cote D'Ivoire adopted a National Action Plan in 2008, followed by Uganda (2008) and Liberia (2009).
4 United Nations Security Council (2008) Resolution 1820, 19 June 2008, UN Doc. S/RES/1820.
5 United Nations Security Council (2009) Resolution 1888, 30 September 2009, UN Doc. S/RES/1888.
6 United Nations Security Council (2010) Resolution 1960, 16 December 2010, UN Doc. S/RES/1960.
7 United Nations Security Council (2009) Resolution 1889, 5 October 2009, UN Doc. S/RES/1889.

8 My analysis focuses on the broadly defined sub-regions of East, South East and South Asia. I do not focus on Central Asia or the broader Asia–Pacific region, thus the Iraq, Kyrgyz Republic and Australian NAPs are not considered in my analysis.

9 PeaceWomen, a programme of the international NGO Women's International League for Peace and Freedom (WILPF) monitors rates of NAP adoption. See www.peacewomen.org for current rates of adoption and access to individual country NAPs.

10 I use the term first-generation NAP to refer to those states that have adopted subsequent revised NAPs following a NAP review cycle.

11 The Troubles, are a colloquial euphemism for the ethno-nationalist conflict which took place in Northern Ireland from the 1960s until the adoption of the Good Friday Agreement in 1998, though isolated incidents of violence have occurred since and sectarian tensions remain.

12 Declaration of the Elimination of Violence against Women in the ASEAN Region issued on 30 June 2004 Jakarta, Indonesia, by the Foreign Ministers.

13 Although Myanmar does not currently have any specific laws on violence against women the Gender Equality Network (GEN), a coordinating body for civil society organisations working on gender based in Yangon, has provided technical assistance to the Ministry of Social Welfare in the drafting of Myanmar's first anti-violence against women law together with the United Nations. As of January 2016, the draft law had yet to be publicly gazetted. For further discussion see Barrow (2015).

14 See section 14 which states that 'The State recognises the role of women in nation-building, and shall ensure the fundamental equality before the law of women and men'.

15 Laws focused on addressing violence against women include the *1997 Anti-Rape Act* (Republic Act No. 8353), the *1998 Rape Victim Assistance Protection Act (Republic Act No. 8505)*, the *2003 Anti-trafficking in Persons Act (Republic Act No. 9208)* and the *2004 Anti-Violence against Women and their Children Act (Republic Act No. 9262).*

16 *Magna Carta of Women (Republic Act No. 9710) 2009.*

17 From the foothills of the Himalayas to the Terai region (plains) with its open, porous borders to India, Nepal is a landlocked state with power and wealth concentrated in the capital city Kathmandu.

18 For example, property of a deceased husband no longer needs to be returned to the paternal family after remarriage and there is no longer the need to reach the age of thirty-five to inherit the property of a deceased husband. As many women marry at an early age in Nepal, this provision proved particularly detrimental to young widows, leaving them destitute.

19 The negative peace paradigm focuses on the direct cessation of armed hostilities, in contrast to the positive peace paradigm, articulated by Johan Galtung (1969), which includes consideration of how structural inequalities within society can be rectified in addition to the cessation of direct hostilities to help to ensure a smooth transition from conflict to a sustainable peace.

20 The National Action Plan of the United Kingdom, for example, does not include any consideration of the conflict in Northern Ireland and the human-rights violations which occurred during the Troubles, including the conflict's specific impact on women.

21 ASEAN comprises ten member states: Brunei Darussalam, Cambodia, Indonesia, Lao PDR (People's Democratic Republic), Philippines, Thailand, Malaysia, Myanmar, Singapore and Vietnam.

22 Article 20(1) of the ASEAN Charter states that, as a basic principle, decision-making within ASEAN should be premised upon consultation and consensus. For further details of the ASEAN Charter see http://www.asean.org/storage/images/ASEAN_RTK_2014/ASEAN_Charter.pdf

23 For example, the ASEAN Convention on Counter Terrorism explicitly upholds the principle of sovereign equality, territorial integrity and non-interference http://agreement.asean.org/media/download/20131229172152.pdf

24 The ASEAN Institute for Peace and Reconciliation held a workshop on strengthening women's participation in peace processes in March 2015 in the Philippines, which was the first meeting to raise awareness of SCR 1325.

Bibliography

Barrow, A. (2009) '"[It's] like a rubber band", Assessing UNSCR 1325 as a gender mainstreaming process', *International Journal of Law in Context* 5 (1), pp. 51–68.

Barrow, A. (2015) 'Contested Spaces During Transition: Regime Change in Myanmar and its Implications for Women', *Cardozo Journal of Law and Gender* 22(1), pp. 75–108.

Bell, C. and O'Rourke, C. (2010) 'Peace Agreements or "Pieces of Paper"? The Impact of UNSC Resolution 1325 on Peace Processes and their Agreements', *International and Comparative Law Quarterly*, vol. 59, pp. 941–80.

Convention on the Elimination of All Forms of Discrimination against Women, CEDAW (18 December 1979, 1249 UNTS 13).

D'Aguirre and Pietropaoli, I. (2008) 'Gender Equality, Development and Transitional Justice: The Case of Nepal', *International Journal of Transitional Justice* 2(3), pp. 356–77.

European Union (2008) *Comprehensive approach to the EU Implementation of United Nations Security Council Resolutions 1325 and 1820 on women, peace and security*, 15671/1/08 REV 1, Brussels.

Fujio, C. (2008) 'From Soft to Hard Law: Moving Resolution 1325 on Women, Peace and Security Across the Spectrum', *Georgetown Journal of Gender and Law*, pp. 215–35.

Galtung, J. (1969) 'Violence, Peace, and Peace Research', *Journal of Peace Research*, vol. 6, no. 3, pp. 167–91.

Global Network of Women Peacebuilders (2011a) *Security Council Resolution 1325: Civil Society Monitoring Report 2011 Philippines* [online] http://www.gnwp.org/sites/default/files/resource-field_media/Philippines_0.pdf

Global Network of Women Peacebuilders (2011b) *Security Council Resolution 1325: Civil Society Monitoring Report Nepal 2011* [online] http://www.gnwp.org/sites/default/files/resource-field_media/Nepal_0.pdf

Government of Nepal (2011) National Action Plan on the Implementation of the United Nations Security Council Resolutions 1325 and 1820 [2011/12-2015/16], Ministry of Peace and Reconstruction [online] http://www.gnwp.org/sites/default/files/resource-field_media/Nepal%20NAP.pdf

International Council on Human Rights Policy (2005) *Assessing the Effectiveness of National Human Rights Institutions*, International Council on Human Rights Policy and the Office of the High Commissioner for Human Rights, Versoix, Switzerland.

National Action Plan (2014) *National Action Plan of the Republic of Korea for the Implementation of United Nations Security Council Resolution 1325 on Women, Peace and Security* [online] http://www.peacewomen.org/assets/file/NationalActionPlans/republicofkorea_nap_2014.pdf

Otto, D. (2009) 'The Exile of Exclusion: Reflections on Gender Issues in International Law Over the Last Decade', *Melbourne Journal of International Law* 10 (1), pp. 11–26.

Philippine National Action Plan on UNSCRs 1325 and 1820: 2010–2016 (2009) [online] http://www.peacewomen.org/assets/file/NationalActionPlans/philippines_nap.pdf

Santos Jr., S.M. and Santos, P.V.M. with Dinampo, O.A., Kraft, H.J.S., Paredes, A.K.R.and Quilop, R.J.G. (2010) *Primed and Purposeful: Armed Groups and Human Security Efforts in the Philippines*, Rodriguez, D. (ed.) A joint publication of the South–South

Network for Non-State Armed Group Engagement and the Small Arms Survey, Geneva, Switzerland.

Swaine, A. (2009) 'Assessing the Potential of National Action Plans to Advance Implementation of United Nations Security Council Resolution 1325', *Yearbook of International Humanitarian Law*, 12, pp. 403–33.

Tan, H. (2011) *The ASEAN Intergovernmental Commission on Human Rights: Institutionalising Human Rights in Southeast Asia*, Cambridge University Press, Cambridge, UK.

United Nations Economic and Social Council for Asia and Pacific (2007) *Promoting Gender Equality in Asia Pacific: Linking the Millennium Development Goals with CEDAW and Beijing Indicators*, United Nations, Bangkok.

United Nations Security Council Presidential Statement 32 (31 October 2002) UN Doc. S/PRST/2002/32.

United Nations Security Council 'Report of the Secretary-General on women, peace and security' (13 October 2004) UN Doc. S/2004/814.

Upreti, B. R. (2006) *Armed Conflict and Peace Process in Nepal*, Adroit Publishers, New Delhi.

Woods, C. (2013) *Classifying South Korea as a Developed Market*, White Paper Report, FTSE Publications.

Part II

Gender, violence and access to justice

6 Sexual assault under cover of national security laws in India

Surabhi Chopra[1]

Introduction: women and national security

This chapter examines the experiences of women suspected of being security threats in India's internal conflict zones. Indian laws on national security grant the executive extraordinary coercive powers over individuals. Women might be affected by these laws as residents in areas perceived as volatile, or as journalists, lawyers and human-rights defenders whose work is constrained by limits on expression and assembly. Women also interact with these laws as partners and family members of suspects and defendants. Of course, security laws most directly affect women when they themselves are suspects or defendants. In this chapter, I focus on how the state interacts with this last category of women who have been suspected, investigated or tried under national security laws in India.

There is considerable literature on how women experience armed conflict (see Gardam 1997; Chinkin 2002). In contrast, research and advocacy on the gendered effects of national security laws and policies is far more limited. This gap is salient. Security-focused legislation has proliferated in the past decade, driven by felt need, by international obligation[2] and by political opportunity. As security laws have grown in number they have also expanded in scope, incorporating loosely defined offences and broad executive powers while reducing the rights of suspects and defendants. Many states have amended immigration and financial legislation to regulate security threats, embedding powers to detain and incarcerate in areas of law that lack many of the checks on executive power contained within criminal law. Some states have deployed military law and the law of armed conflict to combat terrorism. As a result, in many different countries, security laws actually and potentially affect a considerable number of people and can restrict individual rights in profound ways. As such, it is important to understand how these laws interact with structural inequalities and biases, including privilege and disadvantage based upon gender.

In the rest of this chapter, I focus on what happened to two particular women suspected by the Indian state of threatening national security. In 2004, Thangjam Manorama Devi was arrested by paramilitaries on suspicion of belonging to a violent separatist group and found raped and murdered several hours later. I look at her family's attempts to hold the armed forces accountable for her death. I also look at the ongoing criminal prosecution of Soni Sori, an indigenous rights activist in central India accused of membership in a violent radical-left group.

Through my discussion of these two cases I argue that women suspected of security offences are disproportionately vulnerable to sexualised forms of extra-legal violence by state actors. Furthermore, Indian governments have strategically misinterpreted the law to shield soldiers and the police from prosecution. The state's recalcitrance means that victims are forced to pursue justice on their own, facing serious and highly gendered gaps in the law as they do so.

I go on to describe India's legal regime on national security and then discuss what happened to Manorama Devi when she was suspected of threatening national security and Soni Sori's experience in this regard. I end by reflecting upon both cases, highlighting the state's violence and the law's failures, and consider what these imply for women suspected of threatening national security.

National security laws in India

India has multiple, expansive security laws at national level and a further layer of such laws in different Indian states. In addition to counter-terrorism laws,[3] India has laws that allow administrative detention without criminal charge of people suspected of threatening security or public order (section 13, *National Security Act 1980*). Indian law also allows the military to exercise civilian policing powers in areas that are declared 'disturbed' by national or state governments under the *Armed Forces (Special Powers) Act* (AFSPA). AFSPA gives soldiers and paramilitary personnel considerably greater powers of arrest, search, seizure and force than the civilian police have under normal circumstances. For example, the armed forces have liberal shoot-to-kill powers, unfettered by the requirement that force should be proportionate to the threat at hand.

These laws are associated with serious abuses of human rights (see Chopra 2015). Human-rights documentation reveals that custodial torture and biased detention and prosecution under security laws are commonplace in India. Human-rights abuse is facilitated not just by laws that enlarge executive powers while minimising checks and balances, but also by legal impediments to punishing such abuse. Indian law grants a substantial measure of immunity from prosecution to civil servants, police officers, prosecutors and soldiers for acts they might do when exercising national security powers.

AFSPA has the most expansive immunity clause in this regard. No legal proceedings – criminal or civil – can be launched against a member of the armed forces acting under AFSPA, unless the central government permits such proceedings (section 6, *Armed Forces (Special Powers) Act*). This means that the prosecutor on the ground must apply to the national Ministry of Home Affairs in New Delhi for permission to prosecute allegations against military personnel. India's *Criminal Procedure Code* similarly requires the Home Ministry's permission before an official belonging to any of the national civil services can be prosecuted (section 197, *Code of Criminal Procedure 1973*). Thus, a senior police official who sanctions torture in custody could not be prosecuted without express permission from the national government. While junior government personnel are not insulated from criminal prosecution to the same degree, the limited publicly available information suggests that such prosecutions are rare.[4] With this legal context in mind, I examine what happened to Thangjam Manorama Devi and Soni Sori when they were suspected of endangering national security.

The extrajudicial execution of Thangjam Manorama Devi

In 2004, the year that she was extra-judicially executed, 28-year-old Thangjam Manorama Devi worked as a weaver and lived with her parents and siblings in Imphal East district, in the north-east Indian state of Manipur.[5] Her home fell within a disturbed area under AFSPA; all or part of Manipur has been designated as such since 1958 in response to protracted separatist violence.

On 10 July 2004, a group of paramilitary personnel belonging to the Assam Rifles arrived at Manorama Devi's house at midnight. They searched the house, turned up the volume on a portable stereo, locked Manorama Devi's family in the house and dragged her outside, where she was gagged, beaten, drenched with water, attacked with a knife and sexually assaulted. Her family could hear what was happening and had a sliver of a view from a window. After torturing Manorama Devi for about half an hour the Assam Rifles told her to change her clothes. They handed the family an arrest memo and forced them to sign a 'no-claims' certificate stating that Manorama Devi's arrest had been a lawful one. The Rifles took Manorama Devi away and she was found dead and abandoned early the next morning. She had been shot several times. Investigation revealed that she had been tortured and raped before being killed.

Manorama Devi's family complained to the police even before they knew she was dead in order to secure her release. Once they learnt she had been killed they worked to get the official post-mortem report and pressed for the Assam Rifles men to be prosecuted. The Assam Rifles, in turn, lodged a criminal complaint alleging that Manorama Devi was active in a violent separatist group. The paramilitaries claimed that they had been forced to shoot her when she escaped after they arrested her. The police filed a criminal case against the dead woman and began investigating what had happened, on the basis of the Rifles' complaint. Manorama Devi's family refused to claim her body from the morgue until the police investigated her death as a matter of urgency since the family wanted to ensure that her injuries were properly recorded. The police cremated her body without her family's permission.[6]

Manorama Devi was not, by any means, the first person to be extra-judicially killed and tortured by the armed forces. However, her killing was so brutal that it triggered extensive public protests in Manipur (The Sangai Express, 2004). In response, the government of Manipur ordered an official inquiry into her death. The Assam Rifles challenged the official inquiry, arguing that, within India's federal system, the armed forces fell under the constitutional aegis of the *national* government, and the Manipur *state* government could not initiate an inquiry against the actions of soldiers or paramilitaries (*Jagmohan Singh & Ors v. State of Manipur & Ors*. AIR 2006 Gau 33).

The High Court initially agreed with the Rifles and New Delhi, but on appeal reversed its previous decision and, in 2011, it held that the inquiry was constitutional because the Manipur government was responding to a serious disruption of public order, and that maintaining public order is the express constitutional responsibility of the state rather than the Centre within India's federal division of labour (*Jagmohan Singh & Ors v. State of Manipur & Ors*. (2011) 6 GLR 577, paras. 56–9). Refusing to accept public disclosure of the damning report, the central government appealed to the Supreme Court, which has yet to conclusively decide the matter.

The Assam Rifles snubbed queries from the commission of inquiry and the Manipur government; they also ducked criminal investigation, first by refusing to co-operate with the police and then by the simple expedient of moving out of Manipur. In 2010, Manorama Devi's mother and brother petitioned the Gauhati High Court, asking that the government be ordered to compensate them, release the inquiry report and prosecute the individuals who killed Manorama Devi. The petition remains pending. Meanwhile, in legal proceedings at national level about the commission of inquiry, the Supreme Court ordered the Indian Ministry of Defence to give Manorama Devi's family a copy of the contested report, as well as the sum of Rs. 10,00,000 in 2014.[7] The Ministry of Defence complied, though it pointedly classified the money as financial aid not compensation (Imphal Free Press 2015). The perpetrators have not been investigated, let alone charged or prosecuted.

The custodial torture of Soni Sori

Soni Sori is a public school teacher and indigenous rights activist from the central Indian state of Chhattisgarh. She belongs to one of the relatively few middle-class families from her tribal group in the very poor region of Dantewada.

Echoing the experience of many resource-rich regions, mining in Chhattisgarh has brought little benefit to indigenous inhabitants. And, as in other such regions, extreme deprivation combined with disruption by the extractive industry has fuelled non-violent protest as well as violent challenge. The Chhattisgarh government has responded to armed radical-left groups with heavy-handed, hair-trigger policing and severe restrictions on expression and peaceful protest (see *Chhattisgarh Special Public Safety Act 2005*).

In September 2011 the police in Dantewada accused Soni Sori and her nephew, Lingaram Kodopi, of extracting protection money on behalf of a Maoist group from the Essar mining conglomerate (Amnesty International 2012). A police constable from Dantewada admitted to a national news magazine that the police had pressured Sori and her nephew to participate in entrapping an agent of the mining company and had framed them when they refused (Chaudhury 2011). This was not the first time that Sori, her nephew and other members of her politically active family had faced police action (Najar 2014). In 2011, she had several criminal cases pending against her; she had previously been acquitted in five cases for lack of evidence against her.[8]

Fearing what the police might do Sori absconded to Delhi to evade arrest. When she was arrested in Delhi on 4 October 2011 and brought before a court she pleaded not to be sent back to Chhattisgarh. The court refused her request and handed the matter over to the courts in Chhattisgarh, who in turn handed her over for questioning to the police in Dantewada, but warned the police not to torture her. Sori was accused of transferring protection money from a mining company to an armed group.

Almost as soon as the police had Soni Sori in their custody, on 8 and 9 October 2011, they tortured her. She was in evident pain and barely able to walk when she appeared in Dantewada district court on 10 October 2011. She had been beaten and sexually assaulted by the police. Sori was taken to hospital with head and back injuries where she was handcuffed to the bed and barred from contact with journalists. In an interview on 29 July 2014 she recounted being tortured:

> *The superintendent, Ankit Garg, asked me to sign documents that would confirm I was involved with the Maoists. I refused. He then asked the lady constables to leave . . .*
>
> *The police officials started abusing me, calling me a whore and saying I indulge in sexual acts with Maoists. They stripped me naked, made me stand in an 'attention' position and gave me electric shocks on various parts of my body. I still didn't relent. They then shoved red chili powder inside my vagina. By now, I was losing consciousness, but I refused to sign the documents. The cops started inserting stones into my private parts. Many stones – so many that they started falling out. I finally collapsed.*
>
> *The next morning, I could barely move when I was taken to court.*
>
> (Sur 2014)

Sori went on a hunger strike in protest and wrote to the Supreme Court detailing what she had suffered, petitioning the Court for relief. She asked the Supreme Court to transfer her to New Delhi for a medical examination. The Court granted the request in part, ordering that Sori be medically examined in a hospital outside Chhattisgarh, in Kolkota, the capital of the neighboring state of West Bengal.[9] This medical examination confirmed her allegations, revealing sexual and non-sexual physical injuries. A CT scan found stones that the police had forced into her body.[10]

Despite this medical evidence of torture Soni Sori was not granted bail. Instead, the Supreme Court transferred her to a different prison in the capital of Chhattisgarh,[11] and then to New Delhi where she could receive medical treatment.[12] It was almost two years later, in November 2013, that the Supreme Court granted Sori bail conditional upon furnishing a surety and reporting weekly to her local police station.[13] Most onerously, the Supreme Court barred her from entering Chhattisgarh, as a result she was separated from her three young children even after release from prison. Sori was not allowed to visit her family even when her husband died in

August 2013 (Sur 2014). It was not until February 2014 that the Supreme Court ameliorated Sori's bail conditions and she was able to enter Chhattisgarh and return home (Amnesty International 2014). The criminal cases against Soni Sori continue. The government of Chhattisgarh does not appear to have initiated legal proceedings against the police personnel who tortured her.

State violence and failures of the law

In this section, I focus first on women's vulnerability to violence from state actors wielding national security powers. Indian security laws enable violence by the state in general. I argue that women are disproportionately vulnerable to sexual violence and that such violence aims to terrorise not just individual victims but also the communities in which they live. Victims then face an egregious barrier if they report these crimes – although the law does not actually shield officials from prosecution for sexual violence, it has been misused to grant them legal immunity. In addition, the law – even if applied in good faith – fails to capture serious and recurring violence against women. I identify some of these failures below.

Vulnerability to sexual violence

Security laws, with their expanded powers of search and arrest, create far greater room for unlawful violence, sexual and otherwise, than ordinary criminal laws. Soni Sori's and Manorama Devi's experiences suggest that women who are processed under national security laws are highly vulnerable to sexual violence and other forms of physical violence from state actors. Human-rights documentation confirms that the armed forces and the police have committed serious sexual assaults against women when exercising national security powers.

Media coverage and human-rights reports suggest that women suspected of endangering security face unlawful sexual violence even before they are in custody. Soldiers and police have sexually assaulted women while searching their homes. In August 1996, Arubi Devi was raped by two soldiers of the Maha Regiment in her home in Manipur while her husband and child were made to watch (see Begum 2012, p. 278). Lilabati Bahsya and Maniki Bezbaruah were similarly raped in 1998 by soldiers searching their homes for violent insurgents (ibid., p. 279). Soldiers have committed sexual violence in groups, sometimes upon groups of women. In 1987, the army occupied Oinam village in Manipur for four months, torturing and attacking local residents (see Turner and Nepram 2004, pp. 28–9). Many women in Oinam were sexually assaulted; two women in labour were denied medical help and forced to give birth while soldiers watched. In another example of mass sexual violence, in 1991, paramilitaries sexually assaulted at least thirty-seven women while conducting a search operation in Baghmara and Agrungguri villages of the Barpeta district in Assam. Begum reports that these events have never been formally investigated (see Begum 2012, p. 281). A couple of years before the mass sexual violence in Barpeta, a similar episode occurred in Ujanmaidan in the state of Tripura, when the Assam Rifles raped fourteen women belonging to tribal communities in Purba Gobindabari village (see Turner and Nepram 2004, p. 29; Begum 2012).

Manorama Devi, like the women discussed above, was tortured in her own home before she was formally put under arrest. She was attacked where her family could hear what was happening to her. Again, many women have been similarly attacked by the police and armed forces in front of their families or in public. Such open sexual violence suggests, of course, that the police and armed forces feel a sense of impunity when operating under the cover of national security laws. It also suggests that sexual violence is being used to intimidate not just individual victims but entire neighbourhoods and communities, and that the public nature of these attacks on women is deliberate, not aberrant.

Soldiers and the police have been violent when they are at large, but they have also been violent behind institutional walls. Women in custody for security-related offences are, arguably, more vulnerable to custodial violence than women arrested, detained or imprisoned for other types of crime. India's anti-terrorism law allows pre-charge detention for 180 days (section 43D (5) *Unlawful Activities Prevention Act 1967*). Preventive detention laws go further, compounding detention without charge with absence of judicial scrutiny and restricted access to lawyers. These protracted stretches in police custody expose security suspects to a greater risk of sexual violence. In addition, if women seek to expose or challenge such violence, both state and public sympathy for them might be muted because they are accused of threatening national security. The judge who remanded Soni Sori to police custody in 2011 was clearly aware that she was at risk of torture – the police would not ordinarily be cautioned against torturing a defendant in their custody. His willingness to risk a woman being tortured might have been because Sori was accused of a crime against the state rather than another individual. Later, Sori's request for a medical exam outside Chhattisgarh, despite being in pain and needing urgent medical attention, suggests that she feared doctors and nurses within the state would not be neutral when examining her.

State actors exercising security powers have greater legal powers and discretion, and correspondingly more opportunities to breach the bounds of their power. Since the ambit of lawful force under security laws is wider, the penumbra of *unlawful* force administered by state actors correspondingly involves quite extreme violence. As a result, individuals who are investigated or arrested under national security laws are highly vulnerable to extra-legal violence. Women who fall within this group are particularly at risk of sexual violence, both within state institutions and outside them.

It is entirely possible that men processed under security laws are also frequently sexually assaulted by the police and the armed forces, and that male victims do not speak about it. Existing human-rights research does not suggest this; nor do medical records used during past litigation by male victims of human-rights abuses by the police and armed forces. However, it is possible that professionals investigating human-rights abuses may simply not inquire about sexual assault against men because they are not expected to suffer this form of violence.

That said, it is worth noting that sexual violence against women might also be chronically silenced, with only the most serious violence coming to light. The initial post-mortem report on Manorama Devi's body failed to mention the sexual injuries she had sustained. Similarly, the first medical examination report after Soni Sori was tortured catalogued her visible injuries but did not acknowledge the sexual assault she had faced. Women who are sexually assaulted by state actors are likely to face considerable social stigma, often from their closest family members, and have little or no recourse to counselling and support. For example in the case of Arubi Devi, who fought to bring the soldiers who raped her to justice, but even while doing so, was rejected and mistreated by her husband (see Begum 2012, p. 278). Sexual violence that is not witnessed by bystanders; sexual violence short of rape; rape that does not result in visible, external physical injuries; these might all be under-reported or ignored by the police, even when victims speak out.

Immunity provisions as alibi

There is little doubt that the allegations made by Soni Sori and Manorama Devi's family are credible. Medical evidence produced under the supervision of the Indian Supreme Court confirms Sori's allegations of custodial torture. Manorama Devi's family can give eyewitness testimony about what the Assam Rifles personnel who came to their house did. Post-mortem medical reports show that Manorama Devi was sexually assaulted, beaten, knifed and shot several times. Further, an official commission of inquiry has concluded that she was tortured to death.

However, despite the possibility of pressing a credible case in court, the governments of Manipur and Chhattisgarh have not prosecuted the serious crimes committed in either case. For some of these crimes, the state government would need the Centre's permission to prosecute. However, in relation to sexual violence committed in both cases, any statutory insulation from criminal proceedings should, inherently, be irrelevant.

The national government's permission to prosecute is necessary for actions by state personnel that are taken *in good faith*, i.e. actions meant to enforce the law or official policies. Sexual violence, by its very nature, can never constitute an act committed in the service of a law or government policy. Other forms of physical force by the police or military – restraining an individual, shooting at someone, even shooting to kill – will, under some circumstances, be lawful. When considering whether such physical force constitutes an offence a court has to evaluate whether the violence exceeded the threshold of force or was violence permitted under a particular law. In contrast, there is no minimum level of sexual force that is legally permissible in *any* circumstance. Maintaining that sexual crimes cannot be prosecuted without official permission is legally absurd; national and state governments are arguing, in effect, that sexual violence by state personnel could potentially be permitted under Indian law.

This argument is so untenable that legal reform is not really necessary to shift the status quo. The central government simply needs to clarify – and could have clarified many years ago – that acts of sexual violence do not fall within the immunity provisions discussed above, and can be prosecuted without permission from

New Delhi. In 2013 such a clarification was finally included in the *Code of Criminal Procedure*. Section 197 of the *Code*, which provides that the central government's permission is necessary in order to prosecute senior officials, now includes the explanation that such permission is *not* required when a government official is accused of a sexual offence. Dispiritingly, the even wider immunity provision in the AFSPA has not been similarly clarified, despite repeated calls for clarification from civil society and a number of official bodies.

Even without such clarification state governments could apply for permission to prosecute sexual offences committed by soldiers or civilian government functionaries while using national security powers, rather than simply citing legal immunity provisions as a reason for being passive. If the Centre refuses permission, state governments could challenge such a refusal in court, requesting judicial clarification over whether sexual crimes can ever constitute acts done *in good faith*, in pursuit of an official purpose. At the local level, the particular police station that receives a complaint of sexual violence or torture could investigate the offence and gather evidence – after all, legal injunctions on prosecution do not bar *investigating* allegations of serious crime. In failing even to investigate complaints by individuals and their families, the police allow evidence to be lost and destroyed. Particularly in sexual crimes, if medical and forensic evidence is not gathered soon after the offence occurs, successful prosecution becomes very difficult.

The contents of the law fall far short when responding to state violence against women who are suspected of threatening national security. But even the limited potential of the law has been wasted because governments have used provisions on legal immunity as an alibi for inaction. At least as far as sexual violence is concerned this supposed obstacle to legal action is entirely spurious.

Types of sexual violence: recognised and unacknowledged

While, on the one hand, women face heightened risks of sexual violence when they fall under the ambit of national security laws, on the other hand they encounter several barriers in seeking redress. One basic barrier is that particular types of violence are not acknowledged as criminal offences and captured as such by the law and, more fundamentally, might not even be recognised as violence at all.

Rape is, of course, a long-standing offence under Indian criminal law (section 375 *(offence of rape), Indian Penal Code 1860*). However, until very recently, rape was defined to include only penile penetration of the vagina. Soni Sori was sexually attacked in a manner that was not, at the time this attack took place, recognised as rape under Indian law. While the shocking violence Soni Sori suffered – the police forced stones into her body – might have fallen under the offence of 'causing hurt using a dangerous weapon' under the *Indian Penal Code*, this offence does not capture the sexual, intimate, and therefore particularly traumatic, violation at issue.

Indian criminal law was amended in 2013 in the wake of strong public protests after a young woman was brutally gang raped and died as a result of her injuries.

This recent amendment altered the offence of rape to include non-consensual oral, vaginal or anal penetration of the victim's body with parts of the perpetrator's body or with physical objects (section 9, *Criminal Law (Amendment) Act No. 13, 2013*). Had this new offence existed earlier, it would have been able to recognise that sexual penetration with knives and stones was violence as grave as the violence criminalised by rape as it has traditionally been defined. The traditional definition of rape, with its exclusive focus on penile penetration seems to locate the gravity of the violence at issue at least partially in the perceived breach of a woman's chastity, the risk of pregnancy, the possible loss of virginity. When the law recognises that the essence of the offence is the intimate sexual violation of the victim's body, when it privileges the protection of bodily integrity, it is better able to criminalise serious sexual violence.

Just as forcibly penetrating someone was not properly recognised as a crime before 2013, the law similarly fails to recognise other types of sexual violence that have been inflicted by state personnel exercising security powers. In 2011, the act of stripping a woman prisoner in front of other prisoners and guards could only constitute the antiquated charge of 'outraging the modesty of a woman' (section 354 (assault or criminal force to a woman with intent to outrage her modesty), *Indian Penal Code 1860*). This is a mild charge, which carries a potential maximum sentence of two years. It is designed to preserve a woman's 'modesty' rather than protect her rights to dignity and bodily integrity, and simply does not capture the particular act of sexualised violence that Soni Sori suffered in an adequate or specific way. In the Indian context, the failure to recognise stripping another person's clothes as an offence was particularly salient. Public stripping is a form of violence that tends to be directed at women who, like Soni Sori, belong to traditionally *low* castes and tribal communities.

Responding to a petition about the Assam Rifles' occupation of Oinam village in 1987, the Supreme Court used the euphemism 'sexual exploitation' to describe forced provision of sexual services to the paramilitaries (*Manipur Baptist Convention and Anr. v. Union of India* (1988) 1 GLR 433). The Supreme Court took seriously the petitioner's demand for an injunction, but its response was in an entirely paternalistic mode. It said that extracting forced labour 'from the weaker sex' was a grave breach of the law, and positioned itself as the 'protector' of the women involved (*Ibid,*, para. 9). The Court noted with approval that residents of Oinam had restricted themselves to 'the facts', i.e. that particular women had been held in a concentration camp by the Assam Rifles, and found later in 'a dazed and choked condition', but had not been tempted to make 'false and wild allegation[s]' of rape (i*bid*, para. 6). Had the Supreme Court reflected, even in a cursory way, on what genuine consent means it would have discerned that these women had been imprisoned in conditions where uncoerced consent was simply not possible. Therefore each sexual act that women were forced to perform was an act of rape, and this was not just sexual violence but also a particularly invasive and serious form of forced labour. Women in Oinam were also forced to perform highly gendered domestic labour – cooking, cleaning, washing clothes – for Assam Rifles personnel. While not sexual, this too was a form of forced labour. The Court simply did not see such manifest, shocking violence, but did seem to have scrutinised victims' accounts for signs of exaggeration.

To sum up, violence against women, and sexual violence in particular, is neglected in different ways. Police, prosecutors and courts fail to perceive that particular violent acts would fit within established, pre-existing offences. Thus, rape in Oinam village was miscategorised (and trivialised) as 'exploitation'. In addition, violence might not be detected because investigating authorities ignore the likelihood that it could occur. Manorama Devi's lawyers had to press for a second post-mortem report to place her more intimate injuries on the record. Further, particular types of gendered violence are not recognised by the law at all. Such recognition is crucial, particularly for forms of violence that recur, like stripping women of their clothes or forced sexual penetration not captured by the traditional definition of rape. These recurrent, and in that sense *established*, acts of violence can quite easily be delineated as offences within the law. Legal recognition makes it harder for the state to simply ignore or dismiss such violence.

Failure to recognise torture

Recognising specific types of violence as distinct offences would make the law better able to respond to violence against women. At the same time, when state actors are violent there are other fundamental gaps in the law that hinder attempts to hold them accountable. The *Indian Penal Code* stipulates a higher punishment for a public servant who commits custodial rape (section 375 and 376, *Indian Penal Code 1860*) or has intercourse 'not amounting to rape' with a woman in his charge or custody.[14] However, the *Code* did not, until it was amended in 2013, regard sexual violence by state actors in positions of responsibility as an aggravated form of the basic offence at issue.

More fundamentally, Indian law does not criminalise torture as a distinct offence, even though India is a party to the United Nations Convention Against Torture and Other Cruel, Inhuman or Degrading Treatment or Punishment. Just as Soni Sori and Manorama Devi suffered forms of sexual assault not recognised by the law at the time, this violence also simultaneously constituted torture. Recognising the infliction of torture and cruel, inhuman and degrading treatment as discrete, and serious, offences would allow the state actor's entire course of abusive conduct to be taken into account, including actions that might not be pre-existing, freestanding criminal offences but cumulatively intensify the victim's suffering. For example, actions such as the Assam Rifles locking Manorama Devi's family inside their house, or the police handcuffing Soni Sori to her hospital bed, could be captured as a course of conduct that constitutes torture. In addition, creating the offence of torture would allow the law to label abuse by soldiers and the police that does not fit within traditional offences, such as forcing women to perform domestic labour or the horrific act of forcing someone to deliver a child in public, as the Assam Rifles did in Oinam village.

Failure to recognise ethnic bias as an aggravating factor

Just as sexual violence against Soni Sori and Manorama Devi was a form of torture, it might also have been a form of ethnic persecution. The type of violence that Soni Sori faced when she was stripped of her clothes has characteristically been directed at women belonging to disadvantaged castes and tribes in the Indian context. Both Soni Sori and Manorama Devi belonged to minority tribal groups that tend to be stereotyped as primitive. People from north-eastern India, including Manipur, are racially distinct from people belonging to other parts of the subcontinent. Women in north-eastern tribal cultures tend to have greater autonomy and independence than their counterparts in northern and southern India. As a result, they are often stereotyped as sexually promiscuous. We do not know what police and paramilitaries said to each woman or their families or one another while torturing them. However, genuinely reckoning with what happened involves examining whether racial and ethnic bias shaped the devastating violence inflicted on both women.

Investigating whether prejudice was at play is particularly important when state actors commit human-rights abuses while wielding national security powers. In areas where terrorist or insurgent movements are active state personnel might regard the stereotypes that attach to differences of ethnicity, race or religion as intrinsic to the violence they are trying to control. Prejudice and bias, in turn, make it easier to dehumanise entire communities and view them as disloyal, dangerous and, therefore, deserving of brutality. Soni Sori, who had campaigned for indigenous rights for many years, is likely to have been particularly vulnerable to such bias. India has a law that criminalises identity-based violence against individuals from traditionally disadvantaged castes and tribal groups (*Scheduled Caste and Scheduled Tribes (Prevention of Atrocities) Act 1989*). However, it does not appear that the state has investigated in either case whether violence was fuelled by bias.

Failure to recognise misogyny as an aggravating factor

Just as ethnic prejudice motivates violence, so does misogyny. Misogyny is self-evident when women face sexual violence from state actors. However, it is also palpable in non-sexual violence and torture inflicted by the police and armed forces. Post-mortem examination of Manorama Devi's body revealed that the Assam Rifles had shot her on the breasts and genitals multiple times.[15] Some years earlier, when Assam Rifles personnel forced two women to give birth in public in Oinam village, denying them medical health as well as privacy, they were seeking to humiliate and physically endanger both women in a specifically gendered way that could not have been done to a man. When soldiers have assaulted women while forcing their families to watch, or attacked women in public, the victims are being targeted instrumentally, as repositories of family and community pride. When the Supreme Court so easily treats the rape of north-eastern women as 'exploitation', i.e. as coerced prostitution, the court displays both misogyny and racism.

Indian law does not treat misogyny as an aggravating factor when prosecuting and punishing offences. But it should. Just as many legal systems treat racially aggravated violence as more serious than the core crime alone, a full accounting of Manorama Devi's death and Soni Sori's torture requires acknowledging and punishing the prejudice that animated these crimes.

Conclusion: privatising accountability

After Manorama Devi's death public outrage drove the Manipur government to initiate an official inquiry. In comparison, the Chhattisgarh government did not even take the minimal step of establishing a commission to inquire into Soni Sori's experiences in custody. On the contrary, the police officer who supervised the torture of Sori was awarded a national honour for his services to counterinsurgency operations in Chhattisgarh (Sethi 2012).

These two cases demonstrate that state and national governments are passive, if not outright hostile, towards victims of sexual assault and torture by state personnel. As a result, victims and their families are forced to seek accountability on their own. Criminal prosecution is controlled by the state, and civil litigation – suing the wrongdoer – is expensive and difficult. Instead, victims have petitioned the judiciary for relief under public law, arguing that their constitutional rights to life and freedom from torture have been violated.

Manorama Devi's mother petitioned the High Court in Manipur, asking that the state government compensate her and prosecute the individuals who killed her daughter. As discussed earlier, it was not until 2014 that the tangled litigation following Manorama Devi's death resulted in monetary aid for Khumanlei Devi. However, the judiciary has not, so far, ordered the executive to prosecute the perpetrators. Moreover, the money granted is pointedly not compensatory – the Ministry of Defence has not conceded any wrongdoing. Soni Sori has been petitioning the Supreme Court to grant her an unusual remedy, directed towards prosecuting her torturers. She has asked the court to appoint a special investigation team, comprising police officers from outside Chhattisgarh, to investigate her complaints of custodial torture. So far, the Court has ignored her requests.[16]

Litigation in India is expensive, slow and bewildering for the layperson. For example, it took nine court hearings over several weeks to persuade the Supreme Court to order a medical exam for Soni Sori outside Chhattisgarh, ensure the Court's order was implemented by the hospital in Kolkota and confirm that the Court had received the completed medical report. Victims like Soni Sori and Manorama Devi's family navigate the legal system while absorbing the trauma of rape and torture and grieving for a loved one.

Both Manorama Devi's and Soni Sori's cases are so terrible and tragic that they could be considered *sui generis*, unrepresentative of women's experiences under national security laws more widely. However, while these particular, very grave, cases might lie at the end of a spectrum, they alert us nevertheless to women's vulnerability to human-rights abuses under the cover of security laws, and to the challenges victims and their families face in seeking redress.

I have argued above that the content of security laws makes it easier for state personnel to commit human-rights abuses. Gaps in Indian law, some gendered (such as the dated definition of rape) and others general (such as the failure to criminalise torture), mean that violence against women like Manorama Devi and Soni Sori escape recognition. While the law lacks purchase on the types of violence that state personnel have inflicted, national and state governments have reneged on their responsibility to punish violence against women by state actors. Particularly with regard to sexual violence, the executive has amplified legal immunity provisions in a way that is clearly arbitrary.

Mitigating the hazards to women of being a national security suspect requires deep legal reform, checks and balances on executive decision-making and sustained scrutiny and legal challenge by civil society. Discussing such reforms in detail is beyond the scope of this chapter. However, attempts at reform must be embedded in a knowledge of how national security laws actually affect women, in India, South Asia and further afield.

Notes

1 This chapter is a condensed version of an article titled 'Dealing with dangerous women: Sexual assault under cover of national security laws in India', first published in 2016 in the *Boston University International Law Journal* 34(2), adapted here with the journal's kind permission. I first explored some of the ideas during a consultancy project for the International Development Research Centre in August–September 2012 on national security laws in India. I am grateful to the Centre, and in particular to Navsharan Singh for her feedback on my (unpublished) consultancy report, *The Law on National Security in India: When the Exceptional and Normal Intersect* (October 2012, on file with the author). I presented an early draft of this paper at the conference *Gender, Violence and the State in Asia* organised by the Centre for Rights and Justice at the Law Faculty, The Chinese University of Hong Kong. I am grateful to conference organisers Amy Barrow and Joy Chia for inviting me to participate and for their very helpful comments. I would also like to thank Karen Ka Yuet Ng and Ria Singh Sawhney for assisting me in this research.

2 The UN Security's Council's Resolution 1373 obligated UN Member States to take legislative and policy measures to combat terrorist. See UN SCR 1373, (28 September 2001) UN Doc. S/Res/1373. However, SCR 1373 does not emphasise compatibility with international human-rights standards.

3 The current anti-terrorism laws are the *Unlawful Activities (Prevention) Act 1967* and the *National Investigation Agency Act 2008*.

4 There are no publicly available statistics on the number of applications for permission to prosecute government officials, civil or military. As of 1995, no individual from the north-east states had applied for permission to file a civil suit (South Asia Human Rights Documentation Centre 1995).

5 Biographical details about Thangjam Manorama Devi are drawn from the Writ Petition under Article 226, Constitution of India filed in 2010 before the Gauhati High Court by Thangjam Ongbi Khumanlei Devi and Thangjam Dolendro Singh [on file with author] [hereinafter Khumanlei Devi writ petition].

6 Khumanlei Devi writ petition.

7 Rs.10,00,000 was approximately US$ 16,000 at the currency exchange rate on 1 December 2014 (Jaiswal 2014).

8 Order in *Lingaram Kodopi v. State of Chhattisgarh* Petition(s) for Special Leave to Appeal (Crl) No(s).7898/2013, *Soni Sori v. State of Chhattisgarh* SLP(Crl) No. 7913 of

2013, Petition(s) for Special Leave to Appeal (Crl) No(s).7898/2013, Supreme Court of India, 12 November 2013.

9 Order in *Soni Sori v. State of Chhattisgarh* WP(Crl) No. 206 of 2011, 20 October 2011.

10 The medical report is summarised by the Supreme Court in its Order dated 2 May 2012, in *Soni Sori v. State of Chhattisgarh* CRL.M.P. Nos. 1104, 4981 and 8976 of 2012 in WP(Crl) No. 206 of 2011.

11 Order in *Soni Sori v. State of Chhattisgarh* WP(Crl) No. 206 of 2011, 20 October 2011.

12 *Soni Sori v. State of Chhattisgarh* CRL.M.P. Nos.1104, 4981 and 8976 of 2012 in WP(Crl) No. 206 of 2011.

13 Order in *Lingaram Kodopi v. State of Chhattisgarh* Petition(s) for Special Leave to Appeal (Crl) No(s).7898/2013, *Soni Sori v. State of Chhattisgarh* SLP(Crl) No. 7913 of 2013, Petition(s) for Special Leave to Appeal (Crl) No(s).7898/2013, Supreme Court of India, 12 November 2013.

14 Previously, Section 376B and 376C, *Indian Penal Code 1860*; Section 376C, *Indian Penal Code 1860* after amendment by the *Criminal Law (Amendment) Act 2013*.

15 Post-mortem report dated 12 July 2004, Regional Institute of Medical Sciences, Imphal, Ref. PM. No. 211/04 [on file with author].

16 Supreme Court Order in *Soni Sori v. State of Chhattisgarh* WP(Crl) No. 206 of 2011, 2 May 2012.

Bibliography

Amnesty International (2012) 'India: Release Soni Sori on International Women's Day' [online] http://www.amnesty.org/en/for-media/press-releases/india-release-soni-sori-international-women-s-day-2012-03-07.

Amnesty International (2014) 'Amnesty India welcomes bail for Prisoners of Conscience Soni Sori and Lingaram Kodopi' [online] http://www.amnesty.org.in/show/entry/amnesty-india-welcomes-bail-for-prisoners-of-conscience-soni-sori-and-linga.

Begum, A. (2012) 'Rethinking Justice for sexual crimes: Realities in North Eastern states of India', in Katjasungkana, N. and Wieringa, S. E. (eds), *The Future of Asian Feminisms: Confronting Fundamentalisms, Conflicts and Neo-liberalism*, Cambridge Scholars Publishing, Newcastle, UK, pp. 266–83.

Chaudhury, S. (2011) 'The Inconvenient Truth Of Soni Sori', *Tehelka*, vol 8, issue 41, 15 October 2011 [online] http://archive.tehelka.com/story_main50.asp?filename=Ne151011 coverstory.asp.

Chinkin, C. (2002) 'Feminist Reflections on International Criminal Law', in Zimmermann, A. (ed.) and Heinz, U. E. (asst. ed.). *International Criminal Law and the Current Development of Public International Law*. Duncker and Humblot, Berlin, Germany, pp. 125–60.

Chopra, S. (2015) 'National Security Laws in India: The Unraveling of Constitutional Constraints', *Oregon Review of International Law* 17(1), [online] http://ssrn.com/abstract=2441652.

Gardam, J. (1997) 'Women and the Law of Armed Conflict: Why the Silence?', *International and Comparative Law Quarterly* 46(1), pp. 55–80.

Imphal Free Press (2015) ''Defence Ministry releases Rs. 10 lakhs ex-gratia for Manorama's mother as per Supreme Court order', 13 March 2015 [online] http://kanglaonline.com/2015/03/defence-ministry-releases-rs-10-lakhs-exgratia-for-manoramas-mother-as-per-supreme-court-order/.

Jaiswal, A. (2014) 'Help pours in for AAP candidate Soni Sori in Bastar', *Times of India*, 1 April, [online] http://timesofindia.indiatimes.com/home/lok-sabha-elections-2014/news/Help-pours-in-for-AAP-candidate-Soni-Sori-in-Bastar/articleshow/33047960.cms?

Najar, N. (2014) 'Tribal Activist Candidate Poses a Problem for Aam Aadmi', *New York Times*, 27 March [online] http://india.blogs.nytimes.com/2014/03/27/tribal-activist-candidate-poses-a-problem-for-aam-aadmi/.

Sethi, A. (2012) 'Activists shocked at gallantry award for Chhattisgarh cop' *The Hindu*, 26 January [online] http://www.thehindu.com/news/national/activists-shocked-at-gallantry-award-for-chhattisgarh-cop/article2834675.ece.

South Asia Human Rights Documentation Centre (1995) *Armed Forces Special Powers Act: A Study in National Security Tyranny*, New Delhi.

Sur, P. (2014) 'The long and lonely fight: Q&A with Indian tribal rights activist Soni Sori', *Women Under Siege*, 29 July [online] http://www.womenundersiegeproject.org/blog/entry/the-long-and-lonely-fight-qa-with-indian-tribal-rights-activist-soni-sori.

The Sangai Express (2004) 'Protests erupt over custodial death of woman, many nail AR', 12 July [online] http://www.e-pao.net/epRelatedNews.asp?heading=1&src=130704.

Turner, M. and Nepram, B. (2004) *The Impact of Armed Violence in Northeast India: Mini case study for the Armed Violence and Poverty Initiative*, University of Bradford, UK.

7 Public interest litigation on violence against women in Bangladesh

Possibilities and limits

Sara Hossain[1]

Introduction

This chapter examines the use of public interest litigation (PIL) as a strategy to address violence against women in Bangladesh, and its potential and limits. It focuses on two cases, one relating to the investigation and prosecution of *fatwa* violence and the other on medical evidence collection in rape cases where the petitioners were a coalition of rights and development organisations and activists.

The chapter first briefly outlines the framework for legal protection of women's rights in cases of gender-based violence, highlighting some of the constraints to seeking justice, including discriminatory laws and the denial of protection to certain individuals and groups. Second, it discusses how PIL has developed and the extent to which it has been used to address gender-based violence. The third section reviews the two cases, setting out the context and process through which PIL was identified as a relevant strategy, the directions sought from the courts and the responses of relevant state agencies. This section identifies some of the 'successes' that resulted, including: the judicial recognition of the practice of issuing *fatwas* as a form of gender-based violence; the 'two-finger test' as gender discriminatory; greater public understanding of the impact of such violence; and the responsibilities of public authorities. The final section highlights the limits of PIL, particularly where it is not followed by a co-ordinated response from public authorities, sustained activism in the media and by rights organisations, and how these challenges are exacerbated where the issues arise in a more adversarial context involving powerful public or private actors and institutions.

Legal framework for addressing gender-based violence

The *Constitution of Bangladesh*, adopted in 1972 after a nine-month war of independence from Pakistan, was avowedly secular and established the new nation as the People's Republic of Bangladesh, rather than the Islamic Republic from which it had emerged. It guarantees fundamental rights and freedoms, including to life, liberty, equality and non-discrimination on various grounds, including sex and religion, further discussed below.

In terms of specific statutory protections against gender-based violence, colonial-era legislation has been supplemented by a raft of special laws, carving out exceptions to the general criminal law. These have established new offences of violence against women (dowry violence, acid attacks and custodial rape), set up special tribunals for fast-track trials, limited the rights of the accused, put in place protective measures for victims and witnesses and, most recently, civil remedies for victims of domestic violence.[2]

Until the 1980s, colonial-era criminal laws defined the main offences relating to violence against women and relevant procedures. The *Bangladesh Penal Code 1860* sets out offences of violence and sexual violence, such as abduction, kidnapping, trafficking and rape, among others. The *Child Marriage Restraint Act 1929* penalised the offence of child marriage but was little used. Existing definitions of offences either did not recognise certain forms of violence against women, or exposed women from particular communities to the threat of harassment. For example, marital rape is not recognised as an offence, with a very limited exception where a wife is aged below thirteen (Section 375 *Bangladesh Penal Code*) or under sixteen (Section 9 *Suppression of Violence against Women and Children Act 2000*). The new law on domestic violence does define sexual violence but there are not yet reported instances of its use in such cases. Criminalisation of, so-called, unnatural offences meant that lesbian, gay, bisexual and transgender (LGBT) women faced a risk of potential arrest and prosecution (Section 377, *Bangladesh Penal Code*). The definition of the offence of 'outraging modesty' reinforced stereotyped and discriminatory notions and images of women and girls, implying that those who lack 'modesty' cannot face harassment (Section 354, *Bangladesh Penal Code*).

From the 1980s onwards, in the wake of the first UN Conference on Women and in response to increasing activism by women's rights organisations in the country, a series of new laws were adopted that addressed gender-based violence. The *Cruelty to Women (Deterrent Punishment) Ordinance 1983* was soon followed by the *Dowry Prohibition Ordinance 1986*. Instead of a comprehensive review and revision of existing laws, the pattern set for law reform was to carve out an exception by making a special law, defining new offences, enhancing penalties, fast-tracking trials and limiting procedural safeguards for the accused, including imposing restrictions on bail and establishing special tribunals. This model continued to be followed in the 1990s on all laws on violence against women, and in the latest iteration in *Suppression of Violence against Women and Children Act 2000*, amended in 2003 (the VAW Act). The VAW Act defines the offences of: acid attack; rape; rape followed by murder; trafficking; kidnapping and abduction; sexual oppression; dowry related violence or death; and maiming a child for the purposes of begging. The *Acid Crimes Control Act 2002*,[3] the *Human Trafficking (Prevention and Protection) Act 2012* and the *Pornography Control Act 2012*[4] followed a similar pattern. While the fast track procedure and harsher penalties were welcomed, and are still supported by campaigners for victims' rights, concerns have also been raised about whether these are overly draconian and unfairly restrict the rights of the accused to a fair trial. There have also been reported instances of misuse of the law, as false cases are lodged as a part of personal disputes and conflicts, or as political harassment (Goldsmith 2016).

Alongside restricting the rights of the accused, these special laws also include measures for victim protection. The VAW Act provides for holding in camera hearings, prohibiting publication of the victim's name or particulars, and facilitating 'safe custody' for women in a shelter home or designated place other than a prison. It also provides for some restitutive remedies; the special tribunals may direct a convicted offender to pay their fine as compensation to victims, and to pay maintenance to any child born as a result of rape (section 16, *Suppression of Violence against Women and Children Act 2000* (as amended 2003)). The *Human Trafficking (Prevention and Protection) Act 2012* strengthens these protections, and also provides that only women officers may search a woman, and requires a court to adopt a victim-friendly approach to identifying, rescuing, repatriating and rehabilitating any victim/survivor (sections 20(3), 22(3) and 32)

The *Domestic Violence (Prevention and Protection) Act 2010* not only focused for the first time on the prosecution and punishment of offenders, but also sought to put in place civil protection orders for victims. Its preamble states clearly that it is being enacted in pursuance of Bangladesh's ratification of CEDAW. This Act established a new offence of domestic violence, defined to include 'physical, psychological, sexual or economic abuse against a woman or a child of a family by any other person of that family with whom victim is, or has been, in family relationship' (chapter 2, section 3). It also provides for civil remedies, such as compensation orders, protection orders and residence orders, to victims of domestic violence (but limits this to married women in relation to their spouse). In addition to outlining the responsibilities of the Court in protecting victims, the Act enumerates the duties of police officers, enforcement officers, medical service providers and social welfare officers in assisting survivors. Breach of any protection order is punishable by a maximum of a jail sentence, and/or fine, or community service as an alternative at the discretion of the court.

In addition to the above, matrimonial remedies may be invoked in cases of violence against women and girls. In general, these are determined by personal laws, based on religion, which differ depending on whether Muslim, Hindu, Christian or other customary laws apply. They codify gender discriminatory practices embedded in religious doctrine and make it difficult for women to access justice in the event of domestic abuse or other rights violations (Pereira 2002, p. 2). For example, under Muslim, Hindu and Christian personal laws, girls may be validly married as minors with parental consent, although the offence of child marriage is criminalised. Under Christian and Hindu laws, women have limited or no opportunity for divorce and thus may be unable to leave even the most abusive and violent of relationships (Human Rights Watch 2012, p. 2). Discriminatory divorce provisions allow men to obtain divorce more easily than women, and with minimal financial consequences, leaving women economically and socially vulnerable. In the event of divorce, Muslim men are only required to pay ninety days of maintenance to their former spouses or, if the spouse is pregnant, up until the birth of the child.

Efforts have also been made to put in place institutional measures to respond to violence against women. The government's flagship multi-sectoral programme on violence against women (MSPVAW), located within the Ministry of Women and Children's Affairs, has established eight One-Stop Crisis Centres across the country to provide comprehensive care to female victims of violence.[5] While this is a positive step forward, these centres are located in urban or peri-urban areas and are not easily accessible to most, including rural women. The police have also established innovative Victim Support Centres, providing women with counselling services and information about the legal system, the opportunity to register complaints and assist with investigations.[6] Again however, there are still very few centres across the country and women in most districts still lack access to emergency support. Other initiatives include a national hotline on violence against women and emergency shelters, operated by both the government and NGOs. These also remain few in number (less than twenty shelters for a population of 160 million), inadequate for existing needs.

Women remain highly under-represented among the police (less than two per cent), contributing to a lack of gender sensitivity and awareness.[7] Despite some significant appointments there are only six women out of 100 plus judges in the higher courts, with one sitting in the highest court, and less than a fifth of judges in subordinate courts. To date, no woman has ever served as a Chief Justice, Attorney General or Minister of Law (NCSC-USAID 2014, p. 3).

The formal legal system remains enormously overburdened, costly and difficult to access for most women, particularly those living in rural areas (World Bank 2008, p. 11). As of 2013, there were an estimated 2.3 million cases pending in courts around the country, with massive delays involved for all justice seekers (Sarkar 2013). Women who brave the formal court system are faced with significant obstacles: courthouses are extremely crowded; there are no proper waiting or washroom facilities; and many examples of gender bias continue to be reported.

These institutional shortcomings are frequently cited as reasons why women often opt for the *shalish*, or traditional dispute resolution mechanism usually led by local male elders, that also result in settlements which are seen as acceptable to the family and local community and do not challenge or change existing power relationships.

Individual litigation v. strategic litigation: from legal aid to PIL

Despite the various interventions detailed above to put in place a robust legal and institutional framework to address violence against women, it remains the case that fewer than two per cent of women in Bangladesh ever seek any form of redress in such cases (Naved *et al.* 2006, p. 2928)

Many of these cases do not focus on the prosecution of offenders, but on seeking immediate protection for survivors, primarily in the form of claims for financial entitlements due on separation or divorce that occurs as a result of continuing violence. The violence itself, unless very serious, is apparently accepted, seen as a matter of course, and forms the background but rarely the core or substance of the claims. The familiar reasons why women do not seek prosecution and punishment of offenders in cases of violence include stigma, the risk of reprisals and threats and the absence of protection, lack of social security or support beyond the family and community, lack of response or bias within the law enforcing agencies, as well as the cost, distance and time involved in pursing legal proceedings.

Of the tiny minority of women and girls who do seek justice, a significant number are only able to do so if they can secure free legal aid. Some do so through the government's recently re-activated legal aid programme, while others seek assistance from a number of specialised NGOs, focused generally on women's rights or legal services.[8]

Legal aid organisations, in addition to their bread and butter cases on family violence (seeking maintenance and other financial relief), provide support to the prosecution in many cases of violence against women, and have also campaigned for and facilitated the activation and implementation of institutional mechanisms to address violence. In identifying systemic barriers to justice they have also become increasingly engaged in PIL to push for recognition of rights and remedies in cases of violence against women.

PIL differs from individual rights litigation in that it involves invoking the High Court's constitutional jurisdiction for protection of the fundamental rights of particular individuals, groups or communities, resulting directly from the action or inaction of public authorities, where those affected are unable to seek redress due to social or economic disadvantage. In addition to allowing such petitioners, and enabling third party intervenors to assist the court, thus widening access to its remedies, the Court has also acted on its own volition (*suo motu*) in a number of cases. It has allowed for more flexible procedures, directing individuals or organisations to conduct investigations and report back to the court and, in many cases, fashioned new remedies, including compensation (Ahmed 1999; Hoque 2011).

PIL cases generally seek an interpretation of the scope and ambit of particular constitutional rights and related duties of state actors. The Constitution: guarantees the fundamental rights of all citizens to equality before the law; prohibits discrimination by the state on the grounds of religion, race, caste, sex or place of birth; requires the state to adopt special measures in favour of women or children or for the advancement of any backward section of citizens; secures the right to equal protection of the law, life and personal liberty; and gives protections in respect of speedy trial and punishment, including an express prohibition of torture and cruel, degrading, inhuman treatment or punishment (see Articles 27, 28, 31, 32, 35). These cases also invoke Article 21 of the Constitution, which imposes a duty on *all persons* 'to observe the Constitution and the laws'.

In interpreting the ambit of rights, or in fashioning remedies, the Courts may invoke the Fundamental Principles of State Policy.[9] These include the principles of: supremacy of the Constitution; the 'four pillars' of nationalism, socialism, democracy, and secularism; and respect for the dignity and worth of human persons.[10] A recent controversial constitutional amendment that declared Islam as the state religion[11] appears inconsistent with the foundational principles of secularism and human dignity, but has yet to be considered or interpreted by the Supreme Court.[12]

In a number of cases, as we shall see further below, public interest litigants have sought to strengthen their arguments regarding the scope and ambit of the duties of state actors to respect, protect or fulfil women's rights to freedom from violence by reference to Bangladesh's obligations under international human-rights treaties.[13] However, with a few exceptions, no enabling legislation has been adopted to incorporate the provisions of these instruments into domestic law and, as such, they are not directly enforceable (*H.M. Ershad v.Bangladesh* 7 BLC (AD) 67).

PIL has been undertaken in relation to incidents of gender-based violence in the context of forced marriage, forced veiling, sexual harassment in educational institutions, stalking, forced evictions from slums, forced evictions of sex workers and survivors of mass rapes in the Liberation War.[14]

Prosecuting *fatwa* violence

In the early 1990s, public attention first focused on the issuance of *fatwas* against women and girls by the *shalish*, traditional and informal rural dispute resolution bodies. Typically, male village elders would accuse women, and in some cases men, of breaching community norms on sexual behaviour, and impose degrading and humiliating punishments upon them, such as social ostracism, garlanding with shoes, caning or whipping. Where these were reported in the media, women's organisations and human rights or legal aid groups responded variously with public condemnation, protests, local investigations, demands for the prosecution and punishment of offenders and, in some cases, support for victims (Amnesty International 1994; Women Living Under Muslim Laws 1996).

Finally, in 2001, the High Court Division of the Supreme Court of Bangladesh, acting on its own initiative (*suo motu*), took action after a newspaper reported that a local *shalish* had issued a *fatwa* on a woman, subjecting her to humiliating treatment. The Court directed the police to explain why they failed to intervene and to report on the action taken to investigate or prosecute those responsible. Two organisations, the Bangladesh Mahila Parishad (BMP),[15] the country's largest and oldest women's group, and Ain o Salish Kendra (ASK), a human rights and legal aid organisation, intervened in the case and, among others, submitted documents on the pervasiveness of such *fatwa* violence. The police submitted reports indicating that they had investigated and brought charges against several of those involved in the incident. The Court finally held, going beyond all of the arguments made at the Bar, that *all fatwas* were illegal and unconstitutional, and that only courts could give their opinions on matters of law (*The Editor the Daily Banglabazar v. Deputy Commissioner Naogaon*, 21 BLD (HCD) (2001) 45). The judgement resulted in a sharp backlash and violent demonstrations by, among others, Muslim fundamentalist groups and political organisations, with police firing on demonstrators, several deaths resulted.

Within a few months, two men claiming to be *muftis* (persons learned in Muslim personal law) approached the highest court, the Appellate Division of the Supreme Court, seeking to appeal. They had not been involved in the earlier case and had no direct involvement in the incident. However, they succeeded in obtaining permission to appeal on the basis that the judgement, if allowed to prevail, would violate their right to freedom of expression and to issuing and receiving *fatwas* as an integral part of their faith. The two *muftis* argued that all fundamental rights, including the right to freedom of expression – which included both the right to receive and to communicate information, such as *fatwas* – should be interpreted in accordance with the constitutional provision that made Islam the state religion. The case awaited a hearing for almost ten years.

In the meantime, a group of human rights, women's rights and development organisations – the Bangladesh Legal Aid and Services Trust (BLAST), together with ASK, BMP, BRAC[16] and Nijera Kori[17] – initiated public interest litigation directly before the High Court. This time the approach and arguments were very different. The 2001 case was initiated by the judges in reaction to one incident, in contrast, the five organisations drew on their combined experience of campaigning, casework and victim support, and based their arguments firmly on explications of constitutional rights and remedies, and also on the state's obligations under international treaty law. The latter included the state's duty to prevent, prohibit and punish cruel, inhuman and degrading treatment or punishment, and to enforce the universal prohibition against torture.[18] The petitioners also submitted materials by an expert, Professor Khalid Masud, setting out the scope of *fatwas* under *Sharia* law and pointing out the diversity of practice across different countries regarding the recognition of *fatwas*, depending on whether or not the state in question applied religious law and to what extent (specifically whether it applied in respect of criminal law), and on whether there were any authorities recognised by the state as having the power to issue *fatwas*.

Ultimately, in 2010 the High Court found that extra-judicial punishments had been imposed in specific instances cited by the petitioners (including caning, whipping, lashing, a forced *hilla* marriage, forced cutting of hair and exclusion from the village for offences such as 'talking to a man on the road'). It declared the imposition of extra-judicial punishments, including those in the name of execution of *fatwas*, to clearly constitute criminal offences of wrongful restraint, wrongful confinement, hurt to religious sentiment and acts of inducing a person to believe that they would be the object of divine displeasure, all recognised under existing law (sections 354, 342, 295 and 508 of the *Bangladesh Penal Code 1860*).[19] The High Court recognised that the practice of such *fatwas* amounted to:

> *discrimination against women, who are overwhelmingly the subject of such extra-judicial penalties and who are systematically denied recourse to law or legal protection and to protection from cruel or degrading or inhuman treatment or punishment.*

The Court thus shifted focus from interpreting religious law to a secular exercise of identifying the legal and constitutional protections available against acts of gender-based violence resulting from the issuance of *fatwas*. The Court did not attempt to deal with the constitutionality of issuing *fatwas* as such. Importantly, the judges left room for a continuation of traditional or alternative dispute resolution, clarifying that these must be carried out in accordance with the law, and could not involve the imposition of penalties for offences not recognised under Bangladesh law. They directed law enforcing agencies and local government bodies to prevent *fatwas* and to take appropriate legal steps where required, and asked the local government ministry to disseminate public information on such extra-judicial punishments being a crime, and to remind all authorities of their duties to take action to protect victims. The Court also asked the education ministry to include information in the curricula of all educational institutions, particularly *madrassas*, on the supremacy of the Constitution and discouraging the imposition of extra-judicial punishment in any form in the name of executing Islamic *Sharia/fatwa*.

A mere decade after the original judgement, the highest court finally took up the earlier case for hearing in 2011, soon after a widely reported and condemned, nationally and internationally, flogging incident that resulted in the death of fourteen-year-old Hena after she was accused of adultery and subjected to a *fatwa*. At the outset, and in reaction to the reports of Hena's death, counsel for all parties immediately acknowledged that there could be no justification for the issuance of *fatwas* which involved any imposition of punishment and that no authorities could invoke or claim such extra-judicial powers. After hearing all parties the highest court finally disposed of the appeal with a short written order stating that '[*fatwas*] or religious edicts could only be pronounced by persons properly educated in religious matters, but that it cannot affect or violate the rights, reputation or dignity of any person that is protected under the law' (*Mohammad Tayeeb & Anr v. Government of Bangladesh & Ors*, 23 BLT (AD) (2015) 10).

Reforming procedures in rape investigations

Although the VAW Act has brought in significant reforms regarding rape trials, outdated definitions of the offence and discriminatory rules and procedures for collecting evidence, among others, continue to act as a barrier to justice for victims and survivors. The continuing use of character evidence relating to the complainant's past sexual history, permitted by Section 155(4) of the *Evidence Act 1872*, poses a significant challenge. This provides that 'when a man is prosecuted for rape or an attempt to ravish, it may be shown that the prosecutrix was of generally immoral character'.

The introduction of character evidence or the victim's past sexual history is both irrelevant and humiliating for the victim and shifts the focus of the trial from the accused to the victim. An analysis of reported judgements on rape reveals that judges have often referenced the victim's past sexual history, age, divorce status or 'unfeminine' behaviour in their judgements acquitting the accused of rape charges.[20] It appears that:

> *aspects of easy virtue or chastity are recurring themes . . . rape is addressed within frameworks of morality, chastity and honour, instead of being viewed as a crime against an individual and a violation of bodily integrity.*
>
> (Rougerie 2009)

Allowing character evidence to be called to discredit the victim also legitimises the continuing use of discriminatory practices regarding the collection of medical evidence through the so-called 'two-finger test', which remains unaffected by the reforms achieved by the VAW Act. The law requires immediate medical examination of a complainant, and directs physicians to conduct such examinations and to ensure that victims are given copies of their reports.[21] However, the relevant prescribed form still refers to the two-finger test, which is endorsed by the medical jurisprudence textbooks still in use for trainee doctors. It is used to assess any damage to the hymen and vaginal laxity and, based on this, to frame conclusions on whether the victim is 'habituated to sexual intercourse'. The defence then deploy these findings during cross-examination to demonstrate that the victim is sexually promiscuous and thus of immoral character, under section 155(4) of the *Evidence Act 1872* (BLAST 2014).

The continuing prevalence of the use this invasive and humiliating test, and consequently of questions regarding a complainant's past sexual history, serve to deter women and girls from reporting rape or seeking redress. In recognition of this issue, five organisations jointly engaged in filing a PIL to challenge the two-finger test and seek a review of the existing guidelines for collection of evidence in rape cases. The PIL followed a long process of research, consultation and review among concerned activists and legal and medical professionals.

Research by BLAST reviewing records of rape cases in which it was providing assistance to the prosecution on behalf of victims first highlighted the two-finger test as an issue of concern. Subsequently, consultations with prosecutors and then with forensic experts revealed that the test had no scientific basis but continued to be used because courts required such findings to be provided. Some disturbing responses from experts included the views: that if a woman was found 'habituated' to sex, it would be assumed that she was not raped; that married women could not be raped; and that sex workers could not be raped. They also indicated that the two-finger test remained part of the curriculum in medical faculties.

A national conference bringing together medical and legal experts, police officers and victim support specialists, including women's rights organisations with a long track record of working on such cases and on law reform, resulted in the framing of clear recommendations for a review of the guidelines on medical evidence and a repeal of the two-finger test. It also highlighted observations by international and national courts and tribunals pointing to the use of similar tests, including virginity tests, as a form of gender discrimination, a breach of the state's obligations to prohibit cruel and degrading treatment or punishment.[22] These were presented before the then Minister for Women and Children's Affairs.

Further advocacy was undertaken through the submission of memoranda to the Ministry of Health and Family Welfare, and the Ministry of Women and Children's Affairs. When these yielded no response, BLAST served a legal notice on the Ministry of Health and Family Welfare, Ministry of Home Affairs, Directorate of Health Services and the Inspector General of Police. Finally, on receiving no response, it filed a writ petition in the public interest before the High Court. The petitioners included six human rights and women's rights organisations, including BLAST, ASK, BMP, BRAC (all earlier involved in the *fatwa* case), the Manusher Jonno Foundation, Naripokkho, and two scientists, Dr. Ruchira Tabassum Naved and Dr. Mobarak Hossain. They sought a declaration that the test was discriminatory and directions to frame new guidelines, relying on those already formulated by the World Health Organisation.

In its order admitting the petition,[23] the High Court directed the Secretary, Ministry of Health and Family Welfare:

> *to set up a Committee including experts on forensics, criminal justice, public health and experience in providing support to women and girls survivors of violence, to develop a comprehensive guideline for police, physicians and judges or the Nari o Shishu Nirjaton Domon Tribunals on examination and treatment of women and girls subjected to rape and sexual violence, and to submit a detailed report thereof to this court within three months from the date of receipt of this order, for dealing with same in accordance with the law.*[24]

BLAST then followed up with the Ministry by collecting and sending a copy of the High Court's order. A committee headed by the Health Ministry then co-opted civil society members and other experts, which started a process of drafting new court-mandated guidelines (Uzzal 2014). After several internal discussions and consultations, including a review of medico-legal evidence collection guidelines in other jurisdictions, the Ministry drafted a new set of *Guidelines on Medico-Legal Evidence Collection in Rape Cases*. These prohibit the use of the two finger test as a method of medico-legal evidence collection, except where deemed to be medically necessary. In certain cases, such as that of young girls, pregnant and married women, the draft Guidelines prohibit the two finger test in all circumstances. The draft Guidelines refer to the right to health care of survivors of rape and emphasise the need for speedy collection of medico-legal evidence in an environment that is sensitive and friendly to the needs of rape survivors. They also outline in detail the duties of medical officers, police officers and the court in ensuring efficient collection of medico-legal evidence. Notably, the guidelines also seek to establish a monitoring mechanism to ensure their implementation. The Court has yet to consider these draft guidelines.

PIL and its possibilities: punishment, protection, prevention?

In both cases discussed above, the use of PIL made it possible to recognise particular acts and procedures as constituting gender-based violence and to identify the state's responsibility to put in place an institutional response by reworking existing procedures and practices.

While the extreme nature of *fatwa* violence had drawn widespread outrage from the first reported case in the 1990s, similar incidents continued to occur fairly regularly, with no governmental authority giving priority attention to prosecuting or punishing those responsible, even sporadically after the 2001 Banglabazar judgement. Responses from law enforcing agencies remained sporadic at best, and dependent largely on agitation or protest by women's groups or the media. After the 2010 BLAST judgement, with its express denunciation of any forms of extra-judicial punishment and delineation of the duties of law enforcing agencies, it was no longer as easy to escape or evade the responsibility to act in such cases by relying on legal ambiguities. Legal services organisations found the judgement helpful in pushing for accountability by threatening contempt proceedings against law enforcing agencies who delayed investigation of allegations of *fatwa* violence (Ain O Salish Kendra 2014). Development organisations were strengthened in working within communities to prevent the issuance of *fatwas*, again by reminding those concerned of exactly how they would be held legally accountable.[25] Prior to the judgement, *fatwa* violence incidents were sporadically found in the media; after it, they seem to have become rare. All this suggests that the judgement has contributed in some degree to deterring *fatwas* against women.

There has been no movement, as yet, on putting in place the system-wide changes which the Court mandated. No government ministry has issued orders or circulars to direct local government bodies to take systematic action. No changes have been made to the educational curricula. While *fatwa* reports have become more scarce, reports of traditional dispute resolution bodies, or *shalish*, handing down extra-judicial penalties continues, suggesting that change on the ground may only have been semantic.

With the two-finger test case, it is perhaps too early to make an effective assessment. The Ministry's prompt response to the Court's order and its engagement with concerned experts and organisations is clearly a positive development. It has enabled a rethinking of the procedure to reflect the reality of women's experiences of the test, engaging lawyers, forensic experts and women's rights organisations. It has also, through extensive media coverage, achieved some level of public discussion and a change of mindset, at least in some practitioners. It has also led to more discussion around the need to review the underlying colonial laws that justify this practice, with the Chief Justice of Bangladesh and the Chairman of the Law Commission declaring that section 155(4) of the *Evidence Act 1872* demands urgent repeal.[26]

In both cases it is difficult to assess the degree of protection that individual women and girl victims or survivors have secured as a result of the Court's orders. Without more significant changes within the legal system, and in the absence of social security or support beyond the family and community, women and girls are compelled to forego the possibility of justice through accountability or reparation and to accept the lowest common denominator of settlement. While activist advocates can certainly relish the change secured to the letter of the law, it is far more difficult to claim a significant contribution to any change in the experiences faced by victims of gendered violence.

Recognising limits: public interest v. powerful interests

While these two cases resulted in significant achievements, as discussed, they also underscore the limits of PIL as a strategy. In both cases, the resort to PIL reflected a common understanding among petitioners that there was a more than reasonable possibility of securing a win. There was no real confrontation with the state; media support was widely available and helped to engage public discussion and concern.

But PIL petitioners alone cannot drive the pace of change without a proactive Court on the one hand and an engaged Executive on the other. Media activism provides much needed fuel for the PIL engine, and wide initial coverage when a case starts helps to generate discussion and debate. But, with a few exceptions, the reporting and commentary is rarely consistent or persistent. While the PIL case may generate headlines, it is far more difficult to ensure regular follow-ups by journalists on orders or on their implementation.

Also, without close monitoring and follow-up, it is difficult to track how Court directives are being implemented on the ground, or interpreted in ways to defeat their impact. For example, anecdotal examples and a casual survey of news reports suggest that relatively few *fatwas* are now being declared during a village *shalish*. However, while the word *fatwa* itself may not be uttered, extra-judicial punishments are still meted out by the village *shalish* against women for breach of social norms on sexuality.

If the media become increasingly muted and unwilling to confront an increasingly authoritarian executive, and citizens' organisations are also unable to co-ordinate and mobilise for action, the possibility for PIL to serve as an effective tool for accountability comes into question. A strong Executive may, of course, help move inefficient agencies to carry out their legal duties in the face of allegations of state inaction. However, the action necessary to counter powerful interests or actors responsible for gender-based violence on the one hand, and to challenge pervasive gender-discriminatory social norms on the other, can only result from stronger public pressure and citizen engagement, complementing interventions from and through the Courts.

Notes

1 This chapter is based on a paper delivered at the conference on *Gender Violence and the State in Asia* at the Chinese University of Hong Kong on 8–10 May 2014. Thanks are due to Ishita Dutta at BLAST (www.blast.org.bd) for her research assistance, to Nina Sheth for help with citations, and to Dr. Sajeda Amin, Dr. Hameeda Hossain and Dr. Ferdaus Jahan for helpful comments.

2 For reasons of space, this chapter does not discuss the important steps taken in the immediate aftermath of independence of recognising rape in conflict and putting in place measures to assist survivors of mass rape during war under the *International Crimes Tribunal Act 1973*. It also does not address the legal or institutional framework on violence against women applicable in the three districts of the Chittagong Hill

Tracts, which includes both formal courts and traditional justice bodies, where the latter apply the customary laws of indigenous peoples in family disputes.

3 The *Acid Crimes Control Act 2002* creates specific offences involving the use of acid, which disproportionately affect women. It provides for increased penalties, ranging from a minimum of three years in prison to the death penalty, in addition to hefty fine, with sentencing linked to the part of the body affected by the attack. The Act also criminalises attempts, even where no physical, mental or other harm occurs.

4 The *Pornography Control Act 2012* defines pornography as the production and dissemination of documentary, audio-visual materials, graphics, books, periodicals etc., 'which use uncivil dialogue and picture, body movement, naked dance etc. which may create sexual appeal'. It penalises the production, preservation, transportation, marketing, possession or presentation of any kind of pornographic material, and also makes it an offence to force or lure women, men or children to participate in the production of pornography. It increases the maximum penalty for this offence from three months to ten years in prison in addition to a 500,000 taka (USD 6,406) fine.

5 Ministry of Women and Children, One Stop Crisis Centre (OCC), [online] http://www.mspvaw.gov.bd/index.php?option=com_content&view=article&id=188&cmp=1&adfile=1

6 Bangladesh Police, Ministry of Home Affairs, Police Reform Programme Victim Support Center [online] http://www.prp.org.bd/menuvsc.htm

7 Women make up only 1.3 per cent of the Bangladeshi police force, below the average of 8.5 per cent in other least developed countries: United Nations Development Programme, Police Reform Programme (Phase II) Proposal (2009), p. 5 [online] http://www.bd.undp.org/content/dam/bangladesh/docs/Projects/PRP/PRP_Project_Document_Phase_II.pdf

8 Many of these organisations emerged from experiences of engagement in relief and reconstruction during the war and its aftermath, or by individuals closely associated with the independence struggle. Accordingly, they have expressly invoked the resonant language of liberation and work within a broadly secular approach.

9 While these were earlier considered non-justiciable, the courts have subsequently held that they may serve as a guide to the interpretation of particular rights: see Article 8, *Constitution of Bangladesh 1972*; *Kudrat-E-Elahi v.Bangladesh*, 44 DLR (AD) 319.

10 See Articles 7 (supremacy of the Constitution), 8 (fundamental principles) and 11 (democracy and secularism), *Constitution of Bangladesh 1972*.

11 Article 2A, substituted by the *Constitution (Fifteenth Amendment) Act 2011* (Act XIV of 2011) section 4.

12 Article 23A, substituted by the *Constitution (Fifteenth Amendment) Act 2011* (Act XIV of 2011) section 4.

13 Bangladesh is party to core international human-rights treaties, including the 1966 International Covenant on Civil and Political Rights (ICCPR), the 1966 International Covenant on Economic Social and Cultural Rights (ICESCR), the 1957 Indigenous and Tribal Populations Convention (ILO Convention No. 107), the 1965 International Convention on the Elimination of All Forms of Racial Discrimination (CERD), the 1979 Convention on the Elimination of All Forms of Discrimination against Women (CEDAW), the 1989 Convention on the Rights of the Child (CRC), the 2010 Convention on the Rights of Persons with Disabilities (CRPD) and the 2012 International Convention on the Rights of Migrant Workers (CMW).

14 For various judgements see: ASK [online] http://www.askbd.org/ask/category/litigation/; BLAST [online] http://www.blast.org.bd/judgements; and Bangladesh National Women Lawyers' Association [online] http://www.bnwlabd.org/?page_id=5367.

15 See Bangladesh Mahila Parishad [online] http://www.mahilaparishad.org/

16 BRAC is a development organisation that works to alleviate poverty by empowering the poor. [online] http://www.brac.net/

17 For further information on the work of Nijera Kori see [online] http://www.nijerakori.org/
18 The judgement cited these provisions, particularly Article 7 of the ICCPR, 2 and 16 of CAT, and General Comment No. 7 of the Human Rights Committee, as well as CEDAW's concluding comment that violence against women impairs or nullifies the enjoyment by women of human rights and fundamental freedoms under general international law (para. 37). The Court noted that it could refer to these as an aid to interpretation to determine rights implied in the right to life and liberty but not enumerated in the Constitution, and also cited Article 25 of the Constitution (para. 38).
19 *BLAST and others v. Bangladesh and others*, 63 DLR HCD (2011) 1, full text [online] http://www.blast.org.bd/content/judgement/ejp-judgment-8July2010.pdf
20 Chowdhury, N.N. (2015) 'An Archaic Abhorrent Law', *The Daily Star*, 06 February 2015, referring *to Abdul Majid v. State*, 13 BLC (HCD) (2008) 53, at paras. 60 and 66 (divorcee with daughter, raped while asleep in her hut, held to have been 'habituated in sexual intercourse', and to be 'a woman of loose moral character and involved in anti-social and immoral activities'; *Shahin and Others v. The State*, 28 BLD (HCD) 2008, 41 at para. 29 (victim taken away from grandmother at local hotel and gang raped, held to be a 'case of rape of a matured woman who has married twice'); *Sree Pintoo Pal v. The State*, 30 BLD (AD) (2010), 220, at para. 41 (victim domestic held to be 'woman of easy virtue, so her evidence cannot be believed'). Also, see Dutta, I. (2015) 'A "rape shield" law for Bangladesh', *The Daily Star*, 16 June 2015 [online] http://www.thedailystar.net/op-ed/%E2%80%9Crape-shield%E2%80%9D-law-bangladesh-97516.
21 Section 32 of the VAW Act, 2000, and Guidelines for Medical Evidence Collection adopted by the Ministry of Health and Family Welfare. See reports of Naripokkho regarding the process of adoption of these Guidelines. For details, see Basu, A. (2013) *Medical Evidence in Rape Cases: Law and Practice*, BLAST (on file).
22 BLAST, Memorandum on the 'Two-finger Test', presented at National Conference on Medico Legal Evidence Collection in Rape Cases in Bangladesh, 2 February 2013, icddr, b, Dhaka. See also, World Health Organisation (WHO) (2003) *Guidelines for medico-legal care for victims of sexual violence*, Geneva [online] http://whqlibdoc.who.int/publications/2004/924154628X.pdf and *L.N.P. v. Argentine Republic* Comm. No. 1610/2007, UN Doc. CCPR/C/102/D/1610/2007. Human Rights Law Centre (2011) HRLC Bulletin, 'Rights Agenda', Vol 67 – November [online] http://www.hrlc.org.au/files/RightsAgenda_HRLC_Bulletin_November_2011.pdf
23 This Order was recognised, through winning the Silver Gavel at the *Gender Justice Uncovered Awards*, as a leading decision or statement made by a judge in the context of a legal process with a positive impact on gender equality. For more information see [online] http://www2.womenslinkworldwide.org/wlw/sitio/caso-interna.php?idcaso=396&idi=en
24 BLAST, 'Two-finger test on rape survivors challenged', available at: http://www.blast.org.bd/index.php?option=com_content&view=article&id=484
25 Discussion with Faustina Pereira, Director of BRAC's Human Rights Legal Services Programme about use of the 2011 judgement by field workers to prevent *fatwas* being issued or carried out in villages.
26 Liton, S. '143 year old law which allows rape accused to question victims' character needs change', *The Daily Star*, 28 May 2015, quoting the Chief Justice of Bangladesh 'What can be more unfortunate than this when the accused during trial raise question about the character of a woman who seeks justice after losing her honour'. [online] http://www.thedailystar.net/frontpage/143-year-old-law-needs-change-88561

Bibliography

Ahmed, N. (1999) *Public Interest Litigation: Constitutional Issues and Remedies*, BLAST, Bangladesh, Dhaka.

Ain O Salish Kendra (ASK) (2014) *Annual Report*, ASK, Dhaka, Bangladesh.

Amnesty International (1994) *Fundamental Rights of Women Violated with Virtual Impunity* https://www.amnesty.org/en/documents/asa13/009/1994/en/

BLAST (2014) *Research Note: Comparative Laws on the Use of Character Evidence of Victims in Rape Trials*, 8 May 2014 (on file).

Goldsmith, H. (2016) 'Compromising Cases: An Examination of Dispute Resolution through Special Tribunals for Women and Children', *Bangladesh Development Initiative* (forthcoming).

Hoque, R. (2011) *Judicial Activism in Bangladesh: A Golden Mean Approach*, Cambridge Scholars Publishers, Newcastle upon Tyne, UK.

Human Rights Watch (2012) *Will I Get My Dues . . . Before I Die? Harm to Women from Bangladesh Discriminatory Laws on Marriage, Separation and Divorce* [online] http://www.hrw.org/sites/default/files/reports/bangladesh0912ForUpload.pdf

Naved, R.T., Azim, S., Bhuiya, A., Persson, L.A., (2006) 'Physical violence by husbands: magnitude, disclosure and help-seeking behavior of women in Bangladesh', *Soc. Sci. Med.* 62(12): 2917–29.

NCSC-USAID (2014), 'Finding our Voices: Women in the Judiciary and Legal Professions', *Justice for All Program* (unpublished).

Pereira, F. (2002) *The Fractured Scales: The Search for a Uniform Personal Code*, Popular Prakashan, Calcutta, India.

Rougerie, S. (2009) 'Medical Evidence in Rape Case in Bangladesh: Law and Practice', *BLAST* (on file).

Sarkar, A. (2013) 'Backlog of Cases', *The Daily Star*, 18 March 2013 [online] http://archive.thedailystar.net/beta2/news/backlog-of-cases/

Uzzal, M. (2014) 'Deadline over for readying guideline on treating rape victims' *Dhaka Tribune*, 14 February 2014 [online] http://www.dhakatribune.com/law-amp-rights/2014/feb/14/deadline-over-readying-guideline-treating-rape-victims#sthash.Tgrcn2oT.dpuf

Women Living Under Muslim Laws (1996) *Fatwas against Women in Bangladesh* [online] http://www.wluml.org/node/363

World Bank (2008) *Whispers to Voices: Gender and Social Transformation in Bangladesh*, Bangladesh Development Series, Paper No. 22 [online] http://siteresources.worldbank.org/SOUTHASIAEXT/Resources/Publications/448813-1185396961095/4030558-1205418213360/bdgender2008.pdf

8 Dispute resolution and access to justice in rural China

An analysis from a gender perspective

Huang Zhong

Introduction

China's judicial reform over the past two decades has improved the professionalism of Chinese courts and legal staff, and promoted judicial activism and mediation, thus helping to reconstruct the judicial system in both urban and rural areas. Despite unavoidable conflicts between modern state law and rural traditions/customs, judicial intervention has provided residents in rural China with several ways to resolve disputes and access justice.[1] In particular, the grassroots judicial offices (*Sifasuo*) at township level often function as bridges connecting the formal legal system and customary village rules by providing legal assistance, mediation guidance and grassroots legal services. This is especially important for rural residents living around towns who seek remedies through the judicial offices when their grievances cannot be resolved at village level.

Limited academic research exists on rural women's experiences in accessing justice, nor has research explored the particular impacts rural dispute resolution mechanisms have on women, especially those who are more vulnerable due to gender-based violence or customs biased against women. There is also little sound evidence and data showing that rural women have equal access to formal and informal judicial systems when they do experience grievances. This chapter addresses this gap by considering possible factors that facilitate or hinder rural women's access to justice through an examination of their experiences interacting with local judicial offices.

The chapter first provides a historical overview of judicial reform in China, with a focus on how the reform process has affected rural access to justice. It then looks specifically at the role that judicial offices play in bringing law and legal procedures to rural areas through dispute resolution and legal literacy. Turning next to women's rights in Chinese law and policy, the chapter considers the differences between law and practice for rural women. Although Chinese law and policies (such as the *Marriage Law 1950* [amended in 2001], the *Law on Protection of Rights and Interests of Women 1992* [amended in 2005] and the National Programs on Women's development) have emphasised the promotion of gender equality, women, especially those that live in rural areas, still experience gender-based bias and violence which exacerbates their poverty and disadvantage.

Drawing on case studies from the author's in-depth fieldwork in a remote ethnic minority area in Hubei Province, the chapter then examines how township-level judicial offices resolve disputes concerning women's rights through mediation. In particular, the case studies look at the role of judicial offices in the settlement of matrimonial disputes since 'how family disputes are resolved lies at the intersection between the public and private spheres, the crucial nexus where the state's role of shaping citizenship takes place' (Woo 2003, p. 100). Although judicial offices play a significant role in protecting rural women's rights during the resolution of matrimonial disputes, a lack of gender awareness in laws and judicial practices may result in the marginalisation of rural women in their access to judicial processes and eventually prejudice the fulfilment of their rights.

China's judicial reform and its impact on rural access to justice

As early as the end of the 1980s China started to reform court procedures, ensuring professionalism in the judiciary, focusing on enhancing the function of court trials, expanding the openness of trials, improving attorney defence functions and training professional judges and procurators (State Council Information Office 2012). Since 1999 the Supreme People's Court (SPC) has formulated three different five-year plans on judicial reform, which have produced more than one hundred concrete measures on promoting due process, consistency in applying the law, judicial credibility and judicial professionalism.

However, changes in SPC leadership have taken reform efforts in different directions. For example, under the leadership of Xiao Yang, SPC President from 1998 to 2008, justice (both substantive and procedural) and efficiency were specified as the twin themes for the Chinese courts and for judicial reform. However, since Wang Shenjun assumed the SPC Presidency in late 2008, the court's work has shifted, reviving older Party themes that emphasise the political (rather than neutral or independent) and populist (rather than professional) nature of the Chinese judiciary. Following the new Chinese Communist Party (CCP) line of the 'Three Supremes'[2] and the 'socialist rule of law', Wang has stressed the duty of Chinese courts to serve the goals and policies determined by the CCP and to take into account the overall circumstances of Chinese society, thus implicitly downgrading the importance of a strict adherence to legal rules (Gu 2013, pp. 2–3).

Zhu Suli has argued that the shift of judicial reforms in recent years to focus on judicial activism and extensive mediation is designed to meet the challenges that previous reform efforts had (somewhat) failed to resolve, mainly the increasing frequency of conflicts and disputes, the rapid growth in lawsuit-related petitions, and difficulties related to the enforcement of adjudication (Zhu 2010, pp. 5–6). He further argues that, in spite of the significant development of the Chinese judicial system, many reforms, including those stressing the neutrality and independence of judges and the active role lawyers play in judicial processes, are neither applicable nor effective in many regions, especially in rural areas (ibid., p. 6).

Historically, legal traditions in rural areas, like the *Ma Xiwu* method[3] of informal trials, tended to emphasise settling disputes harmoniously and encouraged the adoption of a pragmatic approach that allowed judicial actors to balance the implementation of formal law with ensuring that outcomes were in line with community norms (Whiting and Shao 2014, pp. 226–7). Based on his research on the basic-level judicial system and the investigation of the strategies and techniques of judges in rural China, Zhu argues that effective rural judges are concerned almost exclusively with dispute resolution and rarely use formal law in a conventional manner or play any significant role in the diffusion of central legal norms. Zhu notes that although legal traditions in rural areas are more focused on governance than procedural fairness, they have nevertheless provided grassroots-level judicial officers with effective weapons to solve many kinds of conflicts, thus making an important contribution to the maintenance of social stability at the grassroots of Chinese society (Zhu 2010, p. 33). Furthermore, Zhu argues that the role of rural judges is better understood as a process by which the central government seeks to 'project its power down to the levels where the majority of its citizens live', and that '[i]f Chinese judges do not bring the law to the countryside, the countryside will ignore the law' (Upham 2005, p. 1680).

However, the assertion that rural areas are impervious to 'formal' law has been called into question as Chinese rural society continues to be greatly affected by China's rapid economic development, mass rural–urban migration and ongoing judicial and legal reforms. Socio-legal research into the use of law and legal processes by rural villagers indicate that they clearly see formal law and the judicial system as one method in their toolkit for dispute resolution and the protection of their interests. O'Brien and Li (2006) have observed that aggrieved peasants have adopted a strategy of 'rightful resistance' where rural complainants display loyalty and faith in the central government, its laws and policies, as they seek the help of higher authorities. In villagers' imaginations the central government is relatively upright and sympathetic, while local officials are portrayed as corrupt and despotic, often guilty of trying to keep a lid on conflict by obstructing justice and using intimidation tactics, especially when they are the subject of complaints.

Further, from the villagers' perspectives, the resolution of a grievance typically requires the support of outside authorities far removed from the influence of local cadre (CCP) networks (O'Brien and Li 2006; also O'Brien 1996). A different investigation argues that villagers found local solutions, often with the involvement of village leaders, to be far more desirable and effective. In contrast, the social costs associated with appealing to higher authorities, including the legal system, for help with local disputes tended to discourage the escalation of disputes but also to produce relatively disappointing experiences and outcomes when such routes were taken (Michelson 2008, p. 41).

Anecdotal evidence also highlights other factors that affect whether a rural resident chooses to petition the formal judicial system. In many cases, a party's decision to file a lawsuit, and their achievement of a successful outcome, was largely because they had relatives working in relevant government departments or courts. This reflects the logic of how law is disseminated and used in rural China; people tend to resolve disputes through law or judicial mechanisms only when they can use a relationship or other social mechanism to ensure the outcome. In these circumstances, the law symbolises neither fairness nor justice, but works as a shelter for people with more power and resources (He and Huang 2011).

Finally, so-called, barefoot lawyers (or community paralegals) can also play a positive role in bringing legal tools to rural society. In Chinese legal parlance, barefoot lawyers are self-taught legal activists who have, through personal experience, learnt enough law to engage with the legal system and file complaints (Liu 2002). As the Chinese legal system becomes more professionalised the gap between the legal system and rural society has widened and barefoot lawyers in village society have begun to pave the way for lay people to approach justice. Barefoot lawyers make up for the loopholes in the legal service system in the countryside and re-establish the concept of legal services in village society – legal services based on long-term human relationships instead of money. Therefore, barefoot lawyers have remarkable significance in promoting the rule of law and shaping how rural citizens understand the utility and substance of the law (Ying 2007). However, barefoot lawyers are also sometimes put in difficult situations due to the conflict between state governance of rural society and the spontaneous ways in which interests are expressed in the village (ibid.).

Rural society in China, therefore, is undergoing rapid transition, and its relationship with formal law, and the actors within the judicial system, is constantly evolving. Although the Chinese government proclaimed in 2011 that the 'socialist system of laws with Chinese characteristics' has been established through the enactment of 236 laws, almost 700 administrative regulations and more than 8,600 local statutes (National People's Congress 2011), it is worth noting that the promulgation of laws and the establishment of courts alone is insufficient to establish 'order' based on the rule of law, but that such developments are also reliant on the existence of people who understand how, and are willing, to use these mechanisms (Fei 1998, p. 58). Just as Chinese formal law is increasingly seen as a tool to maintain social order, promote social harmony and secure the development of rural communities, peasants in rural China no longer fear 'the law' or perceive themselves as distant from it, but are attempting to use legal tools to protect their interests. Rather than simply conflicting with local customs, norms and traditions, modern law is trying to integrate, transform and, ultimately, deeply embed into rural social structures (Dong *et al.* 2008).

The development of judicial offices

The establishment of grassroots judicial offices in China started in the early 1980s and expanded to a majority of towns and urban districts through the 1990s. Judicial offices are normally responsible for providing legal counsel and notary services, promoting legal literacy and undertaking dispute resolution in civil cases (You 2005). Government statistics show that China currently has more than 40,000 such offices. These offices undertake a large amount of legal work, for example, between 2004 and 2011: judicial offices solved 2.84 million disputes; assisted in the mediation and settlement of 46.77 million complex disputes; and handled 1.12 million legal aid cases (State Council Information Office 2012).

Though promoting dispute resolution and access to justice on the ground is a laudable achievement, the plight of judicial offices, especially those located in impoverished regions, is still problematic. First, many judicial offices in the central and western regions of China face shortages of human resources. Judicial offices are commonly understaffed, having only one or two staff members where they should be allocated at least one director and two judicial assistants (Fu 2004, pp. 93–4). Moreover, lack of funds and support from both superior judicial bureaus and township-level governments limit the ability of judicial offices to conduct effective legal education activities among rural communities. Meagre incomes also discourage staff members from providing high quality legal services and staying in their positions for long (Tan 2005). Additionally, as judicial offices are, in principle, under the dual management of both township government and county-level judicial bureau, judicial staff are often tasked by local governments to do other work (for example, construction, land ownership registration or even agricultural work), leaving some judicial staff too busy to undertake their actual responsibilities to provide legal services (Chen 2008).

Despite these limitations, judicial offices that mainly work on settling conflicts among rural residents are recognised as an important connection between formal law and rural custom. For example, the Ministry of Justice has affirmed the significance of judicial offices in guiding people's mediation in the community and communicating with the court system (Wang *et al.* 2012).

Unlike mediation conducted by village committees (which is largely informal), mediation in judicial offices is 'quasi-formal' (Li and Xu 2013). Judicial offices document the whole mediation process through a relatively fixed procedure. First, the parties to the dispute give statements of facts about it and also state their preferred solution. The judicial assistant or other relevant staff then obtain the necessary evidence from village leaders or related parties to further explore the facts and specific issues. The judicial assistant will subsequently co-ordinate the parties to reach a settlement. Research has found that, although mediation practices in judicial offices are not always fully in accordance with the law, they do use sufficient local customs to achieve the settlement of disputes and maintain a friendly relationship among different parties (ibid.).

However, there are concerns about the tendency of judicial offices to focus on procedures and norms instead of fact-finding and dispute resolution as they had previously (Tian 2010). Apart from registering and keeping records of mediations, judicial assistants are also required to prepare various forms and statistical tables to provide relevant information on their work for superior judicial bureaus. Although this kind of standard work is necessary, many judicial staff members on the ground complain that the tedious process consumes their energy and time, and affects the already limited resources for dispute resolution (ibid.).

Rural women and the law

The discussion above about the relationship rural villagers have with the law could similarly describe the relationship between rural women and the laws intended to protect them. The Chinese government has promulgated many laws relevant to women's lives (as will be discussed further), but there remains a gap between legislative text and practice. Although the Chinese government is prone to tout its achievements on gender equality and protection of women's rights in laws and policies, Chinese society still suffers from gender inequality problems, such as violence against women and discrimination regarding women's property rights.

Women in rural areas are typically more vulnerable due to poverty and their reluctance to use formal legal remedy mechanisms. Since migration from rural areas to cities has resulted in millions of left-behind[4] women and children, a rural family's traditional functions in production, marriage, provision for the aged and other aspects have weakened and the ability to resist risk has decreased (Fan 2005, pp. 43–4). Migration has exacerbated bigamy, cohabitation, desertion and other unlawful acts, in which cases women and children are more disadvantaged. The household registration and family planning policies are also known to prejudice rural women's rights and welfare. Considering the challenges that rural women face, both in and beyond their family life, there is an urgent need to review whether the law and legal processes in rural China truly provide the equal protection and necessary remedy if their rights are violated.

As Woo suggests, examining the government's family policy, and particularly its policies towards marriage and the dissolution of marriage, can provide an insight into issues of status and inequality, intimacy, violence and philosophies about proper governance in China (Woo 2003, p. 100). Moreover, the process of resolving family disputes presents the interaction between state power, the community and individuals (ibid., p. 101). This is particularly relevant for rural women, who typically only seek help from legal institutions when family disputes arise.

Legal framework for women's rights protections

Since the founding of the People's Republic of China in 1949, the Chinese government has attached great importance to providing legal protection for women. The *Marriage Law 1950* was the first statute enacted by the new communist government and broke with tradition by forbidding the practice of arranged and forced marriages, thus empowering women to initiate divorce proceedings (ibid., p. 106). The Law also established equality between the sexes as a legal concept, introduced freedom for both men and women in marriage, outlawed polygamy and articulated some legal protections for women and children. Subsequently, the *PRC Constitution 1954* stated that 'women enjoy equal rights with men in all spheres of life, political, economic, cultural and social, including family life' (Art. 35) and that '[m]arriage, the family and mother and child are protected by the state' (Art. 96).

In line with the principles established by the Constitution, the *Law on the Protection of the Rights and Interests of Women 1992* was specifically enacted to safeguard women's legitimate rights and interests, to promote gender equality and to enable women to play an active role in society (Rong 2005). Gender equality has repeatedly been held up as one of the basic state policies in promoting social development, with the Chinese government pledging at international forums and domestic events to take concrete measures against any forms of discrimination against women and to protect the equal status and rights of women in the country's political, economic and social life.

China has implemented three rounds of the National Program for Women's Development since 1995. The programmes are designed to promote women's full development and to protect their rights in terms of health, education, economy, participation in decision making and management, social security, environment and law. The programmes have also sought to incorporate gender awareness into the Chinese legal and policy system, including through the drafting and implementation of laws that specifically deal with women's issues. Revisions to the *Law on the Protection of the Rights and Interests of Women* in 2005 aimed to accommodate the rapidly changing economic and social environment and ensure that women's rights were protected. Amendments highlight provisions intended to enhance women's political participation and reinforce women's rights to property by stipulating that female farmers enjoy the same right to contract, to purchase or to own farmland. Moreover, Articles 52 to 54 of the *Law on the Protection of the Rights and Interests of Women 2005* strengthens the government's legal responsibility to protect women's rights through stipulating access to judicial or administrative processes, and providing legal aid and support from women's organisations and other relevant departments.

On paper, the laws relating to family and marriage appear favourable to Chinese women, yet their flawed implementation compromises their effectiveness. For example, consider law and practice related to divorce and property. Both the *Law on the Protection of the Rights and Interests of Women 2005* and the *Marriage Law 1950*, amended in 2001 guarantee the freedom to marry and divorce, state that, in a divorce, special consideration should be given to women and children in the division of property and housing (Li and Xu, 2013, p. 84). The *Marriage Law 2001* and its judicial interpretations also attempt to address some problems faced by women as individual litigants in contested divorces by clarifying grounds for divorce and determining what constitutes joint property (Jiang 2011, p. 25). However, while the 2001 amendment intended to promote the freedom of divorce by formulating a clearer individual property system and allowing for the division of marital estates with a simplified procedure, in practice the law favours the powerful party in the marriage (usually the party with more assets) who is typically a man (ibid., p. 26).

The role of judicial offices in matrimonial disputes

Prior to 2002 villagers seeking a divorce were required to undergo mediation by the judicial assistant in the township judicial office before their divorce could be granted. The parties could only register their divorce with the civil affairs bureau after they had failed to reach a reconciliation through the mediation process and it was determined that 'emotions or mutual affection were broken' between them. However, the amended *Marriage Law 2001* (which came into force in 2002) expanded the freedom of divorce by allowing parties to directly register their divorce with the civil affairs bureau without any mediation if both parties voluntarily agreed to divorce (Art. 31). Since then, the number of matrimonial disputes handled by judicial offices has dropped sharply (Li and Xu 2013, p. 84), but many villagers still seek a consultation with the judicial offices if they have questions regarding their marriage.[5]

Li and Xu indicate that divorce between rural couples is typically accompanied by suffering from poverty, adultery, and violence (ibid., p. 90). Hence the mediation skills and experience of judicial assistants are very important for achieving fairness and justice in the mediation process and decision-making. The typical process of dispute resolution starts with inquiring of one party whether (among other questions): the couple were introduced for marriage or married by free love; the length of their marriage; if there is a child (or pregnancy); the family's financial situation; and their reasons for divorcing. The judicial assistant will then ask the other party the same questions.

Judicial assistants usually settle marital disputes by using both rural customs and state laws. The two main issues in mediation include: (1) the custody of children and alimony – mainly asking about the willingness of both sides, and in consideration of the children's life and education; and (2) the division of family property and debt division (ibid., p. 94). Under Chinese law, the principle related to the division of movable property is that the labour income of the couple is counted as jointly owned property, but land and housing is not included as jointly owned property (ibid., p. 90). For land, following the approach of 'tenure reserved by individual', women who leave the marital property after the divorce may face problems, thus a compromise solution of compensation in accordance with the production of the land might be reached. As for the marital house, Li and Xu found that in almost all divorce cases, women do not claim for housing, with the exception of those who fight for houses for their son's right of succession (ibid., p. 99).

The three case studies presented below are drawn from the author's on-going fieldwork and research, which describe different ways that township judicial offices use law and/or local customs to help vulnerable women settle their matrimonial disputes. Township judicial offices have been chosen because they are the most basic judicial administrative organ, and the first contact that many villagers have with legal processes.

Case study one: reconciling rural customs and formal law

A judicial assistant from J town shared the following case involving a land dispute relating to a woman who had married out of the village she had grown up in and moved to her husband's town (an out-married woman). Her stepfather later subcontracted the family's land to a tea planter without her consent and without compensating her. The woman thus sought help from the judicial office. After taking the case, judicial assistants visited the married woman's stepfather and the village leaders who supported the stepfather. These village leaders believed that out-married women have no right to property from their original family, just like the traditional Chinese saying, 'a married daughter is like spilt water'.

In order to convince the other parties that the out-married woman's claims were valid, the judicial assistants printed out the *Law on the Contracting of Rural Land 2004* and handed it over to the various stakeholders in the village. Article 30 explicitly states that 'if a woman gets married but no land is contracted to her in her new domicile, the party that lets the land shall not withdraw the land originally contracted to her'. The judicial assistants adopted this strategy, saying: 'We must communicate with the village leaders and change their minds first; otherwise there would be barriers in the further work which may harm the relationship between us and the village.' The mediators had to visit the village many times until a compensation agreement was reached between the married woman and her stepfather. There were a few similar cases in other villages, which were also solved by using the *Law on the Contracting of Rural Land 2004*.

Although it took quite a lot of effort, the judicial assistants here were able to successfully persuade parties and other stakeholders to take existing laws into account and reach a compromise. The judicial assistants took rural customs into account but did so without contradicting the core principles of formal law. It is important to note that in these examples the formal law directly addresses the situation facing the judicial assistants. Judicial assistants also prioritised the ongoing relationship between the judicial office and the village by trying to persuade parties to agree with the law, rather than condemning them for violating the law.

Case study two: dealing with the law's blind spots

Judicial offices face challenges in tackling disputes concerning rural women's property rights, especially where the legal system does not address specific scenarios. For example, the judicial office at Y town attempted to mediate a divorce case a few years ago regarding the division of joint property. The out-married woman, the judicial office's client, was seeking to enforce her claim on the homestead, an important part of joint property for a rural couple. Her husband told the mediator that he was willing to voluntarily surrender ownership of the homestead. However, it was located in the village of the husband's family and local custom dictated that a divorced woman must leave her ex-husband's community. Moreover, the *Land Administrative Law 2005* restricts the market-based circulation of land allotted to each rural household for building a house, which meant that the divorced woman leaving the community also had limited means to dispose of the homestead she received from the division of family property during the divorce process. Although the judicial assistants felt sympathy for the woman, the client had no choice but to give up her claim to the land and left her ex-husband's village in the end.

In this case, the judicial assistants were not able to resolve their client's claim in a way that sufficiently protected her legal rights under the letter of the law. Even though both the *Law on the Protection of the Rights and Interests of Women 2005* and the *Marriage Law 2001* state that special consideration should be given to women and children in the division of property and housing, the client's ability to assert her claim was met with structural obstacles in the form of rural custom and, more importantly, the *Land Administrative Law 2005*.

Case study three: gender-based violence in matrimonial disputes

Although gender-based violence remains quite prevalent in rural and urban settings throughout China, there does not appear to be an effective mechanism or clear process by which judicial assistants identify and handle such cases. This is especially true when judicial assistants handle matrimonial disputes, as demonstrated by the author's interview with Miss T.

Miss T., who had graduated from a good law school in Wuhan a few years previously, was still one of the youngest judicial administrative staff in the whole county. As the deputy director of the judicial office at Q town, she was actually in charge of the office and appointed as the legal advisor of the local women's federation, therefore she had more opportunities to engage in different types of dispute relating to local rural women, including several domestic violence cases. In one case, the abused woman came directly to the judicial office for a consultation on a divorce issue and further asked for help in typing a complaint to court since she did not know how to use the computer. The next day, she returned to the office with bleeding fingers, saying that she was caught on the street and beaten by her husband. However, Miss T. did not know the result of her complaint since the abused woman did not ask for legal aid.

Other cases presented similar facts, and Miss T. helped impoverished women get divorces through the court. She recounted that

> maybe because I am a woman too, those female clients were prone to tell their stories with the detailed problems of their marriage. Some of them complained of their alcoholic or gambling addicted husbands with bad temper. One woman seeking legal consultation from the judicial office even told me that she was sexually abused by her husband.

When being asked about how they settled matrimonial disputes, the judicial assistants unintentionally revealed that violence against women commonly existed in many cases. However, unless the client urged divorce, judicial assistants would choose to reconcile disputes between couples, even though there was physical violence or emotional distress in the marriage. An experienced judicial assistant indicated that they usually co-operated with the police in these kinds of cases where the abuse against one party escalated into a crime; 'But if the husband truly repented, we could help to ask the police to dismiss the charge'. Ironically, in recent years there have been several murder cases where, in the end, the abused women killed their husbands.

Judicial assistants therefore may lack awareness of the need to be extra-cautious in cases involving gender-based violence, especially where it is symptomatic of a power imbalance between the two parties that the judicial assistants are seeking to reconcile. Even though the *Marriage Law 2001* and the *Law on the Protection of the Rights and Interests of Women 2005* both prohibit domestic violence and domestic violence is now a ground for divorce, judicial assistants are not particularly sensitive to identifying matrimonial disputes involving violence against women as disputes to be treated carefully. This could have been due to the absence of a national anti-domestic violence law and implementing regulations at the time,[6] but it also points to a lack of understanding and, potentially, a lack of technical skills on the part of judicial assistants.

Conclusion

As judicial administrative staff members have become more professionalised over the past two decades, grassroots judicial offices at township level have gradually played a more significant role in bridging state law and rural custom through dispute resolution and legal literacy campaigns. The head of a judicial office in G town has argued that working in the judicial office now requires certain professional skills, and therefore a degree or a certificate in law is necessary to ensure that parties' legal rights are well protected. He attributes the mediated outcomes that clearly went against one party's legal rights to a mediator's lack of understanding of relevant laws, believing that increasing the legal knowledge and technical skills of judicial officers will be sufficient to improve outcomes for villages, and rural women in particular.

Explaining how judicial assistants should deal with crimes, G town judicial office stated:

> *most judicial assistants know that disputes involving criminal wrongdoing, such as rape, must not be settled by mediation, but in a few individual cases exceptions still exist, especially in remote rural areas . . . Of course, respect for rural customs is important during dispute settlement; however there is a precondition that [rural] tradition does not contravene formal law.*

During the process of mediation in cases involving women's rights, the judicial assistants tend to put the principles of law that stress the protection of vulnerable groups before the rural customs that perpetuate gender-based bias and discrimination, yet their good intentions and ability to solve disputes also play a key role in helping rural women with grievances to seek justice. However, their work is hindered by the conflicts between different laws, a lack of gender awareness within the state law itself (especially some provisions in the law regulating land tenure and transfer), as well as the absence of rules against domestic violence. The problems within formal law itself further hinder the possibility that judicial assistants at the grassroots can further exert activism in helping disadvantaged women clients to access justice, which may eventually prejudice the fulfilment of their clients' rights.

More research into how rural women experience justice mechanisms (both formal and informal) should be conducted in order to better understand how best to protect rural women's rights.[7] It is particularly important to understand how rural women use different systems to enforce and understand their rights as well as: their notions of justice; their satisfaction with the resolutions achieved through the judicial offices or other mechanisms; and whether the law is being used as an instrument for empowerment and, if so, how it is being used effectively.

Notes

1 'Justice' here refers to 'the lay notion of obtaining satisfactory help in efforts to resolve grievances' (Michelson 2008, p. 44).
2 The 'Three Supremes' are the CCP's principles advocated during Hu Jintao's leadership, which involve three layers of meaning: the supremacy of the Party leadership; the supremacy of people's interests; and supremacy of the Constitution and laws.
3 Ma Xiwu (1898–1962) was a senior judge in the Shaanxi–Gansu-Ningxia Communist Base Area during the revolutionary war, who was appointed Vice-president of the SPC in 1954. Ma Xiwu initiated a new trial method characterised by active investigations on the part of judges; holding trials in public spaces, such as in the field or in the village; the involvement of the local community in decision-making and a preference for using mediation (Whiting and Shao, pp. 224–5).
4 Left-behind women and children refers to rural women and children whose husbands or parents left home in rural areas to work or conduct business outside, especially in cities or towns, with absences of half a year at least. They are usually affected by various social, economic and demographic changes that directly or indirectly cause both physical and psychological problems. It was estimated that the numbers of women and children left behind in Chinese rural areas are 50 million and 61 million respectively (Duan *et al.* 2009).
5 Several informants also noted anecdotally that, after the amendments, more couples had gone directly to the court or the civil affairs bureau to seek divorces.
6 China's new National Anti-Domestic Violence Law was promulgated on December 27, 2015 and came into effect on March 1, 2016. No implementing regulations have been issued at time of printing.
7 Unfortunately, this study was not able to explore several key issues relating to the case studies described above due to difficulties with reaching out to rural women clients.

Bibliography

Chen, B. (2008) 'The Difficulties of Grassroots Legal Services in Western Central Rural China' 《中西部农村基层法律服务业的困境》 *Journal of Zhanjiang Normal College*, vol. 2, pp. 26–32 (in Chinese).

Dong, L., Chen, B., and Nie, L. (2008) 'Structural Disorder and Dissemination of Law' 《结构混乱与迎法下乡》, *Social Science in China*, vol. 5, pp. 87–100 (in Chinese).

Duan, C., Zhou, F., and Yang, K. (2009) 'A Survey On Left-behind Women In China' *China.com.cn*, May 7, [online] http://www.china.com.cn/news/zhuanti/fnbg/2009-05/07/content_17738716_5.htm

Fan, Y. (2005) 'Chinese Women and Families in Social Transformation' 《社会转型中的中国女性与家庭》, *The Rule of Law Forum*, vol. 20 (5), pp. 41–7 (in Chinese).

Fei, H. (1998) *From the Soil, the Foundations of Chinese Society* 《乡土中国》 Peking University Press, Beijing, China (in Chinese).

Fu, Y. (2004) 'A Preliminary Review of China's Grassroots Legal Services: Examining the Rural Legal Service Agencies' 《中国基层法律服务状况的初步考察报告——以农村

基层法律服务所为窗口》, *Peking University Law Review*, vol. 6 (1), pp. 86–123 (in Chinese).

Gu, W. (2013) 'The judiciary in economic and political transformation: quo vadis Chinese courts?' *Chinese Journal of Comparative Law*, vol. 1, no. 2, pp. 303–34.

He, S. and Huang, H. (2011) '"Taking Up Law As Arms": How Does The Law Work In Rural Areas? Comparative Study on Four Cases In The Centre Of Hunan Province' 《"拿起法律的武器"：法律何以下乡？—湘中四个个案的比较研究》 *China Rural Survey*, vol. 1, pp. 84–95 (in Chinese).

Jiang, S. (2011) 'Chinese Families In the Context of Judicial Activism' 《司法能动下的中国家庭》, *Beijing Cultural Review*, vol. 1, pp. 24–30 (in Chinese).

Li, X. and Xu, S. (2013) 'Sensibility, Property and "Justice" In Divorce Disputes – A Research Based on Li Town's Data' 《离婚纠纷中的情感、财产与"正义"——基于李镇档案的研究》, *Law and Social Science*, vol. 11(1), pp. 69–104 (in Chinese).

Liu, M. (2002) *Barefoot Lawyers, Newsweek*, March 3 [online] http://www.newsweek.com/barefoot-lawyers-141565.

Michelson, E. (2008) 'Justice from Above or Below? Popular Strategies for Resolving Grievances in Rural China', *The China Quarterly*, vol. 193, pp. 43–64.

National People's Congress (2011) 'Top legislator says socialist system of laws with Chinese characteristics established "on schedule,"' March 11 [online] http://www.npc.gov.cn/englishnpc/news/Events/2011-03/10/content_1640424.htm

O'Brien, K.J. (1996) 'Rightful resistance', *World Politics*, vol. 49, no. 1, pp. 31–55.

O'Brien, K.J. and Li, L.J. (2006) *Rightful resistance in rural China*, Cambridge University Press, New York.

Rong, J. (2005) 'Law Revised to Protect Women's Rights', *China Features*, 20 September [online] http://www.chinese-embassy.org.uk/eng/zt/t213042.htm

State Council Information Office (2012) 'Judicial Reform in China,' October 9, [online], http://english.gov.cn/archive/white_paper/2014/08/23/content_281474983043170.htm

Tan, T. (2005) 'The Logic of the Change and Living Practice of the Organizations – A Political Ecology Review on the Running of the Judicial Organization in Chu Town' 《组织变迁及其生存实践的逻辑——楚镇司法所运行的政治生态学考察》, *Journal of Normal University (Humanities and Social Science)*, vol. 44(1), pp. 118–23 (in Chinese).

Tian, X. (2010) 'The Transformation of Dispute Resolution Mechanisms in Rural Justice Office and the Factors Analysis' 《乡镇司法所纠纷解决机制的变化及其原因探析》, *Contemporary Law Review*, vol. 143(5), pp. 32–41 (in Chinese).

Upham, F. (2005) 'Who Will Find the Defendant if He Stays with His Sheep? Justice in Rural China', *Yale Law Journal*, vol. 114, pp. 1675–718.

Wang, G., Wu, L., Xu, B., Wang, K., and Zhou, Y. (2012) 'A Research Report on the Extensive Mediation System That Is Based on the Improvement of People's Mediation' 《完善以人民调解为基础的"大调解"工作体系调研报告》, *Institute for Justice Administration of the Ministry of Justice* [online] http://www.moj.gov.cn/yjs/content/2012-10/18/content_2787450.htm?node=30053

Whiting, S.H. and Shao, H. (2014) 'Courts and political stability: Mediating rural land disputes' in H Fu and J Gillespie (eds.), *Resolving Land Disputes in East Asia: Exploring the Limits of Law*, Cambridge University Press, Cambridge, UK, pp. 222–48.

Woo, M. (2003) 'Shaping Citizenship: Chinese Family Law and Women', *Yale Journal of Law & Feminism*, vol. 15, pp. 99–134.

Ying, X. (2007) '"Dissemination of Law at Village Level" and "Access to Justice" – A Case Study of "Barefoot Lawyers" in the Villages of China' 《"迎法入乡"与"接近正

义”——对中国乡村“赤脚律师”的个案研究》, *Tribune of Political Science and Law (Journal of China University of Political Science and Law)*, vol. 25(1), pp. 79–94.

You, C. (2005) 'Rural Judicial Office Embedded in the Process of Modernization of the Law'《嵌入法制现代化进程的乡镇司法所》 in Y. Luo (ed.), *Huazhong Law Review* (Volume 2), Peking University Press, Beijing, China, pp. 78–89.

Zhu S. (2010) 'About Judicial Activism And Extensive Mediation',《关于能动司法与大调解》 *China Legal Science*, vol. 1, pp. 5–16.

9 Bringing intersectionality home

Delivering contextualised justice in response to gender-based violence in Hong Kong

Puja Kapai

Introduction

Advocates have long relied on the argument that a state party to CEDAW must necessarily address any impediments to women's enjoyment of their rights. This includes freedom from violence. Drawing on Article 5 regarding the systemic and structural impact of cultural factors on equality, CEDAW General Recommendation 19, which specifically addresses the issue of violence against women and the 1993 Declaration on the Elimination of Violence against Women, advocates emphasise the due diligence obligations of states to ensure an adequate framework to prevent, protect, prosecute, punish and provide reparations against violence, whether it occurs in the public or private spheres, through legal, political, administrative and cultural measures.

Feminist discourse has highlighted the masculinities institutionalised through various cultural structures, including the law. Intersections theory (King 1988; Hooks 1989) has called into question the 'one-size-fits-all' approach, which risks the exclusion of third world women's views, experiences and lived realities in the paradigms for equality (Crenshaw 1989; 1991, p. 1244).

One sphere in which the impact of the failure to incorporate such perspectives is critically apparent is with the measures in place to combat domestic violence. Not all women experience violence similarly nor do they respond to it in the manner anticipated by the law. The effectiveness of measures to combat and address violence is inextricably tied to individual user capacities and their internal cultural response systems, which either drive or discourage certain courses of action. Studies that cut across markers of race, socio-economic background and immigration status have revealed that the existing measures are class-, race- or culture-centric in ways unimagined as relevant before (Lee *et al.* 2002; Dutton *et al.* 2002; Shirwadkar 2004), leaving women of 'marginalised statuses' – such as race, colour, immigrant, persons with disabilities or sexual minorities – most vulnerable to entrenchment in situations of violence. Therefore, seldom do all women have equal access to assistance and protection against domestic violence.

The failure to consider the relevance of measures against women's socio-cultural and religious identities creates a critical 'justice gap' for particular groups of women who may be constrained by internal and external factors in help-seeking.

Substantive equal protection and the fulfilment of the due diligence obligation to address violence requires: locating knowledge and strategies in the lived experiences of all victims of violence; and conducting an intersectional impact assessment of needs and capacities to evaluate the viability of solutions.

This chapter presents a brief overview of feminist theory and uses intersectional analysis to frame the findings from an empirical, mixed methods study on the help-seeking behaviours of ethnic minority and immigrant victims of domestic violence in Hong Kong. It locates the gap between victims' perceptions about violence and their rights and the assumptions underlying laws and policies governing protection against domestic violence, substantiating the existence of the justice gap for ethnic minority and immigrant victims. This signals a failure of the state's responsibility to provide substantive equal protection against violence for all women. The chapter concludes that developing a framework to document the typology of victims of domestic violence is an indispensable first step in plugging the justice gap.

Third wave feminism and substantive equal protection against violence

The inherent masculinities of the law, the under-reporting of crimes such as physical and sexual assaults, and the underutilisation of the full range of the provisions and remedies in relation to gender-based crimes all give cause to examine and understand victim responses to intimate partner violence more fully. The intimate sphere renders the victim particularly vulnerable to specific forms of violence and abuse given the expectations and emotions vested in such a relationship.

Feminist insights pertaining to the struggle for power and dominance and its gendered nature have been mapped across a range of socio-demographic factors (Sirman 1989, p. 7). Men's systemic dominance and control of women is deeply embedded in a culture of patriarchy and is not confined to any particular section of the population (Malik and Lindahl 1998, pp. 409–23; Mauricio and Gormley 2001, pp. 1066–81; Sirman 1989, p. 7).

Existing laws and policies are riddled with assumptions about victims' likely behaviours, including self-identification as a victim of violence – which she recognises as unlawful despite cultural attitudes which condone such violence and the ability and willingness to take necessary steps to seek police and other assistance for self-protection. These expectations are markedly ignorant of the psychological, emotional, cultural, social, and practical considerations impacting the cognitive framing of responses to domestic violence among victims.

While violence against women is not a phenomenon reserved for particular women, its impact on a victim's capacity to overcome family violence in particular at-risk groups is certainly disparate (Anderson 1997, p. 658; Johnson and Ferraro 2000, p. 959) because violence and responses to violence are culturally constructed (Kapai 2012, pp. 346–7; 2015; Liang *et al.* 2005; Saharso 2000, p. 224; Shirwadkar 2004, p. 860).[1] Ethnic minority and immigrant (EMI) women's responses to domestic violence are necessarily informed by personal, cultural and practical constraints, such as immigration status, social networks, mobility or financial dependence. Recent literature provides a compelling account of the failure of general laws against violence to protect all groups of women, calling into question their adequacy and effectiveness in ensuring the short- and long-term viability of any response within the context of an ongoing relationship.[2] Cultural equipment and the lived realities of victims need to be accounted for to understand their motivations and behaviours and to guarantee the relevance and effectiveness of measures.[3]

Certain factors make EMI women particularly vulnerable to domestic violence and becoming entrenched in such situations, significantly affecting their help-seeking behaviour (Menjivar and Salcido 2002; Shirwadkar 2004, p. 860). Internal and cultural factors and values define victims' worldviews of right and wrong and the boundaries of acceptable behaviour, while certain external factors act as enablers or disablers of self-preserving action (Dutton et al. 2002; Lee et al. 2002, p. 531; Saharso 2000, p. 224; Shirwadkar 2004, p. 860).

Varying understandings of what constitute acts of violence across cultures (Amirthalingam 2005; Lee *et al.* 2002) challenge possibilities for an all-encompassing definition which resonates with all victims. Cultural value systems predicated on a belief in the hierarchical nature of a marital relationship that places males at the top of the hierarchy condition women to overlook certain infractions as the 'norm' or 'minor upsets', expecting tolerance, obedience, subservience and understanding on their part. Moreover, troubles within a marriage pertain to a realm in which the law is traditionally neither welcomed nor viewed as effective from a regulatory perspective (Goldfarb 2007, pp. 1487–551; Lewis *et al.* 2001, pp. 105–30). For example, research on the Chinese and South Asian immigrant community in the United States finds a tendency to paint family violence as a 'non-issue' within those groups that have come to be viewed as the 'model minority'. These discrepancies in viewpoint may result from differences in definitions of what constitutes violence, the desire to keep up appearances and the patriarchal structure of these communities (Midlarsky *et al.* 2006, 279–300).

Various situational constraints (external factors) further impact EMI victims' help-seeking behaviours. For example, immigration status (Grosh 2011) contributes to a fear of deportation (Narayan 1995, p. 109), getting into trouble with law enforcement (Menjivar and Salcido 2002, p. 910; Shirwadkar 2004, p. 860) and the consequent loss of access to children (Berinstein *et al.* 2006). The lack of language capabilities (MacLeod and Shin 1993), low levels of education and financial dependence (Shirwadkar 2004, p. 860) and social isolation exacerbate women's dependence on the abuser and tilt the power imbalance even further (Narayan 1995, p. 103). Distrust of law enforcement and frontline responders considered to be an extension of the government tends to undermine access to justice (Latta and Goodman 2005, pp. 1447–8). These indicia place EMI victims at a heightened risk of vulnerability to violence.

Combining this new knowledge with the work of Dobash and Dobash (1979, 1992) and Walker (1977) on the psyche of victims of intimate partner violence helps explain discrepancies in statistics on rates of violence, complaints and convictions. This signals the need for an alternative discourse across disciplines to address the justice gap.

Help-seeking behaviours of EMI victims and competencies of frontline responders in Hong Kong

Despite the steadily growing body of literature that confirms divergent responses to violence among EMI victims as compared with 'local' women in a particular community, corresponding legal and policy measures to apply this knowledge to make full use of newly emerging correlates of violence and vulnerability are yet to be developed. This is an essential and urgent undertaking given the state's due diligence obligation to root out violence against women systematically (Goldfarb 2007).[4]

Unlike the recent emphasis on research into the effects of domestic violence on mainland Chinese women in Hong Kong, very little has been done on the experiences and needs of ethnic minority victims of domestic violence.[5] The studies highlight the impact of cultural values on women's experience of domestic violence. However, the nexus between intersecting factors pertinent to EMI victims, given their other minority statuses and their impact on likely responses, have not been examined.

The data presented in this chapter derives from questionnaires and interviews conducted with EMI victims and frontline service providers[6] working with this community in Hong Kong. They covered their experience: in relation to law and policy to determine whether and how knowledge and understanding of legal rights and perceptions about law enforcement or other frontline responders and the legal system have an impact on the help-seeking behaviours of EMI victims; whether and in what way the cultural value system impacts the relevance of certain measures as appropriate resolutions for domestic violence; and whether frontline responders have the requisite knowledge of relevant laws and policies and cultural competence to offer effective assistance to EMI victims of domestic violence.

Awareness of legal rights and perceptions of discrimination

Although most EMI women were aware that domestic violence was wrong, their awareness of their legal rights to access services was very weak. In some cases, women had been misguided by frontline service providers. Several EMI women complained of racial, religious or other forms of discrimination in the handling of their case but were unaware of their rights to equality and non-discrimination. Others were misinformed that certain services were dependent on their permanent residence status or on filing for divorce from the abuser. Perceptions and experiences of discrimination are rife. Some frontline respondents thought EMI women were not entitled to the same rights or levels of access to social services as Hong Kong Chinese victims. Social workers believe that they should guard against unscrupulous access to public resources. Some social workers blamed EMI victims for their vulnerabilities and recommended that they return to their home countries.

Legal uncertainties also created fear among EMI women. One EMI woman said that the police threatened to arrest both her and her husband since she had also assaulted him, albeit in self-defence. The fact that seeking assistance from front-line service providers did not increase rights awareness and contributed to misinformation is of concern, especially since the findings reveal a critical lack of awareness of relevant provisions among services that are first accessed by EMI victims.

Perceptions and ratings of the performance of the legal system

Ethnic minority victims found the legal system inaccessible to them and expressed particular dissatisfaction with the system's response towards the guilt of abusers, protecting the innocent and its capacity to deliver speedy justice. One victim reported that it took ten years for her to finalise her claim. Others lamented that tactical delays and power imbalances, particularly in the light of a lack of funds, knowledge and the capacity to effectively engage the legal process, severely undermined their prospects for justice.

Victims reported higher satisfaction levels with police performance, notably for their law enforcement abilities, although some expressed reservations about police approachability and fair treatment. For example, one EMI victim complained that the police sided with the abusive partner and failed to protect her. They advised her not to go home due to the risk of violence but did not say when she could return home or where she should go instead, so she eventually returned to her abusive husband. Others shared that although their police complaint initially led to the abuser's immediate arrest, they were released the following day, provoking serious retaliation.

One EMI victim called the police after violent attacks by her husband over several months and said that when the police arrived on the night in question they spoke only to her father-in-law since he was fluent in Cantonese. They did not communicate with her to ascertain her version of events. The police advised her, through her father-in-law, to file a complaint at the police station and leave with them to head to a shelter. She packed her belongings and proceeded to carry her baby with her but the police advised her to leave her baby behind, saying she could pick her baby up the next day. She recollected that it had been two years since she left her baby. Her husband and in-laws have refused to give her access to her child. She felt the police misguided her and have ruined her life. Doubtful of their commitment to helping ethnic minority women, she resolved never to involve the police or social workers in her personal affairs again.

Other EMI victims complained that the police asked them to show them their injuries. When the women requested female officers, they were advised that no female officers were available at that time. They expressed fear over unfair treatment, wrongful arrest and that the police might believe their husband's story given their language limitations. This made them feel very vulnerable. One EMI victim said the police advised her to stay with her husband since the high profile Delhi gang rape made the risk of deportation to India worse than the violence she endured here. Another victim was advised that cultural expectations were she should return to the husband, be a good wife and tolerate the violence.

Perceptions and ratings of the performance of service providers

EMI victims reported that their needs and concerns were not always understood or addressed. They complained of discrimination, a lack of respect for cultural and dietary differences and social isolation made worse by language barriers. They cited the insistence of service providers that they file for divorce before being assisted in accessing compassionate housing, education for their children and other basic needs, as examples of their insensitivity, incompetence and discrimination. Service providers likewise reported that clients had identified shortcomings in their services. Service providers' assessment of their own performance, capacity and competence in handling EMI victims highlighted primarily language and communication barriers and the failure to appreciate EMI victims' cultural needs leading to their inability to survive in shelters.

Service providers had also, in some cases, inappropriately relied on community members from the EMI victims' background to assist with interpretation. This unmediated outreach has backfired, heightening risks of violence and deterring victims from seeking help. One interpreter scolded the victim for bringing shame on her family and threatened to reveal her location to her husband unless she returned home immediately. EMI victims reportedly preferred dealing with occasional episodes of violence over humiliation, isolation and risk of more serious violence if they sought help.

Vulnerabilities, disempowerment and fear

External factors, such as fear of law enforcement and the threat of losing access to one's children due to financial and immigration status dependence, are compounded by poor educational qualifications, absence of social networks and mobility, and a lack of language skills in Chinese or English.

Immigration status and its impact

Many EMI victims were forced to stay silent because they believed their spouses had the power to refuse renewal or to withdraw sponsorship of their visa or undermine their permanent resident status. The threat of deportation and permanent separation from their children deterred them from taking action. The implications of a police complaint on their husband's immigration or employment status (for example, deportation or imprisonment), and concerns about causing unnecessary upheaval in their children's lives led women to sacrifice their safety for the family's sake.

Indeed, social workers expressed that the immigration rules put children and women in a precarious position, exposing them to the risk of continued violence until a more favourable immigration status was achieved. This is particularly true where children risk being taken away from victimised mothers, putting the interests of the child in direct conflict with the mother's safety needs. Several EMI victims waited to achieve permanent resident status before complaining about abuse for the very first time.

Financial dependence on abuser

EMI victims feared they would not be eligible for Comprehensive Social Security Assistance if they left their husbands. Their long-term financial dependence on their spouse and having young children to look after made it almost impossible for them to choose their own safety over their family's needs. They were also concerned about household income if the sole breadwinner was arrested and imprisoned, with destitution impacting their growth and nutrition and disrupting the children's education. Moreover, most participants could not speak Chinese or English and, in the circumstances, were unlikely to find a job.

One EMI victim said the social worker advised her that social welfare services would conduct a risk assessment and take her children away from the abusive environment. When she asked the social worker whether she could bring her children to the refuge, she was incorrectly advised that she could not. Accordingly, EMI victims worry constantly about dealing with the consequences of their complaints, being forced to file for divorce or give testimony against their abusive husband in a criminal case, losing access to their children and their only source of income and being deported if the husband withdraws sponsorship of their spousal visa.

These examples shed light on the complex external factors and considerations underlying the victims' decisions in response to violence. Apart from these, 'internal' factors informed by the cultural or religious value framework of EMI victims make them unlikely to seek help.

Attitudes towards help-seeking against violence in a family setting

Some cultural value frameworks engender an expectation of privacy and secrecy pertaining to the intimate sphere of a marital relationship, which is perceived as impenetrable, sacrosanct and out of bounds to the gaze of outsiders. Complaints about spouses are discouraged, looked down upon and met with rebukes to keep affairs private or are promptly dismissed as fabrications. They worry about breaching the fundamental rule against 'airing one's laundry in public'. One woman said:

> *There are many people to gossip. Even if he was the one who was wrong, eventually, they all talk bad about the wife.*

Ideas of honour, shame and stigma and the expectations of a good, dutiful wife are deeply entrenched in the minds of many EMI women, who see these indicia as signifiers of their success in life. Women transgressing these norms are condemned for bringing dishonour to the family. EMI women are very mindful of how their help-seeking behaviour would be judged by others in their community. One EMI victim said:

> *The people in our community, they blame the woman. Even if the man is having an affair or is drinking and has a high temper, the woman still gets the blame.*

It is they who suffer retaliation, rather than the abuser, in the form of further violence or ostracisation by their extended family and the community. The isolation or expulsion of a woman from her familial or community network is the ultimate punishment and a public pronouncement of her failure as a wife, which would bar her and her children from participation in the community.

A tightly knit community network makes it impossible to prevent news from spreading to their families back home. The consequences of falling foul of these expectations are profound and the costs too high. Victims seemed to prefer an oppressed existence with their kin and support network intact over a marginalised life of isolation and exclusion without them.

Likewise, separation and worse, divorce, are also instigators of social isolation, having a serious impact on family ties, friendships and the future of children. For example, one woman shared:

> *If you separate from your husband, the community also don't want to talk to you because they think you are living alone and independently. That means you are not a good woman.*

Similarly, another said:

> *It's shameful and embarrassing for me. Scared of being thrown out of the house. Do not want a broken home for my children . . . It's like a disgrace for my family.*

Social workers found that some EMI victims avoided counselling or therapy due to a cultural perception of shame associated with seeking psychological or social service support because it implies weakness and an inability to cope with what is viewed in many EMI communities as 'routine' life within marriage.

Help-seeking patterns among EMI victims

By all accounts, EMI victims of domestic violence are unlikely to seek external assistance, support and protection against violence. Their most likely course of action was to seek family support because they would better understand their needs and concerns. However, they also expressed that the experience was not always positive because cultural pressures were often applied to persuade them to stay with their abusive partners.

Institutional competencies: law, discrimination and cultural sensitivity

Despite recognising a growing need for targeted services for EMI victims, institutional and frontline responders indicated a lack of capacity and competence to handle EMI victims' needs effectively.

Knowledge of law

There was an alarmingly low level of awareness among frontline responders of relevant laws pertaining to women's rights, equality legislation, domestic violence and criminal laws. This has serious implications for their ability to effectively assess risks and needs and directly influences the range of options that are made available to victims in very difficult circumstances. This puts clients at risk due to unreliable or misguided advice, which can and has proved fatal to EMI victims.

Language and cultural competencies

Although nearly all participating organisations indicated they had instant access to interpretation services or staff on site to respond to the needs of clients in various languages, language remained a significant barrier to providing quality services. EMI victims complained of poor quality interpretation and were also suspicious of interpreters. Some victims worried about confidentiality issues and the spread of community gossip since interpreters knew them or their families personally. In one instance, a victim was scolded by the interpreter for breaking up her family, instead of having the professional's advice translated for her. In another instance, an interpreter abandoned an on-going interpretation at a hospital out of fear.

In the public hospital system, victims complained there was a four-hour wait for access to an interpreter and, often, nurses and doctors would encourage those accompanying the victims, including children, friends and even husbands or their family members, to interpret. This would lead to restraint in sharing detailed accounts of the abuse and compromised victims' safety, especially if the perpetrator had accompanied her to the hospital.

Seemingly, service providers do not appear to see themselves as having the duty to provide access to interpretation as a matter of right, as reflected by the significant underutilisation of interpretation services, which reported that only ten per cent of their requests came through the social welfare department or NGOs dealing with victims of domestic violence. The usage rate of an instantaneous interpretation video uplink device was at zero per cent.

Finally, some messages risk being lost in translation, particularly where there is a lack of a standardised accreditation and ethics training system for interpreters. This is particularly significant in the counselling context where the need to interpret each statement and the presence of a third party may not be conducive to the development of trust and authenticity, diluting any therapeutic benefits.

Of greater concern however, were EMI victims' criticisms over poor levels of cultural competence. Many women crave a connection with other women who might understand their plight better, having been through such situations before. A frontline service provider said:

> *[EMI] women did not feel confident being referred to a Chinese organisation.*

EMI victims worried that they would be letting their community down by affirming negative impressions and stereotypes. Social workers appeared ill equipped to understand specific cultural factors that impacted how victims thought about the violence, its impact on their marital relationship and their readiness to take certain steps (but not others) to mitigate the violence.

For example, victims expressed that, although they received access to certain temporary services and were informed of their legal rights, these were meaningless without a safety plan consistent with their value framework and which addressed the multiple concerns EMI women fleeing abusive households have. For example, the stigma associated with a married woman spending nights out of the family household would rule out the possibility of staying at a shelter for some. Suggestions of separating from or divorcing a long-time abusive partner may likewise deter them from returning to the services. Most EMI victims therefore eventually returned to the abuser.

Despite awareness of the need to enhance cultural competence, only half of the participating organisations reported that their staff underwent regular cultural sensitivity or competence training. The training materials also raised concerns since some were discriminatory and perpetuated stereotypes about EMI women. Many frontline responders felt that training would not help enhance their cultural capacities stating that 'it was impossible to understand minority cultures'. Others lamented the lack of time and opportunity to enhance service provision.

Addressing domestic violence in Hong Kong: law, policy and practical challenges

In Hong Kong, treaty obligations pertaining to equality and non-discrimination were enacted into domestic law pursuant to the *Sex Discrimination Ordinance Cap. 480, 1995*, which came into effect in 1996, while the *Family Status Discrimination Ordinance Cap. 527* was enacted in 1997.[7] *The Race Discrimination Ordinance Cap. 602* was enacted in 2008 and came into force in July 2009. The Domestic Violence Ordinance was extensively amended into its present form of the Domestic Violence and Cohabitation Relationships Violence Ordinance Cap. 189 (DCRVO) in 2009, to reflect the range of family members who may pose a threat as potential abusers and to extend its coverage beyond married couples and heterosexual cohabitants to former spouses, former cohabitants, immediate and extended family members and homosexual cohabitants.

Although the DCRVO does not define domestic violence, for the wider purposes of policy development in Hong Kong, domestic violence refers to a pattern of coercive control, which includes conduct that manifests itself in forms of psychological, economic, sexual or physical dominance in an intimate relationship.[8] However, for the purposes of police intervention, the definition is narrower, covering only threats of or actual physical violence between parties perceived as having a family relationship, impacting first response and intervention strategies in relation to the reporting and handling of different types of domestic violence complaints. Non-physical abuse and non-serious physical assaults tend to be recorded as 'domestic incidents' by the police.

Domestic violence cases involving serious physical assault are addressed under criminal law under the *Offences Against the Persons Ordinance Cap. 212, 1950* and the *Crimes Ordinance Cap. 200, 1972* without specific legislative provisions that account for the intimate context of the violence and the prospects for repeated or escalated episodes of violence. Additional protection is provided under the DCRVO, which enables protected persons to apply for an injunction against molestation, the intention being 'to provide quick and simple relief to persons who could not and did not wish to take divorce proceedings' and to allow a cooling-off period for couples. The legislation appears to recognise the power dynamic in an intimate relationship and its influence on the victim's reluctance to report the incident to the police, as well as concerns regarding the wellbeing of their children, the potential loss of the family's financial support and any cultural or religious considerations.

Although the low reporting rate in Hong Kong[9] may suggest the prevalence of the 'learned helplessness' psyche amongst Chinese, immigrant and ethnic minority women in the jurisdiction, it has been proposed that victims of abuse are active survivors of domestic violence, where their action or inaction towards help-seeking might be purposeful and strategic, based on various factors (Tiwari *et al.* 2001). For example, many Chinese women abstain from seeking help against violence out of shame of breaking up their marriages, as they usually equate success in life with the success of their marriages (Loke *et al.* 2012). Additionally, in Chinese society and many ethnic minority communities, solidarity of family, including that of the extended family, is very important, creating an expectation of an obedient, respectful and deferential wife. Tension stemming from in-law conflict transfers to the spousal relationship, contributing to the use of violence, especially where sons are expected to side with parents out of filial piety, a strong cultural factor in Chinese society (Choi *et al.* 2012) and ethnic minority micro-communities.

Until the high profile murder–suicides in Tin Shui Wai[10] in 2004, the perception was that the existing provisions and protocols were adequate to ensure the safety of victims of all backgrounds. The failure stemmed from a sense of complacency premised on two misguided presumptions: first, that all victims of family violence experience it similarly and thus existing measures provide access to relevant protection and resources; and second, that safety is the primary concern of victims and they would know where and how to seek assistance and would do so without hesitation. These presumptions ignore the tensions and conflicting considerations that often inform marital contexts and invariably impact coping strategies. The failure to account for the influence of cultural values and social context on reporting and help-seeking patterns highlights an institutionalised ignorance of realities on the ground.

Since 2004 the Hong Kong Government has adopted a three-pronged approach offering preventive, supportive and specialised services, to be achieved through multidisciplinary collaboration between different government departments, third sector organisations, healthcare facilities, police and housing authorities (United Nations 2012). The government has attempted to raise public awareness about these measures through television programmes, such as the 'give a helping hand to your neighbour facing family violence' (Chan 2012, p. 39; The Women's Commission 2009), and the 'Family Support Programme' (Chan 2012, p. 45) to reach target groups through phone calls and home visits as preventive measures. The police were meant to streamline investigation processes through a 'one family one team' policy geared towards greater consistency across intervention strategies and extra protection through access to social workers and temporary accommodation for victims. Medical staff are now trained on domestic violence cases,[11] and specific screening material and risk assessment evaluation is incorporated by social workers, which would lead to comprehensive service provision based on needs (Chan 2012, p. 25).

However, frontline service providers have failed to implement legislative and policy measures. This situation has been further exacerbated by institutional failures. Firstly, there is no standardised screening method adopted by the Hospital Authority to recognise, and ensure care and support for domestic violence victims. In areas where such screening is adopted, a significantly low percentage of medical staff favoured the screening process.[12] In addition, victims of domestic violence who do not enjoy permanent residence also lack access to public resources, such as housing and social welfare, and employment. These increase their dependency on the abusive partner and hinder their ability to and likelihood of seeking help.

The continued use of general legislation to capture and frame all acts of violence perpetuates power-dynamics in a patriarchal and racialised society which extends oppression through its legal framework. It is crucial to recognise that existing measures are specific to race, class and cultural contexts. Service delivery and frontline response models warrant urgent evaluation to ensure the immediate safety of victims and the requisite support.

Towards developing a typology of victim responses to domestic violence

The research findings highlight the complexity of the myriad factors that impact EMI victims' responses to domestic violence. Many layers straddle the raw experience of abuse, the way in which the experience is characterised in the mind of the victim and her innate desire to protect oneself. Racial, cultural and religious identities and value systems converge with external factors, such as law enforcement, immigration, financial independence and social isolation, to render the experience of violence a very different one for the EMI victim, directly impacting the steps she takes towards self-preservation.

Where steps towards self-preservation conflict with cultural values and expectations; EMI victims choose a culturally appropriate course of action, even at the risk of repeat or escalated violence, unless the violence becomes life threatening to them or their children. Cases where women have separated from their spouses despite cultural taboos reflect desperate acts of survival in the face of serious and repeated violence. However, many victims then lead isolated lives and are cut off from their own community and face discrimination and exclusion from mainstream society. Therefore, it is vital to recognise and develop strategies to better understand, inform and predict EMI victims' receptivity to various response measures in light of the unique considerations impacting their help-seeking decisions.

A substantive right to equal protection against violence, and state parties' obligations of due diligence to guarantee such protection, necessitates the identification and obviation of systemic barriers to accessing preventive, protective and punitive means to guard against violence. Moreover, these obligations extend to all persons within their jurisdiction, including immigrants and minorities, and regardless of whether the violence is state-sanctioned or perpetrated by private actors (see e.g. Byrnes and Bath 2008). The due diligence principle makes it incumbent on all states to identify this 'accessibility' gap and to take steps to close this chasm.[13]

Legislation and service models presently do not incorporate any typology of a victim, let alone an EMI victim, into their rubric at all. The large gap between expectations and perceptions of the key stakeholder groups, the barriers to service acquisition and effective delivery, as well as the consequences of misperceptions or ill-advised, prejudicial attitudes on the suitability of interventions, beckon an urgent need to devise a new and dynamic approach to conduct needs and risk assessments to predict victim and perpetrator behaviours.

The construction of an intersectional framework through which to assess EMI victims' experiences of domestic violence, to understand their situational context from a social, political and legal perspective, would serve as a dynamic assessment tool to facilitate the development of corresponding measures to effectively deliver targeted responses to guard against repeat and future gender-based violence. This requires a study of the internal and external factors and their combined effect in producing a unique set of circumstances and constraints to impact the victim's choices and responses to violence. This requires an extensive mapping exercise and screening for each client, starting with the first responder.

The findings serve as the building blocks towards the development of such a typology of help-seeking behaviours of EMI victims so that the responses and interventions in relation to domestic violence can be tailored to suit their specific needs and concerns. An intersectional impact assessment and analysis of EMI victims and their history, based on data collected through various channels of service engagement, should lead to the development of a unique response plan for each client to make equal protection against violence a reality for her and her family. This has important implications for case intake and management processes at NGOs, government service providers and shelters, and for multidisciplinary case conferencing and follow-up work to attend to all the needs of the family that arise as a result of the violence. There are several areas for frontline responders to work together on. All stakeholder groups also need to develop an understanding of the different sources of assistance and support, and the role that different sectors play in protection against and recovery from episodes of violence. In the longer term, facilitating the effective delivery of an integrated response plan will require the development and deployment of multiple competencies and resources and combining integrative knowledge, training and service delivery models.

Conclusion

The effectiveness of the frameworks and institutional capacities for protection against domestic violence are predominantly dependent on individual user capacities and their internal cultural response systems, which either drive or discourage certain courses of action. Cut across markers of race, socioeconomic background and immigration status, international literature and research findings show that existing measures are class-, race- and culture-centric in ways unimagined as relevant before. Findings from multiple studies now confirm that women of colour and immigrant women tend to be most vulnerable to becoming entrenched in situations of violence.

The failure to account for and consider the internal and external conflicts in value systems that these predominant frames of characterising and addressing violence represent for the victims and perpetrators concerned, creates a critical gap in the provision of effective redress against violence for particular groups of women and opportunities for perpetrator rehabilitation.

As the research findings clearly indicate, user capacities and access to the relevant mechanisms for relief against violence are heavily informed by cultural constructs and situational contexts, which, for EMI victims, closely impact their sense of self and their view of their relationship with, and obligations and accountability towards, the family and the broader community to which they belong. These significantly influence their evaluation of their options for relief against future violence.

In order to strive for substantive equal treatment against domestic violence, an intersections analysis of the situational context of victims, which accounts fully for the typology of different victims of domestic violence, must inform approaches and strategies to develop best practices in effective prevention of and protection against domestic violence, to narrow and, ultimately, eliminate this justice gap for an entire community of victims.

To do so meaningfully, there is an urgent need to locate knowledge and effective tools and strategies for violence prevention and redress within the lived realities of the women concerned, so that we recognise that their oppression is not only characterised simply by virtue of their gender but also by other social markers, including race, disability, immigration and socioeconomic status in a system that is still predominantly patriarchal and masculine.

This requires a detailed and systematic review of facially neutral measures, policies, interventions and legal provisions and to question the underlying assumptions and practical constraints that may operate to render them inaccessible to particular groups of women. To treat all victims of violence identically may inadvertently result in unequal protection and constitute a violation of government commitments to eradicate gender-based violence.

Given that a higher proportion of EMI women are victims of domestic violence, and that various factors identified through the literature and empirical research exacerbate their vulnerability, the disempowering factors need to be addressed with urgency. This requires a careful study of the interconnections between factors as 'predictors' of vulnerability for particular groups of victims and an examination of how they can be empowered to minimise the impact of such disadvantages. In particular, the burden placed on them when seeking access to legal or other interventions needs to be mitigated to ensure that they receive timely and necessary assistance and do not spiral into a downward pattern of oppression that the institutionalised incompetence indirectly helps the perpetrator to perpetuate.

Substantive equal access to protections and remedies against domestic violence for all victims must be seen as the relevant benchmark to assess the effectiveness of the state in fulfilling its obligation of due diligence to protect women against violence. The research findings provide evidentiary support for the argument that situational context and cultural factors warrant a complex approach to equality and towards developing inclusive strategies for the effective prevention of and protection against violence.

Notes

1 This is a generalisation given the complexity of factors that impact women's decisions to seek protection and assistance, including length of relationship, severity and regularity of violence and whether the victim believes the perpetrator's rationalisation for the violence.

2 For example, critics have argued against criminal justice approaches towards perpetrators of domestic violence which might put the victim at risk of a more violent attack and questioned the effectiveness of civil remedies such as restraining orders. See, e.g., Crime and Violence Prevention Center, (2005).

3 Poor coordination and the lack of context-sensitive measures contribute to the rise in rates of violence perpetrated against women, largely by people known to them. The failure to follow protocol causes confusion and a poor record of evidence, leading to withdrawal, poor rates of prosecution and conviction and high rates of dismissal in relation to domestic violence. See, United Nations Study of the Secretary-General, 2006.

4 For arguments presented for those who see no value in legal intervention with regard to domestic violence see also Lewis *et al.* (2001).

5 To date, there have only been three such studies, including Hong Kong Christian Service (2007), Tonsing (2014) and Leung and RainLily (2015).

6 The sample included five stakeholder groups: service providers; healthcare workers; social workers (frontline responders from the government and NGO sectors); EMI victims of domestic violence; and non-victims.

7 For a detailed review of the protection of the human rights of women in Hong Kong, see Kapai (2013).

8 This definition reflects the recommendations of various United Nations bodies, including the World Health Organisation.

9 In a 2008 study, the approximate reporting rate of domestic violence cases was only at four per cent (Chan 2012, pp. 19ff.).

10 Between February and April of 2004, a mainland Chinese woman married to a Hong Kong man and residing in Tin Shui Wai reported to the Integrated Family Services Centre, the Social Welfare Department and the Hong Kong Police Department on various occasions, complaining of child sexual abuse and domestic violence. On 11 April 2004 she attended the police station to request officers to accompany her home to check on her daughters, whose safety she was concerned about. Having then rung home several times, she concluded that her husband and daughters were not home. The police decided not to escort her and instead asked her to ring them in the event of an emergency. Later that evening, she and her daughters were found dead in their family home while the husband was found seriously injured. He later died of his injuries. Dubbed a murder–suicide, the incident led to an extensive review into the handling of family violence complaints and frontline sensitivity to high risk factors to prevent such tragedies from occurring in the future.

11 Training is a compulsory part of the Post Registration Certificate Course in Emergency Nursing (Chan 2012, p. 27).

12 Only 53 per cent of nurses and 33 per cent of doctors favoured using the screening process, see Chan *et al.* (2012).

13 The principle of due diligence establishes an obligation, imposing positive duties on state parties to actively take steps to address discrimination, including in the form of violence. See General Recommendation No. 19 (1992) and the Declaration on the Elimination of Violence Against Women (1993).

Bibliography

Amirthalingam, K. (2005) 'Women's Rights, International Norms, and Domestic Violence: Asian Perspectives', *Human Rights Quarterly* 27(2), pp. 683–708.

Anderson, K. (1997) 'Gender, Status and Domestic Violence: An Integration of Feminist and Family Violence Approaches', *Journal of Marriage and Family* 59(3), pp. 655–69.

Berinstein, C., McDonald, J., Nyers, P., Wright, C. and Zerehi, S. S. (2006) 'Access Not Fear. Non-Status Immigrants and City Services' for *Don't Ask, Don't Tell Campaign*, Toronto, Canada.

Byrnes, A. and Bath, E. (2008) 'Violence against Women, the Obligation of Due Diligence, and the Optional Protocol to the Convention on the Elimination of All Forms of Discrimination against Women – Recent Developments' *Human Rights Law Review* 8(3), pp. 517–33.

Chan, KL. (2012) 'Intimate Partner Violence in Hong Kong', in Chan, K. (ed.) *Preventing Family Violence: A Multidisciplinary Approach*, Hong Kong University Press.

Chan, C.C., Chan, Y.C., Au, A., Cheung G.O.C. (2012) 'Reliability and Validity of the 'Extended-Hurt, Insult, Threaten, Scream' (E-HITS) Screening Tool in Detecting Intimate Partner Violence in Hospital Emergency Departments in Hong Kong', *Hong Kong Journal of Emergency Medicine* 17(2), pp. 110–17.

Choi, Y.P., Cheung, Y.W., Cheung, K.L. (2012) 'Social Isolation and Spousal Violence: Comparing Female Marriage Migrants with Local Women', *Journal of Marriage and Family* 74(3), pp. 444–61.

Crenshaw, K. (1989) 'Race, Reform, and Retrenchment: Transformation and Legitimation in Antidiscrimination Law', *Harvard Law Review* 101, pp. 1331–87.

Crenshaw, K. (1991) 'Mapping the Margins: Intersectionality, Identity Politics, and Violence Against Women of Colour', *Stanford Law Review* 43, pp. 1241–99.

Crime and Violence Prevention Center (2005) *Task Force on Local Criminal Justice Response to Domestic Violence, Keeping the Promise: Victim Safety and Batterer Accountability* [online] http://www.ncdsv.org/images/National-evaluation-of-the-rural-DV-and-child-victimization-enforcement-grant-program-vol1_7-2002.pdf

Dobash, R. and Dobash, R. (1979) *Violence against Wives: A Case against the Patriarchy*, Free Press, New York.

Dobash, R. and Dobash, R. (1992) *Women, Violence and Social Change*, Routledge, New York.

Dutton, A.M., Worrell, A., Terrell, D., Denaro, S. and Thompson, R. (2002) 'National Evaluation of the Rural Domestic Violence and Child Victimization Enforcement Grant Program: Volume 1', *US Department of Justice* [online] www.ncjrs.gov/pdffiles1/nij/grants/198128.pdf

Goldfarb, S.F. (2007) 'Reconceiving Civil Protection Orders for Domestic Violence: Can Law Help End the Abuse without Ending the Relationship?', *Cardozo Law Review* 29, pp. 1487–551.

Grosh, O. (2011) 'Foreign Wives, Domestic Violence: U.S. Law Stigmatizes and Fails to Protect "Mail-Order Brides"', *Hastings Women's Law Journal* 22, pp. 84–8.

Hong Kong Christian Service (2007) A research report on the social situations of ethnic minority women in Hong Kong, Project SASA (South Asians Support Alliance), Hong Kong Polytechnic University Department of Applied Social Sciences.

Hooks, B. (1989) 'Feminism: A Transformational Politic' in *Talking Back: Thinking Feminist, Thinking Black*. South End Press: Boston MA, pp. 19–27.

Johnson, M. and Ferraro, K. (2000) 'Research on Domestic Violence in the 1990s: Making Distinctions', *Journal of Marriage and Family* 62(4), pp. 948–63.

Kapai, P. (2012) 'Minority Women: A Struggle for Equal Protection' in Baines, B., Barak-Erez D. and Kahana, T. (eds.) *Feminist Constitutionalism: Global Perspectives*. Cambridge University Press, USA, pp. 336–56.

Kapai, P. (2013) 'The Human Rights of Women in the Hong Kong Special Administrative Region', *William and Mary Journal of Women and the Law* 19(2), pp. 255–300.

Kapai, P., (2015) *Delivering on the Promise of Equal Protection Under the Law: Understanding the Experiences and Help-Seeking Behaviours of Ethnic Minority and Immigrant Victims of Domestic Violence in Hong Kong and the United Kingdom*, Centre for Comparative and Public Law, University of Hong Kong, [online] http://www.law.hku.hk/ccpl/pub/BringingIntersectionalityHome.pdf

King, B. (1988) 'Multiple Jeopardy, Multiple Consciousness: the Context of a Black Feminist Ideology', *Signs* 14(2), pp. 42–72.

Latta, R.E. and Goodman, L.A. (2005) 'Haitian Immigrant Women', *Violence Against Women* 11, pp. 1441–8.

Lee, R., Sanders Thompson, V.L. and Mechanic, M.B. (2002) 'Intimate Partner Violence and Women of Colour: A Call for Innovations', *American Journal of Public Health* 92(4), pp. 530–4.

Leung, L.C. and RainLily (2015) *The Effectiveness of the 'WE Stand' Programme for Female Migrant Workers and Ethnic Minority Women: A Research Repor,*. Association Concerning Sexual Violence Against Women.

Lewis, R., Dobash, R.E., Dobash, R.P. and Cavanagh, K. (2001) 'Law's Progressive Potential: The Value of Engagement with the Law for Domestic Violence', *Social & Legal Studies* 10(1), pp. 105–30.

Liang, B., Goodman, L., Tummala-Narra, P. and Weintraub, S. (2005) 'A Theoretical Framework for Understanding Help-Seeking Processes Among Survivors of Intimate Partner Violence', *American Journal of Community Psychology* 36(1–2), pp. 71–84.

Loke, Y., Wan, M.L., Hayter, M. (2012) 'The Lived Experience of Women Victims of Intimate Partner Violence', *Journal of Clinical Nursing* 21, pp. 2336–46.

MacLeod, L. and Shin, M. (1993) *Like a Wingless Bird: A Tribute to the Survival and Courage of Women Who are Abused and Who Speak Neither English Nor French*, Minister of Supply and Services, Ottawa, Canada.

Malik, N. and Lindahl K. (1998) 'Aggression and Dominance: The Roles of Power and Culture in Domestic Violence', *Clinical Psychology: Science and Practice* 5(4), pp. 409–23.

Mauricio, A. and Gormley, B. (2001) 'Male Perpetration of Physical Violence Against Female Partners: The Interaction of Dominance Needs and Attachment Insecurity', *Journal of Interpersonal Violence* 16(10), pp. 1066–81.

Menjivar, C. and Salcido, O. (2002) 'Immigrant Women and Domestic Violence: Common Experiences in Different Countries', *Gender Society* 16(6), pp. 898–920.

Midlarsky, E., Venkataramani-Kothari, A. and Plante, M. (2006) 'Domestic Violence in the Chinese and South Asian Immigrant Communities', *Annals of the New York Academy of Sciences* 1087(1), pp. 279–300.

Narayan, U. (1995) 'Male-Order Brides: Immigrant Women, Domestic Violence and Immigration Law', *Hypatia* 10(1), pp. 104–19.

Saharso, S. (2000) 'Female Autonomy and Cultural Imperative: Two Hearts Beating Together' in Kymlicka, W. and Norman, W. (eds) *Citizenship in Diverse Societies* (2000), Oxford University Press, New York, pp. 224–42.

Shirwadkar, S. (2004) 'Canadian Domestic Violence Policy and Indian Immigrant Women', *Violence Against Women* 10, pp. 860–79.

Sirman, N. (1989) 'Turkish Feminism: A Short History', *New Perspectives on Turkey* 3(1), pp. 1–10.

Tiwari, A., Wong, M., Ip, H. (2001) 'Ren and Yuan: A Cultural Interpretation of Chinese Women's Responses to Battering', *Canadian Journal of Nursing Research* 33(3), pp. 63–79.

Tonsing, J. (2014) 'Conceptualizing Partner Abuse among South Asian Women in Hong Kong', *Journal of Transcultural Nursing* 25, p. 281.

United Nations (1992) General Recommendation No. 19, CEDAW Committee, 11th session, U.N. Doc. A/47/38.

United Nations (1993) Declaration on the Elimination of Violence against Women, U.N. Doc. A/48/49.

United Nations (2006) Study of the Secretary-General *Ending Violence against Women: From Words to Action*, pp. 1–190 [online] http://www.un.org/womenwatch/daw/public/VAW_Study/VAWstudyE.pdf

United Nations (2012) Committee on the Elimination of All Forms of Discrimination Against Women *Third Report of the Hong Kong Special Administrative Region of the People's Republic of China Under the United Nations Convention on the Elimination of All Forms of Discrimination against Women*, 23 April, CEDAW/C/CHN-HKG/7-8.

Walker, L.E. (1977) 'Battered Women and Learned Helplessness', *Victimology*, 2(3–4), pp. 525–34.

The Women's Commission (2009) *Women's Safety in Hong Kong: Eliminating Domestic Violence. An Update and the Next Step* [online] http://www.women.gov.hk/download/library/report/Safety-Supp.pdf

Part III

Transcending borders and boundaries

Negotiating gender, identity and violence

10 State violence, human-rights violations and the case of *apwint* in Myanmar

Lynette J. Chua and David Gilbert

Introduction

On 7 July 2013, twenty police officers in Mandalay, Myanmar, detained eleven *apwint*[1] at a popular corner around the old Mandalay palace moat (Asian Human Rights Commission 2013).[2] At the police station, the officers stripped off the detainees' clothes, photographed them, hit and grabbed their hair or breasts, questioned them about how they have sex with men, and forced them to frog-hop, sashay, polish officers' shoes and clean tables. Ten of them were released on bail after signing 'agreements' never to visit the same corner at the palace moat or wear women's clothes again. One HIV-positive detainee was sentenced to seven days imprisonment and denied access to her anti-retroviral medication.[3]

This incident is one of countless occurrences of violence in the everyday lives of *apwint* (meaning open in Burmese), a self-ascriptive term for biological males who are gender non-conforming, and identify and appear as feminine. *Apwint* endure police abuse and other forms of state-sanctioned violence and social oppression that harm their socio-economic wellbeing and severely limit their economic prospects. These acts of human-rights violations stem not only from popular religious beliefs and deeply rooted social prejudices, but also from the abuse of power among law enforcement and the judiciary.

Drawing from fieldwork in Myanmar and among exiled Burmese communities,[4] the most extensive on Myanmar's sexual orientation and gender identity (SOGI) minorities to date, this chapter examines the intersection of state and violence against *apwint* in Myanmar. It first reviews the cultural background and conditions related to *apwint*, and explains the social oppression they face. Then it analyses the legal conditions and elaborates on police abuse and other forms of state-sanctioned violence that go unreported and unpunished because *apwint* lack legal protection and distrust the authorities. In doing so, this chapter highlights the larger, endemic problem of arbitrary rule and corruption that permeates all levels of government in Myanmar, a problem that remains unresolved despite the recent transition from military rule to limited civilian governance. Taking these challenges into consideration, this chapter goes on to evaluate efforts to address the human-rights violations against *apwint*.

Cultural background and social conditions of *apwint* in Myanmar

Myanmar's diverse sexual cultures include unique subject positions – also known as categories of personhood – and different degrees of non-conformity to gender and sexual norms. Among them, *apwint* are considered the least gender conforming on the male spectrum and typically suffer the most blatant forms of abuse and discrimination. This section examines the cultural background of *apwint* to contextualise their social status and oppressive conditions, which are intertwined with the abusive legal conditions analysed in the following section.

SOGI minorities who are born biologically male have three core Burmese categories of personhood[5] – *apwint*, *apôn* (*hider*) and *thu nge* (*guy*). *Apwint* act as and appear feminine. At the time of research gender reassignment surgery and silicone breast enhancements were unavailable in Myanmar, but imported hormone replacement drugs, largely from China, were readily accessible and body modification through pharmaceuticals was a common, although not essential, element of becoming and being *apwint*.[6] In contrast, *apôn* identify to varying degrees as feminine and are attracted to men. However, they appear and act as masculine, passing as men in public and certain spheres of life, such as in family and work settings. *Apwint* and *apôn* rarely socialise together; *apwint* see themselves as living in a way that is more authentic and often resent *apôn* for not sacrificing their social standing, economic prospects and familial ties in the way that *awpint* do. The third category, *thu nge*, are gender-conforming and have a sexual preference for *apwint* and/or *apôn*, as well as women, typically as the penetrative sexual partner. They are the primary sexual partners of *apwint*. Some Burmese familiar with English define *thu nge* as 'straight'. However, in the context of Burmese gender codes, 'straight' can signify gender normativity rather than orientation towards the opposite biological sex.[7]

According to Burmese cultural norms, an association with femininity results in a loss of social status, as men's authority (*awza*) and charisma (*pôn*) are 'structurally superior' to women's (Spiro 1997, p. 18). *Awza* is associated with political authority while *pôn* is associated with moral and religious power (Harriden 2012).[8] One's amount of *pôn* is determined by karma through the accumulation of merit in past lives. Since men have greater *pôn* this particular concept of power supports a cosmological view of male superiority to women. In popular belief, being the receptive partner in male same-sex sex, as *apwint* often are, reduces one's *pôn*, resulting in the diminishment of personhood and a loss of respect.

The status of *apwint* is further diminished by dominant religious beliefs, including those of the majority religion of Buddhism. Contrary to Western representations of Therevada Buddhism as enlightened and tolerant, our research finds that Burmese Buddhist institutions and discourse contribute to, and reinforce, the everyday violence that *apwint* face. In Myanmar, the formal institution of Buddhism disallows those who are not 'real men' from entering monkhood, a prohibition applied to *apwint*.[9] Moreover, in Burmese Buddhist thought, life is a cyclical process of birth, death and rebirth, and one's social position is determined by one's karma at birth, as accumulated in previous lives through deeds involving the body, tongue and mind/heart. A prevalent belief is that sexual transgressions in a past life, such as adultery or desiring monks, cause boys to become *apwint*.[10] Hence, the idea of karma makes *apwint* vulnerable targets in the current legal environment by reinforcing a hierarchical view that places them below the status of men and justifies the ill treatment they receive.

Outside the highly exclusionary state religion of Buddhism, *apwint* have managed to establish a firm role for themselves as mediums of spirit (*nat*) worship, which has been integrated into Myanmar's syncretic form of everyday Buddhist practice. However, this common career path does little to address discrimination. Many men, in particular those who adhere to modernist forms of Buddhism, hold spirit mediums in ill repute, seeing them as a dangerous corruption of doctrine and as superstitious.

At home, although there are families who accept or tolerate *apwint*, many others reject their *apwint* children and family members, unable to come to terms with their gender non-conformity or worried about how their *apwint* might negatively impact their social status. Fathers and other male family members often inflict physical violence on *apwint*. One informant's father used to beat her with wire, leaving scars on her forearms. Another informant's father tied her hands to a mango tree at night when she was ten years old. The tree was believed to be haunted and her father wanted to 'bring my braveness out'. During another informant's commitment ceremony, her partner's brothers came and vandalised the place, beat them up and threatened her with a knife to stay away from their brother. Muslim *apwint* report formidable family pressure to enter heterosexual marriage and conform to gender norms. Human rights activists also report cases of sexual assault, stoning and other forms of physical violence against *apwint* in the predominantly Christian Karen refugee camps on the Thai–Myanmar border. Amongst ethnic minority Kachin communities patrilineal inheritance rules have been used to exclude *apwint* from inheriting ancestral lands.

Discrimination against *apwint* is further reinforced by negative representations in Burmese popular culture and media. In Burmese cinema, non-*apwint* actors portray *apwint* with storylines that reinforce sexual and gender normativity and negative *apwint* stereotypes.[11] For example, as a comedic device *apwint* are represented as caricatures, with exaggerated speech and movement and a narrow preoccupation with personal appearance and sex.[12] In dramas *apwint* are treated as objects of pity without the possibility of happiness.[13] Newspapers in favour of liberal reform and democratisation nevertheless use derogatory terminology and even support police action against *apwint*. When reporting the Mandalay incident described in the introduction, these newspapers blamed supposed deviant *apwint* conduct and gave prominence to police statements and other views justifying the crackdown as necessary for the protection of Burmese culture from *apwint* (The Voice Daily 2013; Sai Tha Aung 2013).

Legal conditions and state violence against *apwint* in Myanmar

Despite culturally embedded forms of prejudice against *apwint*, sex in pre-colonial central Burma was largely unlegislated.[14] Regulation of sexuality intensified with laws first introduced during British colonial rule. In 1948, when the Union of Burma gained independence, it inherited the colonial legislation that continues to affect *apwint* today. After a short period of post-independence democracy, the military came into power in 1958[15] and carried over these laws, many of which remain on the books despite the recent transition to civilian governance.[16] This section analyses how repressive legal provisions interact with social prejudices against *apwint* and larger problems within Myanmar's political and legal institutions – abuse of power, arbitrary exercise of authority and corruption – to inflict human-rights violations against *apwint*. It also examines, conversely, how the *lack* of legal provisions and state action combine with cultural norms to perpetuate other forms of violence.

Statutory regulation, abuse of power, and corrupt practices

Following the three Anglo-Burmese wars between 1824 and 1885, what is geographically today's Myanmar fell to British colonial rule. British Burma was first administered as an Indian province. The *Indian Penal Code of 1860*, containing Section 377, was thus extended to it and continued to apply when Burma became a separately administered colony in 1937. Section 377 reads:

> *Whoever voluntarily has carnal intercourse against the order of nature with any man, woman or animal shall be punished with transportation for life, or with imprisonment of either description for a term which may extend to ten years and shall also be liable to a fine.*

The *Penal Code* does not clearly define the phrase, 'carnal intercourse against the order of nature', except to stipulate that penetration would suffice. Nevertheless, similar provisions in other former British colonies have interpreted it to encompass oral and anal sex (Chua 2003; Sanders 2009). Furthermore, since the provision does not explicitly refer to force or involuntariness, it can be interpreted to include consensual adult conduct, whether in public or private.

Even though Section 377 does not single out same-sex conduct or gender non-conforming persons and also appears to cover heterosexual conduct, such as paedophilia, the police in Myanmar deploy Section 377 to persecute *apwint*. Considered male in the eyes of the law, sexual relations between *apwint* and other men are regarded as same-sex conduct. In one case, an *apwint* was working as an attendant at a public toilet reputed to be a cruising ground for *apwint*. A plainclothes officer approached her, said he had a question and took her to the police station. Despite reportedly suffering from a mental illness the *apwint* was charged with Section 377 and sentenced to five years in Insein prison in Yangon, even though she was not engaging in any sexual activity, which is clearly stipulated as a provision.[17]

More frequently than directly invoking Section 377, however, the police persecute *apwint* by exercising, or simply threatening to exercise, their statutory powers of arrest, sometimes in combination with threats of Section 377. Besides the *Penal Code*, British administrators enacted repressive laws to control widespread crime and disorder, which arose at least partly due to their colonial invasion (Callahan 2005, pp. 21–31). These laws include sections 30(d) and 35(d) of the *Rangoon Police Act 1899* and the *Police Act 1945* respectively, provisions colloquially known as 'hiding in the shadows' laws. The *Rangoon Police Act 1899* covers today's Yangon township, and the *Police Act 1945* applies to towns and areas described in government notifications. The two similarly worded sections empower police to arrest without warrant 'any person found between sunset and sunrise, within the precincts of any dwelling-house or other building whatsoever, or on board any vessel, without being able satisfactorily to account for his presence therein'.

Although their maximum prison term of three months is less severe than Section 377's punishment,[18] these laws are extremely powerful because they are so vaguely worded that the police can target anybody they deem to be suspicious or undesirable, such as *apwint*, who are already stereotyped as deviant and criminal. After detaining an *apwint*, the police might threaten to charge her with the 'crime of hiding in the shadows' or escalate it to Section 377 in order to solicit a bribe or sexual favour, or stop her from resisting. These threats usually compel *apwint* to comply. Some want to avoid further entanglement with the law and state actors, whereas others fear the harsher punishment of Section 377 or do not understand its scope; most of all, they distrust law enforcement and the judicial process.

The cases below vary in detail, but each case demonstrates one or more of the most common patterns found in police violence against *apwint* – the detention of *apwint* at public venues popular with them or on the streets at night (hence the laws' notorious nickname), sexual assault, other forms of physical violence, or threats and bribery.[19] According to one case in the town of Monywa documented by activists, police officers detained an *apwint* at a popular *apwint* venue, forced her to perform oral sex, and then took her money away (Equality Myanmar 2012). On a separate occasion at the same venue, when a group of *apwint* refused to perform oral sex and tried to run away, the officers chased after them and beat them up. One of the *apwint* has become afraid of going out at night and has stopped wearing make-up (ibid.).

In other cases, similar to the Mandalay incident of July 2013, the police take the detained *apwint* to the police station first. For instance, in Mawlaymine, an *apwint* in custody agreed to a demand for 35,000 kyat (about US$36.20) in exchange for her release. The officer took her to the back of the station and raped her before letting her go the next day (ibid.). In another case, an *apwint* and her friends were stopped by a police car when they were walking down the street and were put in jail. The police told them to confess to violating section 35(d) of the *Police Act 1945* and threatened to press for longer prison sentences if they did not. Not having any money to bribe the officers, the *apwint* informant offered her necklace, which was deemed to be inadequate. They were charged and convicted under section 35(d) (ibid.).

Most of these detentions end with guilty pleas and do not lead to trial.[20] Even some lawyers advise them not to contest the police because the pleas are believed to mitigate sentences. The litigation process is costly to most *apwint*, and the majority of community legal aid programmes are too poorly funded to sustain trials. After pleading guilty, the *apwint* and her lawyer sometimes also have to bribe the police, the prosecutor and the judge's clerk or judge to obtain a speedier sentencing date and shorter prison term. These bribes usually start from a total of two lakhs or 200,000 kyat (approximately US$207) and go up depending on what the bribers know of the *apwint*'s financial situation.

During our research, nevertheless, we came across an exceptional case that did involve a trial, that of *Second Police Corporal Nay Zin Tun v. Lin Ko Ko* (hereinafter *Lin Lin 2012*) in the Mingalartaungnyunt Township Court of Yangon Division. In December 2012, Lin Lin was arrested under Section 30(d) of the Rangoon Police Act while 'dressed up like a *meinmalya*' on the streets around 10:30 p.m. (*Lin Lin 2012*, Statement of Witness, Defendant). When the patrolling officers asked what she was doing, Lin Lin replied that she was a 'spirit medium' on the way home. In his statement, however, one of the officers claimed that Lin Lin was 'in [a] darkened place' – in front of a high school – and 'could not explain sufficiently the reasons why she was there'. So he said he suspected Lin Lin was going 'to commit a crime' (*Lin Lin 2012*, Statement of Witness, Second Police Corporal Zaw Win Aung). Lin Lin disputed the police officer's claim and argued that she was actually standing at the traffic lights and waiting for a taxi to go home. According to court documents of the trial proceedings, the judge simply stated that Lin Lin's explanation was insufficient and sentenced her to one month's imprisonment with labour.[21]

State actors' abuse of *apwint* continues with impunity in prison. Local activists have documented numerous incidents in which prison guards strip, beat and rape, or compel other prisoners to rape, *apwint* who are segregated within male prisons (Equality Myanmar 2012).[22] *Apwint* inmates are also commonly denied medical treatment. Among those detained in the July 2013 Mandalay incident was Gun San Naw, an HIV-positive *apwint* who had been on anti-retroviral medication for seven years to suppress the progression of the HIV virus. The morning after pleading guilty and receiving a seven-day sentence, Gun asked to contact her family so that they could bring the medication to her. The officer on duty replied that people like Gun 'deserve whatever you've got' and refused to let Gun contact anybody. Gun's health deteriorated as a result of being deprived of medication while in prison (*Gun San Naw (a) Naw Naw v. Republic of the Union of Myanmar* (or) *Naw Naw 2013*, Mandalay State Court, Appellant Brief). Two months after her release, her CD4 cell count, which indicates the health of one's immune system, dropped from approximately 350 to 200 (a count below 200 is one qualification for an AIDS diagnosis).

Other forms of state-sanctioned violence

In addition to the violence perpetrated by statutory regulation, abuse of power and corrupt practices, the lack of legal protection and state inaction result in other forms of state-sanctioned violations against *apwint*. The most commonly reported types of incidents occur in public schools and the workplace. Together they compound the socio-economic discrimination of *apwint* and severely limit their career and economic prospects.

In public schools teachers often ostracise *apwint* or ignore peer bullying. According to one documented case the *apwint* informant was kicked out of class for wearing *thanaka*, a skincare product made of tree bark predominantly used by women in Myanmar (Equality Myanmar 2012). In another instance, the dean threatened to fail and expel the *apwint* informant if she continued to express herself as *apwint* at school (ibid.). One of the first author's informants recounted how schoolmates pulled off her sarong and beat her; teachers ignored her complaints, telling her to sit with the girls instead. Another of the first author's informants could no longer stand schoolmates' name-calling and punched one of the bullies in the face. When she tried to explain her actions to the teacher, she was warned not to do it again or else be 'terminated from the school'.

Because of the violence in public schools it is common for *apwint* to give up on formal education. Without formal qualifications, their employment prospects are further limited. No law exists to prevent employment discrimination. In lower-level office, service and retail positions in Myanmar, men and women are usually required to wear gender-conforming uniforms. *Apwint*, therefore, have difficulty finding employment, unless they suppress their identity and pass off as gender-conforming, biological males. One informant was accused of behaving too femininely and fired from her job at a private company. *Apwint* are also refused employment because of their stereotypes as deviants and HIV/AIDS carriers. Some workplaces even require a negative HIV test as a condition of employment. Needless to say, those who are HIV-positive have difficulty securing jobs or keeping them.

While the *apwint* informant who was fired for being too feminine found new employment with a tolerant NGO, many other *apwint* stay within the well-established self-employment options available to them, such as hair and make-up, spirit mediumship and sex work, which embed them in friendlier communities of like individuals. Since the 1960s *apwint* have increasingly created a niche in spirit mediumship and hair and beauty, with a small minority amassing significant wealth from rich and famous clients. However, the majority of these *apwint* businesses struggle with limited and irregular income. In fact, as a result of the public status of the few wealthy *apwint*, the socio-economic disadvantage of most *apwint* is left unrecognised. The situation is often exacerbated by being ostracised by their biological families and therefore isolated from the attached socio-economic safety net. Furthermore, especially for *apwint* who take up the legally ambiguous occupation of sex work, self-employment involves irregular hours or late-night commutes, thus exposing them to the 'hiding in the shadows' laws, police abuse and corrupt practices.

Addressing the violence

Efforts to address state violence against *apwint* can be divided into two trajectories. The earlier one involves a network of international non-governmental organisations (INGOs), Burmese non-governmental organisations (NGOs) and grassroots-level community-based organisations (CBOs) and self-help groups (SHGs) that work on HIV/AIDS. The other, more recent trajectory is more explicitly human rights-centred and involves a small group of Burmese activists, assisted and funded by international human-rights organisations. In this section, we discuss their efforts and evaluate potential challenges.

HIV/AIDS-centred efforts

During the military regime draconian legislation, such as the *Emergency Act*, the *State Protection Act* and the *Unlawful Associations Act*, limited the freedom of civil-society actors to form associations and mobilise. After its bloody repression of the 1988 student-led pro-democracy protests (Charney 2009, pp. 164–71; Steinberg 2001),[23] the regime imposed more laws, which, together with the older legislation, effectively banned the formation of organisations. The exceptions were for groups conducting only religious and economic activities or those with governmental or military ties.[24]

Although INGOs are also affected by the restrictions they are allowed to work in such limited areas as development and health, including HIV/AIDS. For permission to operate in the country, HIV/AIDS INGOs sign memoranda of understanding (MOUs) with the Myanmar government. Then they typically partner with CBOs and SHGs to implement outreach around the country, funding and providing them with technical assistance, a model that began in the early 2000s. Even though many of these CBOs and SHGs do not have official government permission they are tolerated, presumably because of INGOs' MOU arrangements.[25]

Hence, the HIV/AIDS network of organisations is able to reach out to *apwint*. They include CBOs and SHGs organised for or by *apwint*, who are classified under the HIV/AIDS MSM parlance as a 'key affected population', and are further linked to informal social networks among *apwint*. Through HIV/AIDS prevention and treatment programmes CBOs and SHGs provide safe sex education and counselling services to *apwint*. To help HIV-positive *apwint* who face employment discrimination, some of these groups also provide training on hairstyling, make up and sewing skills that enable them to become self-employed.

The HIV/AIDS-related organisations, therefore, partially address *apwint*'s socio-economic problems, which are worsened by state inaction and the lack of legal protection. The CBOs and SHGs by and for *apwint* help to create a sense of community, and the vocational training empowers them to achieve financial independence and, consequently, reduce reliance on their biological families. Nevertheless, their programmes are limited to health and practical livelihood issues. They do not address structural problems linked to prejudicial norms, abuse of power and corruption. INGOs' MOUs with the government prohibit them from 'engag[ing] in any political . . . activities in conflict with the interests of the Government'.[26] Under the military regime, therefore, these INGOs avoided going beyond their remit of 'health' to advocate for structural or legal reform and especially any open engagement with human rights discourse, cautionary measures that trickled down to and influence the programmes and activities of their partner CBOs and SHGs. It is only after the recent changeover to civilian governance that HIV/AIDS organisations began to provide human rights training to their beneficiaries, including *apwint* communities, and to incorporate human rights discourse into their advocacy work more prominently.

Yet, in spite of the political transition, the relaxation of controls on civil political liberties, the release of political prisoners and the permitted return of exiles, Burmese activists and NGOs remain cautious about human-rights advocacy. The new administration has maintained repressive restrictions on freedom of assembly, with processions only permissible with a police permit, and has arrested activists who protested 'unlawfully'. According to Section 5 of the newly enacted *Right to Peaceful Assembly and Peaceful Procession Act 2011*, permission can be denied if the event is considered a threat to 'security of the State, rule of law, community's peace and tranquillity, and public morality'. While regional parliaments have been established the political system remains unitary in practice, and human-rights abuses in ethnic minority areas are of major concern, particularly in areas of armed conflict in the north and east where there are large-scale development projects (Human Rights Watch 2012; Richards *et al.* 2011, Richards 2012) and in the Bay of Bengal region. *Apwint* in these precarious situations commonly migrate to the cities of Mandalay and Yangon for greater freedom and security. Rights-based advocacy specifically for *apwint* also face the dilemmas and challenges discussed below.

Human rights-centred efforts

Starting in the late 2000s, a few years prior to the political transition, Burmese activists in neighbouring Thailand began to cultivate human-rights awareness among leaders of *apwint* and other SOGI minority communities in towns and cities across Myanmar, many of them from the HIV/AIDS CBOs and SHGs. Using their personal connections, they quietly brought over these grassroots leaders to Chiang Mai, Thailand, educated them about human rights and their inclusion of SOGI minorities (see United Nations Human Rights Council 2011), and empowered them to take up advocacy work. By 2012, these grassroots leaders were able to organise internationally commemorated events, such as International Day Against Homophobia and Transphobia and Transgender Day of Remembrance, to bring attention to the discrimination and violence against SOGI minorities, including *apwint*,in their hometowns.

After the Thai-based activists relocated to Yangon in 2013 they focused on Section 377 of the *Penal Code*. They have since published a study that documents the types of human-rights violations examined in this chapter and advocates for the provision's repeal. They built alliances with the Myanmar Human Rights Commission, which accepted their report on the July 2013 Mandalay incident as a case of human-rights violation, and tried to gain sympathy and support from parliamentary members of various political parties. In addition, they supported the HIV-positive *apwint* detainee to challenge the legality of the police's conduct in the July 2013 Mandalay incident.[27] As this volume went to press, they have started a paralegal programme that trains *apwint* and other SOGI minorities to assist those in their community facing police persecution and criminal prosecution and to document human-rights violations.

However, institutional protection from human-rights abuses and avenues for redress remains weak. Take, for example, the July 2013 Mandalay incident, one of the first public campaigns undertaken by activists. Even though they succeeded in persuading the newly established Myanmar National Human Rights Commission to accept it as a case of human-rights violations, the outcome of their complaint is unclear. Its commissioners are overwhelmed by different types of complaints and cannot investigate all of them in a timely manner. The Commission, though supposedly independent, also lacks the power to impose concrete sanctions that hold responsible state parties accountable.

In addition, the most common form of direct state violence is inflicted through 'hiding in the shadows' laws rather than Section 377. While activists' legal advocacy focuses on Section 377, most of the police abuse they have documented is actually related to these police power provisions; so is the Mandalay case. Activists acknowledge this phenomenon but some position the 'hiding in the shadows' incidents as the consequence of retaining Section 377. They argue that the latter symbolises the illegitimacy of non-heteronormative and gender non-conforming conduct and justifies police persecution of *apwint* using the other laws and broader forms of discrimination and abuse, such as in employment and education. Indeed, in former British colonies, such as India, Malaysia and Singapore, similar Section 377 provisions and other anti-gay laws represent symbols of social disapproval that justify and perpetuate the marginalisation of sexual and gender minorities. Moreover, the British colonial legacy of Section 377 is a recognisable discriminatory law around the world, and thus an internationally resonant platform for local activists to leverage for support and funding.

Repealing Section 377, however, will be difficult. Despite recent legal and political reforms, including the loosening of political censorship, the Myanmar state remains conservative about issues it construes as 'moral'. Newly enacted laws on civil political freedoms, such as the *Peaceful Assembly Act 2011*, still set restrictions on the basis of 'public morality' that maintain a strict regime of sexual censorship. Moral regulation goes hand-in-hand with state imperatives to protect 'religion' and favours social conservatives and the rise of religious and nationalist extremist networks, such as 969. Those who deviate from ethno-national, religious and sexual norms have found themselves the target of violence. If the repeal of Section 377 gains momentum violence against *apwint* could increase, given the heterosexist nature of Burmese radical Buddhist and nationalist discourse, and trends of homophobic nationalism in other post-colonial contexts (see Bacchetta 1999; Boellstorff 2004; Currier 2010; Wahab 2012). The subsequent positive obligation on the state to legislate against discrimination and abuse in families, schools and the workplace will be even more challenging. Besides, legislative reform may not eradicate religious and cultural norms that are deeply heteronormative and gender-conforming, particularly notions of male superiority and the association between *apwint* and karmic wrongdoing.[28]

Emphasis on Section 377 also obscures the endemic problem of arbitrary rule and corruption in Myanmar's political and legal institutions. State violence against *apwint* is merely a symptom of Myanmar's lack of rule of law that results in routine violations of human rights (Asian Legal Resource Centre 2010). The wide statutory police powers, for instance, victimise other socially marginalised groups. Our lawyer informants report similar patterns of violation of sex workers[29] or women who happened to be in the wrong place at the wrong time. In addition, faced with a court system oiled by bribery (Cheesman 2012), *apwint* and other vulnerable classes have little access to justice to address these wrongs. Activists who supported the July 2013 Mandalay case accepted the high probability of losing the appeal. Even if the legislature repeals Section 377 and enacts anti-discrimination laws as part of recent reforms to provide for greater civil-political liberties, state violence against *apwint* could persist if the fundamental problems of corruption and abuse in other branches of government persist.

Conclusion

In this chapter, we examined the everyday violence suffered by gender non-conforming *apwint*, biologically male persons who identify and appear as feminine, in Myanmar. The violence is not only linked to the actions of private parties. State actors and institutions are also complicit in it, as dominant religious beliefs and social norms against gender non-conformity interact with the arbitrary exercise of authority and a culture of corruption to perpetuate violence against *apwint*.

Until recently, violence against *apwint* was absent from national political attention and international human-rights discourse. Within Myanmar, even with the nascent endeavours of a small group of activists highlighted in this chapter, *apwint* face obstacles in mustering open political support for their problems. The suffering of *apwint*, widely regarded as incontrovertible and expected, provokes little local reaction. Although activists have international funding to conduct an impact study on Section 377 (Equality Myanmar 2012), document cases of abuse and violence and occasionally challenge the police in court, they still lack the resources to cover the country's widely dispersed population of *apwint* and the ability to convince the government of the extensiveness of the problem and take action. *Apwint* are generally reluctant to speak out publicly, their fear of repercussions stemming from the legacy of extended and brutal dictatorship, even as some *apwint* activists are gaining confidence as the domestic political environment liberalises. Furthermore, politicians from the NLD and other parties may be willing to listen to activists and express sympathy, but the conservative political climate of moral regulation discourages them from providing *apwint* issues with any visibility, much less prominence, on their political platforms.

The lack of visibility and open support in domestic politics carries over onto the international stage. Myanmar's governmental reports on its international human-rights obligations contain no mention of sexual and gender minority issues. Its submissions to the Committee on the Elimination of Discrimination against Women (CEDAW Committee) treat gender as the equivalent of biological females and do not take into consideration gender non-conformity (see CEDAW Committee 2007).[30] *Apwint*, though not necessarily self-identifying as 'women', are unsurprisingly left out of these official reports. Their grievances are further buried in the romanticised Western image of Myanmar as a tolerant Buddhist nation opening up to the world, a success story of democratisation represented by the enduring images of Aung San Suu Kyi. In fact, it is only with activists' recent engagement with human-rights discourse that the United Nations, foreign embassies, international donors and other INGOs began to notice the human-rights violations against *apwint* (beyond the health focus of HIV/AIDS, in which *apwint* are classified as a key affected population). After the incident of July 2013, for instance, Mandalay-based activists immediately reported the abuse to their Yangon peers, who held a press conference.[31] Otherwise, it would have been written off as yet another everyday encounter. Instead, two months later, the United Nations Secretary General specifically mentioned the incident and recommended the amendment of Section 377 of the Penal Code (United Nations General Assembly 2013).[32]

These small steps, though hopeful, also suggest that the journey towards legal reform for *apwint* will be long and arduous. State violence against *apwint* is connected to broader challenges confronting Myanmar's transition process. The state both actively participates in the violence against them (especially by police) and passively perpetuates it with non-action; meanwhile endemic corruption and abuse of power in the legal system compound the difficulty of exposing and addressing its wrongdoings. The 'conservative' nature of moral politics further hinders activists from asserting their claims openly in national politics. Internationally, the human-rights records of Myanmar's military regime and the new civilian government receive close scrutiny, but the everyday violations of *apwint*'s rights and dignity by low-level state actors are usually overlooked. Yet, there are optimistic signs with the emergence of human-rights activism around *apwint* issues. As Myanmar continues to liberalise, both state and society will have to grapple with whether and how they will accord respect and protection for the human rights of those who are unpopular with religious and social conservatives.

Notes

1 With the exception of names and places, Burmese terms are transliterated following the BGN/PCGN 1970 Agreement. Burmese translated terms are in italics followed by the transliterated term in parentheses upon first usage. English loanwords used in Burmese are also in italics.

2 According to our Mandalay informants, the situation was chaotic. Some people were initially harassed but not detained; others were taken to the police station and then let go without being held under detention. Hence, the total number of detainees varies from account to account. However, most of them, if not all, were *apwint*.

3 While it is common for individuals to use both male and female pronouns, especially since the third-person pronoun in the Burmese language can lack gender specificity, this chapter uses gendered pronouns that refer to individual informants in a way that reflects how they most frequently referred to themselves during interviews and participant observation.

4 The first author has been carrying out fieldwork since September 2012 to study Myanmar's nascent SOGI rights movement and how its activists mobilise human rights. She conducted in-depth, semi-structured interviews with Burmese human-rights activists and legal aid lawyers from various Myanmar cities and Thailand and observations of activist events, as well as collected primary materials from activist groups for analysis. The second author conducted ethnography focusing on sexual minority cultures in Yangon between 2011 and 2013. He used snowball sampling to recruit informants and conduct extended participant observation amongst *apwint* with varied socioeconomic backgrounds in Yangon. He spent time at community events, homes, workplaces, leisure venues and religious festivals. He also conducted qualitative biographical interviews and used discourse analysis to examine film and news media representations of *apwint*. To protect informants, their identities are kept confidential. The authors welcome direct correspondence regarding their fieldwork and research designs.

5 For a detailed study on the subject positions of Burmese sexual minorities, see Gilbert 2013.

6 A small number of *apwint* have been able to access gender reassignment surgery overseas; however, the cost involved is prohibitive to most.

7 The two linked categories of *apwint* and *apôn* provide little space for individuals who are attracted to those with the same sexual orientation and gender identity as themselves. As a result, the more recent subject position of *homo* has been gaining popularity, particularly in urban areas. *Homo* often denotes those who identify as male and are attracted to other *homos* although the term is also used as a synonym for *apôn*. In addition, there is a wider Burmese vocabulary that refers to *apwint* in ways that are generally derogatory. The most common terms are *achaut* and *meinmalya*, which are used both as an insult in public and self-ascriptively by *apwint*. *Achaut* literally means 'something dry', while *meinmalya* literally means 'man acting as a woman'. Within institutional settings, English terms are commonly used to link *apwint* with other gender and sexual categories. Hence, *apwint* are included in 'men who have sex with men' (MSM), an official term used by the Ministry of Health, international non-governmental organisations (INGOs), local non-governmental organisations (NGOs) and civil society networks working on HIV/AIDS. Some *apwint* refer to themselves as *transgender, T.G., or gay*, under the rubric of *LGBT*, or, 'lesbian, gay, bisexual, and transgender', terms that were largely first used by the SOGI minority rights movement that originated in exile in Thailand but have since relocated to Yangon (also see Chua 2015). These activists have also coined an alternative term, *lein tu chit thu* ('those who love the same sex'). As for SOGI minorities born biologically female, compared to their male counterparts they are more atomised and lack common category terms. Although they do use similarly structured subject positions that include the equivalent of *open*, *hider* and *thu nge*, there is only one popular term for female masculinity, *yaukkyalya*. *Yaukkyalya* can be defined as those who 'act like men', and is a term that some female informants consider derogatory. In urban areas, among the diaspora and online, English loanwords such as *tomboy* and *lesbian* are gaining traction.

8 *Pôn* has variously been translated as 'charisma' and 'glory'. Harriden describes *pôn* as 'an innate spiritual quality . . . which resides in the physical body of all male humans'.

9 However, those who 'pass' as masculine can ordain if they stay unnoticed. As for women, with their diminished status in Burmese society, they are fully excluded from monkhood, a prohibition that has been challenged in recent years.

10 This corresponds to a popular belief in Thailand that stigmatises SOGI minorities (Jackson 1998).

11 At least one popular actor has refused to play *apwint* characters because of his homophobic views (Myanmar Daily News 2013).

12 Recent examples include the films *Swè Sa Mè* (*Pull to Eat*), Apyôn (*Smile*), *Pyo Do Maung* (*Guy for Girls*) and *Nauk Pyi* (*Teased*).

13 Examples include *Sèko Taung Wut Min Yaukkya* (*The Nobleman Who Can Wear a Sarong of 19 Lengths*) and *Kanasi Ma Pyôn* (*Kanasi Ma Pyôn*).

14 Although monkhood sex is prohibited and strict Theravada Buddhist ethics aim to reduce material pleasure, including carnal life, such restrictions and beliefs were not the bases for legislation. As in much of Southeast Asia penile adornments, such as the implantation of marbles, were traditional in Burma and used largely for sexual pleasure, demonstrating the permissibility of such values in pre-colonial times. Sex workers held a prominent position in pre-colonial Burmese society, typified by the Burmese term *pyitaungsar*, which literally means 'jewel of the nation'. In the royal court, Burmese kings typically had numerous wives and concubines. According to Fitch, a visitor to Burma in the sixteenth century, the King of Pegu had one wife and a harem of over 300 women (Fitch 2004).

15 The military became a caretaker government in 1958 and then took over following a coup in 1962.

16 Since the country's 2010 elections, a new quasi-democratic political system has come into force and legal reforms have liberalised laws on assembly and procession, trade unions, speech and media. However, legal restrictions on civil political liberties remain in place in legislation such as the *Myanmar Penal Code 1860*, *Code of Criminal Procedures 1898*, *Official Secrets Act 1923*, and *Wireless Telegraphy Act 1933* (see Chua and Gilbert 2015).

17 One of the challenges of conducting fieldwork in Myanmar is the lack of public access to court cases and police records. Information on this Section 377 case came from a lawyer informant who learnt about it from one of the authors' informants and managed to visit the defendant at Insein prison in Yangon.

18 According to Yangon legal aid lawyers, the police also use Section 379 of the *Penal Code*, the provision on theft. As a 'cognisable offence' according to Schedule II of the Criminal Procedure Code, it allows arrest without warrant under Section 54 of the Police Act. Another common proxy law is Section 47 read with Section 34(7) of the Police Act on drunkenness, which also empowers the police to arrest without warrant.

19 Cases reported by activists and legal aid lawyers as this volume went to press are consistent with these earlier patterns based on cases available at the time of writing.

20 Section 61 of the *Criminal Procedure Code* requires police to release somebody in custody after twenty-four hours if there is no evidence or 'no case' against him or her. However, we learn from lawyer informants that detainees are often kept longer than twenty-four hours without being processed in court, pursuant to Section 167.

21 It is unclear how the judge could impose a sentence that includes labour, as the provision does not provide for labour as a form of punishment. However, *apwint* respondents in activist reports commonly recount how they are asked to carry out labour such as floor-cleaning, grass-cutting and carrying rice bags, while serving their sentences. The outcome of the case of *Lin Lin 2012* also illustrates that the most powerful entity in criminal cases is the police, whose words hold sway over judicial personnel (Cheesman 2012).

22 Within the major prisons, *apwint* are placed in separate cells from the gender-normative male population.

23 After twenty-six years of military rule and economic mismanagement, university students led an uprising that spread through urban areas. General Ne Win stepped down, but the military killed approximately 3,000 protestors. In 1990, the military regime – renamed as the State Law and Order Restoration Council and then the State Peace and Development Council – held elections to restore stability. However, when Aung San Suu Kyi's National League for Democracy (NLD) won eighty-two per cent of the seats, the military suppressed the NLD and detained Aung San Suu Kyi under house arrest (Charney 2009; Steinberg 2001).

24 The *Association Registration Law* that came into effect on 20 July 2014 has since superseded these laws. Although it does not criminalise non-registration, its impact is still too early to ascertain (The Irrawaddy News 2014).

25 The Myanmar state at first largely ignored the role of CBOs and SHGs, and publicly acknowledged only local groups that were professional bodies or faith-based. According to the first author's informants, and as reflected in the Myanmar Ministry of Health's *Myanmar National Strategic Plan on HIV and AIDS 2006–2010*, it was not until 2006 that a National Strategic Plan involving the Myanmar government, UN agencies, INGOs and local groups explicitly specified the role of CBOs and SHGs as implementing partners of INGOs.

26 This is a condition in the MOU of an HIV/AIDS INGO where one of the first author's informants works. A copy of the MOU is on file with the first author.

27 The case, dismissed in the lower courts, went on appeal to the Supreme Court, which also dismissed it.

28 While activists have advocated against the use of transphobic and homophobic language in the Myanmar press, they have had limited success.

29 Sex workers potentially face heavier sentencing under the *Suppression of Prostitution Acts* of 1949 and 2008, in which solicitation carries a punishment of up to three years' imprisonment. The Act raises concerns about widespread human-rights abuses by state authorities against sex workers. These include instances of rape, torture, extortion and lengthy prison sentences for those found guilty of crimes under the Act (but since the Act defines prostitutes as biological women, *apwint* cannot be prosecuted for prostitution per se). Legalisation of prostitution was raised momentarily by an opposition MP in the *hluttaw* in July 2013, but was rebuffed by the Deputy Home Affairs Minister, who stated the law was necessary as a deterrent (Nyein Pyae Sone 2013).

30 So far Myanmar is party to only three international conventions related to human rights: the Convention on the Elimination of All Forms of Discrimination Against Women; the Convention on the Rights of the Child; and the Convention on the Rights of Persons with Disabilities.

31 Examples of reports carried by newspapers include The Irrawaddy News (2013), Myo Zaw Linn (2013), Mann (2013). As discussed above, some media reports used derogatory language and supported the actions of the police. Also see the Asian Human Rights Commission report that referred to news reports about the incident (Asian Human Rights Commission 2013).

32 The document refers to *apwint* as 'transgender and transsexual women' in the Mandalay incident. Although these terms cannot completely capture the local sexual subjectivity of *apwint*, activists do use them as approximate translations in their engagement with international actors. Also see endnote 7.

Bibliography

Asian Human Rights Commission (2013) *Burma: Police Torture of Gay and Transgendered People* [online] http://www.humanrights.asia/news/ahrc-news/AHRC-STM-137-2013.

Asian Legal Resource Centre (2010) 'Diagnosing the Un-Rule of Law in Burma: A Submission to the UN Human Rights Council's Universal Periodic Review', *Article 2*, vol. 9, no. 2, pp. 37–72.

Bacchetta, P. (1999) 'When the (Hindu) Nation Exiles its Queers', *Social Text*, vol. 61, pp. 141–66.

Boellstorff, T. (2004) 'The Emergence of Political Homophobia in Indonesia: Masculinity and National Belonging', *Ethnos*, vol. 69, no. 4, pp. 465–86.

Callahan, M.P. (2005) *Making Enemies: War and State Building in Burma*, Cornell University Press, New York.

Charney, M. (2009) *A History of Modern Burma*, Cambridge University Press, Cambridge.

Cheesman, N. (2012) 'Myanmar's Courts and the Sounds Money Makes' in N. Cheesman, M. Skidmore and T. Wilson (eds.), *Myanmar's Transition: Openings, Obstacles and Opportunities*, Institute of Southeast Asian Studies, Singapore, pp. 231–48.

Chua, L.J. (2003) 'Saying No: Sections 377 and 377A of the Penal Code', *Singapore Journal of Legal Studies*, pp. 209–61.

Chua, L.J. (2015) 'The Vernacular Mobilization of Human Rights in Myanmar's Sexual Orientation and Gender Identity Movement', *Law and Society Review*, vol. 49, pp. 299–332.

Chua, L.J. and Gilbert, D. (2015) 'Sexual and Gender Minorities in Transition: LGBT Rights and Activism in Myanmar', *Human Rights Quarterly*, vol. 37, pp. 1–28.

CEDAW Committee (2007) *Consideration of Reports Submitted by States Parties Under Article 18 of the Convention on the Elimination of All Forms of Discrimination against Women: Combined Second and Third Periodic Reports of States Parties, Myanmar*, CEDAW/C/MMR/3.

Currier, A. (2010) 'Political Homophobia in Postcolonial Namibia', *Gender & Society*, vol. 24, no. 1, pp. 110–29.

Equality Myanmar (2012) 'Impact of Section 377 of the Myanmar Penal Code on Discrimination based on Sexual Orientation and Gender Identity' (draft), on file with authors.

Fitch, R. (2004) 'An Account of Pegu in 1586–1587', *SOAS Bulletin of Burma Research*, vol. 2, no. 2, pp. 167–79.

Gilbert, D. (2013) 'Categorizing Gender in Queer Yangon', *Sojourn*, vol. 28, no. 2, pp. 241–71.

Gun San Naw (a) Naw Naw v. Republic of the Union of Myanmar (or) Naw Naw (2013) Mandalay State Court, Mandalay Division.

Harriden, J. (2012) *The Authority of Influence: Women and Power in Burmese History*, NIAS Press, Copenhagen.

Human Rights Watch (2012) *Untold Miseries: Wartime Abuses and Forced Displacement in Burma's Kachin State* [online] https://www.hrw.org/report/2012/03/20/untold-miseries/wartime-abuses-and-forced-displacement-burmas-kachin-state.

Jackson, P. (1998) 'Male Homosexuality and Transgenderism in the Thai Buddhist Tradition' in W Leyland (ed.), *Queer Dharma: Voices of Gay Buddhists*, Leyland Publications, San Francisco.

Lin Lin (2012) *Second Police Corporal Nay Zin Tun v. Lin Ko Ko*, Major Crime No. 982, Mingalartaungnyunt Township Court, Yangon Division.

Mann, Z. (2013) 'Gay Rights Activists to Sue Mandalay Police for Alleged Abuse', *The Irrawaddy News*, 16 July 2013 [online] http://www.irrawaddy.org/women-gender/gay-rights-activists-to-sue-mandalay-police-for-alleged-abuse.html.

Ministry of Health (2006) *Myanmar National Strategic Plan on HIV and AIDS 2006–2010*, Union of Myanmar [online] http://siteresources.worldbank.org/INTHIVAIDS/Resources/375798-1151090631807/2693180-1151090665111/2693181-1155742859198/MyanmarNSP20062010.pdf

Myanmar Daily News (2013) 'I'm Not Going to Play *Achaut* Characters, says Aung Ye Lin', 9 April 2013 [online] http://www.myanmardailynews.org/2013/04/blog-post_6022.html#.U2Xo7a2Sxqc.

Myo Zaw Linn (2013) 'Rights Group to Sue Police for Sexually Assaulting Trans Women', *DVB News*, 15 July 2014 [online] http://www.dvb.no/news/rights-group-to-sue-police-for-sexually-assaulting-trans-women/29901.

Nyein Pyae Sone (2013) 'No Changes to Burma's 60-Year-Old Prostitution Law, Police Chief Says', *The Irrawaddy News*, 10 July 2013 [online] http://www.irrawaddy.org/democracy/no-changes-to-burmas-60-year-old-prostitution-law-police-chief-says.html.

Richards, A. (2012) *Bitter Wounds and Lost Dreams: Human Rights Under Assault in Karen State*, Physicians for Human Rights [online] http://physiciansforhumanrights.org/library/reports/bitter-wounds-and-lost-dreams.html.

Richards, A., Parmar, P. and Sollom, R. (2011) *Life Under the Junta: Evidence on Crimes Against Humanity in Burma's Chin State*, Physicians for Human Rights [online] http://physiciansforhumanrights.org/library/reports/burma-chin-report-2011.html [accessed 28 January].

Sai Tha Aung (2013) 'The Arrests and Charges in Mandalay Are Not Gender Discrimination', *7 Day Daily (in Burmese, on file with authors).*

Sanders, D.E. (2009) '377 and the Unnatural Afterlife of British Colonialism in Asia', *Asian Journal of Comparative Law*, vol. 4, pp. 1–49.

Spiro, M. (1997) *Gender Ideology and Psychosocial Reality: An Essay on Cultural Reproduction*, Yale University Press, Yale.

Steinberg, D.I. (2001) *Burma: The State of Myanmar*, Georgetown University Press, Washington.

The Irrawaddy News (2013) 'Rights Group Condemns Police Arrest of Mandalay Gays', 23 July [online] http://www.irrawaddy.org/latest-news/rights-group-condemns-police-arrest-of-mandalay-gays.html.

The Irrawaddy News (2014) 'Union Government Passed NGO Law', 1 July 2014 [online] http://www.irrawaddy.org/burma/union-parliament-passed-ngo-law.html

The Voice Daily (2013), 'The Start of Action Against Meinmalya at Night Around Mandalay Moat' (in Burmese, on file with authors).

United Nations General Assembly (2013), *Situation of Human Rights in Myanmar: Note by the Secretary-General*, 23 September, A/68/397.

United Nations Human Rights Council (2011) *Report of the United Nations High Commissioner for Human Rights: Discriminatory Laws and Practices and Acts of Violence against Individuals based on their Sexual Orientation and Gender Identity*, 17 November, A/HRC/14/41.

Wahab, A. (2012) 'Homophobia as the State of Reason: The Case of Postcolonial Trinidad and Tobago', *GLQ: A Journal of Lesbian and Gay Studies*, vol. 18, no. 4, pp. 481–505.

11 Legislating inequalities

Gender, sexuality and violence in China

Joy L. Chia

Introduction

The year 2014 marked the sixtieth anniversary of the first Constitution of the People's Republic of China (PRC), which first articulated the principle that women in China enjoy equal rights with men in all spheres of political, economic, cultural, social and family life (Article 96, *PRC Constitution 1954*). In official terminology, this principle is encapsulated in the basic state policy of 'equality between men and women'. Yet, what exactly does that concept of equality entail under Chinese law and policy?

While 'equality under the law' for all citizens is enshrined as a constitutional principle under Article 33 of the *PRC Constitution 2004*, there is no clear articulation within Chinese law and regulations of the definition of discrimination nor how such equality should be protected. Although the Supreme People's Court (SPC) had taken some initial steps towards interpreting constitutional equality under Article 33 it formally annulled its 2001 judicial interpretation and permitted courts to use a constitutional provision as a legal basis for adjudication in December 2008 (Hand 2011, p. 54; Kellogg 2009). The *2011 Regulations on Civil Causes of Action* do not explicitly allow for a cause of action on the grounds of discrimination and most courts have refused to accept discrimination cases on the grounds that they are not listed in these regulations (Webster 2011, p. 664). Furthermore, China's social protection laws, including the PRC *Law on the Protection of the Rights and Interests of Women (LPRIW) 2005*, include broad prohibitions against discrimination or violence but are short laws that are more akin to symbolic statements of policy than any sort of implementable law (Balzano 2007, p. 9).

This chapter considers inequalities in Chinese law and policy at the nexus of gender, sexuality and violence. It starts by examining the inequalities that are embedded in laws that are rarely challenged by the dominant discourse on gender, sexuality and violence in China, and that sometimes even continue to exist in on-going legal reform efforts to address gender-based violence. Although a full treatment of the history of gender relations in modern Chinese history is beyond the scope of this chapter, it is important to note that women's rights and 'equality between men and women' were central to the revolutionary agenda.[1] State feminism manifested in a focus on women as agents of labour productivity, focusing on formal equality among all comrades. However, the post-1949 improvements to the position of women were invariably qualified because of 'the subordination of gender to the supposedly more substantial matters of economic development political power' (Palmer 2007, p. 154).

Within this landscape, equality between men and women has therefore meant that men are held out as the standard by which women are measured, and state policy has largely focused on formal rather than substantive equality (ibid., p. 171). Despite recent efforts by feminists to push the Chinese government towards more progressive gender equality policies, this ambiguous (and problematic) conception of equality has become embedded in PRC legislation and regulations, particularly with regard to its treatment of gender, sexuality and violence. This chapter argues that using male citizens as the standard has privileged the male experience of violence, essentialised violence against women, and overlooked violence where victims and perpetrators fall outside the gendered norms expressed and entrenched in laws. These hidden inequalities have created a hierarchy of violence within Chinese law and practice by meting out different punishments for similar violent acts based on the identity of the victim and perpetrators.

The chapter then examines structural inequalities in the legislative and policy-making process that further exacerbate these disparities by privileging certain groups of individuals above others while shaping public discourse about anti-violence legal reform. How individuals understand, interpret and experience the law and state action is extremely varied, and this is especially true in China where laws are unevenly implemented and many different state actors, with diverse agendas, influence an opaque legislative process. The ultimate inequality, however, lies between the state and its citizens – state imperatives overlie the aforementioned hierarchy of violence among its citizens as the legal framework prioritises state prerogatives over the protection of its citizens' right to equality. As Deborah Davis has noted in the context of marriage and sexuality in the PRC, 'public priorities of the national elite have consistently trumped the preferences of local communities and the personal wishes of individual men and women' (Davis 2014, p. 41). This chapter argues that state interest in controlling specific kinds and consequences of sexuality allows for the tolerance of violence disproportionately borne by women in the public sphere, and that even the best-intentioned legal reform efforts have been stymied by persistent state interests that limit the adoption of comprehensive measures to address gender-based violence.

Legal ambiguities also highlight the fraught relationship that the Chinese state has with violence – either private or state-sanctioned – and raises the question of whether existing legal stipulations on gender equality and government responsibility to stop violence are more rhetorical than actionable. Effective legislative reform requires a clear-eyed view of how political and social culture, identity and gender norms affect individuals' experience of violence as 'harm is inflicted in certain ways and supported by structures and ideologies that permit a specific form of violence to continue in its own precise context' (Fontes and McCloskey 2011).

Gendered laws and gendered violence

Scholarship on legal subjectivity has emphasised how the language and practice of law produces social subjects and categories enshrined in specific identities and social hierarchies constructed by law (Ruskola 2002, p. 205). Laws both shape and reflect a society's understanding of gender and violence, even in framing what kind of violence counts as 'real violence' by determining: (1) what type of conduct constitutes 'violence' that is worth prosecuting; (2) what kind of evidence proves the occurrence of such violence; (3) who is *able to* experience said violence, and therefore is worthy of the law's protection.

Stereotyping within the law

Chinese laws replicate and perpetuate gender stereotypes by framing women and girls as perpetual victims, while assuming that all perpetrators are male. This is especially true where crimes are related to sexual violence. Under Article 236 of the *PRC Criminal Law*, rape is a gendered crime and applies only to women and girls; where the Article discusses further punishment for sexual relations with a child under the age of fourteen years, the legislative text refers only to girls and not boys. Trafficking is also a gendered crime, as Article 240 of the *PRC Criminal Law* only contemplates women or children as trafficking victims. Similarly, until 2015, Article 237 of the *PRC Criminal Law*, which criminalises obscene acts done with force or violence, confined such acts to those perpetuated against female victims. Although recent legal reforms amending the *PRC Criminal Law* have modified Article 237 to be gender neutral, it remains to be seen whether the police and procuratorates will actively prosecute crimes where victims are male. Finally, even when they are not portrayed as victims, other laws only place women in specific roles – for example, administrative sanctions around sex work, as detailed in the *Law of the PRC on Penalties for Administration of Public Security 2005*, assume that all sex workers are female and all those who solicit them are male.

Even Chinese laws that seek to prohibit discrimination or violence against women betray some level of ideological ambivalence about gender equality. For example, the *PRC Population and Family Planning Law 2001* acknowledges that violence against women is often tied to their reproductive functions and prohibits the discrimination and maltreatment of women who bear female babies or who suffer from infertility (Article 22). However, this legislative framing does not challenge or consider the underlying assumption of a preference for sons or the centrality of reproduction in women's identity (and value), but seeks to plaster over a much more deeply rooted inequality problem (Tan 2008, p. 26). Another example of this ambivalence is with regard to how the state has addressed domestic violence. Under the current framework, prohibitions against domestic violence are only found in the laws associated with women, like the *PRC Marriage Law 2001* and the *LPRIW 2005*, rather than more general laws like the *PRC Criminal Law*. In so doing, the government has made domestic violence a women's issue rather than something that concerns everyone.

Invisible violence

The inherent stereotyping that takes place within legislative text also creates invisible categories of individuals who do not conform to gender expectations or heterosexual norms, overlooking types of violence that are inflicted upon them for their perceived deviance from such stereotypes. The current Chinese legal framework ignores violence against male victims and violence against lesbian, gay, bisexual or transgender (LGBT) individuals.

Although current laws prohibiting family violence are supposedly gender neutral and do not specify the relationship between perpetrator and victim, domestic violence is, in practice, largely synonymous with wife-battering, where the violence occurs within a heterosexual marriage, inflicted by a man against his stoic yet helpless wife. Conceptualising domestic violence within a male perpetrator–female victim dynamic ignores male victims of intimate partner violence – although more press was given to the statistic that more than one-third of Chinese women report male-on-female intimate partner violence, the same 2004 national survey indicated that eighteen per cent of male respondents reported female-on-male violence, where fifteen per cent of all surveyed experienced mutual hitting (Parish *et al.* 2004, p. 177).

This framing also ignores the violence experienced by LGBT individuals. A 2009 NGO survey of lesbian, bisexual and trans-identified (LBT) women indicated that forty-six per cent of those surveyed had experienced violence from a same-sex intimate partner (Common Language 2009). However, the existing anti-violence laws and systems at local level generally fail to recognise such violence or offer protection to LBT women when they face such violence (China LBT Rights Initiative 2014). At the time of writing, there is no information about male-male intimate partner violence, which arguably points to the erasure of this issue within society. LGBT individuals also face violence from other family members that is rarely examined; forty-eight per cent of participants in the 2009 survey of LBT women stated they had faced violence from family members because of their sexual orientation, but since most victims of such violence are no longer considered minors, they are not protected under laws protecting minors from parental abuse. Violence against LGBT individuals outside of the home is not even contemplated within Chinese laws. Regulations do not contemplate violence (physical, sexual, emotional or otherwise) against LGBT students in the form of homophobic or transphobic bullying in schools, even though this sort of violence appears to be quite commonplace; for example, a 2012 NGO survey indicated that seventy-seven per cent of 421 students from middle schools, high schools, universities and vocational schools had encountered such bullying (Aibai 2012).[2]

Hierarchies of violence

Finally, Chinese law creates a hierarchy of violence by differentiating among violent acts based on: (1) the relationship between perpetrators and victims; (2) the gender of the victim or perpetrator; and (3) the, so-called, innocence of the victim.

Strangers v. family members

Although family violence is pervasive in China,[3] China has yet to promulgate national anti-domestic violence legislation and only one form of domestic violence – the maltreatment of family members – is currently treated as a crime. Maltreatment of family members has been defined as '[d]urative or frequent family violence'[4] and constitutes a crime under Article 260 of the *PRC Criminal Law* only if the case is deemed 'serious' – that is, 'regular, consistent and continuous' and resulting in what a judge considers to be 'particularly odious physical abuse' (Xue n.d.). The standard for such frequency, as practised by courts, is extremely high, while the law leaves room for judicial discretion in judging the intention of the abuse. For example, in adjudicating a case where a wife was physically abused over the span of her twenty-year marriage, a court refused to find a defendant guilty of maltreating family members because it reasoned that ten instances of battering over a period of twenty years cannot be characterised as 'occurring with high frequency' and further noted that the defendant did not have the intention of maltreating his wife as each instance occurred with good cause as the wife was not obedient to her husband (Yang 2011, p. 251).[5]

By punishing family violence only when it is frequent and flagrant enough to rise to the level of a crime, the law ranks violent acts in the family, signalling that infrequent physical violence does not require legal sanction. The law equates severity with repetition, overemphasises physical injury and places psychological, sexual or emotional violence on a different, and less important, tier. This is further emphasised by how and when the state takes action; maltreatment is only taken up by the state when the victim brings a complaint. As noted by Xue, 'the state will not prosecute . . . unless and until the perpetrator is taken to court for prosecution by the victim . . . [therefore] effectively taking the overwhelming majority of cases out of the arena of judicial remedy' (Xue n.d.). State reticence in prosecuting cases of maltreatment is also carried through administrative sanctions that govern, so-called, lesser incidents of maltreatment. Article 45 of the *Law of the PRC on Penalties for Administration of Public Security 2005* imposes extremely mild sanctions against persons who are accused of maltreating a family member only when the family member demands that the public security organisations 'handle' the matter (perpetrators are to be detained for not more than five days or given a warning). The law also demands that the private prosecutor bear the burden of proof, which is often insurmountable.

A comparison with how Chinese criminal law treats similar conduct against strangers underscores how much leeway perpetrators of family violence are afforded. While a person could be sentenced to up to three years of imprisonment for inflicting bodily injury on a stranger under Article 234 of the *PRC Criminal Law*, a perpetrator of family violence only receives a maximum of two years of criminal detention or public surveillance for maltreatment if the circumstances are serious, and if they are not serious a perpetrator faces no punishment at all (Article 260). If maltreatment of a family member results in serious injury or death, then Article 260 determines that the sentence is two to seven years; conversely, for inflicting severe bodily injury on a stranger, Article 234 states that a perpetrator will receive three to ten years of fixed term imprisonment, while the sentence for causing a severe deformity or death is imprisonment of not less than ten years, life imprisonment or death. The law therefore differentiates between violence inflicted by strangers and violence at the hands of intimates. By imposing more severe punishments for violence outside the family, the law uses male experience of violence as the standard, and implicitly suggests that women's experiences of violence (which tend to be disproportionately inflicted by family members) are less worthy of prosecution and, thus, less important.

Gender of victim or perpetrator

The different treatment of similar conduct based on gender of victim or perpetrator cuts both ways. As discussed above, Chinese law has blind spots regarding certain violent acts, especially those regarding sexual violence, when the victim is a man. Consider the significant disparity in how the legal and administrative system approaches the issue of rape. If a man is the victim of rape or sexual assault, then there are no applicable provisions within the *PRC Criminal Law* (Mountford 2010, para. 58). Until very recently, the only relevant recourse for male victims of sexual assault was Article 44 of the *Law of the PRC on Penalties for Administration of Public Security 2005*, which states that the maximum applicable punishment for molestation or an obscene act against another (i.e. a man) is detention for the maximum of fifteen days. A local court has held that 'sexual invasion between persons of the same sex does not constitute a criminal offence under Chinese law' (ibid., para. 59), while other perpetrators have been released with only official reprimands when police could not charge them with a crime (Wu 2014). In August 2015, the *PRC Criminal Law Amendment No. 9* modified Article 237, which punishes perpetrators of indecent acts involving violence, coercion or other methods, to be gender neutral. This is a welcome change as male victims of sexual assault may now have some redress under the *PRC Criminal Law*; yet it is worth noting that *Amendment No. 9* leaves rape as a gendered crime, which has more severe penalties than sexual violence under Article 237. As previously noted, it also remains to be seen how the Article 237 modification will be operationalised and implemented on the ground.

With regards to the sexual abuse of minors, the October 2013 Supreme People's Court *Opinion on Punishing the Crimes of Sexual Abuse of Minors Pursuant to the Law* differentiated between sexual assault against minors based on their gender. Although child molestation is gender neutral, rape remains a gendered crime which only has female victims. If a male victim of molestation is fourteen years or older but not yet an adult, the act is no longer treated as molestation but rises to an act constituting the intentional infliction of harm, with correspondingly different and harsher penalties.

The contradictory positions here indicate legal ambivalence towards sexual violence against men. Chinese law does not contemplate that men can be victims of rape, but if a rape-like act is inflicted on a young male victim, then it goes beyond the sphere of a sexual crime into physical crime. For example, a 2010 case involving the sexual abuse of an eighteen-year-old man by his forty-two-year-old colleague was prosecuted under intentional injury instead of sexual abuse due to this legal gap (ibid.). This is reminiscent of discourse in international law around sexual violence against men in conflict, where male-on-male rape in armed conflict is under-reported as sexual violence but, when it is reported, is reclassified as torture (Sivakumaran 2007, pp. 254–56).

'Innocents' v. 'non-innocents'

Even as China has undergone significant social transformation in the past two and a half decades, there remains a (state) preoccupation with women's roles in upholding 'social morality' (a sentiment codified in Article 5 of the *LPRIW*) and marriage continues to be promoted as an ideal. This push towards universal heterosexual marriage is further enhanced by family planning policies that only permit 'lawful' children within such marriages. Political rhetoric has called on women to return to their traditional roles, with a corresponding exaltation of particular gender stereotypes (good mothers or chaste virgins) that hardly conform to the everyday experiences of Chinese women.

These gender stereotypes have historically permeated Chinese law, which also acts in part to promote (and enforce) a code of sexual morality by differentiating between those they perceive to be innocent victims and those who have deviated from social ideals. Until the August 2015 *Criminal Law Amendment No.* 9 modified the relevant articles, sex with a girl under the age of fourteen years counted as rape unless the girl was involved in sex work. The PRC *Criminal Law* carved out sex with an underaged sex worker as a separate public order offence under Article 360(2), which imposed a significantly lighter punishment than that of rape. Similarly, in its October 2013 Opinion on punishing sexual abuse of minors, the SPC distinguished between girls who were lured into performing sex acts by gifts or where it was known that someone else was compelling her to engage in sex work, on the one hand, and girls under fourteen who were actively and consensually engaging in sex work, on the other. Perpetrators found to have sex with girls of the latter category were given lighter sentences.[6] The amendment, which came into effect on 1 November 2015, deleted Article 360(2) from the *PRC Criminal Law*. This closed the loophole that allowed adult men to claim, truthfully or otherwise, that their underaged partners were sex workers in an attempt to avoid a rape conviction, while simultaneously subjecting the victim to stigmatisation.

Embedded inequalities and dominant discourses

Although 'women-work' (妇女工作) has been integral to the Chinese Communist Party's revolutionary agenda since the 1920s, state feminism in China is intrinsically conflicted, 'portraying a paradoxical image of a state patriarch championing women's liberation, although with vacillation and inconsistency' (Wang 2005, p. 519). Early PRC legislation, like the *Marriage Law 1950* (which was the first law to be passed by the new Communist government), soundly abolished 'the arbitrary and compulsory feudal marriage system which was based on the idea of superiority of man over woman', and replaced it with a marriage system based on freedom, monogamy and equal rights for women (Croll 1978, p. 230). It is worth noting, however, that the early push for equality within the family has not translated into significant changes in gendered expectations within Chinese society – the practice of virilocal marriage continued unabated, and the introduction of the one-child policy has unleashed forces of a preference for sons which 'manifested in its most extreme forms in a rapid rise in female infanticide' (Howell 1998, p. 174).

The All-China Women's Federation (ACWF) is the organisational embodiment of state feminism, set up to fulfil the two, often contradictory, tasks of promoting the interests of women within the government and the Chinese Communist Party and promoting the interests of the government (and the Party) among women. It serves as a 'transmission belt' which 'pass[es] party policy downwards to its constituency of women and relaying their opinions and demands upwards' to decision-makers within the Party (ibid., p. 171), however, it is worth noting that, in practice, the flow of information is predominantly top-down and therefore, one way (Palmer 2007, p. 171). Within the state structure, it enjoys a 'monopoly of representation' (Howell 1998, p. 172); the ACWF is explicitly granted de jure (and de facto) powers of participation in the policy-making process (Tan 2008, p. 14).[7] The ACWF therefore takes on sole responsibilities for drafting and revising basic laws and legislation that relate to women, as well as government policies and plans for the development of women (ibid., pp. 10–11).

While it can be beneficial to have a designated government-related agency with resources and support for the target population, the political structure and the dual role of the ACWF have had significant impacts on the drafting, enactment and implementation of Chinese legislation. First, just as carving out 'women-work' as a distinct sphere also ensured 'women-work' was separate and subordinate to the Party's 'central work' (Wang 2005, p. 521), ACWF's monopoly over legislation relating to women inevitably distinguishes such legislation as different from other basic laws that affect the general population. As Palmer has argued, the very existence of laws particular to the protection of women's rights and interests 'may have unintended consequences that work against the intention of the law' because such laws identify women as a separate (and socially disadvantaged) group in need of special protection (Palmer 2007, p. 172).

Second, the ACWF's effectiveness in pushing for legislative change is limited as it is ranked lower than a ministry within the state hierarchy and is therefore not granted the authority to take a proactive stance towards creating legislative agendas or making policy. Although the ACWF can criticise current policies or urge government action, any initiative on its part can only be taken with state approval, and the contours of legal reform are somewhat predetermined by when the ACWF is assigned the responsibility to draft or revise relevant laws and policies for the consideration of the State Council.

Third, the ACWF acts as a gatekeeper, determining the content of official discourse about gender and women's rights. As an official state organ, the ACWF does not, and perhaps *cannot*, represent all the demands of all its constituencies, especially those demands which conflict with the state's interest or social/cultural norms (Howell 1998, p. 180).[8] It therefore filters the content of policy documents and, by extension, whose voices are heard at official level. For example, in reporting to the United Nations Committee on the Elimination of All Forms of Discrimination Against Women (CEDAW Committee), the ACWF (which self-identifies as an non-governmental organisation in the international arena) invites Chinese NGOs, experts and researchers on gender issues to participate in writing NGO shadow reports, but very few of those invited include independent women's rights NGOs conducting rights-based advocacy. The ACWF also determines the content of its human-rights reporting on gender issues – for example, excluding groups that deviate from gendered norms about citizenship and moral propriety (like lesbian, bisexual and trans-identified women, sex workers, single mothers, women with HIV/AIDS) in its own CEDAW shadow report. Perhaps even more unfortunately, the ACWF's close reliance on the government has also 'inhibited it . . . from reflecting more broadly on the multi-causal dimensions of gender inequalities' (ibid., p. 177). By claiming to represent all Chinese women, the ACWF also homogenises women into specific, socially acceptable tropes and fails to consider the diversity within its population or take into account the intersectionality of gender and other identities.

As a result, populations which fall outside the mainstream (including LGBT individuals, women with HIV/AIDS, sex workers, rural women and ethnic minority women) are generally under-represented, if not completely invisible, in official policy-making. One reason for this is structural, most ACWF leaders are from the urban and political elites and therefore tend not to identify with, or be from, these marginalised communities themselves. Another reason is the tendency to treat those groups which do appear in official policies (such as rural women, ethnic minority women and women with HIV/AIDS) as objects of charity and concern, rather than as rights-holders. This is further exacerbated by the inability of many advocacy-oriented organisations working with these populations to officially register as non-profit organisations. Although a discussion about the complex civil society landscape in China is beyond the scope of this chapter, it is worth noting that the Chinese government has become increasingly suspicious of advocacy NGOs that generally operate outside of the state sphere.[9] The ACWF has crowded out other more autonomous or independent civil society actors within the women's rights field, in part because 'both the state and the public see that women's issues are already represented by a long-established and powerful force' (China Development Brief 2015, p. 9). The lack of voice within and without the ACWF therefore directly impacts the ability of members of these communities to engage in discussions about laws and policies that directly affect them and their communities (for example, China LBT Rights Initiative 2014, p. 4). The deep inequalities in access to policy-makers among different groups of women have therefore resulted in the continuing marginalisation of some populations within existing legislation.

The ACWF's balancing act between women's rights and state interests also affects public discourse about gender and violence, as treading softly around political considerations has placed emphasis on subjects that are perceived to be politically safe while overlooking those that could be deemed politically sensitive. International human-rights standards recognise that gender-based violence encompasses violence that occurs in both the private and public sphere; CEDAW General Recommendation 19 defines such violence to include 'acts that inflict physical, mental or sexual harm or suffering, threats of such acts, coercion and other deprivations of liberty'. In contrast, violence against women is often interpreted by Chinese authorities to refer only to spousal violence (that is, by a male perpetrator against his wife) to the exclusion of the many other forms of violence that women in China face. In presenting its efforts to stop violence against women in China, the 2012 report that the Chinese government submitted to the CEDAW Committee primarily reported on its efforts to stem spousal violence, demonstrating that the government's own interpretation confines discussions about violence against women to family violence. Family violence in this instance also only refers to violence within families created by heterosexual marriages, rather than de facto families or intimate partners.

While domestic violence continues to be pernicious and pervasive in China, its dominance in the public sphere has crowded out other issues that the state has a responsibility to address and undermines deep thinking on multi-causal, cross-cutting issues beyond domestic violence. Government reports to the CEDAW Committee have never reported on other forms of violence against women, even where NGO shadow reports detail many different forms of violence faced by women in China, including violence against human-rights defenders, sexual harassment in the workplace and sexual abuse of women and girls. There is a paucity of data about other forms of violence and – despite repeated requests by the CEDAW Committee for the Chinese government to improve data collection so as to collect information about all forms of violence against women and to include the information in its CEDAW reports – there is no indication that the Chinese government has taken any concrete steps in this direction.

Gender, sexuality and violence in the state's interest

Beyond the structural inequalities that continue to exist, one of the key obstacles to effective reform efforts that respond to existing violence against women is the desire of the State to control certain gendered activities, often through actual violence or the threat of violence, so much so that gendered violence is sometimes committed in furtherance of specific state interests. Conceptualising violence against women in broader strokes (i.e. beyond domestic violence) challenges government policies and practices in key areas like population control, family planning and sex work, by calling into question why gender-based violence in those contexts is overlooked, or even sanctioned by the state.

Violence in the family planning system

One of the most pernicious forms of gender discrimination in China remains the cultural preference for male children. One study conducted by the ACWF in the

1990s found that the most common source of discrimination and abuse cited by women, especially in the countryside, occurred as a response to not having borne a son (Wang 2009, p. 253). This preference for sons, already rather strong in Chinese culture, was exacerbated by China's transition to a market economy, which resulted in an increased reliance on individual household production. This has particularly affected rural families who find themselves vulnerable if they lack sons to support them in old age (ibid, p. 254).

This situation has been compounded by government policies on family planning that seek to limit population size and advocate a one-child per couple policy. Although the policy is gender-neutral in theory, it is extremely gendered in implementation. These limitations have raised the value of sons and lowered the value of daughters in rural areas. Recognising that family planning policies did run counter to tradition, current law allows for a, so-called, 1.5 child policy, which requires couples to stop bearing children if their first child is a boy but allows them to have a second child after a period of several years if their firstborn is a girl, thereby implying that the girl child is of lesser value. Rather than stemming discrimination against daughters, this policy has inadvertently legitimised gender discrimination within the family and has led to the abandonment of female children or sex-selective abortions. Studies have indicated that the treatment of girl children often depends on the identity and social status of the child, as girls with urban household registrations (where family planning laws tend to be strictly enforced) are rarely abandoned or neglected. In contrast, research concurs that girls are more likely to be abandoned if they are the second or third daughter (ibid., p. 261). Even though Chinese law has criminalised the selective elimination of girls through abandonment, neglect or abuse, these practices have continued unabated.

Beyond failing to combat gender discrimination and violence in families, violence against women also occurs within the family planning system at the hands of state actors in the course of implementing the perceived goals of population control laws. Although Chinese law appears to be gender neutral on the responsibility to practise family planning, in practice, women bear the disproportionate burden in family planning[10] and bear the brunt of the coercive measures that control population growth. Women are subjected to forced monitoring by family planning officials to ensure that they are not pregnant and are using intrauterine devices. In many provinces, family planning regulations even directly prohibit reproduction, recommend that couples with one child undergo sterilisation, or require the termination of pregnancy where the pregnancy violates family planning regulations (China Violence Against Women Concern Group 2014, paras. 9–12). Local government officials have interpreted these regulations to allow for the forced inductions of pregnant women (ibid., para. 10). Moreover, provincial regulations that tie job performance (including promotions and bonuses) to population control create perverse incentives for the use of violence to enforce population control quotas (ibid., paras. 37–9).

Although reforms of domestic regulations by central government have tended towards increased protections of individual civil rights, the state has 'retain[ed] its earlier role of social engineer when it exercises the right to control the reproduction of the nation's population and aligns family policies with goals for national development' (Davis 2014, p. 42). As long as population control remains a 'fundamental State Policy' and an important state tool to 'control the size and raise the general quality' of China's population as articulated in Article 2 of the *PRC Population and Family Planning Law*, it is unlikely that local governmental family planning practices will change. Despite an announced decision by central government to reform its family planning policies by 2016, the relaxation of the policy from one child per couple to two children will likely to do little to stem the use of violence against those women and their families who do not comply with the regulations. This is because the proposed reforms have ignored the use of violence in the implementation of family planning policies, and do not hold state actors accountable for violence committed in the furtherance of population control goals.

Violence in the context of sex work

Another area where violence against women has been tolerated is with regard to sex work in China. While the voluminous discourse about the nature of sex work and whether or not commercial sex work is or is not itself violence against women is outside the scope of this chapter, it is important to note that there is general concurrence that violence and crimes against sex workers should be denounced, and that violence against female sex workers falls under the definitions of violence against women.

Although sex work has a long history in China, the long-established Chinese prostitution system was abolished by the early PRC government in 1949 because it violated socialist norms against gender inequality and the exploitation of women (Meng 2013, p. 52). In state discourse, sex workers have been marked as 'contaminated' and therefore 'requiring rescue, discipline and control' (Asia Catalyst 2013, p. 18; Choi 2011), a mentality that still holds strong in contemporary China. The Chinese government's current approach to sex work continues to rely on early PRC methods, including the closure of brothels, sentencing their owners and pimps to prison and sending sex workers to female rehabilitation centres where they receive medical treatment for venereal disease and education about morality, health, and professional skills (Meng 2013, p. 52). In the 1990s education through forced labour was added to the range of anti-prostitution tools available to the police, as was the Custody and Education system (ibid., p. 53).

Sex work and related activities in China are generally treated as administrative offences rather than crimes. Administrative sanctions against sex work include fines, short-term detention and detention in the Custody and Education system for a term of six months to two years.[11] As violations of the *Law of the PRC on Penalties for Administration of Public Security 2005*, sex work and related activities therefore fall under the remit of the police, which have wide (some say excessive) discretion in the imposition of punishment. Sex workers can be detained without trial by public security organs and often face brutal prosecution after arrest and during investigation. Reports indicate that police brutality against sex workers is par for the course, including violence in interrogation and forced confessions. A recent NGO report provides examples of police violence, including the stripping of sex workers to take photographic evidence of sex work, violence in interrogation and forced confessions (Asia Catalyst 2013, pp. 21–3).

Further, the Chinese government continues to use the Custody and Education system, even though it officially abolished its Re-education through Labour system in 2013. The Custody and Education system is exclusively used as an administrative detention mechanism for both sex workers and their clients, but in practice it is used primarily as a mechanism to control female sex workers, and detainees are disproportionately women. Surveys have indicated that the majority of these detainees were low-income female sex workers who were from rural villages with little or no school education (Meng 2013, p. 73).

Emboldened by the Chinese government's entrenched view that prostitution was a social evil that threatened social stability (ibid., pp. 79–80), police violence against sex workers is rarely raised as a social problem. Neither is violence committed against sex workers by non-state actors, even though it appears to be widespread, if rarely reported due to the illegality of sex work (ibid., pp. 80–1). By framing sex work as a moral failing the government continues to tolerate (and even abet) violence committed against female sex workers in the name of state interests in eradicating crime and social corruption.

Conclusion: institutionalising access to justice for all victims of gender-based violence

More than a decade after it was first proposed to the National People's Congress (NPC), a draft *Anti-Domestic Violence Law* was finally added to the NPC Standing Committee's five-year legislative agenda in September 2013. Legal reform on this front is greatly welcome and a national law will provide consistency in interpretation, and hopefully implementation, of anti-domestic violence protection. At the time of writing, the drafting process for the *Anti-Domestic Violence Law* is on-going and two different drafts have been released. On 25 November 2014, the State Council released the first draft for a month-long period of public comment. This draft contained several important reforms, including the broadening of the definition of domestic violence to include not just physical violence but also psychological violence; and clearer procedures for the application of personal protection orders both during and prior to raising a lawsuit. The second draft, released by the NPC's Standing Committee for public comment in August 2015, included some significant changes to the earlier draft, several of which were backwards steps for reform efforts.

A worrisome development is that the August 2015 draft law revised the definition of domestic violence, and did not include emotional or psychological harm between family members within the scope of domestic violence. The draft further differentiates between different levels of harm, whereby more serious offences are addressed as crimes or administrative harms while less serious cases will be handled through a written warning system. While the August 2015 draft recognises that domestic violence must be dealt with, even when it is not 'serious', it leaves open the question about whether, in practice, the written warning system gives police officers, who have historically been dismissive of domestic violence complaints, the discretion to treat all domestic violence incidents as less serious.

In addition, there are questions about who constitutes the family. While the November 2014 draft defines 'family members' to include 'spouses, parents, children and also other close relatives living together', the August 2015 draft does not include clear definitions of who is considered part of the family. The March 2015 *Opinion on Handling Criminal Cases of Domestic Violence in Accordance with Law*, promulgated by the Supreme People's Court, the Supreme People's Procuratorate, the Ministry of Public Security and the Ministry of Justice, indicate that the expansion of the categories of individuals for whom civil protection orders may be issued is primarily meant to protect the elderly from their abusive children, and minors from abusive relatives. Both drafts have excluded unmarried cohabitating couples – heterosexual or homosexual – with the explanation to the November 2014 draft clearly stating that the drafters did not believe there were real differences between violence in relationships (such as romantic involvements, cohabitation or between former spouses) and violence between ordinary members of the society.

Beyond the specific changes in legislative text through the drafting process, there are several areas of concern regarding the fundamental framing of the *Anti-Domestic Violence Law*. First, the discussions about anti-family violence continue to be framed from a social protection view, and follow the canon of special protection legislation that is 'very much the product of traditional paternalistic state attitudes' (Palmer 2007, p. 152). By seeking to act in the interests of women, children and the elderly as a whole, the laws serve to emphasise the vulnerability of these populations, thus moving the discourse away from equality and rights towards welfare.

There is also the question of what type of violence is protected by the anti-domestic violence legislation and, in particular, whether the type of violence disproportionately faced by particular minority groups would be protected. For example, in the context of sexual minorities, domestic abuse may occur in forms other than physical assault, including psychological, economic, sexual and other forms of abuse. A coalition of lesbian, bisexual and trans-identified (LBT) NGOs recently noted that reported forms of domestic abuse included psychological violence imposed by threats from parents to disown their LBT child; parental threats to commit suicide or self-harm in response to their children's coming out as a means of psychological control; stalking and restricting personal freedom and financial resources; forcing their LBT children to undergo conversion therapy or to be committed to a psychiatric institution; forcing their LBT children to engage in heterosexual intercourse against their will or to enter into a heterosexual marriage (China LBT Rights Initiative, p. 7). In most cases, the parent-child relationship clearly puts such violence within the family, but the affected LBT individuals generally have already reached the age of majority and are no longer treated as minors under Chinese law. How then would such violent acts be treated under the draft law? The violence is not being committed against women by their intimate partners, against minors by their parents or against elderly people by their children. Yet, such violence is very real and should be addressed.

Even if successful, these legal reform efforts are strictly confined to dealing with violence within the family, leaving many other forms of gender-based violence unaddressed. Despite repeated recommendations from the CEDAW Committee that the Chinese government adopt comprehensive legislation on violence against women and girls (a call echoed by international and domestic legal experts and NGOs), the concept of expanding interpretations of gender-based violence beyond family violence has gained very little traction in China.

It is understandable that advocates would seek to push through anti-violence legislation wherever possible, especially where entry points for protection for women are few and far between. Advocates (and policy-makers) must settle for what is possible, rather than what is best, and it is important to recognise that progress is often made through steady steps, rather than leaps. However, the failure of legal reformers either to interrogate the conceptual framework of protection-oriented laws or to challenge structural inequalities significantly impacts their likelihood of success in reaching their stated goals of reducing violence against women and increasing gender equality.

State accountability in the prevention of violence against its citizens is an integral part of ensuring access to justice for victims of such violence. Addressing only one form of gender-based violence to the exclusion of others undermines this system by failing to combat the impunity of both state and non-state actors and therefore perpetuating a climate that is tolerant of gender-based violence at work and in public spaces. In order to successfully prevent gender-based violence, laws and justice systems must first be trusted by its citizens, and state actors must be perceived to be protective agents in order to be used as such. Gender-based violence tolerated or even perpetuated by the state (such as those discussed earlier) undercuts such trust, and sets up public security officials and civil servants as agents of violence. It normalises the use of violence by the powerful against the less powerful, and also condones acts of violence where it can be justified in the furtherance of specific interests.

Legal reform that does not examine the structural inequalities embedded in existing laws and legislative processes runs the risk of perpetuating and even exacerbating the very social inequalities it is seeking to address. Where laws are unequal, discriminatory or render certain communities invisible, access to justice requires more than ensuring that individuals are able to use existing judicial systems. The inequalities embedded in the creation, interpretation and implementation of Chinese laws must be addressed before legal reform can successfully prevent and punish gender-based violence and the discrimination that underpins and perpetuates it.

Notes

1 Feng notes that the 1950 Marriage Law and similar reforms 'repeal[ed] such feudal systems of marriage and family as marriage based on the arbitrary decision of a third

party, a man enjoying higher status than a woman, and ignoring the interests of children, which is an abolishment of the feudal objectionable practices' (Feng 2002, p. 332).

2 The report found that ten per cent of the respondents were victims of direct or indirect attacks and 7.6 per cent were sexually harassed by their classmates and/or teachers.

3 Three in one Chinese women have experienced family violence (overall, 25.1 per cent have faced psychological violence, ten per cent faced physical violence, and 4.1 per cent, sexual violence) while 64.8 per cent of rural women have experienced violence, breaking down the forms of violence experienced as follows: 58.1 per cent (psychological); 29.7 per cent (physical); 29.7 per cent (sexual)) (Guo 2013).

4 Although key terms like domestic violence and maltreatment are not defined in the *Marriage Law 2001* and the *LPRIW 2005*, the SPC has issued judicial interpretations that provide guidance to lower courts on how to interpret the law. The SPC Judicial Interpretation No. 1 of Marriage Law defines maltreatment in Article 1.

5 Yang provides details of this case which demonstrates further ways in which judicial discretion can undermine claims of domestic violence. In this particular case, the wife alleged that she suffered injuries thirty-four times (sixteen of which were supported by hospital records), but the court only gave credence to ten instances (Yang 2011, p. 251).

6 I recognise that this framework begs the fundamental question of whether girls under the age of fourteen are able to consent to sex, much less to sex work.

7 The ACWF's privileged position is enshrined in the *LPRIW 2005* which states in Article 10 that ACWF opinions should be considered when laws, regulations and policies related to important women's interests are enacted.

8 Howell notes that the ACWF's 'financial and political dependence on the party has constrained it in taking up issues that might clash directly with party policy' (1998).

9 For news and analysis on the on-going crackdown against civil society actors, see, for example, Yu 2016; Zeng 2015.

10 China's CEDAW state report indicates that the rates of contraceptive use among women of child-bearing age was eighty-five per cent, as opposed to 15.33 per cent among men (CEDAW China State Report 2013, para. 185).

11 These sanctions are laid out in the *1993 Measure for the Custody and Education of Prostitutes and Clients of Prostitutes* promulgated by the PRC State Council.

Bibliography

Asia Catalyst (2013) '*Custody and Education': Arbitrary Detention for Female Sex Workers* [online] http://asiacatalyst.org/resources/research/.

Aibai Culture and Education Center (2012) Report of the Online Survey on Homophobic and Trans-phobic Bully at Educational Institutions [online] http://www.aibai.com/ebook/library/ebook_aibai/download/2012/11/8/Report%20of%20the%20Online%20Survey%20on%20Homophobia%20and%20Trans-phobia%20Bully(1).pdf

Balzano, J. (2007) 'Toward a Gay-Friendly China?: Legal Implications of Transition for Gays and Lesbians', *Law & Sexuality Review*, vol. 16, pp. 1–44.

China Development Brief (2015) A Longer March: CDB Special Issue on Women's Organizations in China [online] http://chinadevelopmentbrief.cn/wp-content/uploads/2015/03/CDB_Special_Issue_on_Womens_Organisations-March-2015.pdf

China LBT Rights Initiative (2014) *Shadow Report: Implementation of the* Convention to Eliminate All Forms of Discrimination Against Women *in the PRC* [online] http://tbinternet.ohchr.org/Treaties/CEDAW/Shared%20Documents/CHN/INT_CEDAW_NGO_CHN_18361_E.pdf

China Violence Against Women Concern Group (2014) *Submission by the China Violence Against Women Concern Group to the Committee on the Elimination of All Forms of Discrimination Against Women* [online].

Choi, S.Y.P. (2011) 'State Control, Female Prostitution and HIV Prevention in China', *The China Quarterly*, vol. 205, pp. 96–114

Committee on the Elimination of Discrimination against Women (CEDAW) (2013) *Consideration of Reports Submitted by States Parties: China*, UN Doc. CEDAW/C/CHN/7-8.

Common Language (2009) *Survey report on family violence experienced by lesbian and bisexual women in China* (in Chinese, on file with author).

Croll, E. (1978) *Feminism and Socialism in China*, Routledge & Kegan Paul Ltd, London, UK.

Davis, D.S. (2014) *On the Limits of Personal Autonomy: PRC Law and the Institution of Marriage*, in Davis, D.S. and Friedman, S.L. (eds.) *Wives, Husbands and Lovers: Marriage and Sexuality in Hong Kong, Taiwan and Urban China*, pp. 41–61.

Feng, X. (2002) 'A Review of the Development of Marriage Law in the People's Republic of China', *University of Detroit Mercy Law Review*, vol. 79, pp. 331–98.

Fontes, L.A. and McCloskey, K.A (2011) 'Cultural Issues in Violence against Women' in Renzetti, C.M., Edleson, J.L. and Bergen, R.K. (eds) *Sourcebook on Violence Against Women (2nd Edition)*, SAGE Publications, Thousand Oaks, California, USA, pp. 151–68.

Guo W. (2013) 'Supreme People's Court Prepares Trial Guidance on Domestic Violence-Related Criminal Cases' (最高法拟出文件指导涉家暴刑案审), Jan. 16 [online] http://news.china.com.cn/live/2013-01/16/content_18208301.htm

Hand, K. (2011) 'Resolving Constitutional Disputes in Contemporary China', *University of Pennsylvania East Asian Law Review*, vol. 7, pp. 51–159.

Howell, J. (1998) 'Gender, civil society and the state in China', in Randall, V. and Waylen, G. (eds) *Gender, Politics and the State*, Routledge, London, UK, pp. 166–84.

Kellogg, T. (2009) 'The Death of Constitutional Litigation in China?' *China Brief*, vol. 9, no. 7, The Jamestown Foundation [online] http://www.jamestown.org/programs/chinabrief/single/?tx_ttnews%5Btt_news%5D=34791&cHash=da4e942eff#.Vlo_T3arTDc

Meng, J. (2013) *On the Decriminalization of Sex Work in China: HIV and Patients' Rights*, Palgrave Macmillan, New York, USA.

Mountford, T. (2010) *The Legal Position and Status of Lesbian, Gay, Bisexual and Transgender People in the People's Republic of China* [online] https://www.outrightinternational.org/sites/default/files/395-1.pdf

Palmer, M. (2007) 'On China's Slow Boat to Women's Rights: Revisions to the Women's Protection Law, 2005', *The International Journal of Human Rights*, vol. 11, no.1–2, pp. 151–77.

Parish, W.L., Wang, T., Laumann, E.O., Pan, S. and Luo, Y. (2004) 'Intimate Partner Violence in China: National Prevalence, Risk Factors and Associated Health Problems', *International Family Planning Perspectives*, vol. 30(4), pp. 174–81.

Ruskola, T. (2002) 'Legal Orientalism', *Michigan Law Review*, vol. 101, pp. 179–234.

Sivakumaran, S. (2007) 'Sexual Violence Against Men in Armed Conflict', *The European Journal of International Law*, vol 18, no. 2, pp. 253–76.

Tan, L.Y. (2008) 'Changing Mindsets: How China's Abnormal Sex Ratio Is Turning Its Government into a Champion of Gender Equality', *Asian Journal of Comparative Law*, vol. 3, pp. 1–31.

Wang, L. (2009) '"Missing Girls" in an Era of "High Quality": Government Control over Population and Daughter Discrimination in Reform-Era China', *Social Transformation in Chinese Societies*, vol. 4, pp. 245–70.

Wang, Z. (2005) '"State Feminism"? Gender and Socialist State Formation in Maoist China', *Feminist Studies*, vol. 31, no. 3, pp. 519–51.

Webster, T. (2011) 'Ambivalence & Activism: Employment Discrimination in China' *Vanderbilt Journal of Transnational Law*, vol. 44, pp. 643–709.

Wu, N. (2014) 'Chinese man accused of raping another man walks free due to loophole in criminal law', *South China Morning Post*, September 25 [online] http://www.scmp.com/news/china/article/1600213/chinese-suspect-who-raped-another-man-walks-free-due-loophole-criminal.

Xue, N. (n.d.), *Women's Self-Defense and Legal Reform in China: Discussing from Women Victims' Oral Accounts* [online] http://www.iolaw.org.cn/global/EN/showNews.asp?id=24660.

Yang, H.C. (2011) 'Impact Litigation in China: The Procurator as a Legal Avenue for Cases in the "Private Family Sphere" of Domestic Violence', *Pacific Rim Law and Policy Journal*, vol. 20, pp. 237–64.

Yu, V. (2016) 'Charity workers in China say NGOs being "pulled out by the roots"', South China Morning Post [online] http://www.scmp.com/news/china/policies-politics/article/1903724/charity-workers-china-say-ngos-being-pulled-out-roots.

Zeng, J. (2015) 'Guo Yushan and the predicament of NGOs in China', Probe International [online] 21 May, http://journal.probeinternational.org/2015/05/21/guo-yushan-and-the-predicament-of-ngos-in-china/

12 PathFinders

Supporting access to justice for pregnant migrant workers and their children in Hong Kong

Kay McArdle[1]

Despite a world-class public healthcare system and perceived independent rule of law, Hong Kong's laws, policies, practices and institutional mechanisms fail to provide adequately for the human rights and access to justice of migrant workers, especially of migrant domestic workers who are pregnant. With their employment frequently unlawfully terminated precisely because they are pregnant, migrant domestic workers and their children can become prone to the worst forms of abuse, homelessness, poverty and even trafficking. Social and cultural stigmas exacerbate these problems. Access to public healthcare is denied to former migrant domestic workers who have lost their jobs and is also denied to their Hong Kong-born children. Ambiguous employment contracts, labour, health and immigration policies shroud in uncertainty the maternity rights and obligations of both pregnant migrant workers and their employers.

By the end of 2013, Hong Kong employed more than 320,000 foreign domestic workers (Census and Statistics Department 2014, p. 43) of whom about half came from Indonesia and nearly all of whom were women. This population is employed by around just ten per cent of Hong Kong's private households and forms approximately four per cent of Hong Kong's population (Tam and Tong 2012, p. 247). Based on typical employment and retirement age norms and trends, most migrant domestic workers in Hong Kong are of prime reproductive age, namely between twenty-five and forty years old. Non-governmental organisations (NGOs) working with migrant domestic workers have noted the significant legal, economic, social and cultural challenges and barriers they face, which are often intensified and more apparent during pregnancy and after the birth of a child. In 2014, around fifty per cent of the working women served by PathFinders, a Hong Kong NGO working with Hong Kong's most vulnerable children and their migrant mothers, were either unlawfully dismissed from their employment because they were pregnant or resigned because they were not adequately informed as to their maternity entitlements.

This chapter describes and analyses the legal and policy landscape regarding migrant domestic workers in Hong Kong from PathFinders' perspective. Relying on primary data and research collected by PathFinders, the chapter begins by outlining the economic and social context within which migrant domestic workers' lives and work are situated, before discussing the legal framework that has ostensibly been set up to protect them. The chapter then discusses systematic gaps that exist within the current system and details experiences of significant numbers of women and children who fall outside both legislative and policy safety nets. Finally, the chapter concludes with a number of policy recommendations to help rectify the dire consequences of what appears to be a systemic anomaly or oversight.

Economic status of migrant domestic workers

Migrant domestic workers form a critical part of Hong Kong society. This majority female population is vital to maintaining Hong Kong's position as a global economic hub. The employment of migrant domestic workers allows employers to maximise income-earning opportunities (double income families) by alleviating the pressures associated with taking care of the household, children, the elderly, the sick or disabled and pets. The arrangement also allows the Hong Kong Government to effectively outsource care services for infants, children, the infirm and the elderly at a reduced cost outside the state-paid health and welfare systems. Migrant domestic workers are employed on standard employment contracts (*Form ID407*)[2] at government-approved minimum wage rates that fall significantly below the statutory minimum wage levels applicable to other employees in Hong Kong. While PathFinders is not aware of any publicly available analysis of the economic savings and social value that the migrant domestic worker population brings to Hong Kong, there do exist recommended approaches for determining those values in the broader context, notably by the International Labour Organisation's (ILO) work on domestic workers (ILO 2011) and in the Domestic Workers Convention No. 189 (ibid. 2011b) and Recommendation No. 201.[3]

Migrant domestic workers come to Hong Kong mainly from Indonesia and the Philippines. In mid-2013 and February 2014, Hong Kong received its first migrant workers from Bangladesh and Myanmar. Other sending countries include India, Nepal, Malaysia, Pakistan, Sri Lanka and Thailand (Census and Statistics Department 2013, p. 43). Economic opportunity is the key driver for migrant domestic workers to come to Hong Kong. The flows of labour migration in Asia and the Pacific are typically from lower-income countries, including South and South East Asia, to countries or areas, such as Hong Kong, that have labour shortages and offer higher wages.[4] According to World Bank figures, international migrants remitted more than USD 550 billion in earnings globally in 2013, of which USD 414 billion flowed to developing countries.[5]

Many migrant workers leave their families, including their own children, to work abroad to generate remittance income to send to their families, boosting the standard of living and opportunities for their home communities and children. According to the World Bank estimates of Hong Kong's international remittances in 2013 were USD 666 million outbound.[6] It is unclear what proportion of this total was attributable to migrant domestic workers as opposed to other migrant workers. In a macroeconomic sense, migrant domestic workers perform a crucial function, and Hong Kong has clear guidance and legislation on how such workers may enter and work in Hong Kong. However, the personal experiences of individuals suggest that, in practice, the current legislative and policy framework insufficiently protects migrant domestic workers.

The majority of migrant domestic workers arrive in Hong Kong already heavily in debt as a result of extortionate agency fees (Amnesty International 2013, pp. 61–5). The employment agencies that hire migrant domestic workers frequently adopt exploitative and unfair practices, including requiring workers to sign a loan agreement in their home country, thereby circumventing Hong Kong's legal limits on agency fees of ten per cent of one month's salary (around USD sixty). Many migrant domestic workers reportedly pay in excess of USD 3,000 – fifty times the legal maximum – and many work abroad for longer than anticipated to repay agency fees. The Fair Employment Agency, a foreign domestic worker employment agency based on a social enterprise model, was a welcome development in 2014.[7] Moreover, migrant domestic workers' terms of employment fall short of their economic contributions to Hong Kong society. While certain universally applicable statutory labour rights (for example, annual leave, rest days, sick leave and anti-discrimination laws) apply to migrant domestic workers, they are excluded from Hong Kong's *Minimum Wage Ordinance Cap. 608, 2010* (section 7) and pension provisions under the *Mandatory Provident Funds Schemes Ordinance Cap. 485 Schedule 1, 1995* (Schedule 1).

As of 1 May 2015, the statutory minimum wage was HKD 32.5 per hour.[8] Excluded from the statutory minimum wage, migrant domestic workers receive woefully inadequate and discriminatory hourly-equivalent wages. The average working day for migrant domestic workers is estimated to be around sixteen hours (Haufman 2014), which, at the current legal domestic worker minimum wages rate of HKD 4,110[9] is equivalent to just HKD 7 per hour (around USD 0.90). Further, a 'live-in' requirement applies to all migrant domestic workers. This is contained at clause 3 of the contract (*Form ID407*), which states that 'the worker shall work and reside in the employer's residence'. How this live-in requirement is supposed to operate in practice with maternity, sickness and other statutory leaves under the *Employment Ordinance Cap. 57, 1997* is unclear and the subject of great concern for PathFinders and many other NGOs who work on the frontline with migrant domestic workers.

Social and cultural background of migrant domestic workers

The economic shortcomings of the migrant domestic worker employment scheme foster a culture of dependency amongst migrant domestic workers in relation to their employers and employment agencies. There is a significant power imbalance and inequity from the start of the working relationship. Migrant domestic workers cannot effectively choose or vet their employers. The employer chooses their migrant domestic worker, typically via an agency, thus power resides with the employer and the agency.

Migrant domestic workers are left with little freedom to leave sub-optimal or even abusive working conditions for fear of agency fee reprisals, as well as losing their immigration status and their ability to work in Hong Kong again. As far as PathFinders is aware, there is no government blacklist of employers who abuse migrant women, though in recent years there have been several incidents of alleged torture and abuse reported to the authorities. However, PathFinders is aware that certain consulates do maintain employer blacklists.

Between 2012 and mid-2015, PathFinders' clients disclosed thirty-one incidences of emotional, physical and sexual violence that occurred in a domestic employment context. The attacker was either the employer or another household member the migrant domestic worker was hired to serve. In three of these cases the violence resulted in pregnancy.

Justice Centre Hong Kong and Liberty Asia's report *How Many More Years a Slave*, (2014, p. 14) cites a 2013 survey of foreign domestic workers conducted by the Mission for Migrant Workers:

> *well over half of those surveyed stated that they had suffered verbal abuse, one in five had suffered physical abuse and 6% had suffered sexual abuse. An earlier 2005 study found that 93% of those surveyed reported employment agency overcharging, more than half underpayment of salary, 45% reported denial of rest days, 57% denial of statutory holidays, 40% a confiscation of passport and employment contracts and 57% long working hours.*

Once in Hong Kong, the restrictive living and working arrangements and extreme working hours[10] combine to isolate migrant domestic workers, limiting their ability to share knowledge about their rights and to meet with the agencies and NGOs who can help them. Alone, afraid and disempowered, their choices are either to remain in sub-optimal employment relationships to retain access to wages and public healthcare or to terminate their contract. If migrant domestic workers choose to terminate their contract, they are required to return to their home country within two weeks, this is provided that they are in a position to afford the airfare and/or have not had their passport retained by their employer or the employment agency.

Alternatively, migrant domestic workers may stay in Hong Kong by paying to extend their visa status lawfully and paying for their own accommodation, food and transport while bringing a claim against their defaulting employer and in many cases, seeking a new employer. However, some migrant domestic workers remain in Hong Kong unlawfully. Destitute, homeless and in violation of their visa's terms of stay, these migrant domestic workers are increasingly vulnerable to crime, physical and drug abuse, poor housing conditions and are susceptible to trafficking and the most dangerous elements of society.

The pregnant, migrant women workers who seek support from PathFinders typically fall into the latter category above. Such migrant workers are often technically 'immigration criminals' when they first come to PathFinders because they have overstayed their visas, breaching the 'condition of stay' imposed by the *Immigration Ordinance Cap.155, 1997*. PathFinders has helped 475 women who were undocumented or overstayers. Frequently, their pregnancies are too advanced for them to fly, based on airline policies, and/or they do not know how to obtain the required doctor's certificate to be able to fly since they are denied access to public healthcare.

PathFinders' case workers first assist these women to surrender to the immigration authorities immediately to stabilise their legal status. This may or may not involve criminal proceedings against the women for breach of the conditions of their stay and for remaining in Hong Kong unlawfully. Some proceedings result in imprisonment for the mother and her child, typically, stays in prison with her until the age of three. Some children are born while the mother is in prison.

Already disadvantaged economically and legally, migrant domestic workers, the majority of whom are women, face further prejudice. These women are defined by an employment status in which domestic work is undervalued and migrant workers are considered somehow 'other' or 'lesser' in Hong Kong, a conservative and largely patriarchal society. Migrant workers are, by definition, transient and struggle to integrate within local communities, particularly if their Cantonese or English language skills are poor. As a result migrant domestic workers are perceived and treated as outsiders. This perception is exacerbated by their ethnicity and restricted earning power. These cultural attitudes, assumptions and preferences pervade public services.

PathFinders' clients frequently face discrimination and prejudice when dealing with labour, immigration and health departments and the police. They are publicly humiliated by verbally abusive staff, have to deal with judgemental officials or are pressurised to settle claims by Labour Tribunal officers who openly deride them and side with the employer. In many cases little allowance, if any, is made for the fact that the woman is speaking her second or third language and without any legal assistance. PathFinders' requests to have a 'McKenzie friend', a person who sits in court with a litigant, have been repeatedly denied. Clients of PathFinders report how they are treated not as humans but as machines, with little or no thought being given to their psychological or emotional wellbeing.

While abuse of any kind is reprehensible, what makes it worse is that many incidents of chronic verbal, physical and mental abuse during the employment relationship go unreported.[11] The victims are often conditioned to believe that the abuse is normal, do not know what to do, or are deterred by the ineffectiveness or absence of victim protection and reporting mechanisms; this is combined with a deep fear of the consequences of speaking out, loss of income and costs of proceedings to obtain justice and compensation – not only for themselves but also for their families. Some women are financially responsible for as many as ten family members in their home country and need to work. Alternatively, some women prefer to leave Hong Kong as soon as possible to put their bad experience behind them. Further, these women are frequently not believed and reports of substantiated, successfully prosecuted abuse cases have only recently begun to appear in the Western and Chinese media.[12]

This commoditisation of migrant domestic workers does little to support them as women, colleagues and homemakers. These women are not only violated, they are disenfranchised, unsupported and impotent. Significant educational, linguistic and cultural barriers prevent them from understanding and asserting their rights, while employers and employment agencies are either unaware of, or do not fully understand, their obligations. Pregnancy compounds these factors and places both woman and child at extreme risk. In PathFinders' experience it is precisely when a pregnant migrant domestic worker and her baby are at their most vulnerable that they face and endure huge and insurmountable barriers to survival and support. Many women report that abuse and prejudice worsens when they became pregnant. Further, the women's employment is often terminated because of their pregnancy and then, as a direct consequence of this unlawful dismissal by the employer, these women lose access to Hong Kong's public health and welfare services having lost their employed status. Significantly, by comparison, refugees and torture claimants, and their children, do have access to these basic health and welfare services while the determination of their status claims are pending.

Migrant domestic workers also face considerable moral condemnation, with their right to be pregnant at all being brought into question. To illustrate, at a March 2013 Legislative Council Manpower Committee hearing, Liberal Party Youth Committee Member, Harris Yeung, suggested 'that MDWs should not be permitted to live out as they would only become pregnant' (Hong Kong Helpers Campaign 2014). Campaign organisations, such as the Hong Kong Helper's Campaign, have suggested that accidental pregnancy is not the issue that should concern employers, but that the focus should be on access to affordable family planning education. Under international law, the Universal Declaration of Human Rights (UDHR) clearly states that all persons 'without any limitation due to race, nationality or religion, have the right to marry and to found a family' (Article 16, UDHR). At local level, the *Employment Ordinance Cap. 57, 1997* also guarantees female employees the right to have a child. For migrant domestic workers who are pregnant or who have given birth in Hong Kong, it is the combined, frequent and systemic abuses and, in practice (if not at law), denial of real justice and access to it, that conspire to ensure that they and their children remain in the lowest echelons of Hong Kong society.

Laws and policies relating to migrant domestic workers

Migrant work is a global phenomenon and these issues affecting migrant domestic workers are not exclusive to Hong Kong. The ILO estimates that of '52.6 million [migrant workers] worldwide – more than four out of five of them women – are employed as domestic workers' (ILO 2013a), 'of these, 21.5 million (41 per cent) domestic workers are in Asia Pacific' (ILO 2013b). Despite the significant numbers of migrant workers, the report found that the rights and conditions experienced by domestic employees and other waged workers in Asia lagged behind those in other regions, leaving Asian migrant workers particularly vulnerable to exploitation. Compared with Latin America, where three-quarters of migrant domestic workers benefit from statutory limits on the maximum number of weekly working hours, only one per cent of domestic workers in Asia Pacific are protected. Further, only twelve per cent of migrant domestic workers are covered by statutory minimum wage legislation. In terms of pregnancy protection, the majority of migrant domestic workers (seventy-six per cent) in Asia Pacific are not entitled to maternity leave and its associated benefits.

Hong Kong has ratified a number of international legal instruments including: the United Nations International Covenant on Civil and Political Rights (ICCPR); the International Covenant on Economic, Social and Cultural Rights (ICESCR); the Convention on the Elimination of All Forms of Discrimination Against Women (CEDAW); ILO Convention No. 29 concerning Forced or Compulsory Labour; ILO Convention No. 105 concerning the Abolition of Forced Labour; and the UN Convention on the Rights of the Child (CRC). The ICCPR has been formally incorporated into the *Bill of Rights Ordinance Cap. 383 1991* and is referenced in the Basic Law, Hong Kong's constitutional legal framework.[13]

In September 2013 ILO Convention No.189 concerning Decent Work for Domestic Workers came into force. This Convention seeks to extend basic labour rights and protections to domestic workers. Short of ratification, ILO Convention No.189 is already acting as a catalyst for improved labour and social rights for domestic workers globally with several jurisdictions having recently passed legislative reforms, including Singapore which has finally introduced a rest day for migrant domestic workers every seven days and has mandated training for employers of migrant domestic workers.[14] Despite this limited progress, employers in Singapore are still permitted by law to terminate the employment contract of a pregnant employee who is a migrant domestic worker.[15]

To date, the Government of the Hong Kong Special Administrative Region (SAR) and the Central People's Government in Beijing have not indicated a willingness to ratify ILO Convention No.189, although the Philippines, a major sending country of migrant workers, is a signatory. However, the Hong Kong Government's shift towards collaboration with the Indonesian Consulate[16] for educating newly arrived migrant domestic workers on their employment and other rights and obligations has been well-received, especially in the wake of the 'contemptible' treatment of Indonesian domestic worker Erwiana Sulistyaningsih 'whose abusive former employer was sentenced to six years in prison' (Lau and Chan 2015) in February 2015. Global media coverage of the case drew attention to the situation of migrant domestic workers in Hong Kong with international outrage and condemnation of the treatment of Erwiana and domestic workers more generally.

By contrast it must be noted that, to a large degree, migrant domestic workers in Hong Kong do enjoy predominantly the same statutory labour rights and benefits as other employees, with certain exceptions. The contract specifically states that migrant domestic workers enjoy, 'entitlements under the *Employment Ordinance Cap. 57, 1997*, the *Employees' Compensation Ordinance Cap. 282, 1997*, and any other relevant ordinances' (Clause 16, *Form ID407*).

The *Employment Ordinance Cap. 57, 1997* confers, amongst other things, rights to annual leave, sick leave, maternity leave, severance pay, long-service pay and protection from unfair dismissal. Migrant domestic workers are also protected by Hong Kong's criminal laws and its four anti-discrimination ordinances: *Sex*

Discrimination Ordinance Cap. 480, 1995; *Disability Discrimination Ordinance Cap. 487, 1995*; *Family Status Discrimination Ordinance Cap. 527, 1997*; and *Race Discrimination Ordinance Cap. 602, 2008*. These ordinances, broadly speaking, provide protection to migrant domestic workers during their stay and employment from discrimination, harassment and victimisation on the grounds of sex, marital status, pregnancy, disability, family status and race.[17]

However, the Hong Kong Immigration Department's Standard Employment Contract (*Form ID407*) fails to state what rights and protections are specifically denied to migrant domestic workers. Section 7 of the *Minimum Wage Ordinance Cap. 608*, adopted in 2010, is a recent example where migrant domestic workers are specifically excluded.[18] While the Hong Kong government is still deciding whether or not to introduce standard working hours legislation, PathFinders anticipates that migrant domestic workers will almost certainly be excluded. Further, employers are not required to make pension provisions for migrant domestic workers under Hong Kong's otherwise largely universally applicable *Mandatory Provident Fund Schemes Ordinance (Cap. 485)*.

Given how many migrant women of prime reproductive age are employed as domestic workers, it is curious that their contract fails to specify the entitlement to maternity protection and benefits. This is despite the fact that Form ID407specifies: 'The Helper shall be entitled to all rest days, statutory holidays, and paid annual leave as specified in the Employment Ordinance, Chapter 57' (Clause 6, *Form ID407*). By comparison, the sample contract provided on the Hong Kong government's website for hiring local domestic workers, clearly sets out maternity rights and states: 'The Employee is entitled to maternity leave and maternity leave pay according to the provisions of the Employment Ordinance'.[19]

Terminating the employment of a migrant domestic worker (or indeed of any eligible female employee) on the basis that she is pregnant is, prima facie, unlawful and carries both civil and criminal sanctions under the *Employment Ordinance Cap. 57, 1997*. Unfortunately statistics on employer prosecutions for such unlawful dismissals are lacking. Further, under the *Sex Discrimination Ordinance Cap. 480, 1995*, sanctions also apply if a pregnant worker is treated less favourably or any condition or requirement is applied which is unreasonable and which would be impossible to comply with because of pregnancy.

In PathFinders' experience this prohibition against the termination of employment on the basis of pregnancy is something employers, agencies and migrant domestic workers themselves are either not aware of or choose to ignore. The lack of clarity, practical guidance and policy leads to uncertainty on the part of both employer and employee during pregnancy, maternity leave and beyond.

In addition, the lack of data maintained by the Hong Kong SAR government about foreign domestic workers is inadequate as it relates to women's health, maternity, childbirth, immunisations and adoption. PathFinders is aware of more cases of pregnant, migrant domestic workers giving birth in Hong Kong, as well as adoptions, than are currently on public record.[20]

Correspondence from the Labour Department to PathFinders stated that the live-in requirement applies during statutory maternity leave. If this is indeed the case, such a situation exposes mothers and nursing infants to unsuitable living conditions, potential abuse and custodial violence. Thirty per cent of live-in migrant domestic workers do not have their own private room and are made to sleep in unsuitable places, including bathrooms, kitchens and, in some cases, in the same room as an adult male member of the household (Mission for Migrant Workers 2013). More nebulous is what should happen at a practical level once the baby is born. Clearly communicated policies and practice guidelines are regrettably absent. Questions include, for example, whether requiring an employee to live in the employer's home during maternity leave potentially constitutes forced labour, sex discrimination and/or a fundamental breach of human rights.

The status of newborn infants and whether they are also subject to the live-in rule is unclear, leaving newborns at risk of being separated from their mothers. The newborn is not party to the employment agreement or the Immigration Department's 'condition of stay'. If employers do not have the space, or desire, to accommodate a newborn, there is little consideration as to what the viable alternatives may be or whether an employer should be criminally liable for failing to house a domestic worker during maternity leave. Migrant domestic workers are often hired to take care of children and the elderly. There is no guidance on whether employers are able to hire another migrant domestic worker on a short-term basis as maternity leave cover or whether the live-in rule would also apply. The above questions all assume that the migrant domestic worker is still employed and living with her employer. In PathFinders' experience, the consequences of unlawful termination of employment on the basis of pregnancy can be catastrophic for both mother and infant.

Employers must notify the Immigration Department within seven days of the termination of a migrant domestic worker's employment.[21] The, so-called, Two-Week Rule means that upon termination of employment, a migrant domestic worker loses her visa status and has two weeks from the date of termination within which to find a new employer or to leave Hong Kong. This two-week period applies only to migrant domestic workers and typically not to other 'skilled' migrant or expatriate workers. It is a blanket rule and its application does not take into account the lawfulness or otherwise of the termination of the employment, whether civil and/or criminal claims are in progress and does not make allowances for pregnancy.

Migrant domestic workers who have their employment contracts terminated are denied access to public health services as soon as the employer completes the online notification process.[22] The exception to this rule is if there is an emergency or a life-and-death situation, in which case these homeless, destitute, pregnant women are charged penalty rates (around HKD 100,000) for giving birth. In PathFinders' experience, the Hospital Authority seldom grants fee waivers and the women are deemed to fall outside the Samaritan Fund's eligibility criteria by virtue of the fact that their permission to remain in Hong Kong has expired or ceased to be valid.[23] Further, regular first-world standard perinatal care is not classified as emergency care, thereby putting both mother and child at risk.

During these two weeks, migrant domestic workers are not entitled to work or to receive any basic living or financial support, even in instances where the employer has unlawfully dismissed them. Two weeks is insufficient time to seek and obtain legal redress when, for example, the time from first appointment to filing at the Labour Tribunal is twenty-five days and from filing to first hearing is a further twenty-five days (Amnesty International 2013, p. 95). Moreover, during this time, migrant domestic workers are not permitted to work, and would need to pay personally to renew their visa and depend on others' charity or on NGOs to provide room and board. This meagre time period effectively violates the worker's successful access to and pursuit of justice. The consequences of a lack of practical support and challenges in finding new employment are the key reasons why these women do not initiate or then persist with legal action against their former employers. Put simply, it is too difficult, expensive, time-consuming and stressful. The system is stacked against migrant domestic workers legally, linguistically and culturally. On top of all these hurdles, the women who come to PathFinders are pregnant or nursing an infant, unemployed and, typically, homeless.

Conversely, the employer, even with civil and criminal claims pending against him/her or their household, can in practice proceed with hiring their next migrant domestic worker. Employers are only prevented from doing so where the female migrant worker has had the courage to provide evidence to, and convince, the Director of Immigration that the eligibility of the employer should be called into question (Hong Kong Immigration Department 2015). Despite this, and based on PathFinders' experience, it is extremely unlikely for a pregnant, migrant domestic worker to file a report against the employer in the current justice framework, even where the pregnancy arises as a result of the employer's rape of the worker or where there has been significant abuse.

Laws in practice: systemic gaps and consequences

By mid-2015 PathFinders had helped over 2,800 vulnerable children in crisis and their migrant mothers. These women and children fall through the legislative and policy safety nets intended to protect the most vulnerable in society. PathFinders collaborates with NGOs, policy-makers, legislators, consulates, government departments, international agencies and other key stakeholders to address the systemic gaps and root causes that give rise to the shocking and avoidable situations these women and children find themselves in. Some of our major successes to date involve narrowing these systemic gaps, which fall into three broad areas, specifically, (i) immigration, (ii) healthcare and (iii) employment. The following PathFinders case exemplifies the complex cultural, legal and social situation in which migrant domestic workers find themselves upon termination of their employment contract:

> *Nia, a 31-year-old Indonesian domestic worker, was unlawfully dismissed by her employer when she gave notice of her pregnancy. Although Nia's boyfriend was a permanent resident of Hong Kong, he was unable to support her and her unborn child.*

Heavily pregnant and with no access to prenatal check-ups, Nia was living on one meal a day and suffered verbal and physical abuse from her boyfriend. She was both afraid and unable to return to Indonesia, fearing her family's disapproval. Nia was in hiding, scared and taking refuge nightly in an internet cafe when she heard about PathFinders. *At that time she was 7 months' pregnant.*

PathFinders *found her a safe place to stay and gave her food and clothing. We provided counselling and told Nia of her rights, obligations and options for the future. We helped her extend her visa in Hong Kong, connected her with pro-bono legal support for labour claims, arranged pro-bono prenatal care and, once her daughter was born, helped her obtain a Hong Kong birth certificate and Indonesian identity papers.*

(PathFinders 2012)

At a time when many people celebrate the news of their pregnancy and the arrival of a child, Nia was isolated, abused and had little hope for her own or her baby's future.

Immigration

A key gap arises when a migrant domestic worker overstays their working visa and becomes an undocumented migrant. As in Nia's case this commonly occurs once a migrant domestic worker becomes pregnant, quite often with a mixed-race child conceived outside of wedlock, and is afraid to, or is unaware of, how to return home. Unsupported, these women are regularly turned away from government departments and some NGOs because they lack valid documentation. Their passports have often been confiscated by either the employment agency or their employer on arrival in Hong Kong; their Hong Kong Identity Card (HKID) becomes invalid within two weeks of their employment contract being terminated, often they have their HKID cards stolen, or they sell them in desperation as a means to survive.

Many do not fully understand Hong Kong's immigration and legal systems; as a result many migrant domestic workers are unaware that they have only two weeks in which to find new employment if they are dismissed or that they must proactively surrender to the Immigration Department once they have overstayed in order to legalise their immigration status. Many of the women we see at PathFinders fear surrendering because they have heard that they will be strip-searched and put in prison where they will be raped. In PathFinders' experience, if a women surrenders to the Immigration Department, as opposed to being arrested by the police, it is more likely that she will be released on bail with recognisance papers rather than be detained or imprisoned.

Another key loophole in the immigration system is the status of children born to undocumented migrants. Usually, birth records are transferred from public hospitals to the Birth Registry in a matter of days. However, in a case similar to Nia's, because the extortionate hospital bill had not been paid the hospital delayed transferring the birth records. To apply for a birth certificate and to extend her own visa, the mother was then pressured to pay the hospital bill by the Birth Registry and given only a one-day visa extension each time at a cost of HKD 190 each day. Despite being born in Hong Kong, unless – as in Nia's case – the father is a Hong Kong resident, the child automatically inherits the immigration status of the mother. As in Nia's case, a mother who is not legally married to the baby's father is required to go through several hurdles at the Birth Registry to secure the baby's right to Hong Kong resident status. There is a presumption that the husband of the mother, if any, is the birth father.

To rebut this presumption, the Birth Registry required, in one case, both birth parents to undergo DNA testing at a cost of HKD 5,000. This is not practical if the father has absconded, as many do. As a result of intensive lobbying to, and collaboration with, the Birth Registry, PathFinders' clients can now secure a Hong Kong Birth Certificate for their babies using a statutory declaration signed by both birth mother and birth father stating that they were in an exclusive relationship during the relevant period. In 2014, thirty-nine per cent (PathFinders 2014c, p. 5) of the children PathFinders helped and whose immigration status was determined became Hong Kong residents under either their father's visa or their mother's working visa. Were it not for the interventions by PathFinders these undocumented babies and children would not be able to access medical care at public hospitals other than emergency services.

Without certification by the relevant consulate of a Hong Kong birth certificate in Hong Kong, these children may be denied a home country identity (i.e. their mother's home country, where the children have never been) and, in turn be excluded from social and welfare services, thereby placing their entire future at significant risk.

It is important that women are able to prove the paternity of the biological father, particularly if the father is a Hong Kong resident, since Hong Kong residents directly pass on their immigration status to their children. However, migrant domestic workers are often denied access to justice. PathFinders has successfully brought appeals against rulings by the Director of Legal Aid in instances where Legal Aid had been denied to assist the child to prove the father's paternity. However practical problems can then arise when the mother is granted custody and her child obtains Hong Kong residency yet she does not have the right to remain and work in Hong Kong.

For those women who are not in a position to support their child, access to adoption services in Hong Kong has proved challenging. Children born to migrant domestic workers who have overstayed their visa had historically been excluded from the Social Welfare Department's adoption pool. Working with pro-bono lawyers, PathFinders referenced refugee case law that confirmed that, for adoption purposes, undocumented children born to migrant domestic workers in Hong Kong are considered Hong Kong residents.[24] In 2012, 'PathFinders' babies' formed 7.4 per cent of the Hong Kong Social Welfare Department's adoption pool and 4.7 per cent in 2013. Prior to establishing that these children could be adopted in Hong Kong they were often abandoned or left with other undocumented men or women to be looked after and sometimes sold to traffickers. In several instances, PathFinders' clients have been offered cash for their babies.

PathFinders has also encountered cases of sixteen-year-old children who have lived in Hong Kong their entire lives and are undocumented, unimmunised and uneducated. These children live in the shadows of mainstream society without access to public healthcare, welfare or education. Without an identity and social welfare protection, they can easily fall prey to abuse, neglect, severe poverty and trafficking. PathFinders is working to find ways to ensure that these babies and children have an identity, free of charge, and are registered as existing. The existence of such children was recently brought to the fore by the Repulse Bay suicide case, where a fifteen-year-old girl who was undocumented, committed suicide (Lo 2015). More generally, the UN Committee of the Convention on the Rights of the Child's Concluding Observations regarding Hong Kong in October 2013 raised concerns regarding undocumented children of migrant workers and said that the best interests of the child are not 'fully reflected and incorporated in key child-related acts and policies' in Hong Kong (Committee on the Rights of the Child 2013, paras. 29 and 31).

Healthcare

While employed, migrant domestic workers have access to Hong Kong's impressive, heavily subsidised, public healthcare system, the same as any other lawful resident. However, unlike other residents, such access ceases once their employment is terminated. Without a working visa, migrant domestic workers are classified as 'Ineligible Persons' and are no longer entitled to access public healthcare, even when their dismissal is unlawful, except in emergency circumstances when they are charged penalty rates. Pregnancy can and does lead to specific health vulnerabilities. Perinatal care is denied since it does not qualify as emergency care, which puts the life of both mother and baby at risk and violates the human right to the highest attainable standards of physical and mental health. Further, this denial of public healthcare extends to: sex education; safe, effective and affordable family planning; and protection from preventable and communicable diseases, notably including immunisations.

These services are vital to a woman's sexual and reproductive health rights, enshrined in CEDAW and in the World Health Organisation guidelines. Commitments by states to guarantee these rights have further been affirmed in the Program of Action of the International Conference on Population and Development (1994) as well as in the Beijing Declaration and Platform for Action (1995).

Obtaining legal documentation for mother and child is the first and most significant step towards them gaining access to essential health services. Yet the cost of a Hong Kong Birth Certificate can be prohibitive. There is currently no fee waiver or alternative social aid mechanism offered by the Birth Registry. This in turn results in failures to, or delays in obtaining Birth Certificates.

Critically, without a clear immigration or legal status and with no right of abode, these women's babies are also considered to be 'Ineligible Persons' for public healthcare purposes. The baby has no right to receive post-birth medical follow-ups, including basic immunisations. This creates a risk not only to the immediate family, but also to the wider Hong Kong population via contagious diseases more often associated with less developed economies. At the most practical level, prenatal check-ups identify whether the mother is carrying AIDS, Hepatitis B and other diseases which can be passed on to a newborn. In Nia's case, when she did access public healthcare facilities to give birth, she was presented with a bill of HKD 90,000 as if she were a private patient. She could not possibly pay this extortionate fee, nor was a fee waiver granted and nor was she an 'Eligible Person' to qualify for help from the Samaritan's Fund. There is currently no mechanism to direct the bill to the defaulting employer, but for whose unlawful actions migrant women workers such as Nia would not be placed in this situation.

Employment

The key trigger for a downward spiral of events, as in the termination of Nia's employment, is a breach of section 15 of the *Employment Ordinance Cap. 57, 1997*, which carries both civil and criminal penalties for the employer, as well as an established breach of section 8 of the *Sex Discrimination Ordinance Cap. 480, 1995* which gives rise to potentially significant damages claims. Employment Ordinance-related claims must be pursued in person at a Labour Tribunal without legal assistance. Conversely, *Sex Discrimination Ordinance Cap. 480, 1995* claims benefit from Legal Aid, which means that proceedings can largely be conducted by a lawyer on their client's behalf. For PathFinders' extremely vulnerable and poor clients the latter option is preferable as it allows the women to seek legal redress while continuing with their lives and looking after their newborn infant.

Had Nia decided to pursue civil claims in the Labour Tribunal and/or the District Court, she would technically have been permitted to work, but the reality is that no one would have employed her at seven months' pregnant. Without a job, Nia would have had to pay for her own accommodation and food while pursuing her claim. She would also have had to pay to extend her visitor's visa, typically every two weeks at a cost of HKD 190, despite having no income herself or for her family. In stark contrast, former employers can notify the Immigration Department online that the employment has been terminated and immediately hire another domestic worker.

Even when migrant women do bring labour claims and cases, they face prejudice, humiliation and discrimination by insensitive and poorly trained frontline staff and officers. Women are often denied the opportunity to seek advice or support while their claims are being processed. Further, women are belittled by former employers and by government and judicial officials through processes which are conducted exclusively in Cantonese. Migrant domestic workers are regularly forced into signing unfair and prejudicial settlement agreements that are often presented in Cantonese with little explanation or guidance as to any alternative solutions or, critically, the negative impact of settlement clauses that are drafted far too broadly to the employer's unfair and significant advantage. Further, women experience derogatory and racist remarks in addition to judgemental attitudes towards their pregnancy and perceived morals.

Statistical data from government departments on women and children, particularly migrant domestic workers, is severely limited in Hong Kong despite the substantial size of the population. While migrant domestic workers do have specific HKID card numbers, for which data exists and is capable of being obtained and analysed, the principal institutional mechanism for the advancement of women in Hong Kong, the Women's Commission, excludes the migrant domestic worker population from its annual statistical review (Women's Commission, 2013). PathFinders has sought to gather significant and reliable data to demonstrate the size and depth of the specific issues that their frontline staff encounter on a daily basis. Understanding and awareness of the inadequacies of the existing legal framework of protection for migrant domestic workers could be enhanced if large-scale and longitudinal data was publicly available, including, for example, the number of migrant women that give birth every year in public hospitals and the number of migrant workers' children who are able to acquire a Birth Certificate and/or become Hong Kong residents.

Data on differences in access to social welfare systems (for example, accommodation, food, living allowance, visa charges and medical fees) and how this varies between pregnant, domestic workers whose work has been unlawfully terminated, refugees and torture claimants would give a clearer indication of how migrant domestic workers fare alongside other vulnerable sectors of Hong Kong's population. At present it is unclear how many migrant domestic workers receive perinatal check-ups in the public healthcare system or, indeed, how many babies are born each year to migrant domestic workers, including those who have become immigration criminals and given birth in prison.

Conclusion

The lives of the migrant children and women helped by PathFinders are complex and affected by multiple local and international laws, policies and practices. Migrant domestic workers in Hong Kong find themselves in a catch-22 situation on becoming pregnant. Economic factors and dependency drive their vulnerabilities, and social and cultural stigmas exacerbate their problems. Limited or unclear protection at law and in practice offers meagre financial and practical support. The fact that vulnerable victims of unlawful activity often become criminally liable themselves demonstrates that the justice system is failing.

However, PathFinders remain optimistic that the situation for migrant domestic workers can be improved by a continued, concerted and collaborative effort between all key stakeholders to ensure that no child born in Hong Kong is born in crisis and that the migrant mothers of these children obtain effective and lasting access to justice. As reports of migrant worker abuse and discrimination have increased it is clear that the challenges are significant. Based on PathFinders' experience of working directly with migrant domestic workers and their children, a number of actionable recommendations for changes in legislation, practice and policy are suggested.

Before or shortly after the arrival of the migrant domestic worker in Hong Kong migrant workers would benefit greatly from on-line, mandatory, language-appropriate information/training about their health, labour, discrimination rights and recourse options. Such training should include culturally appropriate information about female health, sex education and where to go for advice; it should also specify that employers cannot lawfully require a migrant domestic worker to be forcibly given a contraceptive injection against her wishes. Equally, employers should receive appropriate information about their rights and obligations in relation to hiring and employing a migrant domestic worker. While information does exist, it tends to come from multiple government departments and portals, and is disparate and unclear. Specifically in relation to pregnancy protection, *Form ID407* should be amended to state explicitly that migrant domestic workers are entitled to statutory maternity leave and protection against discrimination under Hong Kong's labour, discrimination and criminal laws.

In Hong Kong, culture and gender sensitivity and awareness training needs to be delivered to government and judicial officials and to front-line staff regarding how to deal with migrants and ethnic minorities respectfully, equitably and humanely. This should include where to ask for help or where to refer complex cases to when staff do not know the answer. Further, The Family Planning Association and women's health clinics must also address their own service provision to migrant domestic workers. Services need to be made more easily accessible and user-friendly to migrant workers, for example opening hours on Sundays when the majority of domestic workers have their statutory rest day.

To counter cases of abuse and discrimination, publicity of employer prosecutions would act as a deterrent. A significant challenge in cases of abuse is that employers often continue to hire migrant domestic workers without any legal redress being taken against them. Given the vulnerability of women working in a domestic setting within private households, it seems imperative that the Hong Kong Government develops a database to map and track incidents of abuse and abusive employers to prevent recidivist abusers from effectively 'importing' and abusing more vulnerable women, and men, from overseas. The current live-in requirement and its implications for maternity, perinatal and postnatal care of migrant domestic workers is yet to be adequately scrutinised by the relevant government departments. In this regard, multi-lingual government-endorsed cross-departmental guidelines should be developed and published on how best to successfully manage the pregnancy of a migrant domestic worker. This should include a specific discussion around the treatment of the live-in requirement during all statutory leaves, including maternity.

Inevitably, even with such protections in place, cases of discrimination towards pregnant migrant domestic workers will continue, however, appropriate reforms of laws and policies could help to reduce, rather than exacerbate discriminatory experiences. First, 'emergency' services and/or sickness should be re-categorised, to specifically allow pregnant migrant domestic workers, and their Hong Kong-born babies, reasonable access to essential medical services before, during and after pregnancy. This access to public healthcare would also encompass the specific needs of pregnant women and newborns for essential perinatal and child care and mitigate against public contagion risks. Alternatively, if it is not feasible to re-categorise such emergency services, the government should seek to ensure that a medical fee waiver is granted. A relevant comparison might be made to Hong Kong's granting of public healthcare access to refugees and torture claimants who have claims and status determination pending. Regardless of their immigration or documentary status, all children in Hong Kong should receive essential vaccinations and an identity.

At present, Hong Kong lacks a consistent approach to visa extensions for migrant domestic workers accessing Hong Kong's justice system. Ideally, visa extension fees should be waived while civil and criminal claims are in process. Social security support and support for victims of criminal activity should be provided to migrant domestic workers who are required to stay in Hong Kong but not allowed to work while their claim is being processed. Alternatively, claimants should be able to return to their home country and be brought back at the government's expense for court and tribunal hearings.

While addressing the systematic gaps that exist within the current system would vastly improve the experiences of women and children who fall outside both legislative and policy safety nets, a cultural shift in societal attitudes is inherent to strengthening migrant domestic workers' status in Hong Kong. The Government currently relies on migrant workers to provide essential care services, effectively outsourcing welfare services. Analysis and publication of the economic savings and social value that the migrant domestic worker population brings to Hong Kong (ILO 2011) would help to raise awareness of the significant value and important role played by migrant domestic workers.

Notes

1 This chapter is written with the research and editorial support of several PathFinders colleagues, including Jennifer Meehan, Kylie Uebergang, Louise Robinson, Amelia Allsop, Jenny McAlpine, Rachel Ganly and Luna Chan. The author would also like to thank Professor Nicola Constable for her helpful comments and suggestions.
2 *See Standard Employment Contract for Migrant Domestic Workers ID407* [online] http://www.immd.gov.hk/eng/forms/forms/id407.html
3 See Relevant ILO instruments on Domestic Work [online] http://www.ilo.org/travail/areasofwork/WCMS_151734/lang--en/index.htm
4 International Organisation for Migration [online] http://www.iom.int/asia-and-pacific
5 Migration Policy Institute Global Remittances Guide [online] http://www.migrationpolicy.org/programs/data-hub/global-remittances-guide
6 See World Bank Annual Remittances Data Outflows (as at October 2014) [online] http://go.worldbank.org/092X1CHHD0
7 Fair Employment Agency [online] http://www.fairagency.org/
8 Statutory minimum wage, Labour Department [online] http://www.labour.gov.hk/eng/news/mwo.htm
9 GovHK: Hiring Foreign Domestic Helpers [online] http://www.gov.hk/en/residents/employment/recruitment/foreigndomestichelper.htm

10 There is currently no legislation on standard working hours in Hong Kong, which leaves migrant domestic workers who work in a domestic setting in the private sphere particularly vulnerable. See Hong Kong Helpers Campaign [online] http://hkhelperscampaign.com/en/maximum-working-hours/

11 PathFinders has also made submissions to the Legislative Council's Panel on Welfare Services Sub-Committee on Strategy and Measures to Tackle Domestic Violence and Sexual Violence to highlight the domestic and sexual violence endured by our clients in an attempt to provide deterrents and solutions. See PathFinders Submissions [online] http://www.pathfinders.org.hk/public/resources/pathfinders-material/

12 See for example 'Foreign Domestic Workers in Hong Kong' http://www.scmp.com/topics/foreign-domestic-workers-hong-kong; also Proctor, J. 'Nanny who was "virtual slave" wins $55K in B.C. human rights case' *CBS News* (1 April 2015) [online] http://www.cbc.ca/news/canada/british-columbia/nanny-who-was-virtual-slave-wins-55k-in-b-c-human-rights-case-1.3018672

13 PathFinders made a number of submissions in 2013 and 2014 to the relevant United Nations' Treaty Monitoring Committees in respect of ICESCR, CEDAW and the CRC (see PathFinders 2013, 2014a and 2014b).

14 Singapore Ministry of Manpower, eligibility requirements Female Domestic Worker work permit [online] www.mom.gov.sg/foreign-manpower/passes-visas/work-permit-fdw/before-you-apply/Pages/default.aspx

15 Singapore Ministry of Manpower, notification requirement regarding change to a Female Domestic Worker work permit http://www.mom.gov.sg/passes-and-permits/work-permit-for-foreign-domestic-worker/notify-mom-of-changes

16 See Press Release 'Labour Department to step up collaboration with Consulate-General of Republic of Indonesia in HK to promote rights of foreign domestic helpers' (24 June 2014) [online] http://www.info.gov.hk/gia/general/201406/24/P201406240875.htm

17 Equal Opportunities Commission, *A Guide for Foreign Domestic Helpers and their Employers* [online] http://www.eoc.org.hk/EOC/GraphicsFolder/showcontent.aspx?content=A+Guide+for+Foreign+Domestic+Helpers+and+their+Employers

18 S. 7(3) of the *Minimum Wage Ordinance Cap. 608, 2010*, specifically states: 'This Ordinance does not apply to a person who is employed as a domestic worker in, or in connection with, a household and who dwells in that household free of charge.'

19 See Clause 11, Sample Employment Contract, Labour Department [online] http://www.gov.hk/en/residents/employment/recruitment/localdomestichelper.htm

20 Legislative Council, Press Release, 'Maternity support for persons entering Hong Kong on employment visas', 11 February 2015 [online] http://www.info.gov.hk/gia/general/201502/11/P201502110818.htm

21 See Online Notification of Premature Termination of Employment Contracts of Foreign Domestic Helpers, GovHK [online] http://www.gov.hk/en/residents/employment/recruitment/terminateforeignhelper.htm

22 *See Hospital Authority Ordinance Cap.113, 1990*, Gazette Reference G.N. 5708, Part 1 (i) on Revisions to List of Charges [online] http://www.gld.gov.hk/egazette/pdf/20131739/egn201317395708.pdf

23 *See* Samaritan Fund Eligibility Criteria (b) [online] http://www.ha.org.hk/visitor/ha_visitor_text_index.asp?content_id=212018

24 *RE NTH (AN INFANT) (1996)* 1 HKC District Court; Adoption Case NO 99 of 1995 before GILL DJ 4 September 1995.

Bibliography

Amnesty International (2013) *China: Exploited for profit, failed by governments: Indonesian migrant domestic workers trafficked to Hong Kong*, 21 November [online] https://www.amnesty.org/en/documents/ASA17/029/2013/en/.

Census and Statistics Department (2014) *Annual Digest of Statistics (2014 Edition)*, 43 Hong Kong Special Administrative Region.

Committee on the Rights of the Child (CRC) (2013) *Consideration of Reports submitted by States Parties under Article 44 of the Convention:* China, UN Doc. CRC/C/CHN/CO/3-4 (29 October 2013).

Haufman, K. (2014) 'Hong Kong's Hidden Shame: Why Foreign Domestic Worker Abuse is So Rampant', Coconuts HK, 18 July [online] http://hongkong.coconuts.co/content/hong-kongs-hidden-shame-why-foreign-domestic-worker-abuse-so-rampant

Hong Kong Helpers Campaign (2014) '2. Enforce Maximum Working Hours' [online] http://hkhelperscampaign.com/en/maximum-working-hours/

Hong Kong Immigration Department (2015) *Quick Guide for the Employment of Domestic Helpers from Abroad* (ID(E) 989 (3/2015), Eligibility Requirement [online] http://www.immd.gov.hk/pdforms/ID(E)989.pdf

International Labour Organisation (ILO) (2011) 'Measuring the economic and social value of domestic work' [online] http://www.ilo.org/travail/whatwedo/publications/WCMS_156071/lang–en/index.htm

International Labour Organisation (ILO) (2013a) 'Domestic workers across the world: Global and regional statistics and the extent of legal protection' [online] http://www.ilo.org/global/publications/books/WCMS_200962/lang–en/index.htm

International Labour Organisation (ILO) (2013b) *Asia leads world in domestic worker numbers, but legal protection, working conditions lag*, 9 January 2013 [online] www.ilo.org/asia/info/public/pr/WCMS_201084/lang–en/index.htm

Justice Centre Hong Kong and Liberty Asia (2014) *How Many More Years a Slave: Trafficking for forced labour in Hong Kong* [online] http://www.justicecentre.org.hk/framework/uploads/2014/03/JCHK_Report_final_spreads.pdf

Lau, C. and Chan. T (2015) 'Erwiana's former boss jailed for six years as judge calls her behaviour "contemptible"' *South China Morning Post* 27 February 2015 [online] http://www.scmp.com/news/hong-kong/article/1724621/hong-kong-employer-who-abused-indonesian-maid-erwiana-jailed-six

Lo, C. (2015) 'Girl, 15, dies in fall from Repulse Bay tower; parents arrested for 'ill-treatment" *South China Morning Post* 7 April 2015 [online] http://www.scmp.com/news/hong-kong/article/1758631/girl-15-dies-after-fall-repluse-bay-building-parents-arrested

Mission for Migrant Workers (2013) *Live-in Policy Increases Vulnerability of Female FDH's Vulnerability to Various Types of Abuse* [online] http://issuu.com/mfmw/docs/primer_live-in_english

PathFinders (2012), *Annual Report 2012* [online] http://www.pathfinders.org.hk/public/wp-content/uploads/PathFinders-2012-Annual-Report_Digital_final_revisedEmails.pdf

PathFinders (2013), *Submission to the UN CRC Committee* [online] http://www.PathFinders.org.hk/public/wp-content/uploads/PathFinders_UNCRC_2013Sep.pdf

PathFinders (2014a), *Submission to the UN CEDAW Committee* [online] http://www.PathFinders.org.hk/public/wp-content/uploads/PathFinders_UNCEDAW_2014Jan.pdf

PathFinders (2014b), *Submission to the UN ICESCR Committee* [online] http://www.PathFinders.org.hk/public/wp-content/uploads/PathFinders_UNICESCR_2014Mar.pdf

PathFinders (2014c), *Annual Report 2014* [online] http://www.pathfinders.org.hk/public/wp-content/uploads/PathAR2014_23_6_1650.pdf

Tam, S.M. and Tong, Y. (2012) 'Migrant Women and Ethnic Minority Women' in Choi, S.Y.P. and Cheung, F.M. (eds.) *Women and Girls in Hong Kong: Current Situations and Future Challenges* Hong Kong Institute of Asia Pacific Studies, The Chinese University of Hong Kong.

Women's Commission (2013) *Hong Kong Women in Figures* [online] http://www.women.gov.hk/download/research/HK_Women2013_e.pdf

13 Women against women?

Rural women leaders' role in addressing gender-based violence in China

Gao Wei

Introduction

This chapter explores the role of rural women leaders in achieving access to justice and rights protection of women villagers in China. It examines how rural women leaders interact with the grassroots justice system and the power structure behind it at institutional and cultural levels. A specific focus is placed on the role of women leaders in dealing with family planning and domestic violence, scenarios which both involve entrenched gender stereotypes and possibly also severe cases of violence against women. The chapter furthermore envisions the opportunities open to rural women leaders and other practitioners to cope with these problems.

Although existing academic literature in China and abroad has discussed the rural justice system in China and its effects on rural people's access to justice, little attention has been paid to the way in which the rural justice system particularly impacts upon women. This is especially important in cases of gender-based violence, such as family planning and domestic violence, which are strongly affected by the power imbalance between men and women generated by gender-biased traditions and their continued presence in the rural dispute resolution process. Most research on gender and law in China has focused on theory, looking primarily at legislation and the corresponding mechanism design, with less discussion on how law and justice are understood and experienced at rural level during its implementation or through local dispute resolution processes, for example, through community mediation or grassroots judicial offices.

Even less research has explored the role of rural women leaders in the rural justice system and the inherent dilemma that they face in executing their work. There have been in-depth studies on women's political participation in rural China, but none have considered how women leaders are involved in dispute resolution and interact with the law. Part of the reason is that, in reality, women leaders' participation in dispute resolution may not be as active as that of male leaders due to their marginalised status in village governance structures. This chapter argues that women leaders do participate in dispute resolution at village level and have the potential to make a greater contribution to improving the rights of women villagers and their access to justice in rural China.

Drawing on needs assessment surveys and legal research and training programmes with rural women leaders in a rural county in Hubei Province, this chapter uses rural women leaders' experiences as a framework to examine how, on the one hand, injustice is executed and backed by power manipulation and, on the other hand, how justice could be reconstructed. The chapter starts by placing rural women leaders in the power structure of village governance and analysing the resulting gender implications. It then describes rural women leaders' roles in dealing with cases involving violence against women, and articulates the power dynamics in those scenarios. Finally, it draws lessons from my own experience working with rural women leaders through programmes run by the Wuhan University Public Interest and Development Law Institute (PIDLI) to demonstrate how legal empowerment is possible and has the potential to change the power structure from the bottom up to advance rural women's rights in China.

Rural women leaders in China: the 3 in 1 reality

Rural women leaders occupy a unique position in grassroots justice systems. On the one hand, they are usually the first institutional point of contact when women in rural communities encounter gender-related disputes, such as with marriage and domestic violence; on the other hand, they are state agents who implement the government's laws and policies on family planning, a task which could also involve violence against women. As female members of the communities themselves, their perceptions of gender relations can affect the way in which they work, especially how they attempt to resolve disputes. Their position in the village governance power structure has left them too marginalised to represent the interests of fellow women villagers. Formal law has shown its weakness in providing effective remedies in cases of violence against rural women, in part because the law itself does not contain the elements necessary to protect rural women or because the implementation measures are not effective enough, especially in rural areas. However, rural women leaders are probably the only agents who have sincere concerns about women's rights in rural China and our research has shown that these women leaders have the potential to be empowered and actively involved in the cause of advancing rural women's rights. In doing so, rural women leaders have to negotiate their various roles and identities as: (1) village committee member; (2) rural women's representative; (3) specialist family planning cadre; and (4) woman in rural communities herself.

Village committee member

The village committee is a mass autonomous organisation elected by the villagers and administered at township level in mainland China. The *PRC Organic Law on Village Committees 2010* authorises village committees to set up sub-committees in charge of people's mediation, public security, public health and family planning as needed, and village committee members can serve on sub-committees. Villages with a small population are not required to set up sub-committees and responsibilities can be shared among members of the village committee. In reality, the members of village committees usually carry multiple responsibilities. In many villages we have been to in Hubei, the village head also acts as mediation director and public security director.

Several laws in China address women's political participation at rural level. Article 6 of the *PRC Organic Law on Village Committees 2010* stipulates that women should be among the members of the village committee, while the *PRC Law on the Protection of Women's Rights and Interests 2005* stipulates that women are entitled to appropriate representation on the village committee. The *PRC People's Mediation Law 2010* also requires that there are women members on the people's mediation committee. The inclusion of women members in the village committee is to:

> *ensure gender equality. It, on the one hand, guarantees the political rights of women by enabling them to participate in leading the village and, on the other hand, it is necessary to protect the legitimate rights and interests of rural women, elderly and children. Women cadres are able to speak for women and other disadvantaged groups in the village so as to prevent abuse against women and the elderly, and to maintain family harmony and reduce rural disputes. Women cadres are also helpful in carrying out tasks regarding family planning and public health because they are closer to women and are in a better position to manage and mobilize rural women.*
>
> (Zhang 2006, pp. 23–4)

It is not explicitly provided in the *PRC Organic Law on Village Committees 2010* that women members should only be in charge of women's affairs, and it is without any indication (at least not from an analysis of the text) that such a person has to be a woman. However, it has become common practice that, as long as there is a woman member of the village committee, she is usually called the 'women's director'. Though it varies from village to village, generally the women's director's tasks are only concerned with women's affairs such as family planning and the care of disadvantaged groups and not significantly related to village governance in general.

Rural women's representatives

Women's leadership in rural China is also realised through the women's federation system. The All China Women's Federation (ACWF) is a mass organisation with the mandate to represent women's interests and rights and promote gender equality. Though labelled as a non-governmental organisation, the ACWF is actually led by the Chinese Communist Party and thus enjoys semi-official status. At township or village level, the ACWF takes the form of a women's congress (*funu daibiao dahui*) and is supervised by ACWF. As listed in Article 11 of the *Work Regulations on the Organization of Women's Federations at Village Level 2010*, the main tasks of the women's congress include: promoting rural women's participation in village governance; representing women villagers and participating in the decision-making process with regards to public affairs in the village; protecting the rights and interests of rural women and children; educating the community about laws and regulations that impact women and children; and preventing and eliminating domestic violence.

Specialist family planning cadre

Implementing family planning policy is one very important mandate for rural women leaders. The family planning policy in China dates back to the 1970s and was introduced to control population growth. With a complicated legal and policy framework, the policy is usually called simply the One Child Policy. In reality, couples do have the chance to have more than one child given specific conditions. Generally, couples need to apply for birth permits before they conceive a baby and unplanned pregnancies are often required to be terminated. If an unplanned child, the couple has to pay a high penalty in the name of 'social support fees' and local governments often require that these couples undergo sterilisation procedures. In practice, such forced sterilisation is borne by the woman and not her husband. In addition, unplanned children may face difficulties in accessing an entitlement to social welfare and, as a result, are disadvantaged in various aspects of life.

To ensure the local enforcement of provincial family planning policies, every village is required to have a specialist family planning cadre (*jisheng zhuangan*) to assist the work of the township family planning office, including: disseminating family planning information; collecting information on women of childbearing age; ensuring use of contraceptive measures; and issuing birth permits, collecting fees and penalties. In practice, the village head and secretary do not get involved directly in family planning work, and it is mainly the family planning cadre, usually a rural woman leader, who is in charge of this issue and directly engages with villagers (Zhang 2015).

Juggling multiple roles: the 3 in 1 reality

Each of these roles (the women's congress director, the village committee member and specialist family planning cadre) is distinct and carries specific responsibilities, but in practice it is common for one woman leader to hold the three positions concurrently. Among the female training participants and interviewees that I engaged with, almost all of them had the three abovementioned work titles simultaneously.

Several researchers have made similar observations in other parts of the country. Liu Xiaohong's research on rural women's political participation in sixteen villages of eight counties in two provinces of central China in 2000 found that, in most cases, the woman who serves as the women's congress director will also be elected as the women director on the village committee. Should another woman be elected as a village committee member without a specific position, the village committee would typically appoint her as the women congress director, replacing the original director and ensuring that there was only one woman on the village committee. Although the women's congress director should technically be elected by the women villagers, in practice she is usually appointed by the village heads (Liu 2002, p. 113). In this sense, villages satisfy the requirement of the *PRC Organic Law on Village Committees 2010* to include women members in the village governance structure while limiting the actual number of women leaders in the locality. Similarly, research on family planning structures in rural villages have found that only large villages have full-time family planning cadres, while, in most villages, the family planning cadre also includes the village women director, village hygienist or accountant (Zhang 2015, p. 167).

Situating rural women leaders' role in women rights protection: institutional dilemmas and cultural traps

Marginalised in the village governance structure

The seeming inclusion but actual exclusion of women in village governance structures can be illusive. Enshi county, where we carried out projects, was proud to share that they had a very high ratio of women leaders (approximately thirty per cent), and we were told that most rural women leaders attending our training were village directors or village party secretaries. However, during subsequent visits and interviews in the villages, it was discovered that almost all of them were only deputy directors or party secretaries, and not the top leader in their village. In those cases, there are usually only two village cadres on the village committees; while the head is always male, the woman in most cases holds a concurrent position as women's director.

Providing a shortcut for rural women's congress directors to join the village committee helps women to sit on the village committee and guarantees that there is gender diversity on the committee, at least in terms of numbers. However, such representation is more for the sake of formality. This arrangement keeps the number of rural women leaders to the minimum and women's representation is thus superficial. The systemic design of a 'women's director' on the village committee has built a solid wall between the elected women cadres and the mainstream village governance circle. Women directors are expected to take care only of 'women's issues', as the position title literally indicates. Therefore, they do not have real leadership power. Furthermore, this gendered division of labour in the village committee renders the election a competition between women themselves, which hinders the organisational strength of women as an interest group (Guo and Ming 2013, p. 36).

Research has shown that villagers are ambivalent about voting for women during the village committee elections. Most villagers interviewed stated that they only voted for women because someone had to do the family planning work in the village. Others did not vote for women due to several gendered stereotypes. For example, on the assumption that rural women leaders only worked on family planning, villagers preferred to vote for other (male) leaders who were assumed to have authority in financial and economic interests. Others recognised that women generally lacked influence within the village and were therefore either unlikely to get voted on to the committee by other villagers or would not be able to do much once they obtained the position (Liu 2002, p. 116; Guo and Ming 2013, p. 36). This low expectation of women in turn hinders the zeal of women elites to participate in elections, in part because of the recognition that winning an election is likely to result in an assignment of responsibilities similar to those of a women's congress director (Liu 2002, p. 113).

This gendered labour division further impedes rural women leader's from representing women villagers and somehow creates hostility among women towards each other. Rural women villager's attitudes towards rural women leaders also show that institutional marginalisation can reinforce cultural marginalisation. Our research in Enshi County, Hubei Province, supports this to some extent. When asked about the challenges rural women leaders' faced in their work, quite a few mentioned that women villagers did not understand the work of rural women leaders and showed no support, and that some villagers even looked down on women leaders. During a series of work experience sharing sessions, rural women leaders' comments similarly reflected that: 'Women naturally appear less powerful. When you are on site trying to mediate a dispute, people won't listen to you because you are a woman.' A young women director newly graduated from university stated: 'I am responsible for family planning. But because I am a woman and young, I have no influence.' Many women leaders shared that they have to take care of the elderly and children at home besides their work and it is very difficult for them to meet both responsibilities as family caregiver and woman leader.

Although the law may be well-intentioned in trying to increase women's political participation at grassroots level, rural women leaders remain marginalised in the village governance power structure. The purpose of such laws is to ensure that women are able to participate in decision-making on village public affairs so that a gender perspective is taken into consideration. Including women in the village governance structure acknowledges that gender equality concerns both males and females (and even other genders) and indicates that every decision regarding the village could impact on men and women differently. However, the nature of the rural women leaders' work has not helped them realise that purpose in practice. The relevant regulations, such as the *Work Manual for Village Committee Cadres* and the ACWF's *Work Regulations on the Organization of Women's Federations at Village Level*, emphasise the women leaders' role in advancing the interests of women and other disadvantaged groups, such as the elderly and children, but also unintentionally signals that these are only women's issues and women leaders would do better to just focus on women's issues. Consequently, women leaders are marginalised in the village governance structure. This marginalisation in turn reinforces the cultural attitudes that women are only good at caring for the disadvantaged and should not be involved in 'male issues', such as property disputes or land contracts.

Contradictory identities: state agent or protector of women?

In China, the family planning policy comes from the state and the power extends to the grassroots. When state power reaches ground level, it is rural women leaders (and other village cadres) who exercise power in families. In this case, rural women leaders apparently choose to identify themselves more as a state agent rather than as a defender of women's rights. Not only do women leaders not have substantial power in the village committee, as discussed, but they are also dependent on it. This somehow places women leaders on the opposite side of women villagers and their families. Villagers probably know that decisions are not made by the women directors, but since they expect the power of the male village heads to benefit them in other aspects of life, they can opt to vent their anger strategically against women leaders.

The grassroots implementation of China's family planning policy can sometimes involve brutal violence against women, for example forced abortions or sterilisation. Rural officials have been known to mobilise the police or local militia to take coercive action against women who have not voluntarily terminated their pregnancies or undertaken sterilisation as required by regulations (Li 1995, p. 164). A lack of specific statutes to punish government officials, or others acting in an official capacity, who abuse the rights of women and girls allows local officials to use violence to achieve their aims, especially when they are under a great deal of pressure to achieve the rigidly assigned quota (ibid., p. 156). Prosecutions of local officials who authorised violence or took no action to prevent violence against women in family planning have rarely taken place, according to interviews with Chinese lawyers, family-planning officials and international human-rights monitors (ibid., pp. 156–7).

Further, the policy also causes violations of the rights of female children. First, it triggers social practices such as female infanticide and the abandonment of infant girls (ibid., p. 146). Second, in some regions couples are allowed to have a second child if the first-born is a girl. As Li Xiaorong describes it:

> *This policy gives official legitimisation to sex discrimination by codifying it into governmental birth regulations. It sends the public the message that exceptions to the restriction on birth rates are permitted if the survival of male lineage in the family is endangered . . . A female first-born seems a less-than-whole baby and needs to be supplemented by a second child in order to count as much as one male firstborn.*
>
> (ibid., p. 160)

Over the years, the situation has changed and violence against women in this regard has decreased to a great extent. In the past two decades, the government has taken some steps to try to reduce the violence through legal and policy reform. Article 4 of the *Law of the People's Republic of China on Population and Family Planning* stipulates that 'the people's governments at various levels and their functionaries . . . may not infringe upon the lawful rights and interests of the citizens' when implementing the family planning policy. The Chinese government has also relaxed its family planning policy since 2013 in some pilot cities and allowed couples to have two children if either of the parents is an only child. More recently, in October 2015, the Chinese government announced plans to ease its family planning policy so as to allow two children per couple.

Despite this relaxation of rules, forced abortions and female infanticide are still not unheard of in rural areas. In its Concluding Observations to the review of China's combined seventh and eighth periodic report, the Committee on the Elimination of Discrimination against Women (CEDAW) stated that it remained 'concerned about the persistence of deep-rooted stereotypes regarding the roles and responsibilities of women and men in the family and society', noting that such stereotypes were 'reflected in the tradition of son preference which, because of sex-selective abortion and other illegal practices such as forced abortion and sterilization and the infanticide of girls, results in an adverse sex ratio' (CEDAW Committee 2014, para. 24). Such government intervention is also very much part of contemporary practices – where the author has worked, women are still required to undergo contraception procedures (such as the mandatory use of intra-uterine devices) so as to ensure that they do not have more children than allowed by the relevant regulations. Since family planning policy imposes a limitation on individuals' rights to reproduction and involves heavy monetary penalties or bodily harm, it remains a focal point of state–society conflict (Michelson 2010, p. 212).

Tasked with the implementation of family planning policy, women directors do face resistance from women villagers in their work. When asked during a training session to share the challenges they encounter in their work, one of the groups of women leaders reported that 'family planning is the most difficult among women leaders' tasks, some women still possess the patriarchal ideology that boys are better than girls, so they are resistant against birth control and do not want to use [an intra-uterine] ring' and that 'the key to succeed in our work is to get the support from women villagers'.

Rural women leaders (both women's director and women's congress directors) are supposed to represent the rights and interests of rural women. They are usually the first institutional point of contact when women in rural communities encounter disputes, especially gender-related ones, such as in marriage and domestic violence. However, they are also state agents who implement the government's laws and policies with regard to family planning. Consequently, rural women leaders only get to work closely with childbearing-age women and do not have much support from other villagers. In addition, women of child-bearing age generally do not like rural women leaders due to the nature of their work, such as the collection of fees for violating family planning policies, forced gynaecological check-ups and even measures involving violence against women (for example, forced insertion of a contraceptive ring or enforced sterilisation). When villagers are not satisfied with the family planning policy and its implementation, the first people they blame are the women directors (Liu 2002, p. 114). In these ways, rural women leaders lose the villagers' trust and support.

This contradiction of identities has previously been raised in discussions of village cadres in general. Xu Yong has described the dual role of village cadres acting as both state agent and 'family head', where family mainly refers to the village. The state and villagers hold different expectations of village cadres and such expectations grow stronger over time. However, the interests of the state and villagers are not always the same. Where these interests conflict, village cadres tend to identify themselves more as a state agent than a family head, because they have been used to an inherited top-down style of administration (Xu 1997).

This theory could also be applied here. State policies on family planning and gender equality are sometimes in conflict with each other and send mixed signals to the rural women leaders tasked with implementing them. On the one hand, the state imposes family planning policies in rural areas which, in fact, aggravate the preference for sons by conditionally allowing a second child when the first-born is a girl. On the other hand, the government also promotes the idea that family planning is a strategy to combat the preference for sons and thus it is an important cause to which rural officials should be devoted. Rural women leaders therefore might find themselves confused as to the day-to-day implementation of their responsibilities. We assume that they expect to speak for women villagers, but, due to the rural power structure and women leaders' reliance on the resources of the village committee, it is possible that sometimes they have to neglect or even act against the interests of women; these dynamics are then further compounded by rural women leaders being soaked in the discourse about the 'great social cause' promoted by family planning, and being given only specific (and draconian) tools for managing the population goals within their communities.

An additional complication is that women leaders also have a third identity, namely that they, like the majority of ordinary women villagers, grow up within their communities, get married, go through their fertile periods and take care of their (matrimonial) families. Their roles as rural women leaders also make it difficult for them to reflect on their own experiences as women villagers. This is clearly demonstrated in individual interviews with rural women leaders. For example, one rural women leader shared her story:

> *I personally do not want to use the ring either. I still got pregnant after I had undergone the surgery and I had to go and suffer from another surgery to terminate the pregnancy.*

This case is not atypical among the interviewees, and it is clear that women leaders, as women themselves, are sympathetic to the complaints of women villagers. Many leaders have received complaints from women villagers that use of the intra-uterine ring has worsened their health in different ways. Women leaders also mentioned a case where, despite using the government-mandated contraceptive ring, a women villager got pregnant and therefore asked for compensation from the village. The village did not provide any compensation and the woman refused to use a ring ever again.

Whether a woman's resistance to sterilisation measures is based on a preference for sons or due to a fear of pain or worsening health conditions, it is more problematic that women are deprived of their rights to make decisions about their own reproduction, and such limitations on their reproductive freedom could even take a violent form. One story shared by an interviewee manifested women's subordination in the family:

> *Most of the male villagers are fine. They send their wives to attend the meeting regarding family planning. But some of them still hold firmly the traditional 'son preference' idea and insist on having more children. So they won't allow their wives to our family planning meeting and do not accept the induced abortion surgery.*

Here, women are not even seen as subjects with a say on this issue. Lack of awareness in this regard makes women leaders see those who do not co-operate as troublemakers. This again creates more conflict between women leaders and their fellow women villagers.

Trapped in the traditional rural justice system

Despite the above mentioned discontent with rural women leaders, my research shows that many women villagers will still turn to rural women leaders for help in cases of family disputes, such as divorce, support for children or the elderly, even domestic violence. This is not surprising since it appears that women villagers (as well as male ones) have also internalised the idea that these issues are within the mandate of women leaders. According to my interviews, if villagers encounter disputes relating to property boundaries or the ownership of forests, males in the family would go to the male village heads, who are believed to have greater authority and ability. Yet, when the opposing party is a male within the family, women villagers feel women leaders are the only ones who could understand their experience and would not automatically be on the husband's side. Research has also demonstrated that women in rural areas have a stronger preference for resolving the dispute through mediation, as compared to men, because women tend to seek external authority outside of the home due to their subordinate status in the family and most disputes are usually about intra-household disputes (Read and Michaelson 2008).

The rural justice system in China is quite informal and does not have the same procedures and substantial norms as the formal legal system. As a result of a combination of traditional culture and development in rural society, disputes have become more complicated and diverse. Where local norms are unable to successfully solve all disputes, state law is used. Nonetheless, traditions are maintained in some rural areas, particularly in more remote areas and where accessibility to formal justice is limited; mediation is still the mainstream method to solve disputes. Unlike the previous elders' governance, village cadres and grassroots judicial agencies have become the mediation authority backed by state law. Even when the official judicial system is resorted to, the village committee is the first institutional point of contact for most villagers.

A cultural analysis of mediation indicates that it can reflect cultural values and, to some extent, it can also reproduce specific power relations and social structures

(Qiang 2001, p. 2). In this context, gendered notions, which are deeply influenced by culture, will repeatedly present themselves in mediation – not only in the substance of the case, but also in the process of the mediation itself. In addition, observers have argued that mediation has been upgraded within the official judicial system in China because it is an effective tool for the penetration and operation of power (Zhu 2012, p. 32). Dispute resolution in China's rural areas, therefore, takes on a greater complexity with regard to how it interacts with state law and the villages' autonomous norms.

Many have discussed the potential disadvantages of mediation (Cobb and Rifkin 1991; Field 1998). One potential issue is where mediation happens between two unequal parties and where the process does not effectively address these inequalities. In some cases the power imbalance may be reinforced through the mediation process and severe consequences may occur if violence (especially violence within the family) is overlooked. In particular, experts have argued that mediation is not appropriate in cases involving violence or threats of violence. Since violence involves a serious power imbalance, it is difficult to change the power relationship during imbalanced mediation sessions. This is especially problematic where the mediation is seen as a private, closed process rather than the, arguably, more open and public venue offered by trials; dealing with domestic violence in a 'private forum' could perpetuate the view that abusers can avoid punishment by conducting themselves 'appropriately in a mediation environment' (Eliades 1999).

Nevertheless, mediation remains a typical mechanism for dispute resolution in rural China, and the process by which rural women leaders tend to interact with the justice system. Although many scholars have conducted in-depth research on grassroots mediation in China, there is no specific analysis on the role of women or women leaders in mediation. This is partly because most women leaders are still alienated from the justice system (both formal and informal) in rural China. This is supported by information collected through training sessions during which many women leaders described their work as being largely about family planning. Further, most women rural leaders have had no previous experience of mediating a dispute. In a workshop with around thirty participants, typically only two or three senior women leaders had much experience in handling disputes.

Although the marginalised status of rural women leaders often makes them invisible in the rural justice system, in some cases they do play a role in rural women's access to justice and rights (be it positively and negatively). Rural women leaders also have the potential to change the current gender-equality landscape in rural areas in China but only when their awareness about gender-equality principles and substantive rights are enhanced.

Domestic violence against women is one typical example worth exploring. Nationwide research on domestic violence in rural China indicates that domestic violence is pervasive in rural communities, with 62.02 per cent of respondents saying that domestic violence has happened in his/her community over a period of two years (Chen 2007, p. 93). In contrast, most women leaders I interviewed thought that there were no cases of domestic violence in their area, or that such occurrences were very rare. During the interviews, women leaders told us that 'some women villagers do not want to share even if they have experienced violence', while more than one leader said that 'times have changed and nowadays it's always the wife who batters the husband'. These responses from rural women leaders may be due partly to assumptions that the only 'real' domestic violence is physical violence and a lack of awareness of how violence can manifest itself in other forms (such as psychological violence, sexual violence or economic control). It is also possible that interviewees were reluctant to share such issues in front of an outsider, such as myself.

Most women leaders we interviewed use mediation to deal with domestic violence and they generally tried to reconcile married couples. A typical strategy is to use 'back to back' mediation (i.e. talking to the disputants separately) and a dispute is considered as resolved if the husband promises he will never do it again. It is not known whether there is a repeat of violence in those cases. In the minds of rural women leaders reconciliation is probably the best solution for everyone. Moreover, it is still a common perception that perpetrators of domestic violence usually have a 'good reason' for what they have done. For example, in our survey of rural women leaders (and some male leaders) in Enshi county, where our pilot project was conducted, one third of respondents thought 'the victim must have done something wrong in the first place' for domestic violence to occur. In such cases, the mediator her/himself could be the source of power imbalance between perpetrator and victim.

However, it is not easy to come to the simple conclusion that rural women leaders should just tell every woman suffering domestic violence to divorce her husband and put him in jail. Issues regarding women's rights rarely exist in isolation, they are linked to others and one can never solve a single problem without looking at the context. In cases of domestic violence, it is very much related to the accessibility of the appropriate justice system and the woman's economic situation. One reason that rural women do not want to leave their husbands, or the reason rural women leaders do not suggest they should do so, is because women villagers own fewer economic resources than their husbands. Rural women usually are not allocated lands when they get married and move to live with their spouses (ibid.). Further, knowing little about the laws that govern marriage and its dissolution, rural women are often are disadvantaged in the division of property in divorce proceedings. Finally, emotions and emotional attachment are also important. Putting aside questions about the awareness levels of the victim and whether their emotional dependence is actually economic dependence, rural women leaders also confront the real pain of women villagers when they provide support on issues relating to domestic violence. As a result, rural women leaders are squeezed between traditional culture and state power in the process of trying to resolve disputes, even as they seek to address these very complex issues.

Viewing rural women leaders as agents of change: a legal empowerment action

Despite all the challenges, rural women leaders have great potential to act as change agents to improve the substantive situation of women in rural China.

Most of these leaders are sincerely concerned about the women's rights issues they deal with on a day-to-day basis; they are also positioned within rural power structures as probably the best agents who have sincere concerns for women's situations in rural China, and with great potential. It is important to explore how women leaders could be empowered to make changes starting from within their communities.

Since 2006 PIDLI has been working on access to justice issues in rural China. Its strategy is to work with grassroots legal aid workers (including lawyers and township/village leaders) so that they can provide better legal services to rural residents. This is in line with the idea of legal empowerment first stipulated by Stephen Golub in the field of international development, which defines legal empowerment as 'the use of law to increase the disadvantaged population's control over their lives' (Golub 2001). Legal empowerment adopts a bottom-up approach which emphasises the potential and ability of the disadvantaged groups to activate changes, address current imbalanced power relations and achieve equal enjoyment of rights. Legal empowerment methods include, but are not limited to, the provision of legal services such as litigation, non-judicial representation, education of communities and paralegals and related activities like organising the community and the use of media.

Although PIDLI's legal empowerment programmes have resulted in successful cases where rural residents received legal remedies in cases of land disputes, work-related injuries and so on, we observed that the number of women among training participants was extremely low. Given the discussion above, the situation of rural women has manifested their disempowerment in the power structure and a lack of rights awareness; legal knowledge and confidence have made it difficult for them to get out of this powerless state. Therefore, PIDLI started to work with rural women leaders in 2012 and carried out pilot training projects in Enshi County, Hubei Province in 2012 and 2013.

The 2012 training with women directors focused on building gender awareness among rural women leaders and introducing them to notions of gender equality and rights. The training content included gender sensitivity, mediation skills, handling frequently-occurring dispute cases (including cases of domestic violence), legal self-study methods and women leadership-building. The 2013 follow-up training sought to further enhance the group's awareness of rights and gender equality, and also improve their dispute resolution skills. It was also hoped that these training sessions would help rural women leaders form a support network in the field.

Some positive changes were witnessed during the training sessions. First, the training increased rural women leaders' awareness of gender equality and rights. Surveys taken before and after the training indicate that rural women leaders now have an enhanced level of awareness in regard to gender equality and rights of rural women and other disadvantaged groups, such as the elderly and children. For example, trainees who initially thought that that 'men beating their wives is normal' had given up this idea by the end of the training. In addition, more trainees agreed that all kinds of domestic violence (not only physical) should be eliminated.

Training with rural women leaders has enhanced their capacity to use the law to serve the community. The training feedback has shown that trainees have learnt practical legal knowledge and case-handling skills, especially in regard to the rights of women (marriage, property rights upon divorce, domestic violence), the elderly (support and inheritance) and children. One trainee shared that she was able to solve a dispute immediately after training using the knowledge learnt about non-marital cohabitation.

Conclusion

Power imbalance permeates the structures and processes related to women's access to justice and rights in rural China. The power imbalance affects multiple levels in the form of state law and policies, village governance structures and cultural perceptions and, in practice, these reinforce each other. When rural women leaders' role in the process is examined, in many cases, the power imbalance and injustice experienced by rural women is, ironically, carried out or exacerbated by rural women leaders.

Understanding the complex power structures within which rural women leaders are expected to perform these conflicting roles will not only allow us to better understand how to enhance rural women leaders' ability to speak for women within their village but also how to assert themselves within village governance structures. Our research indicates that rural women leaders have shown a potential to contribute to the advancement of rural women's rights through legal empowerment, which raises their gender awareness and enhances their ability to engage in rural dispute resolution. Recognising that women leaders' perceptions of gender relations directly impacts the way they work and attempt to resolve disputes, legal empowerment programmes can also train women leaders to use existing legal tools to protect the rights of women in their village. This chapter suggests that an empowerment process for rural women leaders offers the possibility of turning the 'women against women' model into a 'women for/with women' model, thus helping to transform bottom-up power and changing the gender-equality landscape in rural China.

Bibliography

CEDAW Committee (United Nations Committee on the Elimination of Discrimination against Women) (2014) Concluding observations on the combined seventh and eighth periodic reports of China, UN Doc. CEDAW/C/CHN/CO/7-8.

Chen, W. (2007) 'Study on Domestic Violence in Rural China' 《我国农村家庭暴力调查研究》, *Law and Business Studies*, vol. 6, pp. 91–101 (in Chinese).

Cobb, S. and Rifkin, J. (1991) 'Practice and Paradox: Deconstructing Neutrality in Mediation', *Law & Social Inquiry*, vol. 16, no. 1, pp. 35–62.

Eliades, D. (1999) 'Power in mediation – some reflections', *ADR Bulletin*, vol. 2, no. 1 [online] http://epublications.bond.edu.au/adr/vol2/iss1/2.

Field, R. (1998) 'Family Law Mediation: Process Imbalances Women Should be Aware of Before They Take Part', *Queensland University of Technology Law Review*, vol. 14, no. 2, pp. 23–39.

Golub, S. (2001) *Legal Empowerment: Advancing Good Governance and Poverty Reduction in Law and Policy Reform at the Asian Development Bank*, Asian Development Bank, Manila.

Guo, J. and Ming, L. (eds.) (2013) 'Research on Rural Women's Political Participation – Examples of the Pilot Program Experience in Hebei and Heilongjiang 《农村妇女参政问题研究 – 以河北、黑龙江试点经验为例)》, Chinese People's Public Security University Publishing House, Beijing (in Chinese).

Li, X. (1995) 'License to Coerce: Violence against Women, State Responsibility and Legal Failures in China's Family Planning Program', *Yale Journal of Law and Feminism*, vol. 8, pp. 145–91.

Liu, X. (2002) 'Women's Congress at Village Level and the Role of Women in the Village Committee Election' 《农村村级妇代会组织与妇女在村委会选举中的地位》, *Journal of Central China Normal University (Humanities and Social Sciences)*, vol. 41, no. 6 [online] http://www.chinaelections.org/article/101/74307.html (in Chinese).

Michelson, E. (2010) 'Family Planning Enforcement in Rural China: Enduring State-Society Conflict?' in Oi, J.C., Rozelle, S., and Zhou, X. (eds.), *Growing Pains: Tensions and Opportunity in China's Transformation*, Shorenstein APARC/Brookings Institution Press, Baltimore, US.

Qiang, S. (ed.) (2001) *Mediation, Legality and Modernity: Mediation in China* 《调解、法制与现代性：中国调解制度研究》 China Legal Publishing House, Beijing (in Chinese).

Read, B.L. and Michelson, E. (2008) 'Mediating the Mediation Debate: Conflict Resolution and the Local State in China', *Journal of Conflict Resolution*, vol. 52, no. 5, pp. 737–64.

Xu, Y. (1997) 'The Dual Role of Village Cadres: State Agent and Family Head 《村干部的双重角色：代理人与当家人》 *Economic and Society*, vol. 8 (in Chinese).

Zhang, S. (2006) 'Work Manual for Village Committee Cadres' 《村委会干部工作手册》, China Legal Publishing House, pp. 23–4 (in Chinese).

Zhang, Z. (2015) 'Law, State and Society in the PRC: A Case Study of Family Planning Regulations Implementation at Grassroots Level in Rural China', PhD thesis, Department of Law of the London School of Economics and Political Science, UK.

Zhu, S. (2012) *Sending Law to the Countryside: Research on China's Basic Level Judicial System* 《送法下乡：中国基层司法制度研究》, Peking University Press, Beijing (in Chinese).

14 Law, inequalities and diverse vulnerabilities

Client-perpetrated violence against female sex workers in Hong Kong

Susanne Yuk-ping Choi

The number of studies of client-perpetrated violence against female sex workers has grown rapidly in recent years. Client-perpetrated violence is an important issue because violence directly impinges on the basic human rights of sex workers and has significant negative consequences for the mental, physical, sexual and reproductive health of female sex workers (Day and Ward 2004), as well as being an obstacle to the practice of safe sex, making it difficult for women to enforce any agreement to use a condom and impinging on the right to justice for sex workers (West and Zimmerman 2002; Human Rights Watch 2013). On the other hand, studies of client-perpetrated violence based on biased samples may not reflect the working conditions of sex workers across different settings and venues; they may overemphasise the victim status of this population and produce erroneous conclusions and thence flawed policy-making (Weitzer 2005). The variability in work venue, market segment and geographical location poses a challenge for researchers to achieve an understanding of the types, prevalence and severity of client-perpetrated violence against sex workers (Chapkis 2000; Weitzer 2000; Vanwesenbeeck 2001; Monto 2004).

This chapter synthesises data from participant observation, archival searches, a community survey and in-depth interviews to answer the following questions: how do work arrangements and other contextual factors affect vulnerability to client-perpetrated violence; how do laws related to sex work affect sex workers' experiences and produce inequality and variability in vulnerability among this population? The precarious legal status of the sex industry has made it virtually impossible to ensure representative sampling in studies of sex workers. In this chapter we hope to illuminate the complex relationship between the legislation and client-perpetrated violence against female sex workers. Previous studies of violence against sex workers have drawn attention to differences between indoor and outdoor workers. Our comparison of experiences of violence victimisation in sex workers revealed considerable diversity across the wide range of work settings we investigated and demonstrated that future studies should move beyond comparisons of indoor and outdoor sex work and seek to analyse the hierarchy of the sex industry and its diversity. Thus far the legal debate about sex work has revolved around the issue of legalisation v. criminalisation (Farley 2004). Our findings demonstrate that this dichotomous framework limits our understanding of the complexity, inconsistencies and contradictions of legal provisions related to sex work (Bungay *et al.* 2010). We develop the concept of diverse vulnerabilities to argue that instead of legalising or criminalising sex work, laws often function to create inequalities between different groups of sex workers and expose them to different degrees and types of vulnerabilities, thus serving as a mechanism to marginalise all sex workers (Choi 2011a).

Indoor v. outdoor

While studies have shown that female sex workers experience multiple forms of violence from pimps, strangers, intimate partners, police and clients (Dalla *et al.* 2003; Church *et al.* 2001; Lowman 2000), it is clients who have been identified as one of the main perpetrators of violence against female sex workers in certain sex work venues and locations (Choi *et al.* 2008; Choi 2011a). So far the most consistent finding is that streetwalkers tend to be more vulnerable to violence than indoor workers (Dalla 2002; Church *et al.* 2001; Weitzer 2009; Lowman 2000; Whittaker and Hart 1996; Pyett and Warr, 1999; Hart and Barnard 2003). Church *et al.* (2001) found that, in comparison with workers in saunas or call girls, women who worked on the streets in the UK reported much higher rates of robbery and physical violence and sexual violence by clients (see also Whittaker and Hart 1996). Lowman and Fraser (1995) reported similar differences between streetwalkers and escorts in Canada; streetwalkers were more likely to have been robbed, kidnapped, physically harmed and sexually assaulted. Similar discrepancies in violence and victimisation between indoor and outdoor workers were also reported for Australian and United States samples (Perkins and Bennett, 1985; Perkins 1991; Perkins and Lovejoy, 1996; Prince 1986).

A survey of 200 female sex workers in the southwest of China found that streetwalkers were significantly more likely to report violence victimisation by a client in the previous year than indoor workers recruited from hair or beauty salons, massage parlours, karaoke bars, saunas and nightclubs (Choi *et al.* 2008). The reasons for outdoor workers' greater vulnerability to client-perpetrated violence are complex and related to several risk factors, including lack of protection from co-workers, inability to control the location of an encounter, the need sometimes to conduct the transaction in a car and the higher prevalence of drug and alcohol use during work (Kinnell 2004; Simić and Rhodes 2008).

However, Hong Kong, the field site of the present study and a Special Administrative Region of China, deviated from this pattern. On 14 March 2008 a 35-year-old woman working in a one-woman brothel was killed by a client. Over the subsequent two years another eight female sex workers in Hong Kong were murdered by clients or men pretending to be clients. Eight of these nine victims worked in one-woman brothels and one was a call girl (Chen and Choi 2010). Were the murders of these eight women 'isolated incidents' or is the extreme vulnerability of women working in one-woman brothels in Hong Kong due to structural factors?

Data

This study synthesises data from four sources: twenty-five field visits to sex work venues, including one-woman brothels, karaoke bars, nightclubs, saunas and hair salons in Hong Kong between December 2006 and December 2008; a survey conducted by a local NGO in 2006/2007 on client-perpetrated violence among 106 female sex workers from four settings (street; one-woman brothel; nightclub; karaoke bar); and fifty-four in-depth interviews with female sex workers from different sex work venues (eight worked in karaoke bars; eight in dance bars; eight in hair salons; twelve in one-woman brothels; seventeen on the street and one as an escort) between March 2007 and September 2010. Our data not only cover female sex workers who work in different settings, but also with diverse ethnic backgrounds. For example, our in-depth interviewees include nineteen local-born Chinese women, twenty-four mainland Chinese-born women, seven Thai women and four Filipinas. Finally, our data also include a comprehensive survey of legal provisions related to prostitution; we analysed the legal framework for prostitution in Hong Kong to assess how legal provisions influenced sex workers' vulnerability to client-perpetrated violence across different work settings.

The sex industry in Hong Kong

The sex industry in Hong Kong is a highly stratified field by setting, locality, clientele and fees, age, ethnicity and migration status of the workers. At the time of our field research the nightclubs and karaoke bars in the tourist areas of Tsim Sha Tsui and Jordan (both in Kowloon) were the high-end of the industry, predominantly serving clients from the international and Chinese business elite. Women working in these settings were generally younger and most were Chinese, born either in mainland China or in Hong Kong. Some of the mainland Chinese-born workers had gained residency status through marriage to a Hong Kong man, but others held a tourist or business visa and were thus at risk of arrest for overstaying their visa, entering Hong Kong illegally or violating their visa conditions. In these high-end establishments a madam or manager matches the 'girls' with clients in return for a cut of their fees. Women working in these establishments had two sources of income: drinking and entertaining clients within the club; and providing sexual services to clients. Fees for drinking with clients ranged from HKD 110[1] to HKD 135 per hour, and sex service charges were usually above HKD 1,500 per two hours or per encounter. Sexual services were provided inside the rooms of the establishment or in hotel rooms paid for by the client. Clients paid the establishment rather than paying the sex worker directly. Women were paid by the establishment either weekly or bi-monthly, often in cash.

The middle tier of the sex industry hierarchy consisted of dance bars scattered around the Wan Chai (on Hong Kong Island) and Tsim Sha Tsui business districts with high-rise office buildings and hotels. As well as dance bars, there were many pubs, nightclubs and eateries providing non-Chinese food. All the dance bars had English names like 'Hawaii', 'King', 'Country 88', 'Romance', 'Bunny Club' and

'Cheers Club' because their clientele were mainly non-Chinese expats, travellers and sailors. Their exteriors were decorated with flashing yellow, green, red and blue fluorescent lights hanging around the door and a dark textile curtain separating the interior of the bar from the vibrant, busy street outside. Three or four women would stand outside the curtain wearing tight tops, which revealed their cleavage, miniskirts and high-heeled black leather boots. Inside the bar, the lighting was very dim; so dim that it felt almost dark. The women working in these dance bars varied widely in age (eighteen to forty-two years old according to the women we talked to during field visits), but were predominantly of Thai or Philippine origin. Most of the Thai women had Hong Kong residency and/or relatives (husband, ex-husband, sisters and so on) living in Hong Kong and spoke some Cantonese; most of the Filipinas were in Hong Kong on a six-month work visa and communicated with the research team in English. According to the women, their clients were mostly non-Chinese men. These women called themselves 'bar waitresses' and their income came from commissions for selling drinks to clients, tips from clients and fees for sexual services (HKD 700–1,500 per sexual transaction) which were usually provided at another venue, for example in a hotel. Clients had to pay both the establishment and the sex worker; they paid the establishment for the woman's time and the woman for sexual services.

The karaoke nightclubs, massage parlours and saunas concentrated in the Yau Ma Tei and Mongkok districts, in Kowloon, represented the lower rungs of the hierarchy of the sex industry in Hong Kong. Often several businesses were situated in the same building whose entrance and lobby would be filled with colourful (typically yellow) advertising signs displaying the names of the venues and the fees for different time segments, for example, tea dance and night dance, or different services, for example 'HK$360 for full services'. Some signs carried pictures of women in bikini tops or showing off their shoulders and cleavage. In one of the buildings we visited, when we stepped out of the lift we were greeted by an automatic announcement in a woman's voice offering 'plentiful of beautiful women, reasonable charges, in modern time, not waiting time' (excerpt from field note, original in English, 7 December 2013). All these establishments had Chinese names: some containing auspicious words such as 'prosperity', 'profitable' or 'popular'; some had names meaning 'modern time' or 'new era'; and others used dance names (e.g. 'Waltz') or city names (e.g. 'Madrid'). The workers in these venues were a mixture of women born in mainland China and locally born Chinese women and the fees were cheaper, ranging between HKD 200 for a blowjob to HKD 500 for full service (massage and intercourse). The women were also older; many had worked in higher-end settings and moved down the industry hierarchy as they aged. In these settings, clients paid the cashier at the counter rather than paying the sex worker directly. Undercover police investigations and police raids were frequent and the women had devised various tactics to avoid being arrested, such as never asking directly if the client wants sexual services, only hinting.

At the bottom of the sex industry hierarchy there were three types of work settings: hair salons, one-woman brothels and streetwalkers. Most hair salons providing sexual services were located on the first floor of rundown residential buildings in the Yau Ma Tei district, in Kowloon. Their signs used words such as 'women', 'massage', and 'skilful'. Aside from the signs hanging at the entrance, there were usually no other exterior decoration. Inside the flat, 'service areas' were partitioned off using white or beige cotton curtains. Most hair salons had between two and four women working each shift and were open round the clock. The age range of the hair salon clientele was wide, although older clients (men in their sixties or older) were in the majority. Vaginal intercourse was not usually performed; clients usually asked for blowjobs or hand jobs. The fees in these establishments were cheap, ranging from HKD 80 for a hand job to HKD 150 for a blowjob. Most women working in these venues were older, with the age range being from late thirties to over sixty years.

The only legal form of prostitution, one-woman brothels could be found in every district of Hong Kong and tended to be concentrated in two or three old, rundown buildings in the district. Our research team identified fifty-one one-woman brothels in three buildings in Tsim Sha Tsui (field note, 18 January 2008) and fifty-seven one-woman brothels inside a single building on another street in the same area (field note, 1 February 2008), and thirty-five one-woman brothels in three buildings in Kwun Tong (30 January 2008). The brothels were roughly fifty to sixty square feet in size, just big enough to hold a double bed, a small table, occasionally a massage chair or plastic chair, and a shower and toilet area. Most one-woman brothels hung a red or pink light bulb outside the door as a sign and had installed a video camera for safety reasons. The women put up paper signs using phrases such as 'Queen of blowjobs', 'Local Woman', 'Massage', 'Cute Mandy, Good at Massage', 'With Body, Give you Energy', 'Big breast lady from Xinjiang [in North China], Good Services, Skilful Hands and Plenty of Time'. We inferred from the prevalence of these signs that many of the women working in these brothels were not aware that section 147 and section 147B of Hong Kong's *Crimes Ordinance Cap. 200*, enacted in 1972, prohibit one-woman brothels from displaying signs advertising prostitution (field note, 29 November 2007); one woman we visited on 30 January 2008 complained that she had been arrested because the police found a paper sign saying 'freshly arrived beautiful lady'. She felt that it was unfair because she worked the brothel in shifts and had not stuck the paper there (field note, 30 January 2008). During our field visits to one-woman brothels in six districts (we visited some districts several times), we met far more mainland China than Hong Kong born women. The services provided in one-woman brothels included massage and various sex acts, prices ranged from HKD 200 to HKD 500, depending on the services provided.

Streetwalkers could be found in the tourist districts of Hong Kong, for example Wan Chai and Tsim Sha Tsui, and in rundown districts such as Mongkok and Sham Shui Po. The population of streetwalkers included women of different nationalities, sexual orientations and ages. In the tourist areas streetwalkers were predominantly Thai, Filipina and mainland Chinese and there were transgender and cross-dressed sex workers. In rundown districts the majority of streetwalkers were mainland Chinese women. The locals in some rundown districts had nick-named the areas where streetwalkers recruited clients 'horse circuits' and men

Table 14.1 Diversity of the sex industry in Hong Kong

Work setting	*Presence of co-workers*	*Sites of sexual transaction*	*Payment method*	*Demographic background of worker*
High-end karaoke bars and nightclubs	Yes	Inside the establishment or hotels	Client pays the establishment	Women in their late teens or twenties, mainland Chinese or local
Dance bars	Yes	Hotels or client's place	Client pays the establishment	Filipina or Thai of all ages
Medium-end karaoke bars, massage parlours, saunas	Yes	Inside the establishment	Client pays the establishment	Women in their thirties and forties, mainland Chinese or local
One-woman brothel	No	Inside the establishment	Client pays worker directly	Mainly women in their thirties or forties, mainland Chinese or local
Low-end hair salons	Yes	Inside the establishment	Client pays the establishment	Mainly women in their forties or fifties, mainland Chinese or local
Streetwalking	No	Hotel or client's flat	Client pays worker directly	Women of all ages, ethnic groups, transgender

would gather around and gaze openly, passing comments on them. Streetwalkers complained of frequent police raids and arrests and mistreatment by passers-by, who sometimes spat on them. Streetwalkers usually conducted their business in clients' flats or in rented hotel rooms. They were paid by the client on entrance to the venue for the sexual transaction.

In sum, the sex industry in Hong Kong is a hierarchal and heterogeneous space; sex workers in different settings vary in work arrangements, including the presence of co-workers, sites of sexual transactions and payment methods. They also differ in demographic backgrounds and legal status. While many mainland Chinese women are working illegally, the Philippine workers obtain the, so-called, 'entertainment visa' that allows them to work legally in dance bars. Table 14.1 summarises the different sex work settings in Hong Kong and the variation in work conditions.

Reports of client-perpetrated violence

Analysis of the 2006/2007 NGO survey clearly showed stratification in sex workers' vulnerability to violence according to the work setting (see Table 14.2). In the survey 14.2 per cent of female sex workers reported that they had been robbed,

Table 14.2 Client-perpetrated violence reported in the 2006/2007 survey

	Karaoke bar, nightclub, dance bar (n=40)	*One-woman brothel (n=36)*	*Streetwalker (n=30)*	*Total N=106*
Forced or coerced into certain sexual acts	14 (35%)	6 (17%)	8 (27%)	28 (26.4%)
Physical violence	4 (10%)	7 (19%)	3 (10%)	14 (13.2%)
Robbery	2 (5%)	3 (8%)	10 (33%)	15 (14%)

13.2 per cent had experienced client-perpetrated physical violence at some point and 26.4 per cent had been forced or coerced into performing sexual acts during the previous six months. Sex workers in different settings were vulnerable to different types of victimisation. Sex workers in karaoke bars, nightclubs and dance bars reported the highest rate of being forced or coerced to perform unwanted sexual acts with clients (thirty-five per cent); sex workers in one-woman brothels reported the highest rate of client-perpetrated physical violence (nineteen per cent) and streetwalkers reported the highest rate of robbery (thirty-three per cent).

The survey provided a glimpse of the scale and vulnerability to different types of violence across sex work settings. Our data suggest that in Hong Kong, rather than being generally less vulnerable to client-perpetrated violence, the type of client-perpetrated violence to which indoor workers are most vulnerable varies according to the work setting. This renders the indoor v. outdoor classification inadequate for capturing the complexity of female sex workers' experiences of violence and other crimes. In the next section, we use our in-depth interview data to illustrate the tenuous nature of the traditional distinction between indoor and outdoor settings. In particular, the experiences of sex workers in one-woman brothels, an indoor setting, were similar to those of sex workers in other indoor settings in some respects, but similar to those of streetwalkers in others.

Contextualising violence

'Being forced or coerced to perform unwanted sexual acts with clients' was the form of offence most prevalent amongst sex workers in high-end settings such as karaoke bars, nightclubs and dance bars. All sex workers whom we interviewed set boundaries and refused to perform certain sexual acts: certain parts of their bodies were not for sale: most refused to provide anal sex; some did not do oral sex; some would provide oral sex but did not allow clients to ejaculate inside their mouth; some workers refused to kiss clients; and most forbade digital penetration. However, clients in high-end settings often attempt to incentivise the woman to consent to something she would not normally consent to, such as anal or unprotected sex. Sometimes women in high-end settings accept the higher fee reluctantly because they do not feel that a continued refusal would be respected.

Other times, they turn down a higher fee but are forced to perform the unwanted act. Women reported that drunken clients are particularly likely to refuse to respect their boundaries and resorted to using violence to get what they wanted. The following interviews illustrate the contexts in which these violations occurred.

> *I have been kissed against my will by a number of clients . . . I told them that I didn't do kisses . . . Some just disregarded my resistance and kissed me.*
>
> (Interviewee no. 38, karaoke bar)

> *An Indian guy beat me the whole night. He hit me . . . He banged my head like a ball. He was so drunk. I was green then. I had just turned twenty, I did not have much experience. He wanted to fuck me hard. I got really freaked out when he put his fingers inside my vagina. At the end, he wanted to pull the condom off. I yelled at him. I said 'fuck you'. But then he said that he would give me a big tip. When we were finished, I asked for the extra money but he refused. He kept saying 'no', 'no', 'no'. He wanted to grab me and I had to run [out of the room].*
>
> (Interviewee no. 30, dance bar)

Although sex workers in high-end settings reported the highest rate of being forced or coerced to perform unwanted sexual acts, this does not mean that this type of violence is uncommon among sex workers in low-end settings, such as one-woman brothels and outdoor settings. In fact, seventeen per cent of one-woman brothel workers and twenty-seven per cent of streetwalkers in the survey reported being forced or coerced to perform unwanted sexual acts in the previous six months. Our in-depth interview data showed that the dynamics of sexual violence differ somewhat across settings. While clients in higher-end settings tend to first use incentives when they want women to perform unwanted acts, clients in low-end settings may promise a higher fee in exchange for performing unwanted sexual acts and this is not paid. Sex workers would then report this as robbery. In other instances, clients in lower-end settings do not even bother trying to incentivise women, but resort to physical force straight away. The following quotes from streetwalkers and one-woman brothel workers are cases in point.

> *I insisted that he put on the condom, but then he pulled it off. I refused to continue [with sexual intercourse] and we ended up fighting . . . you see that guy was drinking. He finished the whole bottle of rice wine and he could not ejaculate.*
>
> (Interviewee no. 14, streetwalker)

> *We took a shower together and then we started [intercourse]. I was first facing him and then I was facing down. But gradually he started to curse me. He pinned my hands down and started to work the back [anal sex]. It was painful.*

> *I struggled but I couldn't move. The pain was excruciating. I wanted to yell for help but somehow no voice was coming out of my mouth . . . It was a terrifying experience. I was so scared that I did not do business for two months.*
>
> (Interviewee no. 1, one-woman brothel)

> *I had to escape from the room because the client wanted anal sex . . . I don't do anal. I wanted to pick up my clothes but he refused to let me go. I had to push open the door and shout for help. Even then he refused to let go of me . . . At the end I managed to open the gate and escaped. I was yelling for help really loud, so he did not follow.*
>
> (Interviewee no. 39, streetwalker)

Sexual violence violates the bodies and dignity of sex workers and reflects a client's lack of respect for sex workers and their boundaries. Sex workers in Hong Kong as a group are animalised, the slang term for a sex worker is 'chicken' (*ji*). The men who purchase services from sex workers maintain a double standard; it is all right for them to buy sex but women who sell sex are 'unworthy' and their bodies can be violated. Although sex workers in high-end settings charge clients higher fees, they do not seem able to escape the stigma attached to the occupation. This may also partly explain why high-end indoor workers are not exempt from client-perpetrated sexual assault.

Analysis of data from the 2006/2007 survey showed that sex workers in one-woman brothels were particularly vulnerable to client-perpetrated physical violence. Our in-depth interviews showed that sex workers in one-woman brothels and streetwalkers were equally vulnerable to client-perpetrated physical violence due to two work setting-related factors, refusal of payment and lack of co-worker protection, which do not apply to sex workers in venues such as karaoke bars, nightclubs, dance bars, massage parlours and saunas. Clients in nightclubs and bars pay the cashier before being allowed to take a worker out to complete a sexual transaction. Prices are set by the venue and the fee is paid to venue employees, such as cashiers or managers, which minimises disputes between clients and sex workers over payment.

In contrast, sex workers in one-woman brothels and streetwalkers receive payment directly from their clients, they usually request payment before service to avoid payment refusal and violent confrontations with clients. However, the request for payment is usually made after the client enters the venue (in the case of one-woman brothels) or after the worker and her client enter the location agreed for the sexual act (in the case of streetwalkers) and this creates opportunities for payment refusal and violent confrontation.

> *We were already inside the room. I asked him to pay first. He said that he would pay after sex. I didn't know him and asked why should I trust him? I insisted that he pay first. He refused and grabbed me. I kicked him and ran out of the room.*
>
> (Interviewee no. 25, streetwalker)

> *I wanted to check if he had money. He showed me a fifty-dollar note and then rushed me to take off my clothes. I wanted to see his money first. He didn't have money so I asked him to leave. He refused to leave and used his hands to hold my neck, choking it.*
>
> (Interviewee no. 24, one-woman brothel)

The isolation and lack of protection from co-workers also makes sex workers in one-woman brothels particularly vulnerable to client-perpetrated physical violence. Previous studies have shown that the presence of other sex workers or staff at a venue acts as a powerful deterrent to client-perpetrated violence, and provides crucial support for sex workers when violence does occur (Choi and Holroyd 2007). Third parties can act as 'capable guardians' (Miethe *et al.* 1987) and restrain potential offenders. A woman from a hair salon explained why she chose to work there instead of in a one-woman brothel:

> *There are four of us here. You won't be left alone. There won't be times when you would be completely vulnerable. If you are alone, on your own, there are many occasions when you would be vulnerable and defenceless. When you take a shower, for example. Here [at the salon] things are open. The beds are separated only by a curtain; there are no rooms. If something happens, the woman in the next bed would surely hear you.*
>
> (Interviewee no. 37, hair salon)

Sex workers may also be protected by venue personnel such as managers and madams. The law categorically views venue managers, madams and pimps as evil exploiters living off the earnings of sex workers. One of our respondents from a dance bar also complained that she was pressurised by her madam to have sex with a client when she was freaked out:

> *You don't have a choice. If the customer is willing to pay, you have to go . . . even if you don't fucking like it . . . you still have to go . . . even if we are fucking freaked out you know.*
>
> (Interviewee no. 30, karaoke bar)

However, there is also evidence that the presence of managers or madams in bars reduces the number of occasions when sex workers come into direct conflict with clients.

> *I think before he came into our club he was already drinking. When I chatted with him, he was very rude and started to slap my leg like that [makes a loud noise by slapping her own lap]. . . So I told the madam that this guy was dangerous and not to ask girls to sleep with him.*
>
> (Interviewee no. 45, bar)

> *They had already paid and I was ready to go out with them. But then they started to fight [near the bar]. So I went back to the bar and told the madam that I would not go because I was scared.*
>
> (Interviewee no. 43, bar)

The experiences of these women suggest that a categorical view of venue staff deviates from the complex interactions between sex workers and these people; they may be a source of exploitation and coercion, but they may also be able to offer genuine protection and useful services to women, depending on the context.

Legal provisions related to sex work in Hong Kong

How can we explain the diverse vulnerabilities of sex workers in different work settings? We argue that the pattern of vulnerability is directly and partly related to the laws on prostitution in Hong Kong, which take a very complex and contradictory position on prostitution. Although prostitution itself is not illegal, sex workers have a very precarious legal status. Prostitution is often grouped with 'unlawful sexual intercourse' or 'unlawful sexual acts' in the *Crimes Ordinance Cap. 200, 1972*. Thirteen sections of the *Crimes Ordinance Cap. 200, 1972* variously prohibit: control over persons for prostitution (section 130); causing prostitution (section 131); causing or encouraging prostitution of, intercourse with, or indecent assault on, a girl or boy under 16 (section 135); causing or encouraging prostitution of a mentally incapacitated person (section 136); living on the earnings of another party's prostitution (section 137); use, procurement or offer of persons under eighteen for production of pornography or for live pornographic performances (section 138A); keeping a vice establishment (section 139); letting premises for use as a vice establishment (section 143); (as a tenant) permitting premises or vessels to be maintained as a vice establishment (section 144); (as a tenant) permitting premises or vessels to be used for prostitution (section 145). The police have the power to search premises in cases where they suspect someone of living on third party earnings from prostitution (section 151). A 'vice establishment' is defined as 'premises being used by two or more persons for prostitution' (section 117), which means that the only legal form of prostitution is one-woman brothels operating on premises owned by the woman herself.

All other forms of sex work, including sex work in nightclubs, karaoke bars, massage parlours, saunas and hair salons, are illegal because they involve more than one sex worker in the same venue and/or because a third party, for example, the owner, manager, madam or pimp running the establishment, is involved and takes a cut of the income from sex work. People working in these settings, including the sex workers, are therefore frequently the target of undercover police investigations and raids to determine whether they are providing sexual services on the premises. The police also frequently conduct raids to check whether establishments are using individuals from groups specifically protected by laws against prostitution, for example under sixteen-years-old and mentally incapacitated persons (sections 135, 136, 138A, 140, 141 and 142 respectively, *Crimes Ordinance Cap. 200, 1972*).

The Hong Kong government also operates a stratified work visa system for migrant sex workers. Women from the Philippines can apply for a work visa which will enable them to work legally as waitresses in dance bars (which also provide sexual services, see above) in Hong Kong, but there is no similar option for women from mainland China; they can apply for a tourist visa (usually seven to fifteen days), or a business visa (usually one to three months) or a two-way permit (usually for three months if an immediate family member, such as a husband, is a Hong Kong resident). These restrictions on mainland Chinese women means that a sizeable proportion of sex workers from mainland China working in Hong Kong are illegal workers; in police raids on sex work establishments such as nightclubs, karaoke bars, massage parlours and saunas they are often arrested and charged with 'breaching a condition of stay' (section 41, *Immigration Ordinance Cap. 115, 1972*). In Hong Kong in 2003 over 10,000 mainland Chinese women were arrested for sex work and charged with 'breaching a condition of stay', 'over staying' or 'entering Hong Kong illegally'. In 2004, 109 law enforcement operations against illegal prostitution were conducted by the police (Laidler *et al.* 2007).

Although under the existing legal code a one-woman brothel is the only setting in which prostitution can take place legally, one-woman brothels are often put under police surveillance and subject to legal challenge. Section 147A of the *Crimes Ordinance Cap. 200, 1972* prohibits one-woman brothels from displaying any signs advertising prostitution, while section 147B grants a police officer with the rank of chief inspector or above authority to remove or take away a sign which he or she 'reasonably believes . . . is displayed in contravention of section 147A'. The majority of women working in one-woman brothels rent rather than own the premises and the sections of the *Crimes Ordinance Cap. 200, 1972* about letting premises for use as a vice establishment (sections 143, 144, 145) criminalise anyone who rents an apartment for use as a one-woman brothel. This means that many sex workers in one-woman brothels risk eviction if the owner finds out that the premises are used for prostitution. High property prices in Hong Kong and economic constraints make it difficult for workers in one-woman brothels to purchase their own premises.

The criminal law in Hong Kong also prohibits activities such as soliciting for an immoral purpose and loitering for the purpose of soliciting for any immoral purpose (section 147, *Crimes Ordinance Cap. 200, 1972*). The law against soliciting means that streetwalkers are at high risk of being arrested by the police. Together these laws constitute a disadvantageous legal environment that exposes sex workers in different settings to various legal challenges and creates inequalities among sex workers. Vulnerability to different types and degrees of violence and access to justice also varies according to the work setting (Table 14.3). In these various ways, the law constitutes a mechanism for state-sanctioned inhibition and marginalisation of prostitution.

Table 14.3 Legal prohibitions related to sex work in Hong Kong

Types of prohibition	*Legal provisions*	*Work settings affected*	*Types of sex workers affected*
Control over persons for prostitution	S130	Karaoke nightclubs, massage parlours, saunas, hair salons	Mainland Chinese women without work permit
Causing prostitution	S137	Karaoke nightclubs, massage parlours, saunas, hair salons	Mainland Chinese women without work permit
Living on earnings of prostitution of another party	S139	Karaoke nightclubs, massage parlours, saunas, hair salons	Mainland Chinese women without work permit
Keeping a vice establishment	S143	Karaoke nightclubs, massage parlours, saunas, hair salons	Mainland Chinese women without work permit
Letting premises for use as a vice establishment	S144,S145	Karaoke nightclubs, massage parlours, saunas, hair salons, one-woman brothels	Mainland Chinese women without work permit
Displaying any signs advertising prostitution	S147A	One-woman brothels	Mainland Chinese women without work permit
Prohibition against soliciting	S147	Streetwalking	Mainland Chinese women without work permit, Thai women, transgender individuals

Diverse vulnerabilities and the law

Legal provisions related to prostitution in Hong Kong have created an inequality among sex workers and a variation in vulnerability according to national origin and sex work setting. Rather than drawing a clear distinction between what is legal and what is criminal, the current legal framework has made most sex work settings legally or socially precarious. For example, although one-woman brothels are the only legal form of sex work in Hong Kong, they deprive the women who work in them of protection from co-workers and venue personnel, thus exposing them to high levels of client-perpetrated violence. Venue personnel such as managers and madams are not necessarily parasites living off the earnings of sex workers, they may play a useful role in protecting sex workers. To ensure that sex workers are not exploited or pressurised by venue personnel it might be better to grant sex workers employment rights so that they can leave an unsuitable employer rather than banning categorically all employment of sex workers, as the law currently does. The existing regime, which criminalises individuals who own or run sex work venues, is clearly ineffective, with most sex work venues operating as entertainment venues to evade the legal prohibitions relating to use of premises for sex work.

Sex workers in venues other than one-woman brothels (nightclubs, dance bars, karaoke bars, massage parlours and hair salons) are protected from client-perpetrated physical violence to a certain degree by the presence of co-workers and venue personnel, but they are subjected to frequent police raids to establish: whether sexual services are being provided on the premises; whether underage children are involved in sex work; and whether illegal migrant workers are working in the establishment. Even when client-perpetrated violence does occur, sex workers in these venues are inhibited from reporting it to the police because they are not supposed to be selling sex in these venues. This is particularly the case for mainland Chinese sex workers, whose illegal status deters them from reporting client-perpetrated violence to the police as they fear deportation. It also makes them vulnerable to extortion, as this respondent reported:

> *He said he was a plain-clothes policeman. He asked to see my ID card. He checked my ID card and told me that it was illegal for me to work because I haven't got permanent residence . . . I was terrified and asked him to let me go. I said 'Please let me go. I have a few hundred dollars with me; I could give them all to you'. He said it was too little . . . at the end he forced me to go to the cash machine and withdraw three thousand dollars for him before he let me go.*
>
> (Interviewee no. 24, mainland Chinese streetwalker)

This respondent did not know whether the man who extorted money from her really was a policeman. She was so afraid of being deported that she could not imagine reporting the crime to a law enforcement agency. Similarly the laws on soliciting have made streetwalkers a frequent target of police operations and created tremendous fear of law enforcement agencies among this population. Even when they are victims of crime many streetwalkers do not feel that they can count on the police to help them.

Because it makes most sex work legally precarious through one means or another, we argue that the law casts a shadow over all sex workers and causes them to doubt whether they can rely on protection from law enforcement agencies when they experience violence at the hands of clients. Given that the law also has a symbolic significance, which is reflected in social attitudes (Choi 2011b) and influences how citizens understand and interpret particular behaviours (Boittin 2013), it is clear that the restrictions on legal sex work further stigmatise and marginalise this population. The current legal framework thus deprives sex work of social legitimacy and implies that sex workers are unworthy of legal protection when they are violated by clients (Scambler and Paoli 2008).

In highlighting the heterogeneity of client-perpetrated violence experienced by sex workers we do not seek to perpetuate the view that sex workers are passive victims. We are cognisant of the strategies that sex workers use to minimise their exposure to violence and violations; for example, all the sex workers we interviewed screened clients to avoid troublemakers. Drunken clients are often avoided because sex workers believe that men under the influence of alcohol take longer to ejaculate and some cannot ejaculate at all. Alcohol also tends to make clients more prone to anger, less restrained and more difficult to reason with. Other screening criteria include tattoos, provocative language and gazing at female sex workers in an unfriendly way. Streetwalkers choose the venues for their sexual transactions carefully to minimise the risk of violence or robbery. Certain locations, such as big and expensive hotels, are preferred because streetwalkers believe that clients who can afford to stay in big hotels are less likely to refuse payment. If possible, streetwalkers avoid going to the home of a client. Some workers in one-woman brothels avoid night work or are extra-vigilant at night. Although there is no clear evidence that night work is less safe than day work, workers generally feel safer and more in control during the daytime. Some sex workers hone their communication skills and attempt to boost their self-confidence and assertiveness so that they can manage and diffuse conflicts with clients more effectively. However, regardless of how careful and vigilant sex workers are in screening clients and selecting a venue, no matter how good their communication skills, sex workers in all settings are exposed to various forms of client-perpetrated violence, and sex workers as a group still suffer shockingly high rates of homicide and other crimes. Their trade remains under the shadow of social stigma and this is why, when violence occurs or when their rights are breached, sex workers usually just endure it instead of seeking help from law enforcement agents.

Our concept of diverse vulnerabilities summarises the key two findings of this chapter. First, it shows that sex workers' experiences of client-perpetrated violence vary according to the work setting and on this basis we suggest that future studies of violence against sex workers should go beyond comparisons of indoor and outdoor and seek to explore and understand the diversity of sex work. Second, by demonstrating the ways in which the current legal framework makes sex workers in all settings vulnerable to different types of client-perpetrated violence and robbery in one way or another, our findings highlight the need for a more sophisticated debate about the legal climate for sex work, one which goes beyond the legalisation v. criminalisation dichotomy. Ill-conceived legalisation does not reduce the vulnerability and marginalisation of sex workers. As we have shown, the current legal framework makes all sex workers vulnerable in different ways, and so it serves more as a mechanism for state-sanctioned inhibition of prostitution than as a means of protecting sex workers from harm.

Note

1 100 Hong Kong dollars is equivalent to around thirteen USD, eight British pounds sterling or ten Euro.

Bibliography

Boittin, M. (2013) 'New Perspectives from the Oldest Profession: Abuse and the Legal Consciousness of Sex Workers in China', *Law & Society Review*, vol. 47, pp. 245–78.

Bungay, V., Johnsona, J.L., Varcoea, C. and Boyd, S. (2010) 'Women's Health and Use of Crack Cocaine in Context: Structural and 'Everyday' Violence', *International Journal of Drug Policy*, vol. 21, no. 4, pp. 321–9.

Chapkis, W. (2000) 'Power and Control in the Commercial Sex Trade', in Weitzer, R., (ed.) *Sex for Sale: Prostitution, Pornography, and the Sex Industry*, Routledge, New York.

Chen, W. and Choi, S.Y.P. (2010) 'What has the Government done to Prevent further Violence against Female Sex Workers?' *Ming Pao*, April 15, (in Chinese).

Choi, S.Y.P. (2011a) 'State Control, Female Prostitution and HIV Prevention in China', *China Quarterly*, vol. 205, pp. 96–114.

Choi, S.Y.P. (2011b) 'Heterogeneous and Vulnerable: The Health Risks Facing Transnational Female Sex Workers', *Sociology of Health & Illness*, vol. 33, pp. 1–17.

Choi, S.Y.P., Chen, K.L. and Jiang, Z.Q. (2008) 'Client-perpetrated Violence and Condom Failure Among Female Sex Workers in Southwestern China', *Sexually Transmitted Diseases*, vol. 35, pp. 141–6.

Choi, S.Y. and Holroyd, E. (2007) 'The influence of power, poverty and agency in the negotiation of condom use for female sex workers in mainland China', *Culture, Health & Sexuality*, vol. 9, iss. 5, pp. 489–503.

Church, S., Henderson, M., Barnard, M. and Hart, G. (2001) 'Violence by Clients towards Female Prostitutes in Different Work Settings: Questionnaire Survey', *British Medical Journal*, vol. 322, pp. 322–3.

Dalla, R.L. (2002) 'Night Moves: A Qualitative Investigation of Street-level Sex Work', *Psychology of Women Quarterly*, vol. 26, pp. 63–73.

Dalla, R.L., Xia, Y. and Kennedy, H. (2003) 'You Just Give Them What They Want and Pray They Don't Kill You: Street-level Sex Workers' Reports of Victimization, Personal Resources, and Coping Strategies', *Violence Against Women*, vol. 9, pp. 1367–94.

Day, S. and Ward, H. (2004) 'Approaching Health through the Prism of Stigma: Research in Seven European Countries', in Day, S. and Ward, H. (eds.) *Sex Work, Mobility and Health in Europe*, Kegan Paul, London, New York and Bahrain.

Farley, M. (2004) '"Bad for the Body, Bad for the Heart": Prostitution Harms Women Even if Legalized or Decriminalised', *Violence Against Women*, vol. 10, no. 10, pp. 1087–125.

Hart, G. and Barnard, M. (2003) '"Jump on Top, Get the Job Done": Strategies Employed by Female Prostitutes to Reduce the Risk of Client Violence', in Stanko, E.A., (ed.) *The Meanings of Violence*, Routledge, London and New York.

Human Rights Watch (2013) '*Treat Us Like Human Beings': Discrimination against Sex Workers, Sexual and Gender Minorities, and People Who Use Drugs in Tanzania*. [online] http://www.hrw.org/sites/default/files/reports/tanzania0613webwcover.pdf

Kinnell, H. (2004) 'Violence and sex work in Britain', in Day, S. and Ward, H. (Eds.) *Sex Work, Mobility and Health in Europe*, Kegan Paul, London and New York.

Laidler, K.A., Petersen, C. and Emerton, R. (2007) 'Bureaucratic Justice: The Incarceration of Mainland Chinese Women Working in Hong Kong's Sex Industry', *Internal Journal of Offender Therapy and Comparative Criminology*, vol. 51, pp. 68–83.

Lowman, J. (2000) 'Violence and the Outlaw Status of (Street) Prostitution in Canada', *Violence Against Women*, vol. 6, pp. 987–1011.

Lowman, J. and Fraser, L. (1995) *Violence Against Persons who Prostitute: The Experience in British Columbia*, Technical Report TR1996-14e., Department of Justice Canada, Ottawa.

Miethe, T.D., Stafford, M.C. and Long, J.S. (1987) 'Social Differentiation in Criminal Victimization: A Test of Routine Activities/Lifestyle Theories', *American Sociological Review*, vol. 52, pp. 184–94.

Monto, M. A. (2004) 'Female Prostitution, Customers, and Violence', *Violence Against Women*, vol. 10, pp. 160–88.

Perkins, R. (1991) *Working Girls: Prostitutes, Their Life and Social Control*, Australian Institute of Criminology, Canberra.

Perkins, R. and Bennett, G. (1985) *Being a Prostitute: Prostitute Women and Prostitute Men*, George Allen and Unwin, Sydney.

Perkins, R. and Lovejoy, F. (1996) 'Healthy and Unhealthy Life Styles of Female Brothel Workers and Call Girls (Private Sex Workers) in Sydney', *Australian and New Zealand Journal of Public Health*, vol. 20, pp. 512–16.

Prince, D. (1986) *A Psychological Study of Prostitutes in California and Nevada*, unpublished doctoral dissertation, United States International Univ., San Diego, California.

Pyett, P. and Warr, W. (1999) 'Women at Risk in Sex Work: Strategies for Survival', *Journal of Sociology*, vol. 35, pp. 183–97.

Scambler, G. and Paoli, F. (2008). 'Health work, Female Sex Workers and HIV/AIDS: Global and Local Dimensions to Stigma and Deviance as Barriers to Effective Interventions', *Social Science & Medicine*, vol. 65, pp. 1–15.

Simić, M. and Rhodes, T. (2008). 'Violence, Dignity and HIV Vulnerability: Street Sex Work in Serbia', *Sociology of Health & Illness*, vol. 31, pp. 1–16.

Vanwesenbeeck, I. (2001) 'Another Decade of Social Scientific Work on Sex Work: A Review of Research 1990–2000', 12 *Annual Review of Sex Research*, pp. 242–89.

Weitzer, R. (2000) 'The Politics of Prostitution in America', in Weitzer, R. (ed.), *Sex for Sale: Prostitution, Pornography, and the Sex Industry*, Routledge, New York.

Weitzer, R. (2005) 'New Directions in Research on Prostitution', 43 *Crime, Law & Social Change*, pp. 211–35.

Weitzer, R. (2009). 'Sociology of Sex Work', *Annual Review of Sociology*, vol. 35, pp. 213–34.

West, C. and Zimmerman, D.H. (2002) 'Doing Gender' in Fenstermaker, S. and West, C. (eds.) *Doing Gender, Doing Difference: Inequality, Power, and Institutional Change*, Routledge, New York.

Whittaker, D. and Hart, G. (1996) 'Research Note: Managing Risks: The Social Organization of Indoor Sex Work', *Sociology of Health & Illness*, vol. 18, pp. 399–414.

Conclusion

Amy Barrow and Joy L.Chia

> There is no thing as a single-issue struggle because we do not live single-issue lives.
>
> (Audre Lorde, *Sister Outsider: Essays and Speeches* 1984)

As Audre Lorde, a 'Black Feminist, Lesbian, Mother, Warrior and Poet'[1] captures in her writing, it is impossible to frame the struggle against gender-based violence as a single-issue. A central aim of this book has been to situate the role of the state in analyses of how gender and violence are manifested in several Asian jurisdictions. In editing this book, we were struck by how difficult it was to categorise our chapters and the central issues that they deal with; it became abundantly clear that the relationship of the state with gender and violence in Asia is best considered through robust, multi-layered frameworks, which acknowledge that gendered violence is often experienced at the confluence of multiple issues and identities. Such framing is particularly important when examining the underlying structural context within which gender-based violence is perpetrated and the possible reasons for the failure of states to prevent, investigate and punish such violence.

International human rights norms have an important role in framing how gendered violence can be understood and eliminated in local contexts, and are especially important in increasing the sensitivity of state institutions and actors to the multiple and intersecting forms of violence faced by women and girls. Within Asia, state parties to CEDAW have sent mixed signals regarding their commitment to the advancement of gender equality by subjecting their obligations under CEDAW to reservations on core articles of the treaty, in essence undermining the spirit and intention of the Convention. Chinkin's comprehensive overview of the international human rights framework (Chapter 1) highlights the importance of accountability mechanisms while articulating how access to justice is an essential precondition to the protection of all individuals' rights.

Even where international norms are accepted and filtered down to the national level, the implementation of these norms is inherently problematic as gender-based violence often intersects and interacts with other forms of identity-based violence, whether this violence is based on factors such as caste, class, marriage status, race, ethnicity, sexual orientation, gender expression or disability. Though intersectionality is a major theme running through the book, several authors have examined in detail how these tensions play out in legal and policy responses to gender-based violence. Gurung and Thapa (Chapter 4) have explored the limitations of framing conflict-affected women as a homogenised group through a case study of the experience of single women (widows) in Nepal. Kapai's examination (Chapter 9) of the help-seeking behaviours of ethnic minority and immigrant women in Hong Kong, gives a sense of the inadequacy of a 'one size fits all' approach by states in their bid to eliminate domestic violence.

As the book's chapters succinctly demonstrate, responses to gender-based violence across jurisdictions in Asia have been marred by a lack of accountability and political will to address these acts of violence as well as the underlying causes of gender discrimination. Such inertia is compounded by the failure to identify certain forms of violence as gendered violence, either due to customs that have normalised such acts or because populations are marginalised to the extent that their experiences of violence are rendered invisible. As important as it is to hold states accountable for the gendered violence perpetrated by non-state actors (as articulated by the due diligence standard), it is likewise important to scrutinise the ways in which gendered violence is perpetuated, both actively and passively, by the state through its laws and policies, or by state actors in the implementation of such laws and policies. As Chia describes in her analysis of Chinese legislation (Chapter 11), entrenched gender stereotypes in laws and policies can undermine well-meaning legal reform efforts by privileging certain forms of violence over others, and by ignoring violence that falls outside of typical gendered narratives of victimhood. Legislation and policies must recognise the different types of gender-based violence that occur within each context, as well as the different populations that are affected by such violence. Choi (Chapter 14) highlights how laws and policies can even create inequalities *within* vulnerable populations by differentiating between members of a particular group (in this case, sex workers) according to other characteristics, such as national origins and work settings.

State-sponsored violence against women can also be overlooked when such violence is written into laws or when violent acts are permitted as responses to violations of laws. This book has made clear that state actors may themselves be complicit in the manifestation of violence against women and that framing gender-based violence as family violence obscures, and ultimately ignores, such violence. Gao's analysis of rural women leaders in China (Chapter 13) gives an indication of the complex, and conflicting, social roles that they must navigate not only as protectors of women's rights through their representation of women villagers, but also as state actors tasked with implementing family planning policies. Through the implementation of state regulations, rural women leaders may inadvertently perpetuate gender-based violence against the women that they seek to protect. Further, as explored by Chopra in her critique of national security laws in India (Chapter 6), women accused of security offences are disproportionately vulnerable to extra-legal violence (often sexual in nature) by state actors.

Significantly, a lack of reporting and documentation has made it difficult to map gender-based violence in its multiple forms and this invisibility has contributed to the lack of accountability of both state and non-state actors. The difficulty of producing evidence-based reporting on sexual violence is particularly challenging in situations of armed conflict and its aftermath, as highlighted by Gomez in her analysis of state accountability for gender-based violence in the Sri Lankan war (Chapter 3). Given the complexity of recording data on sexual and gender-based violence, particularly in states where judicial and state infrastructures are weak, civil society organisations play an integral role in documenting gender-based violence. However, given the often qualitative nature of such reporting and the lack of 'hard' data, states, and international organisations, are reluctant to accept such data as evidence. This is indicative of the privileging of quantitative data over qualitative data by states, which contributes to the invisibility of gender-based violence.

In developing the concept of state obligations under the due diligence standard in the context of violence against women, the Special Rapporteur on Violence Against Women, Rashida Manjoo, in her 2013 report to the Human Rights Council, has pointed to the 'lack of state accountability for social structural deficiencies . . . that create environments that are conducive to acts of violence' (Human Rights Council 2013, para. 20) against individuals because of their actual or perceived gender. This is another major theme of the book, which has analysed instances of structural violence and their gendered impact on the experience of violence and on mechanisms for redress. Shackel's examination of the post-conflict transition experiences in Timor-Leste (East Timor) and Sri Lanka (Chapter 2) highlights the pitfalls of characterising violence against women in conflict as extraordinary, which fails to acknowledge that women experience violence before, during and after such conflicts, and absolves states from their responsibility to consider how state structures allow gender-based violence to be perpetrated with impunity. Chua and Gilbert discuss the structural factors that normalise, and even encourage, violence against sexual minorities in Myanmar by state and non-state actors (Chapter 10). By focusing on the situation of the *apwint*, the chapter highlights how ordinary laws, and lawlessness, disproportionately affect the gender non-conforming *apwint* community when they are exacerbated by social stigma and gendered discrimination.

Even if willing to prevent violence, state actors and governments may nevertheless lack the resources and capacity to respond adequately. Huang's chapter on rural justice mechanisms in China (Chapter 8) underscores how judicial agents and legal institutions may themselves be ill-equipped to address the gap between law on the books and the practical realities of the communities such laws purport to impact. State actors are often themselves embedded in political and social contexts which undermine their capacity to identify and respond to gender-based violence or gender discrimination, and Huang's chapter demonstrates that law reform efforts must also address these deficiencies.

Governments themselves may likewise find their best intentions stymied by a lack of resources and capacity. As explored by Barrow (Chapter 5) in her analysis of Asian National Action Plans (NAPs) to implement UN Security Council

Resolution 1325 (SCR 1325), the progressive, broad-ranging and aspirational goals articulated in the Nepalese and the Philippine NAPs have been hindered by the absence of gender budgeting and inadequate financial resources. While developing states may find that additional resources need to be mobilised from donor partner organisations so as to fulfil states' commitments to the spirit and intention of SCR 1325, this may lead to a lack of ownership and detract from the state's primary responsibility to implement the resolution.

In the face of inadequate government resources, civil society actors can make meaningful contributions to address gender discrimination and gender-based violence through community organising, and through legal and policy advocacy grounded in practical experience. Several chapters present case studies that explore the rich and diverse ways in which frontline organisations' work with under-represented groups may strengthen access to justice by empowering those groups within society and increasing their visibility. McArdle's chapter on the experiences of PathFinders (Chapter 12), which provides services to migrant children and pregnant, migrant domestic workers in Hong Kong, illustrates how civil society organisations can empower marginalised women to confront structural gender-based violence perpetuated by immigration and employment laws. In examining the experiences of the Bangladesh Legal Aid & Services Trust (BLAST), Hossain offers an insight into how public interest litigation may be used as a tool to combat gender-based violence (Chapter 7). However, there remain limitations to public interest litigation as a strategy to secure rights and gender equality as the success of public interest litigation cases is often reliant on multiple drivers such as a proactive court, an engaged executive and consistent media coverage to heighten awareness.

State responses to gender-based violence need to recognise not only the multiple forms in which violence manifests itself, whether physical, psychological or economic, but also consider the diversity of women's experiences and other factors at play, such as immigration status, personal laws and religion. Civil society actors can help educate such responses by increasing the visibility of marginalised or vulnerable groups and helping to amplify voices that have historically been silenced by structural discrimination. Yet, it is worth noting that increased civil society participation in policy-making regarding violence against women is a necessary but insufficient condition for more effective state responses. Many civil society organisations operate on shoestring budgets and have limited capacity to expand successful projects on a country-wide scale. Funding streams for many organisations are vulnerable to spending cuts, particularly in times of financial insecurity, or shifts in the interests of government and private donors. Any injection of resources on the part of the state has to be sustainable, yet increased civil society engagement should not be treated as an opportunity to outsource state responsibilities to its citizens, especially those who are most marginalised and in need of state protection.

States also need to apply a gender-specific lens to evaluate how state structures, including laws, policies and state actors, may actively contribute to the perpetuation of gender-based violence. Gender mainstreaming, a gender equality strategy adopted at the UN in the 1990s, does not appear to have delivered on its promise to empower women and achieve gender equality. While well intentioned, the process of implementing gender mainstreaming often becomes a tick-box exercise by those in power who may lack the requisite gender sensitivity. Further, it is clear that gender should not be isolated from other aspects of identity, and that awareness of the intersection and interaction of multiple facets of identity, such as class, disability, sexuality and race, is increasingly important in the design of equality and diversity strategies.

Further, though the Beijing Declaration and Platform for Action 1995 called for the creation and strengthening of existing institutional mechanisms for the advancement of women (section H), it noted that in many cases the effectiveness of such mechanisms had declined. Institutional mechanisms play a critical role as a bridge between the state and civil society, but these mechanisms must be centralised to enable the effective diffusion of policy advice on gender equality and diversity. Further, the structure of these mechanisms must be based on the Paris Principles (UN General Assembly 1992) with clear lines of accountability. Rather than the marginalisation of gender and its seeming alignment only with women, gender should be mainstreamed in the work of national human-rights commissions that are impartial and independent of the state.

The elimination of gender-based violence is multi-layered and requires the sustained commitment of state and non-state actors at both macro and micro levels. Greater resource allocation is needed to better train those on the frontline, including medical staff, lawyers, the judiciary and the police. Macro and micro level documentation of gender-based violence is important, not only through statistics that present the landscape of gender-based violence but also the acknowledgment and recognition of evidence-based reporting of a qualitative nature, which is often overlooked.

This book reveals that there is much more to be done to better understand and address gender, violence and the state in Asia. As states continuously draw and redefine the boundaries of the public and private spheres, it is critical that scholars, practitioners and activists continue to engage with these shifting borders so as to uncover and confront invisible and overlooked forms of gender-based violence. Yet, it is most important that anti-violence laws and policies should remain centered on the lived experiences of those affected by violence, so that efforts to eliminate gender-based violence reinstate choice and agency to help individuals live their multi-issue lives to the fullest capacity.

Note

1 For further information about the work of Audre Lorde see the Audre Lorde Project http://alp.org/about/audre.

Bibliography

Human Rights Council (2013) 'Report of the Special Rapporteur on Violence against Women, its causes and consequences, Rashida Manjoo' (14 May 2013) UN Doc. A/HRC/23/49.

UN General Assembly Resolution (1992) 'National Institutions for the Promotion and Protection of Human Rights' (20 December 1992) UN Doc. A/RES/48/134.

Index